CHASING SHADOWS

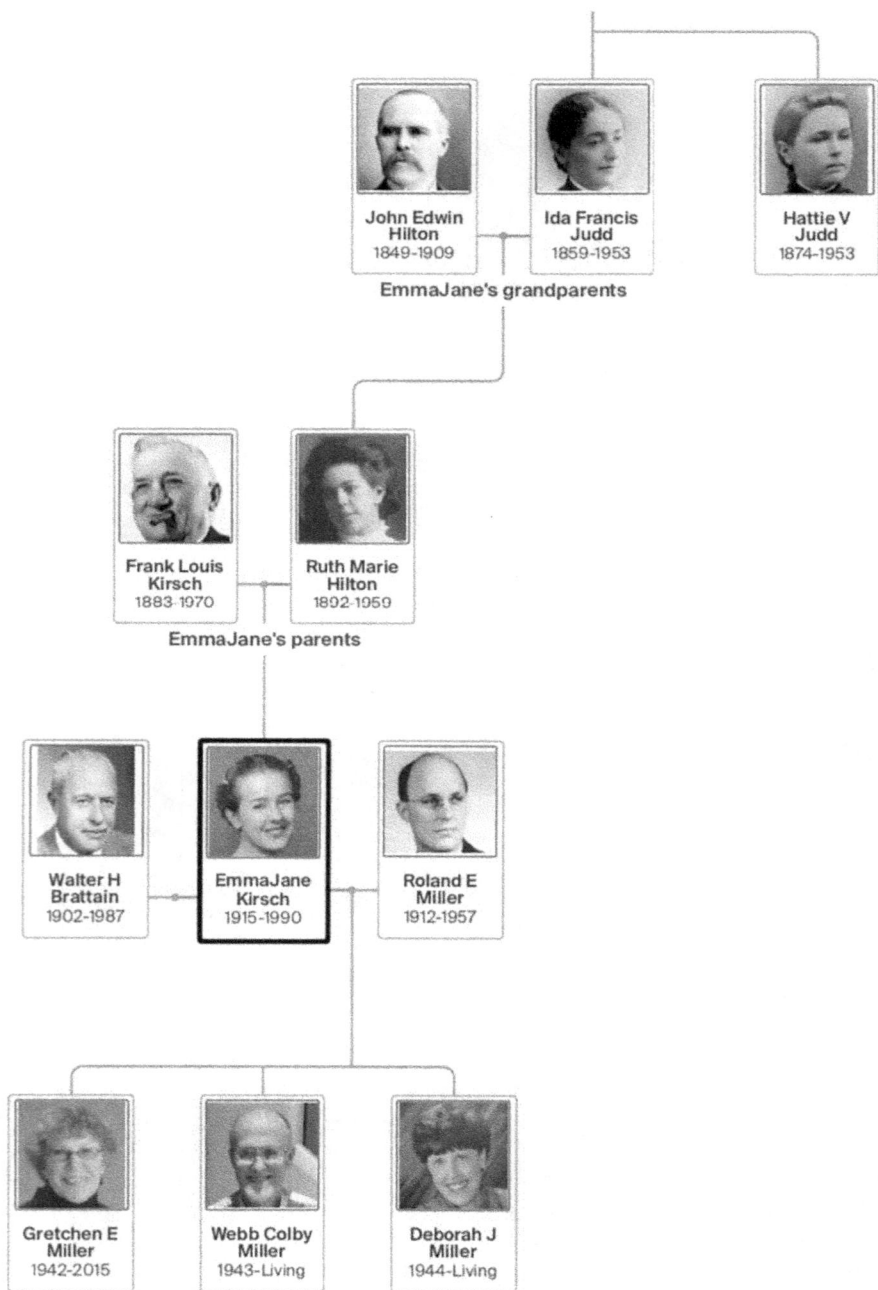

John Edwin
Hilton
1849-1909

Ida Francis
Judd
1859-1953

Hattie V
Judd
1874-1953

EmmaJane's grandparents

Frank Louis
Kirsch
1883-1970

Ruth Marie
Hilton
1892-1959

EmmaJane's parents

Walter H
Brattain
1902-1987

EmmaJane
Kirsch
1915-1990

Roland E
Miller
1912-1957

Gretchen E
Miller
1942-2015

Webb Colby
Miller
1943-Living

Deborah J
Miller
1944-Living

CHASING SHADOWS

Reconstructing a Family through Letters

A Memoir

Debi Miller Bonds

&

Webb Colby Miller

KITHARA PRESS

2023

To our family and future generations

ἐλθέ: καὶ σκιὰ φάνηθί μοι: ἅλις γὰρ ἐλθὼν κἂν ὄναρ γένοιο σύ. . .

[Come back! Appear to me as a shadow, or a dream will be enough. . .]

—Euripides, *Heracles*, 494-495

In all of us there is a hunger, marrow deep, to know our heritage—to know who we are and where we came from. Without this enriching knowledge, there is a hollow yearning. No matter what our attainments in life, there is still a vacuum, an emptiness, and the most disquieting loneliness.

—Alex Haley

Contents

Preface

Beginnings

Memoir isn't the summary of a life; it's a window into a life, very much like a photograph in its selective composition. It may look like a casual and even random calling up of bygone events. It's not; it's a deliberate construction.

—William Zinsser

Mother's request in the early summer of 1963 seemed innocent enough: would I transcribe her grandmother Ida's handwritten memoirs? I was immediately interested. "Transcribe" sounded vaguely exotic, as if she were entrusting me with something both challenging and near to her heart. The image of my new Olympia typewriter popped into my mind. I loved the look of that machine—lavender gray with a sandpapery finish that felt good to the touch. I could see myself tapping away, expertly flipping the carriage return at the sound of the bell, the perfectly typed pages piling up by the typewriter. I felt useful and important.

I waited for Mom's instructions as she handed me the photocopied sheets covered with Ida's semi-legible handwriting. When she told me that all she wanted me to do was type the text of the story—probably so she wouldn't have to do it herself—my fantasy crumbled: I was chained to my chair, sweat pouring off my forehead, wads of paper littering the floor.

I remembered Ida, whom we called Nanmy, from times we would visit my grandparents in Seattle. I was four or five years old. In contrast to her daughter (my grammie), who was effusively warm and loving, Nanmy seemed an enigma: a large, grim presence, cloaked to her ankles in heavy, dark fabric. When she moved, there was no visible body motion beneath her layers. She glided from room to room like a tall ship over a calm sea. It's no wonder I felt put off by her "memoirs."

I flipped through the pages casually, seeing only a relic from the distant past. I felt neither connection to her sentences nor to her indecipherable penmanship. Her descriptions, sentiments, and ruminations left me cold. I must have typed about a third of the text before my patience ran out. Having just graduated from high school, I was eagerly looking forward to escaping from Walla Walla, Washington to a new life at the University of Idaho. I barely had time for my immediate family, let alone family history.

Years later, I would wonder if Mother had more in mind than merely passing on her grunt work. Did she hope I would develop even a slight interest in individuals who had long fascinated her? Whether she knew it or not, Mother's directive had planted a seed that would eventually take root in my mind, bearing the fruit of my passion for our family's history.

Although that day marked the beginning of my pilgrimage into what I call the "family thicket"—that extraordinary web of letters, photographs, diaries, newspaper clippings, and other memorabilia—there were many dry spells during which I was busy living my own life. But there were also times that aroused my interest in our family history, as when Mother would invite me along on car trips to places with links to her past or to meet distant relatives.

One such adventure took place in the mid-1970s when I was living in Idaho Falls. Mother, having arrived for a visit, suggested that she and I drive to the Mormon Library in Salt Lake City, where she could continue her genealogical research in detail. This was perhaps the first time I tuned into her ongoing passion for family history.

In 1983, not long after Chris and I had moved to Nebraska, Mother invited me to drive to Fox Lake, Wisconsin, to locate Nanmy's childhood home. Although much had changed since Nanmy's day, Mother seemed delighted simply to be in Wisconsin even without the promise of any obvious discoveries. She was inspired by some of Nanmy's descriptions in her written narrative, as I was to be many years later.

In 1985, Mother and I drove to her birthplace, Abilene, Kansas, where she introduced me to some of her relatives and pointed out the house where she was born. I loved how animated she became as she shared newly discovered genealogy links with Edna Daniels and her daughter, Helen Farley, relatives on the Hilton side. Almost thirty years later, I would experience a similar energy and excitement upon finding information about Hattie, Nanmy's youngest sister, discoveries that would forever change and enrich the way I viewed my family.

As Mother and I headed north into Nebraska, she casually mentioned that it wouldn't be out of our way to visit Fullerton, in Nance County, where her parents had been married in 1911. While there, we could check at the county courthouse for their marriage certificate. Although eager to get home, I agreed. The courthouse was a long one-story building that had replaced the imposing Victorian brick courthouse built in 1894. Flanked by two flagpoles, metal benches, and wastebaskets, it looked more like the entrance to a grade school than a seat of government. Inside, a woman at the counter greeted us. Mother asked if the courthouse still held records from early in the century and handed her a paper on which she had written her parents' names and wedding date. Taking the paper, the clerk nodded and disappeared around a corner. She returned in a few minutes carrying a document. I felt my breath catch in my throat as she unfolded it and handed it to Mother.

I could imagine the youthful duo—Ruth, barely nineteen years old and the more mature Frank, twenty-eight—walking into the venerable 1894 courthouse that spring day, eager to begin their life together. And here we were, seventy years later, seeing the certificate that may have lain untouched since their wedding. Mother studied the paper silently and handed it to me. I stared at their signatures, running my hands over the sheet, mingling my fingerprints with theirs. I was catching the fever to know about our past.

By the time Mother and I pulled into our driveway that night, my interest in the Fullerton courthouse discovery had fizzled. I didn't really have time for those kinds of pursuits right then. Besides, one genealogy enthusiast was surely enough for the challenging task of following historical links—trails that more often than not went nowhere.

In 1986, Mother decided to move from her mansion on Alvarado Terrace in Walla Walla to a small condominium in an unfamiliar part of town. Having lived alone since Walter's move to a Seattle nursing home a few years earlier, she had often considered downsizing. But it was a hard decision to walk away from the house in which she had lived for forty of the best years of her life. Worse, she had no idea where to begin sorting out what to save from the many rooms piled with memorabilia.

Growing up during the depression, Mother never learned to jettison. The house bulged from top to bottom with decades of accumulation: a collection of books rivaling a Carnegie library, a stash of fabric that could have stocked a small store, and thousands of old letters, news clippings, and documents spanning four generations of family history.

Assuming that Mother would be in charge, I offered to help. But she had come to a crossroads with no signs to point her in the right direction. The enormity of the job had brought her to a standstill. Faced with the Herculean job of separating four floors of important memorabilia from years of generic accumulations she could discard, Mother and I switched roles. For the first time in my forty years as her daughter, I became the adult who would direct activities, set deadlines, and keep the packing going. Stepping into my new role, I forged a plan: we would spend the next six weeks working our way around the house from room to room. Mother could decide what she wanted to take with her. We would pack those items and leave the rest for the mother–daughter team who made their living holding estate sales. They would sort through the remaining items to sell or toss. There was no guarantee this would work; she agonized over the hundreds of decisions—some especially difficult—that she had to make as we progressed. But there seemed to be no other way to do it. We would stand or fall together!

Each day delivered new and interesting stuff I had never known was there. I was totally unprepared, though, for what I saw when she opened a hand-carved trunk wedged against the back wall of the basement storage room. Following her, I felt like I was in a *film noir*.

The naked light bulb cast a harsh, jagged shadow where we stood. She knew exactly what she was looking for and where she would find it, even though she hadn't been in that part of the basement for years. I was confused when she pulled out what appeared to be mere folds of moss-green cloth. Was this what she dragged me down here to see? As she turned back a corner of that dull fabric, revealing an iridescent blue border, the room lit up in Technicolor! This was a creation that could have belonged to royalty. Nanmy had stitched together the elaborately embroidered fabric pieces into a crazy quilt in 1884. The diversity of color and texture along with her stunning designs piqued my interest in my great-grandmother. How could the same person who crafted this eye-popping quilt have penned the lackluster memoirs Mother asked me to transcribe two decades earlier?

My offer to help organize these heirlooms had led me to the discovery of more links to our past buried within the papers and photographs. On one occasion I saw a strange intensity in Mother's eyes as she handed me the file of Dad's editorials and a small stack of love letters he wrote to her during the summer of 1937. One of the most painful moments for both of us was opening boxes full of cards and letters—hundreds of them—sent during Dad's brief illness and after his death. As she opened each one, she quickly resealed it and went to the next. Perhaps that was the moment when I stepped into her shoes as family historian.

For the first time, I saw my mother struggling to balance the weight of the past with her continuously unfolding present. I understood her love of distant cultures and her sense of personal history. I could see that sorting the latter was too big a job for her. I had a brief thought that it would at some point be up to me to take custody of all this. The thought vanished as quickly as it had come.

Looking back, I can scarcely believe that she lived less than four more years after moving out of that house. Both of us believed—expected—that she would live at least another twenty. Neither of us had any idea of the importance of our work that summer. Had Mother died before the big move, I doubt that I would ever have been able to locate the treasures we unearthed, some of which resided in

boxes full of random, worthless items. For example, one morning we
were looking through boxes in what had been Webb's room on the
third floor. I saw her pull out a handful of her mother's letters from a
box stuffed with *Woman's Day* and *Good Housekeeping* magazines.
Our careful sifting through her possessions in 1986 prepared me for
the sorting I would do years later.

The summer after Mother's death in 1990, I conducted a second
round of downsizing with Chris, Gretchen, and Gretchen's daughter
Deborah's help. The same mother–daughter team that had done the
1986 sale organized the estate sale at Rustic Place. Gretchen took a
few boxes to Portland. Chris and I drove home to Nebraska with
our own stash of documents and dishes—Rosenthal, Wedgewood,
and hand-painted china from Nanmy's collection—in two vehicles
(one a rented van), communicating with each other by CB radio. We
unloaded the family history boxes and shoved them against the back
wall of our basement. There they stayed for the next seventeen years.
Sometimes they seemed to call to me, reminding me that I wanted
someday to do something with them. Just not right then.

In 2007, I finally took the plunge. I unpacked all the boxes and
dove into Mother's genealogical treasures. For most of June I breast-
stroked my way through a Sargasso Sea of jumbled piles—decades of
letters and postcards; records of births, deaths, and marriages; pass-
ports, journals, photos, circus memorabilia, and more. I covered every
available surface in our big room and living room with them. Trying
to make order out of chaos, I first decided to put together everything
associated with a particular person. It quickly became clear that I
would have to ask of each item, "Is this worth saving?" My son, Scott,
questioned my willingness to get rid of any cards and letters sent to
his grandfather during his illness in 1956. When I showed him the
huge stack I was keeping, he was amazed by the outpouring of love
and encouragement his friends and colleagues sent to him—physical
evidence worth saving. After labeling and repacking the documents,
I put them in plastic tubs where they would wait until I was ready
to do some serious archaeology.

I was beginning to make sense of what lay buried in those tubs and boxes. But even more important, as I read the letters and documents, I began to see that there was a reason I had them. They were not really mine, but they were mine to take care of and to make sure that the stories they contained would not die but be passed on to future generations.

Mother was the nexus between me and the family history. Had she not kept all this material, there would have been nothing for me to do. Watching her going through her treasures, I imagined her editing her life story, sorting out the chaff and keeping the essentials—the written record of her relationships, told in journals and letters to and from her parents, Dad, and then Walter—writings she would never discard. She saw value in keeping all that, but it is not clear that she ever had the idea to organize it into a book. As much importance as she attached to her family's past, the allure of her next big adventure always took priority. Maybe I had reached the place where I could pick up where she left off and write a real memoir.

Why Now?

This is a book I put off writing for more than fifty years because I wanted it to be perfect, which it is not and could never be. In almost every family there is someone like me who desperately wants to write such a story and is forever kept from it by fear of failure.

—Ted Kooser, United States Poet Laureate,
Lights on a Ground of Darkness

In 2009, Chris and I retired from college teaching and moved to Henderson, Nevada. As we settled into our new home, I deposited the family history tubs in the guest room. I soon began pulling out items to photocopy, thinking that, like pieces of a thousand-piece puzzle, they would come together to capture the total picture of the Kirsch–Miller–Brattain family. But my initial writing attempts led nowhere. I didn't know where to start. I was on the outside looking in. They all seemed to be living fascinating lives in some distant country, and every now and then I would get a postcard or telegram about what they were up to. I had my puzzle spread out before me, but there were too many missing pieces. How could I use these inert documents and my scattered memories to bring my family members to life? And most importantly, how would I join their party?

In January of 2012, I arrived at a clearing in the thicket from where I could see a path forward. Thumbing through a course catalog from the University of Nevada, Las Vegas, I saw that Chris Cutler, an instructor, was offering two classes in memoir writing, levels I and II. This seemed like the perfect solution: here I could learn to piece together Mother's saved treasures into a coherent, readable format. I was eager to move my project along and didn't want to string things out. I asked if I could take Levels I and II at the same time. Chris cautioned me against doing so. "In my experience," she wrote, "people do best when they start with the novice writing level and then continue onto level II." Undeterred, I signed up for both and was ready to begin the following week.

I marched into the first class armed with my notebook and my mental outline of how to organize my material. I had the fixings for an instant memoir project. Bursting with excitement, I was trying my best to remain calm. But I still viewed the finished product as a packet of assembled documents to which I would add explanatory notes.

Chris gently pointed out the absurdity of my strategy. If all I wanted to do was to pull items out to copy for a booklet, I didn't need to spend time and money on memoir classes. I could cut and paste on my own. Her classes involved telling personal or family history through the narrator's lens. Therefore, I would have to be the central voice in my project. Sure, I could choose certain items as the foundation for my project, but I would need to add my own memories, reflections, and musings. The classes would be helpful in that I could give and receive feedback about writing submitted by all members. Who knows, I might even get ideas about how to proceed. My initial plan quashed, but hope alive, I returned the next day to meet the students in the level II class.

Unlike Ted Kooser, I was not looking for perfection. Instead, even though I was taking writing classes, eager to do something—anything—with the family history in early 2012, I was still miles from knowing how to begin, what questions to ask, or where to look for answers. Living fingers had typed and penned those words in letters and diaries. Faded photographs captured the solemn faces of real people frozen in a moment of time, but not the vibrant persons inside. Their vacant looks did not speak to me. No breath issued from their nostrils. Who in life were these people whose DNA I carry? How could I empathize with them, feel what they felt? More than anything else, that was what I really wanted to do. I wanted that connection. But it seemed that the more I wanted to break through this paper barrier, the more impenetrable it became. The harder I pushed, the more it pushed back (like the Monster from the Id in the sci-fi film *Forbidden Planet*). I needed a different approach.

Over the next few months, I began to develop a way that looked promising. Although the entire family history archive was important, some photos and documents made an indelible impression on me. There were records of life-changing events, for example Gramps's 1911 letter to Ida Hilton and Mother's early entries about Dad in her 1936 college diary. And there was Gramps's photo of Belle, a baby elephant, climbing out of his friend's car. Such discoveries would become waypoints along the arc of my story, helping to bring their long-silent voices to life.

Faced with this accumulation of written letters, journals, and photographs, my job was to find the real person behind each document. I might compare my work on the family history to that of the archaeologist, or even the forensic psychologist. Initially I imagined only skeletons being lifted from their graves. Gradually discovering the living persons behind them has involved educated guesses, searching for clues that might help identify and breathe life into them. Only by gathering key documents relating to each person would I begin to see beyond their surface meaning to the personalities of each.

I first would have to imagine a scene in which he or she produced that letter or article and then a further scene inspired by its content.

What could it tell me about the person who created it? For example, I might be reading an editorial Dad wrote. I then imagined the pile of virgin paper stacked adjacent to his typewriter, him snatching a piece up, hurriedly popping it in behind the carriage, with the automatic turn-and-a-half to get the paper lined up and ready to receive his ideas—an act as familiar to him as brushing his teeth—then the click-click-click-ding as the ideas begin to flow, as deftly onto the page as if deposited by an artist's brush.

Spurred on by Chris's advice to make it personal, I had to figure out how to position myself in the family narrative. This had to be more than just the story of my ancestors; I needed to know what I inherited from these individuals that makes me who I am. If I were to succeed in writing a memoir, I could not make myself invisible. It would be their story from my point of view. Above all, I would have to examine my own past judgment of and lack of empathy toward my parents and grandparents. Although time had softened those feelings, writing about my family taught me that I needed to revisit and resolve such judgments before I could portray them fairly. The story of how I came to understand my feelings about my father, mother, and stepfather takes up a good portion of the book. Their letters and other writings shed light on things I have wondered about over the years and revealed things about my parents that I did not know. These new revelations have in turn given me new insights into myself.

The idea of being a witness has been the compass guiding my way through the family thicket. It is like coming home to my family. I imagined what I might learn about Mother and Dad if I could secretly observe them before and after they met, after their marriage, and again as Dad went from his beginnings as a reporter to editor of his paper, where his creativity as a journalist resulted in a Pulitzer nomination, an upward journey that added neon to Mother's incandescent life as well.

Finally, I was *in* the family history thicket, with real people in real time. I could hear their voices calling me. I was straddling two realities: my own life, relationships, and activities, and my life in the context of the riches of my family's past. I became invested in their personalities and everyday lives. I had to reconstruct them, filling in the gaps with my own memories and reasoned inferences.

Webb, my brother, has his own story, in the Prologue, about how he came to be my co-author. His collaboration and contributions have added immeasurably to both the book and my experience of researching and writing it.

Debi Miller Bonds, 2012–2023.

Introduction

Why Letters?

*I didn't have time to write a short letter, so I wrote
a long one instead.*

—Attributed to Mark Twain

*Sir, more than kisses, letters mingle souls;
For, thus friends absent speak.*

—John Donne

Saving letters holds special importance in our family. The family history boxes are full of them. Reading them, I imagine their journey from the writers who addressed and mailed them, to those who read and saved them, coming to rest at last in my family history tubs. When Mother was in college, she even kept copies of her own letters to her parents. She and I exchanged many letters during the final twenty years of her life. I have almost all of them; even the ones I wrote to her came back to me. These letters are more than a record of events and activities in the lives of the writers. They are skeleton keys to the personalities, hopes, and desires of real persons in my own past and clues to who I am as well.

In his book *Writing about Your Life*, William Zinsser advises memoirists to "think small," to complement major life events with ordinary incidents that can give voice to universal themes. It is these self-contained moments, he contends, that can—when described effectively—speak to larger truths. In writing about my family, I am discovering that letters embody these "larger truths" and can speak for themselves. Dad's letters in particular provide a window into our familial themes of connection, commitment to kin, and community.

As a newspaper writer, Dad knew the power that words have over people. He understood the audience for whom he was writing and could move from logic and persuasion to self-deprecating humor accordingly. He had a gift for drawing readers into not only what he had to say, but also to his verbal style. But it is through the warmth and wit of his personal letters that he is most alive to me. Reading them, I can tilt my head and eavesdrop as he rehearses his message. During those moments, I recognize the voice I so love but have not heard for more than sixty years.

Dad's letter to his future mother-in-law, written after his first visit to their Seattle home, is full of warmth and clever originality, conveying his appreciation while adding a dose of charm. (The full letter appears on p. 151.)

January 10, 1937

My dear Mrs. Kirsch,

. . .

I wanted to thank you again for your extreme kindness to me during my stay in your home. It is a rare faculty to be able to make a person who is more or less a stranger feel so completely at ease, and you may believe that it was appreciated by me. Of course, I felt as though I ought to know you already, from everything your daughter had told me, but first meetings are apt to be a little strained, the more particularly when it suddenly dawns on you that your only girl is bringing home a boy for you to cast the eagle eye upon. Well, I can only say that I have never enjoyed any visit more, and that I hope to be able to continue our grand friendship for a long time. (Yes, Mrs. K., I AM crazy about your daughter. Is it a surprise?)

. . .

Yours,
Roland

When writing to his fiancée, Dad abandoned all professional pretense to "play" to his audience of one. During their month-long separation in August 1937, Dad wrote twenty-six letters to her. I can picture the late-night setting at the *Walla Walla Union-Bulletin*: Dad is at his desk at the paper. He is itching to type. The amorous words are ready to spill out onto the page. He had already made up his daily whimsical greeting before noon. During those weeks he will produce at least a dozen noms d'amour such as "Darling Mrs.-to-be," "Dollin," "M'Love," "'Lo Josephine," and "Darling Emmy."

Since much of what I knew about my family members who died between 1953 and 1990 came from letters, it seemed natural for me to join that conversation by writing my own letters to them directly, as if they could read them. I could imagine Dad, for example, opening and reading my note. He would be right there in my mind as I wrote. He and I could be virtually together for a one-on-one interaction. Even though he had died decades earlier, my emotional link to him was intact. I could easily resurrect the longing for him that fueled my life for years, ignited on that Monday in 1957. I even knew some of what I wanted to say to him.

At age eleven, I was just beginning to learn how to use my limited composition skills. I wanted to tell him how desperately I needed him to come home. But I thought he would also want to know that I was living a normal, happy life. I wrote about school activities, my social life, the weather, and my pitiful typing skills. I thought news from home would help him pass the time until he returned, cured from this nameless illness that was disrupting our lives.

I wrote the first of my two surviving letters to Dad on a pink letter sheet. I loved that pastel combo. It was as if the satiny paper could convey my loving message better than my clumsy words. A few days later I addressed my letter to Grammie and Gramps's Seattle house, knowing that they would deliver it to him.

October 14, 1956

Dear Daddy,

I will be very very glad when you get home.

Tomorrow we are having a big Social Studies test. Patty Holt was in town and I talked to her on the phone.

I am glad that you liked my card.

The stationary [*sic*] I am writing on Mother brought me from Seattle. Mrs. Craig [family helper] has been very nice to us.

> Love & kisses,
> Love Debby

P.S. Will write again soon.

October 17, 1956

Dear Daddy,

I am not a very good typer so please excuse me for my mistakes. I will sure be glad when you get home.

It is raining quite hard tonight. But lately the weather has been fairly nice outside, but it rained once or twice since you left.

We sure have had a lot of tests lately. We had dancing the other day for the first time this year.

If you get a chance to see Valdeen [daughter of grandparents' neighbors] please say hello for me and also, please tell Grammie and Gramps hello.

We had our first basketball game tonight and it didn't turn out very well. We played Jefferson and at the end of the game the score was as follows, Green Park [elementary school I attended], 28, Jefferson, 34,

I will write again soon,

With Love,
Debby Jane

Reading those early pleas I wrote to Dad, I relive the longing I felt at the time, begging him to come home. I had no room then for probability or chance-taking. I needed him.

Comparing the simple words I wrote to Dad as a kid with his own eloquent and witty writing, I was driven to take another stab at composing a letter to him. I wanted to prove that, while I got some things right in my 1956 letter to him, I could also write from a position of empathy and awareness of his extraordinary life. (He would not have used "extraordinary" to describe his accomplishments, but I get to.) This was the perfect opportunity to replace regret with gratitude and respect—and to show that although I'm in a different league as a wordsmith, I'm following in his footsteps.

I love letters that are back-and-forth conversations. Even when one of the letters is missing, the reply can leave few questions as to what the sender might have written. For example, in May of 1911, days before Frank (Gramps) and Ruth (Grammie) were married, his soon-to-be mother-in-law mailed a letter to Wymore, Nebraska, where Gramps had set up his carnival. Although Nanmy's letter is lost, I have his, in which he defends his devotion to young Ruth and commitment to care for her. Nanmy may have questioned his thinking about marrying young Ruth, a comment he inferred was a dig at his line of work. Gramps's response to Nanmy affected me strongly. It infuriated me that he had to defend himself against Nanmy's accusations that he wasn't good enough for Ruth. I wanted to step in and tell Nanmy off, then realized that Gramps had done it his own way when he suggested that she might be coming from a position of ignorance about the kinds of people who run traveling shows.

During the first term of the memoir classes, I decided that letters would be the heart of my project. I would begin by simply quoting family members' letters all or in part and make observations about them. The second way developed out of Chris Cutler's insistence that I had to be the central voice in my narrative. I would write to selected family members, recreating their stories as seen through my eyes.

The third and most challenging way was to compose letters impersonating certain family members, where no such letters survive. Most of those I wrote as part of the story of my great-aunt, Hattie Judd. Although the letters are fictional, I based them on real events and situations. They are my way of further understanding the persons involved.

My research began by going through the material I had organized, supplementing it with library and Internet research, while going to class and submitting samples of my writing.

To whom would I write? I initially wanted to limit my project to five individuals: my grandfather, my grandmother, my great-grandmother, my father, and my mother. They comprised most of my accumulation of family material. That might have worked had I completed my work the first year. But in early 2013, I learned of my great-aunt Hattie's story, which I had to tell. Two years later, my dear sister, Gretchen Miller Kafoury, died unexpectedly in the middle of the project. It was a non-issue—I had to write to her. And there would be more discoveries in the following years that would lead me to write two more letters—to my brother, Webb Colby Miller, and to my late stepfather, Walter Houser Brattain. (Our brother Bill died near the end of my writing. I'm grateful that Karen, his daughter, wrote about her parents in Chapter 12.)

My goal became the creation of a living memory for these individuals, a glimpse into their lives that could capture some of their stories for future generations. Writing these missives has been a great gift to me. Through these letters, I am reconstructing the meaning of my own life through theirs.

—Debi

Prologue

Brother and Sister
Letters to Each Other and to Our Younger Selves

To the outside world, we all grow old. But not to brothers and sisters. We know each other as we always were. We know each other's hearts. We've shared private family jokes. We remember family feuds and secrets, family griefs and joys. We live outside the touch of time.

—Clara Ortega

Debi and Webb seen celebrating their most recent chapter in the family history.

Dear Debi,

Now that we are completing the family-history book, I find I have a lot to say about the project. I'll describe how my involvement unfolded, then make some observations.

Early in my life, I realized that Mom was something of a pack rat. After all, there was a small, treasure-packed room in the basement that I entered only two or three times in my many years living in the house. I didn't appreciate the full extent until I saw the fifteen-or-so large tubs of papers that you inherited from her. Apparently, our mother saved almost all correspondence; an extreme example is the stack of long letters that our father had received from an admirer, the mysterious (at least to me, and maybe to Mom) Helen, as well as other friends; the letters are all dated several years before Dad met Mom. Who saves letters from a family member's old friends? Oops—you've kept them for thirty years.

After you had hauled the tubs around for twenty-some years, I was pleased and relieved to hear that you were starting to boil them down to something that our kids might find useful. (I'm curious to see how much of the original materials will get passed on to them.) A few years ago, you mentioned your supportive writing group and the progress you were making, but at that time it was just a passing interest of mine—something to keep my sister occupied and happy.

Things changed a few years ago when I visited you and Chris. Something—maybe seeing the enormity of the task facing you, or perhaps my direct exposure to how it energized you—lit a fire in me, though I was unclear how to interface with your project.

The point of entry that I finally recognized was though my curiosity about our family genealogy. Buried in the tubs, I found the information that Mom and our paternal grandmother had recorded. I remembered Mom talking about visiting places in Connecticut where her ancestors had lived. For Grandmother Pearl, hindered by loss of a family bible in the Chicago fire of 1871, investigating ancestry often involved the time and expense of visiting out-of-state courthouses. I thought it would be much easier for me, using the Internet. Besides satisfying my own curiosity, I wanted to pass information about the family tree on to the next generation—to give them something like I wished I had gotten from my mother and paternal grandmother. My hope was that this information would support and augment what you produced.

I worked on this in the fall of 2015, and finished a draft of my final report during a week-long visit to you the following February. Chris produced excellent pictorial renditions of family trees. I enjoyed this effort so much that I later spent some time exploring the heritage of our children's other parents. The Kafoury and Fox (Fuchs) lineages came to this country just a few generations ago, and I didn't have much luck tracing backwards from wives. I remember starting to look at the Agenbroads, but don't recall why I gave up.

Looking into the ancestors of my current wife, Nancy, I hit pay dirt. Her parents came from a part of Maine where families tend to remain for generations. Also, there are numerous books about early settlement of southern Maine, including York and Brunswick, typically written between 1880 and 1910, that can be found on the Internet. Frankly, her ancestors are more interesting than ours, including swashbucklers as opposed to the farmers and sedentary types in our tree. Her first direct ancestor in this country (William Hilton, no known relationship to our Hilton ancestors) came in 1621 on a small supply ship, one year after the Plymouth settlement, and another (Edward Johnson) came the year after that. By contrast, our lazy ancestors didn't begin coming here until what early-American historians call the Great Migration, starting in 1630. Nancy had ancestors killed by Indians, while another (Johnson Harmon, grandson of Edward Johnson) led troops that massacred Indians and killed the French priest inciting them. (But who are we to point fingers, since we are related to Aaron Burr?)

I was also fascinated by the family history of our stepfather, Walter Brattain. Most of his ancestors came from Germany or Scotland relatively recently, though the Brattain lineage goes back to John Brattain (born 1720) of North Carolina, who was either born there or came from Scotland around 1750, depending on whom you believe. However, Walter's recent ancestry is a story worth telling in some detail, and this year I have done so in a chapter on "Young Walter."

My week with you in February, 2016 was magical for me, and I was eager to make this a February tradition. (The timing is clearly ideal, so I can "warm my feathers" during the depth of a Pennsylvania winter.) I spent much of the 2017 visit learning what I could about Dad's childhood, and writing a summary. Unanswered questions remain, such as: How did he come to be born in the tiny burg of Milton-Freewater, Oregon, whereas his family lived in St. Louis? I know Dad's family took trips to the West in the summer, but Dad was born in January. I also explored the content of his many editorials for the *Walla Walla Union-Bulletin*. I know that these were a main focus of his professional life, and wanting to honor his legacy, I read through his editorials and wrote a brief description of his main theme. My final effort that year was to start writing about Walter's early life, a topic that we both kept revisiting until quite recently. Unfortunately, I had to cancel a 2018 trip at the last minute, when I started radiation treatments for prostate cancer.

During my February 2019 week in Las Vegas, I tried my hand at your letter-writing approach to recording family history. I found this perspective to be immensely satisfying, even cathartic; there was much I wanted to say to Dad. I imagined having a conversation, with the current version of Webb talking to Dad frozen in time by his death. When I asked myself what he would want me to talk about, the answer was: myself. If I had died when Andrew was thirteen, I would want to know how his life unfolded thereafter. Also, thinking in terms of my intended audience, especially my children, I would have loved finding such a letter from Dad to his father. In addition to learning about me, I know that Dad would be overjoyed to hear the news about his sister Marian that I recently added to my letter.

When you suggested, in the summer of 2019, that I write a "letter to myself," it seemed like an excellent idea, though for months I was unsuccessful in getting going. Finally, a few weeks before my 2020 visit, I saw how to proceed; starting with a photo of me and you, taken not long before we learned of Dad's illness, I remembered what I could of the worries from those days (not easy to do, given how idyllic our childhoods were), and addressed them. This exercise got me to think about my childhood more deeply than ever, leaving me more appreciative of Kid Webb.

Also before the 2020 visit, I drafted a letter to Mom, again writing to a parent frozen in time by their death. During her life, I told her repeatedly that I appreciate and love her, but I wanted to express this more completely and emphatically. Finally, I got a jump on my letter to you, the one you are now reading.

The 2021-2023 visits were canceled because of COVID, though

progress continued as you connected with Hattie's living descendants and polished your letters to near perfection. The deaths our two siblings left me feeling like the project needs to be wrapped up; it will happen in 2023. (A classic approach/avoidance conundrum: what on earth can I do in the winters of 2024 and beyond to attain even a fraction of this excitement and satisfaction?)

This January I got re-invigorated about my description of Dad's childhood and started learning more about his siblings, Marian and Raymond, and another occasional household member, Clara Colby Thoms. This activity has been very rewarding. I especially enjoyed identifying and contacting two of Marian's daughters, Virginia and Marianna, who could share insights into Dad's childhood because they were blessed to have fifty years of conversations with a parent who grew up in that household. Moreover, it brought me closer (if that is even possible) with you. The piece on Young Roland is my favorite contribution to our project.

A few weeks ago, it finally sunk in that you actually want to turn some of our writings into a book; before now I didn't take this seriously. I still haven't come to want a book, other than that I love to see you even more excited about our project. However, I made two changes to what I had written to ease the transition to book form. First, I found quotations to start each piece, for consistency with your style. Second, I put captions on photographs and adjusted the text so that photos can be migrated relative to words to eliminate wasted space.

After you drafted numerous potential family-history documents, and I drafted a few, we metaphorically spread them out on a table and decided which to keep and how to organize them. Both of us have occasionally written essays, as opposed to letters to an individual, and I proposed that we each contribute at most one "Dear X" letter to any given family member. (After seeing your letters to Gretchen and Gramps, AKA Honeychile, I felt no need to write to them—anything I said would pale in comparison to what you wrote. In other cases, I imagined writing a letter, but came up empty-handed.)

Material that we wanted to retain, but which seemed out of place in our letters, was put into an essay. I believe that our winnowing of potential material tightened up the presentation, and our separation of ideas into letters and essays organizes the material effectively.

This completes a summary of my involvement with your family-history project. However, be patient, I still have several points to make.

My main reasons for working on this project were to (1) learn more about my nearest relatives, (2) get in closer touch and enliven my feelings about some of them, and (3) deepen my connection to you by pursuing shared goals. I've often heard that teaching about an idea is the best way to understand it. For me, writing about my feelings is the best way to clarify them, pursuing reason number two. Indeed, writing and revising are critical for everything I want from participating in this project. Given how many people keep a diary, maybe I'm not unique in this.

All three aims were met by addressing our needs to resolve sixty-year-old issues about Dad's death. Your letter to Dad says, "my goal is to restore, renew, and revise my connection to you." That encapsulates both of us in a nutshell. Frequently, words sent to you about some aspect of family history drew an enthusiastic response: all goals met. In addition, the electricity of your letters has energized me, and some of your observations have affected what I wrote. For instance, you expressed a deep interest in the White House dinner for Nobel Prize winners (1962). When thinking about my letter to Mom, I remembered sitting by Ted Sorensen, JFK's speechwriter, at a celebratory dinner in 2010. Contemplating how Mom would have loved being there with me, and how you would react to this thought, nearly overloaded my circuits as I wrote about it.

In some cases, I investigated a topic of interest to me, but either did not attempt to write about it, or later discarded my writings. For example, to explore the interest in ancient Egypt shared by Mom and Kathleen, I spent many hours watching YouTube videos and DVDs from the library, which didn't yield fodder for my letters. Similarly, I read your books on the Rosenbergs, consulted other sources, and jotted down some ideas, but nothing came of it. Also, I read Dad's

My target audience, the next generation. From the left: Scott Agenbroad, Ross Brattain, Karen B., Brenda A., Andrew Miller, Sarah M., Mari M., Katharine Kafoury, Megan M., Deborah K. Photograph taken at the Reed House on the Manzanita, Oregon, beach, perhaps around 1980.

The audience, from around 2000. Deborah, Megan, Katharine, Mari, Sarah, Andrew, Brenda, Karen, Scott, Ross, and the final addition, Kathleen Miller.

Megan and her great-grandfather, Frank "Honeychile" Kirsch.

editorials, identified the most common theme, and wrote about it, but the result didn't excite me. A final example concerned the enjoyment of detective novels, which I share with Dad; I spent weeks reading some written between 1935 and 1957. Still, these efforts fulfilled the goals of learning more about our family and sharing an interest with you.

Another goal has been less important. I am hoping to produce a few entertaining family-history documents. My target audience is our children and possibly other relatives. The audience is so small that it fits in a photo.

I've sent my children some of our drafts, but so far the feedback has been meager. Apparently, their current interest in family history is like mine was at their age, which is to say imperceptible. On the bright side, I've erased the unpleasant thought that the huge pile of family records, which you inherited from Mom, would be dumped in their laps; maybe we can just leave behind a small book. I will be pleased if any of them decide to learn more about ancestors they barely, if at all, remember.

Despite their low interest to date, the goal of pleasing and inform-ing our kids has occasionally affected which drafts I kept. Just recently, while revising a description of Dad's childhood, I was reminded how much I learned from Dad's tabular summary of that period. About the same time, when Dad's niece Virginia asked for information about our home life, I realized I had almost nothing on the subject to offer either Virginia or our kids. That's when I decided to polish my letter to myself, which at least describes the internal life of one family member.

In the last 100 years, society has "progressed" from Helen's long and beautiful handwritten letters to 140-character impulses broadcast to a million followers. However, modern technology may also spur the revival of traditional family and local histories, like *Walter Merryman of Harpswell, Maine and his Descendants* by Rev. Charles Nelson Sinnett (1905) and *Histories of York County, Maine* by W. W. Clayton (1880) (among the books I used to reconstruct Nan's family tree).

Left: Webb seen composing his letter to Mom. Right: Webb and Chris return from adding 5,000 steps to their Fitbits.

More examples can be found in the chapter on our family genealogy. These books were probably handwritten (with considerable effort), then professionally typeset and published (at considerable cost).

The availability of word-processing and self-publishing tools has substantially decreased those burdens. Also, the Internet makes reconstruction of the family genealogy relatively easy and rewarding. I hope that my chapters on Young Roland and Family Genealogy illustrate those points. Of course, one is free to follow in Grandmother Pearl's footsteps and traipse around the country in pursuit

Debi and Webb, probably plotting how to annoy Gretchen.

of information about some long-lost relative, as illustrated by your marvelous letter to Hattie.

Modest computer resources and skills are adequate for everything I did on this project. I worked on an Apple laptop computer with an Internet connection. Genealogy studies relied on paid subscriptions to websites Ancestry.com, Newspapers.com and AmericanAncestors. org. Text was prepared with Microsoft Word, and images were viewed and cropped with Preview. The graphical tree of family members leading off this book was created with Ancestry and Preview, and the two figures in the Young Walter piece were created with Preview. The trees in Appendix II were drawn with Word. (In addition, Chris used InDesign to prepare the book for printing.)

To anyone reading: I recommend that you dive into family history at some point in your life. I've had an absolute blast doing it. Another recommendation is that you take this plunge together with others in your family; sharing the project with my sister was necessary for me both to start and to complete the effort, and provided me with years of joy.

After the five-star reviews by you and Chris, I was pleased when my 2018 Christmas present from Nan and Kathleen was a Fitbit wristwatch for counting steps. I only wear it in the winter, since getting exercise during the rest of the year is no problem for me, and it became a pivotal part of my writing process. Formulating my contributions frequently corresponded to working on my goal of 10,000 steps every day, either up and down my long driveway at home or around your Las Vegas neighborhood. For instance, the contents of my letters to Mom, to you, and to me were largely planned in my driveway, in the weeks before my 2020 visit.

Debi, you have been the one constant in my life. Other people, places, and interests have come and gone, but you've been present from my earliest memories until now. We shared a bedroom for our first few years, and there's nothing like whispering when you're supposed to sleep to build a partners-in-crime friendship between two kids. On the other end of my life, you've become my best friend, other than Nan, and brought me huge bonuses of purpose, excitement and joy as we documented family history. Between those times, you were always present, sometime close and sometimes distant, but always available. Come to think of it, our life-long interaction reminds me of a hammock: high on each end and comforting in the middle.

I know I've told you repeatedly that I appreciate and love you. With this letter, I want to express this even more completely and emphatically. Our family history project has let me, in your words, restore, renew, and revise my connection to you.

—Webb

Notice the custom-made belt depicting the woolly mammoth genome that my daughter Kathleen gave me! More on this later.

> *Do you know what friendship is? . . . It is to be*
> *brother and sister; two souls which touch without min-*
> *gling, two fingers on one hand.*
>
> —Victor Hugo

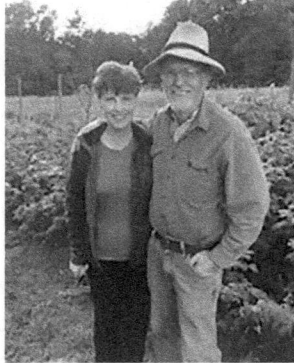

Debi and Farmer Webb by the raspberries, State College, Pennsylvania.

Dear Webb,

When your daughter Kathleen and you visited us in late 2015, I did not expect you to shatter my long-held biases—that you were both insensitive and blind to how others saw you. But you did so in only a few sentences.

I was standing at the kitchen sink, finishing up preparations for dinner. I had made some comment about it having been thirty years since you visited us at home. Rather than apologizing for your absence, you said, "The thing is, Debi . . . I don't need people. I don't socialize. I have no friends. I am a lousy brother and father. And I have limited tolerance for grandchildren. I'm a schmuck, your basic recluse . . . but I'm happy."

I didn't anticipate what came next. "In fact, I rarely think about our past or our parents . . . maybe one time in every two or three months."

I hardly knew how to make sense of that. I had convinced myself that you weren't much interested in keeping in touch with family. But what didn't fit with my sense of you as a clueless, insensitive person was your claim that you were a "lousy" brother and father—a "schmuck."

Even when you added that you were happy despite your aloofness, I chose to focus on your awareness of its effect on the rest of the family.

My second shock came just before you left for the motel that night, when you told me how happy you were to hear the joy in my voice when I would talk about my family history discoveries. In responding to my feelings, you showed a level of empathy in stark contrast to what I had experienced in our prior conversations in which I rarely felt understood.

Cracks were forming in my portrait of you as the remote brother, fissures that might allow me at last to ask you the questions—ones I had explored with Gretchen—I had wanted to ask for years. What was it like for you when Dad died? How did his death impact your life? How had your thinking about Dad changed over the years?

I did ask you those questions at breakfast a couple of days later, quickly adding that you didn't need to answer them right away. My invitation for you to delay your response was a way of buying time for me to prepare to hear your answers. Your revelations might stun me once again.

But, like a contestant in a rigged game show to whom someone had slipped the questions in advance, you were ready with the answers: "After Dad died, I shut myself off from everyone, including Mom. Especially Mom. I decided that to feel as close to anyone ever again could leave me open to the unbearable pain of future losses. It wasn't worth it."

Your revelations were like a knock to the side of my head.

For almost sixty years I had thought of myself as the one in the family who suffered most after Dad's death. I was the youngest, the neediest, the loneliest Miller. I assumed that everyone else knew that about me as well. Especially you.

Suddenly you were straight-up telling me about how Dad's death had rocked your world, how you had become guarded about all your relationships as a hedge against future debilitating losses. Gretchen had long ago set me straight about the devastating impact of Dad's death on her life; but for years I thought that you more or less sailed through this time and came out pretty much unscathed. Even though

I no longer thought of our reactions to Dad's death as a competition for most miserable, your disclosure bumped me out of any would-be lead. No one was going to give me the trophy for the biggest hurt, the most widespread destruction.

And there was more: you talked about what happened when you did think about Dad, about the memories and emotions that overwhelmed you, and about how they temporarily wiped out your ability to focus on anything else. You added that the experiences weren't all bad—they could be powerful reminders of your past and ongoing connection with Dad. You stressed that you could choose when to unleash those memories.

You spoke simply and clearly, without histrionics, letting me in on what I came to see as your private narrative, your own hellish journey. Your powerful words and imagery brought into focus your experiences of loss, exposing what my emotional distance from you had prevented me from seeing. How did I miss that you had been processing Dad's death your entire life thereafter?

Just before you and Kathleen left Henderson, you said, "I wonder if Dad would be proud of me, would approve of how I have lived my life."

Even though you had expressed this to me more than once in the past, I was again incredulous. You completed a Ph.D. in mathematics and had been on the faculty at several universities. Time magazine included you and colleague Stephan Schuster in their list of the 100 individuals who most influenced the world in 2009 for sequencing the DNA of the woolly mammoth. By every yardstick you were successful. Yet you remained unsure of how to answer the question "Would Dad have approved?" Your question suggested that you were driven to achieve, seeking his approval on one level while knowing on another that, no matter how hard you tried, he would never be able to give it to you. It made me wonder how your attitude toward your life work might have been different had Dad been alive to see what you have done.

Following that visit, I was able to overcome my biases of how you should have reacted to Dad's death, lived your life, and related to me.

Setting aside my judgment about you now seemed so easy, natural, and right. As my former, limited and limiting, picture of you shrank away, I was flooded with childhood memories of you, flashbacks of being your little sister.

You gave me two childhood gifts: connection and compassion. We spent a lot of time together, especially before we formed our own friendships. By being my companion, you gave me a chance to learn how to feel close to someone else. We didn't need to talk about what we felt towards each other. I loved chumming around with you as I watched how you interacted with others and the world around us. I admired and envied your curiosity about nature and your unusual ability to figure things out by yourself. It was as if you could come up with the answer to most any question just by thinking about it. Perhaps you in turn thought it was your duty to be a kind of protector to me.

Gretchen and Webb, Arch Cape, Oregon.

I think we both saw Gretchen as an in-charge person, at the helm of her life and others'. She was the quintessential first child: responsible, conscientious, and organized. I faced tough competition as the youngest Miller, with a knockout and talented sister and a brilliant brother. You and Gretchen seemed to have been born with creative paths unrolling easily before you. Seeing no path I could call my own, I waited for others to tell me which direction to follow based on what they thought best suited me.

I sought ways to connect with both of you. When I sensed you had mischief on your mind, I signed up. I was always ripe for shared shenanigans when things got quiet.

Mother had a certain radar, a gift for detecting secret plans even before we showed up with our guilty expressions. Whenever our wheels started rolling, she was poised to monitor our activities. One day when we were about six and seven, we decided to cut each other's hair. Although I can't remember who came up with the idea, within seconds we had selected a pair of shears from the sewing room and eyed one another for places to snip. I grabbed a small chunk of your hair from the back and chopped. When it was your turn, you cut a lock closer to my face.

If Mother found clippings where no clippings should be, she would be on to us. Surely tucking the snipped hair under some underwear in back of a dresser drawer would be safe. But of course what is missing can also be evidence, a fact that strangely did not occur to us.

We slipped into the kitchen where Mother was preparing dinner. "What have you two been up to?" she demanded, immediately seeing the results of our mischief. Not waiting for our protestations of innocence, Mother scolded us for using scissors around our faces and eyes. Soon, however, she quit her reprimand as suddenly as she had started, perhaps realizing that our sister's teasing would serve to discourage us from repeating that prank.

A few years later we decided that your clarinet could be a tool for something besides music. With an inflated balloon and your horn, we had everything we needed for a game of baseball. What damage could one possibly cause knocking a balloon around? You pitched a perfect strike, and I swung with enough force that the bell of the instrument flew off like a meteor and collided with the wall, leaving a crater the size of Delaware. My sense of horror at what I had done was overridden by my pleasure at having lobbed a home run for the first time in my life. That we might get in trouble was simply the price we would have to pay for a few moments of fun. The dent in the wall seemed more indicative of misbehavior than any possible damage to your horn.

Although the instrument incident took place after Dad's death, it was an exception to the direction our distancing relationship was heading. By then we seemed to be fleeing down separate and lonely roads. Whether this was normal for siblings approaching adolescence, or that his death had upended our sense of family unity, or both, I can't say. We were not equipped to offer emotional support to each other. Had I paused for a moment to truly peer behind Gretchen's or your external façade, I might have discovered that your worlds had been shattered as violently as mine.

Although I have spent years studying death and bereavement, I have never heard of a child dying of grief upon a parent's demise. The bottom line is that I wonder how we survived Dad's death. It's as if the gouge into our core could have stopped any of us from breathing our way into adulthood.

Mom and Dad's final month together at the Seattle hospital would have given them time to discuss her future, the decades she—then only forty-one years of age—would live. Dad made it clear that his greatest concern was for his children's welfare. To that end, he asked our close friends Dorothy and Clyde Robinson to assist Mother in caring for us, a pledge they made and kept until their deaths.

Had we been able to spend part of those final weeks with Dad— rather than being "held captive" at home in Walla Walla with Grammie and Gramps—he might have given us some guidelines for living without him. What kinds of directives could he have issued to make the years without him easier than they were?

If Dad had told us to be kind to one another, I might have listened. Empathy could have kept me close to you during our growing-up years. Had I been more compassionate, I might have seen you as innocent rather than aloof, cautious rather than calloused, skeptical rather than withdrawn.

I used to think that if I could learn one questionable detail about

Dad's life—some minor human infraction—that insight would suffice to knock him off the pedestal on which I had raised him. Wouldn't it have been easier to grieve the death of a human than a superman, one who had little in common with the world of fallible humans I saw everywhere?

For sixty years I have waited for Dad to return. I am still waiting. It's as if, sifting through the layers of family history, I might find Dad peeking out from underneath one of his letters, editorials, or playful photographs.

Webb, I will be ever grateful that you found your way into this project, allowing us to reconnect on the deep level I cherished from our childhood. May our re-commitment lead to more conversations with our own children and grandchildren as we continue to discover more gems of information from our diverse family history.

I love you!

—Debi

PS: I love the following piece you sent me a few years ago, a vignette about Dad's death. The frightening intensity of your private grief takes my breath away each time I read it. You call it "The Box." —D.

February 2017

My Dearest Sister Debi,

My life has been immeasurably enriched since you led me "into the family thicket." You've become my best friend and provided what is becoming the high-point of my year—the February week in Las Vegas. Trying to imagine what long-departed family members thought about various topics has emphasized to me that one should pull out all the stops when communicating with the living family. As part of telling you about my inner life, I'll do my best to describe what to me is the most striking facet of my response to Dad's death.

For over thirty years, beginning with his death in 1957, my most treasured childhood memento was a small box, visible only to me, similar to but slightly larger than one designed to hold a wedding ring. A hinged spring on the back of the box allowed me to snap open the lid. Sometimes the box seemed to be covered in red or light-colored velvet; other times it was dark and smooth. I imagined that I kept it in a drawer just deep enough to hold jewelry, watches and other personal effects.

That box imprisoned my pain over our father's death, shielding me from any random disruptions of my life that it might cause, but making it quickly available whenever I chose to let it out. Upon opening the box I would invariably be flooded by a blinding light of laser-like purity permeating all of my senses—I would be aware of no other images, sounds or thoughts. As long as I kept the box open I was connected to a reality far more meaningful than my day-to-day existence. That light was the reality of my overwhelming sense of loss for my father.

I treasured my box more than any of my material possessions. I felt that to give it up would leave my life diminished. And more importantly, it would separate my father even farther from me and his brief existence in the world.

But it was also a reminder that if I completely loved someone, something would cause them to leave me. When my first marriage failed, I had the perverse satisfaction of knowing that I was correct in drawing that conclusion.

Over time, I opened the box less often, perhaps only a couple of times per year near the end of those thirty years. I had come to feel that my need to hold on to the box was definitely contributing to my inability to completely surrender to another person. It was no easy task for me to convince myself that Dad would want me to let go, let alone actually do so. Success has made possible nearly 30 wonderful post-box years.

Just now, as I tried to share all this with you, I was pleased to see that even after nearly 30 years of not visiting the box, it remains possible and indeed rewarding to make the trip.

Love, your adoring brother, Webb

Penn State University Creamery.

Oh Webb! Do you really need a table in the document?

Webb and Nan Miller in Tucson, Arizona, Mineral and Gem Show—[Debi to vendor:] "Hey! This is my brother—he sequenced the woolly mammoth genome and you're selling their teeth. He needs one, so do I!"

> *These are the quicksilver moments of my childhood*
> *I cannot remember entirely. Irresistible and emblemat-*
> *ic, I can recall them only in fragments and shivers of the*
> *heart.*
>
> —Pat Conroy, The Prince of Tides

Hello Webb,

When Debi proposed that I "write a letter to myself", it seemed like an excellent if novel idea. However, for a few months I was unclear how to start. Now, with the approach of February 10, 2020, and my annual trip to see Debi and Chris, I've been energized. My only—minor—struggle has been with using words like "you", "I" and "us." I've settled on using "you" when talking about ages zero to twelve, "I" when referring to my current situation, and constructs like (1) "you" plus future tense verb or (2) "I" plus past tense verb for intermediate events.

The pre-pubescent Webb with 360-day-younger sister Debi, perhaps around 1955.

I have many photographs of you, but the youngest age where I feel we could have a truly meaningful conversation is found in one of you and Debi and another of you and Dad, taken on the same day. You are perhaps eleven or twelve years old. You look perched on the precipice to adulthood, and old enough to make sense of what I'll say. Also, I think this is before The Attack of the Hormones, so you should be able to pay attention.

Webb with his father, taken the same time as the previous photo.

I'm very curious to hear what you have to say in this conversation, but given the circumstances, I'll go first.

If you haven't already realized it, you'll come to see that your own childhood is amazingly peaceful and safe. However, some of my memories of you involve your concerns or worries, and I want to talk with you about those that will echo through much of your later life. Of course, the trauma of having your adult front teeth knocked out had some long-term consequences, but they were foreseeable and unimportant. Also, you have a sense of guilt over not-infrequent bursts of anger, such as the time you slammed the back door so hard that the window broke. In later life, you will almost never give in to anger, so I'll ignore that issue, too.

Of your concerns that continue into adolescence and beyond, the first one I remember involves your stuttering. Our father's mother was a born educator, and when you were just three or four she began teaching you to read. Our parents asked her to stop when they became aware of your stuttering, in hopes that relieving your performance anxiety would solve the problem. Unfortunately, that didn't work. Indeed, the problem won't ever completely go away. Reading out loud, especially to strangers, will be essentially impossible. This will adversely affect your professional life, though it won't stop you from being quite successful at it. The problem won't completely disappear until you start reading to your grandchildren. The upside is that stuttering will keep you humble, knowing that at any moment you might be unable to complete a sentence. No worries about morphing into a Silver-Tongued Devil.

I also remember that you sometimes felt unworthy. For instance, around age eight you got a chemistry set as a Christmas present, and cried because you felt undeserving of something so wonderful. I think this was a variant of the well-known impostor syndrome. You will continue to occasionally feel undeserving of a particular success. But don't worry: I once heard an expert on the syndrome say that its presence is a good indicator of, and perhaps a contributor to, success in life. For instance, in his experience, the most successful personal relationships occur when both people feel that their partner is out of their league. That is, they feel like an impostor, and hence stretch to be the best partner they can be. With a job, if one feels out of their depth on a project, they will often work harder than if they feel totally competent. I find this quite believable, and these benefits may also accrue from the humility brought on your stuttering.

Maybe this is the year Webb got the chemistry set.

I remember a third recurring concern. At around age twelve you noticed an article in, as I recall, *Popular Mechanics*, describing how to build a contraption where one person would operate a homemade air pump, allowing someone at the end of a hose to breathe underwater. Your father provided some funds to buy parts, including a rather expensive diving mask, and went to a local cannery in search of the specified size-303 metal cans. As with a number of other projects, you didn't complete it, but instead chased after the next shiny object. These failures typically left you feeling inadequate.

You'll probably be glad to hear that, before long, it will become evident that you did inherit the ability to remain focused on a project until completion, which will turn out to be a cornerstone of your professional life. Another characteristic will be that you prefer to work on projects that are not at all popular, at least when you take them up. These two traits, *i.e.,* an unswerving focus on a novel project, will be evident when you reach your majority. However, there is tension between them: you can get obsessed with a project that is unpopular for the good reason that a substantial breakthrough is elusive or impossible. For you, the remedy will be that even if a project gains a modicum of success, a need to explore a new frontier will eventually get you to shift to a radically different project. Such moves from being an expert in one field to a novice in another naturally disrupt professional advancement, but you'll be driven by a need for excitement. In the course of a forty-plus-year career, you will change professional focus three times. The popular wisdom about the third time has merit (spoiler alert).

I don't recall how much of a concern it is for you, but I know you sometimes wonder how smart you are. Of course, some adults sound smarter, but it is unclear how much of that springs from longer fact-gathering and brain development. There's a danger that you might be demoralized when you leave your small-town and peer-focused bubble, and bump into superior intellects, so let me put that to rest. Eventually you'll learn that many people are smarter than you (and me), some of them far smarter. Rather than you finding it depressing, it will be (as it should) a source of pride for you given your attainments. After all, a self-made man has more reason to be proud than does an equally-achieving person born with the proverbial silver spoon.

In summary, some of your current worries will instead turn out to

benefit your later life. However, I'm a bit concerned that you will conclude that your adulthood will be as relatively carefree as your youth,
leaving you more vulnerable to any future adversity. Don't make that
assumption. I promise that you will experience your full quota of the
pain and heartache, as memorialized by poets and country singers. I
leave it to you to navigate those waters.

You will make it through all of these adventures, ultimately reaching your "angle of repose." There is a wonderful book of the same
title by Wallace Stegner, but the phrase originally came from geology,
and refers to the steepest angle at which loose material will no longer
slide. I imagine a pile of gravel, with steep sides being buffeted by the
elements—wind, rain, ice, etc. Eventually the sides relax (slump) to
their angle of repose. That is how I see my life, finally reaching my
angle of repose. And who knows? In that long run of peaceful and
happy years you may even develop a deep and rich relationship with
the younger sister in that photograph.

1019 Alvarado Terrace, Walla Walla, Washington.

Maturity is the ability to live fully and equally in
multiple contexts; most especially, the ability, despite
our grief and losses, to courageously inhabit the past, the
present, and the future all at once.

—David White, *Consolations: The Solace, Nourishment and Under-*
lying Meaning of Everyday Words

[During memoir-writing sessions in 2019, our instructor, Chris Cutler, suggested writing a letter to a younger version of ourselves. At first, the idea of writing to myself felt strange. I didn't see the point of writing to some version of me that I had left behind. But when I came across two familiar childhood photos taken the summer of 1951, I saw a way forward. Instead of a pudgy kid sporting a dorky expression, I suddenly saw a young girl with whom I could empathize, one for whom I felt compassion. I realized I might have something to say to her. She was not some goofy stranger. She was me.]

Dear little Debby-in-braids,

You don't know me yet, but someday you will. I think I know you, though. From my mid-seventies, I have a panoramic view of your life to come. What could I tell you about your future that might resonate with the little-girl you? To help me find an answer, I have chosen two black and white photos from a summer day in 1951. In one, taken on the patio of 1019 Alvarado Terrace, you are holding onto the railing, leaning back, smiling over your shoulder at the photographer. In the other, you are looking in the mirror, appearing ready about to cut off your braids with a giant pair of scissors. You are wearing a favorite yellow and brown patterned dress, one your mother made. Folded pigtails, a bow tied around each plait, give your thin hair some bulk.

Your dad proposed the idea for the patio stance, as well as the upstairs mirror shot. He liked to add a playful quality to many otherwise generic poses, a behavior you will inherit. This may be your last day with long hair. Someone—maybe you—will cut off your braids, and your mother will tuck them into an envelope, which will end up in one of the family history boxes. You are taking a step toward growing up, toward maturity. You're ready for first grade at Green Park School.

As you progress through the elementary grades, music will be a fun part of your school life. Your early training will include piano lessons from Miss Hanna and violin from Mr. Cassel. You will be a member of a violin quartet called "The Violets." At school assemblies, you will march onstage single file, performing simple tunes to the accompaniment of Mr. Cassel at the piano. Those ensemble experiences are fine and much preferable to playing solo. You can hide—a "shrinking" Violet?—behind more proficient players. Even so, you will feel a little strange being on display before an audience. It will feel artificial. (A great contrast to times when you love attention as you do tongue tricks or, eyes covered, correctly name random notes others play on the piano. You are not fooled—you have perfect pitch, another link to your dad.) Still, you will think that the Violets must be pretty good if you play in public. But wait. Fifty years later you will reconnect with your fourth and fifth grade teacher, Sally Helmer. She will delight in telling you she found listening to your early efforts at Green Park excruciating! Nothing playful about her comment. Don't feel bad—remember, you will have to take only a fourth of the blame for the cacophony. But you will learn how to improve your showing. Your favorite musical activity will be playing simple duets with your dad. Next to him, you will be dimly aware of the gulf between his beautiful cello tone and your scratchy attempts. But he won't seem to mind and knows you are new at this. These musical moments will forge a special relationship between the two of you. You will never be a soloist but will find your place in ensembles throughout your musical life.

In junior high, you will put away your violin for almost two decades, a decision you will come to see as a survival strategy. Fortunately, you will reconnect with your fiddle and discover a commitment to practicing you never had as a child. For twenty years you will search for your voice—a means of expressing through the strings of your fiddle—what lies within you. You will obsess about finding the rich tone that parallels the music that courses through your veins. While playing duets with Chris, who will be your teacher and then (dare I tell you) your husband, you will in time come close to creating true music but will never be satisfied with your tone. When standing beside him, you can absorb his energy while focusing on his tone rather than your own. By yourself, the beautiful music you hear in your head will remain beyond your power to produce on the violin.

One of your challenges will be growing up with siblings who seem to have already discovered their niches in academic and social life and parents who appear to excel at everything. Comparing your talents or skills to those of your brother and sister, you will seem to fall short. Your sense of self-worth will be long in coming; for years you will look to others for approval and validation. At last, when you are in graduate school, you will realize that you are no longer pursuing grades or degrees in order to impress someone else. This will be wonderfully liberating and will make you free to find your own voice.

Your mother's death, when you are forty-five years old, will throw you into adult orphanhood. After writing your Ph.D. dissertation on the experiences of several women who, as adults, have lost their mothers, you will learn that your ultimate writing experience awaits you. Stories of your ancestors known and unknown lie dormant in the letters and photographs saved by your mother. As you work your way through their writing and bring them to life in your mind, you will ultimately be able to weave elements of their lives into your own.

In the process of retelling their stories, you will finally experience congruence. (That's a fancy way of saying your own life story will begin to make sense to you.) Your memoir will reflect your deepest thoughts and feelings. Words will bring you the expressive tool you could not find in playing music. It won't come easily. You will agonize while shaping those thoughts into words that can adequately express them. Your search will bring deeper meaning to your life by connecting with others—beginning with your children and grandchildren—balancing what was, what is, and what might be. Those discoveries will enhance how you will relate to everyone in your life.

Although you will start this pilgrimage into the family history by yourself, you will have help: Webb will write splendidly about aspects of the family history you never would have—and Chris will take on a jaw-dropping commitment, editing and preparing the book for print. Both are welcome gifts as you bring your work to fruition.

Be kind to yourself. You will be reconnecting your past to your present for the rest of your life.

I'll close with a quote that you will not understand for years, but please hold onto it until you can appreciate the futility of listening to my predictions for your life. You will create your own meaningful narrative. Safe travels.

> *No one can build you the bridge on which you,*
> *and only you, must cross the river of life. There may be*
> *countless trails and bridges and demigods who would*
> *gladly carry you across; but only at the price of pawning*
> *and forgoing yourself. There is one path in the world*
> *that none can walk but you. Where does it lead? Don't*
> *ask, walk!*
>
> —Friedrich Nietzsche

Scenes from forty years with Chris.

Wedding Rehearsal, Walla Walla, 1982.

Married 20 years.

Denver, Colorado, married 30 years.

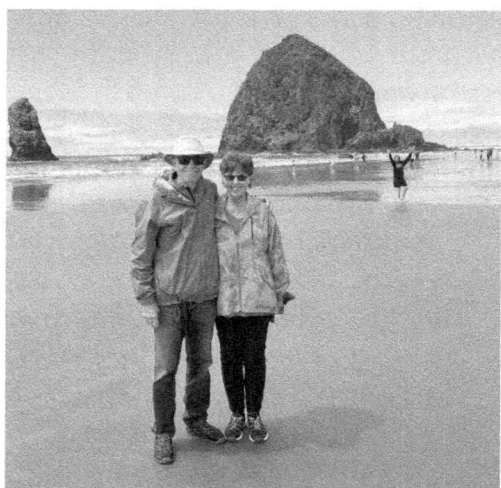

Cannon Beach, Oregon, married 40 years.

CHASING SHADOWS

Frank

Elephants love reunions. They recognize one another after years and years of separation and greet each other with wild, boisterous joy. There's bellowing and trumpeting, ear flapping and rubbing. Trunks entwine.

—Jennifer Richard Jacobson

Why the hell shouldn't I run away with the circus?

—Sara Gruen

Dear Honeychile!

I remember well that summer of 1961. Mother, Webb, Bingo [our beloved cocker spaniel], and I returned to Walla Walla from two years in Chatham, New Jersey. You knew the story: Mom had thought it might work for us to move east so she and Walter could live together. Although Webb went along with it, he wasn't too keen on the idea, largely because he disliked being thrown into unfamiliar situations. For me, it was traumatic. I rebelled in subtle and not-so-subtle ways. I rang up big phone bills talking to my friends back home. I wore makeup and started smoking. Without saying so, I made it clear in a thousand ways that New Jersey wasn't a good fit for me. Ultimately, I got my way, and we moved back to Walla Walla so I could finish my junior and senior years in high school. But there was another reason Mom would have wanted to come back: you had been widowed just months before we left. I know she was worried about you. I wish I had been more tuned into your grief.

You were a master at hiding your sadness. You had decided that life on the open road was the best medicine and that maybe I could

Honeychile and Debi arrived in Seattle.

Karen Viestenz, Debi, and Sharon Transeth arrived at Aunt Mari's on Mercer Island, WA.

Honeychile's travel companions 50 years later, still eager for another road trip.

be your traveling companion. Together we hatched one such plan that year: we would convince Mother to let you drive two dear friends and me to Seattle for a few days with Walter's sister, Mari. Karen, Sharon, and I were giddy teenagers, and you were the perfect chaperone, providing some supervision without really tuning into our incessant teenage banter. After we arrived in Seattle, we took pictures. Standing next to you, I look innocent enough. You, your hat at a rakish angle, look ready for adventure.

For years, you still burned with that same eagerness for egress. I remember the night before a trip in the mid-1960s that Mom, you, and I were to make to Seattle. Hours after you had gone down to your basement bedroom, Mom and I were saying goodnight in the kitchen, both ready to sleep for a few hours before our early-morning drive.

Just as one of us reached to turn off the main light, we heard your footsteps climbing the narrow basement stairs. With each step your hard leather soles tapped the metal stair nosings, announcing your approach.

Mom and I giggled, knowing that in seconds you would appear in your rumpled suit and hat. Your internal alarm would have gone off before we even set ours. According to basement time, we were due to head out for Seattle.

As you reached the top step, you paused to steady yourself before entering the kitchen.

"Dad!" Mother chided, "Debi and I haven't even gone to bed."

After some prodding and repeated promises that we would leave by eight o'clock, you returned to your bedroom to wait for dawn. Sleepless, no doubt.

You had a strange, almost radar-like way of knowing where advertisers would hang posters for certain upcoming events in store windows. I loved when you would call out, "Debi, let's go out! I need to check on something." You would then direct me to drive down Alder Street in Walla Walla before turning left on 2nd or 3rd Street, where you inevitably would spot a small circus poster. How did you know where to find them? I never really asked, preferring to think of you as a kind of magician possessed of secret knowledge, an image I formed when we would visit you at your carnival.

One poster you found induced us to attend the Carson & Barnes Circus in Walla Walla. I remember sitting next to you high in the stands when we heard the voice of Kirby Grant, the star of the TV show "Sky King," over the loudspeaker. After he welcomed the audience and introduced the president of Whitman College, Grant called out your name: "Fra-aank KIRSCH!" All eyes turned to you as you stood up and modestly doffed your hat. At that moment I caught sight of how others saw you: the influential, revered, former circus owner. I was proud to be your sidekick!

Every kid has at least two grandfathers, but not everyone's grandfather owns a traveling circus. Mine did. To me, you and the circus were synonymous. If there is a "circus gene," I inherited it. But I also inhaled my share of circus dust. And developed a lifelong love of elephants—but more about that later.

In my mind I'm a child again, walking through the entrance to your traveling circus—"Western Shows"—in Burien, just south of Seattle. It is the gateway to another world, self-contained, far removed from, but somehow explanatory of, my child's world. In that world, the carousel, the Ferris wheel, the Tilt-A-Whirl (my favorite ride), the tent show, and the game booths full of enticing toys all combine to entertain, edify, and amaze. The hustle and bustle fills my ears. I feel insignificant among the surging crowd as I pass by the "joints" [concession stands], where sweaty men in shirtsleeves shout at the crowds to try their luck at ring tossing and ball throwing. "Step right up! Walk this way! Sir! Win the prize for your young miss! Everyone walks away a winner!" I think, winning is easy! I don't notice that the same stuffed toys hang on the joints' canvas walls day after day. Players almost never win the giant prizes. Most get ultra-cheap prizes known as "slum," which cost about a buck fifty a gross. I move quickly from joint to joint looking for the perfect toy, the very prize I need to take home. Of course, setting your heart on a giant stuffed

The Miller kids at Gramps' Western Show about 1951.

toy is normally a poor strategy when the game is rigged against you. But I am not your typical chump or mark. I'm family. The boss's granddaughter. All the agents know it. It doesn't matter that I throw balls that always miss the stacked pins or that I toss dimes that only bounce before sliding off the edges of the flattened glass plates. They know who I am and make sure that I don't walk away empty-handed.

Although I feel a surge of joy when they hand me a coveted toy, your generous crew give me the biggest, most enduring prize of all: the gift of belonging. I feel at home there, a real member of your circus family.

I came along rather late in your career. As the youngest of three children, I often felt a lack of direction compared to my brother and sister, who seemed grown-up to me even as kids, even though we were only a year or so apart in age from each other. I was always searching for my proper place. As you got to know me, you may well have thought I needed something I could fit into, a place where I felt fulfilled and got special treatment. Everyone working in the traveling show business is there, it seems, because they didn't find their place in the nine-to-five world of ordinary society. The carnival is a world unto itself, a fraternity with its own hierarchy and rules of behavior. Somehow, my connection to you earned me an honorary place in that society, a place where I could be myself and not how anyone else wanted me to be.

Although the details of how you became the Honeychile I knew and loved are sketchy, I can reconstruct a basic outline of your life before me through your letters, photos, and scrapbooks.

Your life story could be summarized in the two pictures above. As a young boy, you allowed yourself to be dressed in a dapper wool tweed suit, handsomely fitted to your small size. You wore a printed silk bow that someone had carefully tied under the broad, starched collar. The jacket's parallel pleats added charm and style to your fetching look. Even your future persnickety mother-in-law, already an accomplished seamstress, would likely have approved of this proper look for the son of an Abilene, Kansas, doctor.

I see in your young expression a resolve to face the unknowable future. Although you appeared not to be looking at anything in particular, in your mind's eye you might have been focusing on something in Abilene or beyond its borders.

The second photo, taken decades later, shows you decked out in one of your three-piece tweed suits, complete with a starched shirt and printed silk tie. You could have just been to the same barber who knew how to tame that front tuft of young-boy hair for the camera. In contrast to the youthful photo in which you faced the unknowable, here you knew just what you could find. I see evidence of wanderlust but without the mischievousness I detect in many of your other pictures. Perhaps the absence of a cigar tamed you a bit. When you held a cigar in your mouth, your lips held a mischievous curl. It was as if you knew some things that the rest of us might not. But you were generously willing to share your secrets with anyone ready to come along on the ride.

Frank L. Kirsch, circa 1963.

My favorite picture of you flaunts your playfulness, sparkling eyes, and a mouthful of mischief just behind that unlit cigar. How did you get away with that cigar-chewing behavior? Although all of us in the family teased you about your "vile habit," we seemed to accept a "see-gar" as part of your outfit. You wore a dapper suit and a colorful pre-tied bow tie sprinkled with white polka dots. You combed and parted your hair, flattening it to the right, and all strands stayed in place except for the front tuft that popped up, proudly independent.

Mother kept flamboyant newspaper and magazine articles about you. In one written in 1959, Frank Lynch of the *Seattle Post-Intelligencer* interviewed you (whom he called "Mr. Carny") in a piece titled "Midgets and Giants and Jingle of Coins." Lynch posed the kinds of questions I wish I had asked you during the last ten years of your life. You told him about your father, Martin, who came to America from his native Germany, where he had graduated from medical school, ultimately settling in Abilene, Kansas. Although you might have followed in your father's path, fate had determined otherwise. The number one American showman of the turn of the century, Charles Wallace Parker, also lived in Abilene. The lure of the outdoor show business won out and you followed Parker's lead.

Your sense of intrigue with the circus could have started during your early months of working for the Parker Amusement Company, where you sanded wooden merry-go-round horses that would soon metamorphose into fiery steeds, destined for one of his prized carousels [also known as Carry-Us-Alls]. Those smooth, brightly adorned ponies, moving up and down to the rhythm of the calliope music, could transport riders young and old to a dreamlike world. The carousel's angular momentum was enough to keep the stationary world spinning by. Reflecting on this time for you, I can see how these carousels might well have set your career in motion. Perhaps you were already thinking about your future with the circus as you worked on those ponies as a thirteen-year-old.

Although your father expected you to become a doctor and serve the community as he did, you came up with your own idea of service. You saw the traveling show as a way of healing people, by bringing to life their fantasies and giving them live entertainment that had more power to heal than any prescribed elixir. You saw the immediate, positive impact on the faces of those attending a show or even strolling through the carnival lots. Walking among exhibits, both enticing and strange, attendees shuffled along through sawdust that almost served as a brake, a physical force that kept one from moving too quickly. Despite the slowed walking pace, there was an excitement in those crowds, a palpable lure to come closer, to be curious, and to check out the sideshow promises.

At age nineteen, you first "hit the tanbark" [joined a traveling show] as a trombone player in the circus of Walter J. McDonald, Abilene's other leading citizen. From there you and your horn moved from company to company like the changing seasons. What melodies of life did you learn along with the tunes that you performed in town after town? What stories could you have told about your fellow musicians, who likely were as entertaining after the show as they were under the tent? How many of them also kept the show business embers stoked during the coming decades?

You flourished as an itinerant performer, but less so as a bachelor. When Ruth Marie Hilton came into your life, you began a courtship in which you wrote to her for at least two years before deciding at age twenty-eight that you and she should get married. In one of the earliest surviving missives—from 1909—you teased and tempted her with your playful language and banter. Your letter sounds like a delightful improvisation—a conversation in which little was said but a good deal was communicated—as if the real letter to her was written between the lines, intended only for Ruth's eyes.

There was one potential problem standing in your way. Barely nineteen years old, Ruth would have let you know that her mother had powerful ideas about her proper marriage age and what sort of man she should marry. In a letter now lost, Ida likely questioned your qualifications as a husband, given your chosen profession with its constant travel and subculture. As you replied to Ida about your plans, choosing your words carefully (I wonder if this was a second

Frank and Ruth in Cedar City, Nebraska, the day after their wedding, May 17, 1911.

Frank and Ruth with Ida Hilton (Ruth's mother), taken the same day.

or third draft), you gently took issue with her assessment of you and your chosen career, as well as your plans to marry Ruth.

Wymore [Nebraska], May 7, 1911

Dear Mrs. Hilton:

No, I will not consider the letter as a lecture. Just as you say, everything is to be considered. I expect a happy life, why should I not? I think Ruthy a very broad minded girl. I will do all in my power to make her happy. There is only one thing I had in my mind, you could have against me and that's the "show profession" which I know numerous have.

But Mrs. Hilton, do you not think that could be termed ignorance? I think there are just as good people in the profession as there are out.

If it's up to me, I should like to meet you at Central City [Nebraska] the 17th [one day after the wedding in Fullerton, Nebraska] and if you have any suggestions to offer, I would be more than pleased to hear them. Hoping you and I will see that same light of happiness in Ruthy's face forever.

I remain

Sincerely yours, Frank

Although I have found no documents to account for your educational years, the photographs you kept from your early musical ventures could tell a similar tale. The images of the bands, laid side-by-side, seem to form a progression, as if several of you entered the profession as peers, advancing from one group to another at the completion of each season. In rehearsals and performances the musicians honed their technical skills and endurance before advancing on to the next band. A better band.

Abilene, Kansas, 1903. Frank is in back row, second from right.

You kept these pictures as a reminder of the beginning of your professional identity. Standing uniformed with your fellow band members, you send a tacit message: "We are members of a tight-knit fraternity of musicians and speak the same language. Some of us will continue through different bands, reuniting season after season to entertain across the Midwest. Our improvisations—those moments when we leave behind the notes on the page—tell you our individual stories."

Your musical history in photographs begins in 1903 with your stint with the C. W. Parker Amusement Company. Subsequently you performed as a member of the Blondin Show, the Lewis & Clark Great Western Shows, and ultimately your own, the Kirsch Show.

In reading one of the newspaper articles, I learned that you acquired the rights [likely in 1912 or 1913] to "The Cattle King: King of the Cow Punchers (A Melodrama)," along with two Pullman cars, which you named after your parents, Emma and Martin. With your own show and your own coaches, the parallel steel rails became your ticket to tour the Midwest. Finally, your parents, mother-in-law, and others could look at you and say, "Now, there's a man of substance."

When you toured by train with your band and tent show, people were eager to see what you brought to town. Entertainment of any kind was hard to come by for most rural villages and towns, and the occasional traveling show—rare, but at least more frequent than Halley's Comet—was cause for celebration. But along with the appeal of novelty came high expectations. Not willing to settle for mere amusement, they wanted to be carried away to foreign lands, to witness spectacles beyond their imagination.

You pasted small newspaper clippings [without dates, but likely during the 1912-1913 seasons] into a hard-cover composition book, write-ups from your tour with the Lewis and Clark's Western Show, and subsequently, with your own. Your company, the Kirsch Show, traveled several seasons.

Among the clippings is an Abilene newspaper article touting your show:

> A good sized crowd attended the western play "The Cattle King" held last night in the large tent on South Cedar Street. The show was a story of Arizona life well staged and interesting and was well put on by a good sized company. It was far above the average run of Western plays given this city and pleased those present. The company carries a good band and both the band and the orchestra which played at the show were good. Two concerts were given by the band yesterday, one at noon the other in the evening. A feature of the concerts was a western song with a band accompaniment. Neither money nor time have been spared in making the show a first class tent show and Frank Kirsch, owner and manager, of this city is to be complimented for the first class company and aggregation he has secured.

One of the newspaper clippings from Saratoga, Wyoming described the Pullman cars in which your company traveled:

The Kirsch Show, traveling with two railroad cars named after Frank's parents, Martin and Emma. Frank is standing on the far right with his trombone.

A Splendid Show Company—The play, "The King of the Cowpunchers," staged here Tuesday night by the Lewis & Clark company, attracted a full house and everybody went away pleased with the performance. The company travels in its own cars, one a baggage and dining car, the other a sleeper, and stages its plays in a large tent capable of seating 700 people. They pitched their tent by the side of the railroad track and the setting was pleasant in every way. The company is one of the cleanest we have ever seen—fine young men of excellent character and sweet, healthy, lovable women, living up to the very highest of which they are capable. The play is a fine one. Never for one minute, either in the play or in vaudeville does any act or word border on the smutty or obscene but all is free from any untoward suggestion. It is a play where one can take the family and sit down to the evening knowing that there will be nothing to offend the etiquette of a pure home life. The play is a strong one of Western life on the ranch, something we are all familiar with, and the players are all of them excellent. *The Sun* can most heartily endorse the play as well as the company and both are exceptionally good.

*He goes out for an automobile ride every day. The
Old Lady has given him the car. She gives him whatever
he wants.*

—Jean de Brunhoff, *Babar the Elephant*

And now, about those elephants…

According to the legendary showman P. T. Barnum, "When
entertaining the public, it is best to have an elephant." You took that
message one step farther by making it personal. Your quote could
have been: "When entertaining your grandchildren, it's best to know
an elephant."

Belle and Honeychile outside of the Berry house.

You and your close friend Morgan Berry shared a passion for
elephants. Morgan was well known among circus owners and zoo
personnel for importing exotic animals, and elephants were one of
his success stories. In 1952, he bought a young, orphaned calf in
Thailand and named her Belle. Just three months old, Belle traveled
with her new owner on a steamer from Bangkok to Seattle.

Belle moved into Berry's Seattle residence in the Fremont District
and soon became family. In his book *Packy & Me*, zoo veterinarian
Dr. Matthew Mayberry writes: "Morgan had learned from India's
mahouts [elephant owners] that the bond between elephant and man
can be extremely tight, lasting a lifetime. . . . Knowing this, Morgan

raised 35-inch, 185-pound Belle as if she were his daughter." Belle, reportedly, was potty-trained and had the run of the house. Although she slept in the basement on her own pile of hay, she occasionally climbed to the second floor during the night to tell her owners with a tap of the trunk that she needed a snack. After treats, Belle would creep back downstairs and tuck herself into bed.

Belle was quite an attraction in the neighborhood and could often be seen on her stroll with Mrs. Berry, sometimes stepping on the backs of Mrs. B's shoes. But it was the car rides that got the most attention.

Morgan Berry helping Belle out of his car.

Morgan and Belle drove around Seattle in a Cadillac convertible or a sedan, her trunk wrapped around Berry's neck.

When Belle was about one year old and weighed more than 600 pounds, Morgan decided it was time to move her to Seattle's Woodland Park Zoo. I can imagine how painful that was for the family when Belle climbed into the trailer. Belle was later taken to the Portland Zoo.

In 1962, Belle gave birth to Packy, a male whose arrival sent waves of excitement around the country. Packy was the first elephant born in captivity in the United States in over forty years. *Life* magazine ran a spread about the birth. Our family tracked the mother-son

L to R: Front row: Noah Barranco, Sydney Agenbroad.
Second row: Lauren Woodard, Devin B., Brenda B., Scott A.,
Third row: Bob Lee in Elephants, Debi, Chris
Back row: Ross Brattain, Karen Brattain, Tracy A.

Debi with Noah, Sydney, Lauren and Devin. Packy
is just behind the hedge between Debi and Lauren.

Packy, age 53.

duo throughout their lives and frequently caught sight of them at the Oregon zoo.

Although you, like Morgan Berry, loved elephants, you stopped short of insisting that a calf come live with you and Grammie at your whimsically named home, "Kirsch's Poor Farm," in northwest Seattle.

Today, your grandchildren and great-grandchildren adore stories from your adventurous life, keeping them alive by retelling them in their own way.

I recall one such moment when Chris, the Gramps of this generation, and I were playing puppets in our loft with grandsons Devin, ten, and Noah, seven. We all had a puppet on each hand and were having a grand time breathing life into those stuffed figures. Suddenly a memory of the circus flooded my mind. I laid down my elephant and hedgehog puppets on the mini sofa and jumped up to grab a picture of you from the closet nearby. I returned holding the poster-sized photo in which you were sporting one of your chewed-but-never-smoked stogies in your mouth and looking mischievous as ever. [See p. 9.]

"Hey guys," I called. "Check this out! This is a wonderful picture of my dear Gramps, known as Honeychile. His real name was Frank, and he had a really great face. Don't you think?"

Devin excitedly interrupted, "Mimi, sometime I want to tell you about my grandfather! My grandfather had a circus!"

"Wow! That's so neat! Just imagine, owning a circus. . . And you know what? That guy was this guy! He's the one in this picture; he's the same guy! Honeychile is our circus grandfather!"

Devin's eyes flashed in a moment of insight, as his mind began to piece together key fragments of his mental puzzle, adding a face to his "grandparent," the one who loved elephants.

In 2015 I took the elephant stories to school. Mrs. Field, second grade teacher of your great-great-grandson Noah's class in which I volunteered, invited me to give a program, to tell stories about Belle and Packy. I had a great time with the kids, sharing pictures of you and the elephants. They giggled when I held up the picture

Mrs. Field's second grade class, 2015
(Noah directly in front of Debi).

Noah decorating elephant cookies.

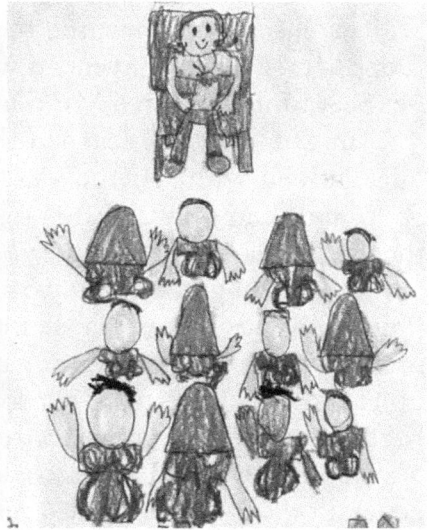

Addison St. Pierre's detailed
drawing includes Debi's elephant
pendant and earrings.

Packy's 2015 birthday cake.

Noah's drawing of Packy
stepping on his cake.

of Morgan supporting Belle's forehead to prevent her from falling trunk-first onto the pavement while exiting the sedan. Following the questions—everyone wanted to know what it was like to live with an elephant—Noah passed out elephant cookies that he and I baked and decorated. They all loved the photo of Packy appearing to step on his birthday cake. Afterward, Mrs. Field invited her students to write me a thank-you note and draw a picture, one of which, by Addison

St. Pierre, superbly captured the moment. Noah began his note with "Dear Mrs. Bonds" and ended with "Your friend, Noah." How could I expect him to call me Mimi in front of his peers or even on paper?

In 2016, when I learned that Packy, then fifty-three, had been quarantined with tuberculosis, I knew I needed to take Brenda and Scott and their four children to see him. Granddaughter Lauren had the great idea to contact the zoo. Bob Lee, elephant curator, agreed to meet us, suggesting that we ask a staffer to call "Bob in Elephants" if we didn't see him when we first arrived at the new Elephant Lands area. Bob gave us a VIP tour and, since we weren't allowed direct access to Packy, he took photos of him using my camera. Sadly, in February 2017, just months after our visit, Packy died.

Honeychile, your stories continue to spread throughout the younger generations. Another great-great-grandchild has fallen in love with tales of your life. A few years ago Chris and I were having breakfast with my grand-niece Tia in Hector's Diner in New York, around the corner from the Whitney Museum. We were enjoying a traditional greasy-spoon breakfast (I think you would have enjoyed it!) and sipping coffee. Across the street we watched a well-dressed young woman unsuccessfully coaxing her large black dog to walk. Our conversation drifted to you, the circus, and elephants. Tia was fascinated by your story and excitedly made me promise to send it to her. I could imagine your mischievous nod of approval as we talked about you.

If I could magically make you appear for even one afternoon—the scene is one of your shows, and you are with your friend, George "Slim" Lewis—I could learn about the essence of you by following you and eavesdropping on your conversation. Slim's arm is around your shoulder as the two of you walk the midway, each trying to top the other's circus stories.

In his 1961 book *The Ape I Knew*, Slim expressed his opinion of you: "To all good show people, but more especially to Frank L. Kirsch and William R. 'Ketrow' Peters, who collectively gave to the outdoor show world and presented to the American public, for over one hundred years, clean Carnival and Circus entertainment."

Lewis judged individuals based on his view of their honesty and fairness. He had ample opportunity during his seasons with American United Shows to learn the difference between honest operators like you, who ran their shows with compassion and equity, and those who merely separated gullible marks from their money.

After your death, Slim paid tribute to you in the March-April 1970 edition of *The White Tops* (published by The Circus Fans Association):

> Ahll out and ahll ova that's all for today folks, but there will be another show tomorrow, where and which tomorrow who knows? But there will, there has to be, for the show must go on and on forevermore. The curtain comes down but to rise again, if not here on earth then somewhere in the endless universe.
>
> On February 27th in a hospital at Walla Walla, Washington, the curtain came down for Frank Louis Kirsch, who spent the greater part of the 86 years he put in on this life's stage in the outdoor show business. The curtain falls for all of us, today, tomorrow, perhaps the next, but for men like Frank there can be no finale, for if there is then we all have performed in vain.
>
> For almost 40 years until he retired in 1960, Frank was the owner and operator of the Western Shows, a small carnival he toured mostly in western Washington cities and towns. The Western Shows Midway was one of the few carnival midways of his time a family could enjoy an hour or two of merriment on, without being hustled out of their last penny by some gaffed up flat joint.
>
> Frank was born in Abilene, Kansas, in 1883, during a period after the Civil War when the Yankees and the Rebels joined hands there to develop and build the West. For several years before he traveled west to establish his home in Seattle and organize the Western Shows, Frank owned and operated a two-car railroad circus complete with elephants that traveled throughout the Middle West and southern states, this was about 1913, '14 and '15.
>
> During recent years Mr. Kirsch was a charter member and past president of the Northwest Showman's Club; past president of Jack Bell Tent No. 90 of the Circus Fans Association of America; a member of the Pacific Coast Showman's Association, and for many years, a Mason.
>
> Frank's wife, the former Ruth Maria Hilton, whom he married in 1911, died in 1959. He is survived by his daughter, Mrs. Walter H. Brattain of Walla Walla and 4 grandchildren. He was buried in Walla Walla on Tuesday, March 3, 1970.
>
> —George W. "Slim" Lewis

I grew up adoring you without understanding what it was about you that transfixed me. You seemed to be a grand mix of innocence and mischievousness. You came across as being on the verge of maturity, but not quite there. Part of it was your youthful zest for what was just around the corner. You changed, however, when you stepped onto a carnival or circus lot. You became responsible, grounded, and wise. It was as if even the scent of the circus could ignite your imagination and could transport you home. Honeychile, your magic lives on.

I love you,
Debi

Carrying on the tradition: Debi with granddaughters Sydney, Hope Lowis and Liya Lowis, with elephants at Omaha's Henry Doorly Zoo, 2022.

Debi and Tia, NYC 2016, where Honeychile's story first captivated Tia.

2

Hattie

*Our brightest blazes of gladness are commonly kin-
dled by unexpected sparks.*

—Samuel Johnson

Debi and I met only a few of our relatives. We knew three grandparents and our maternal great-grandmother, Ida, but no aunts, uncles or
cousins. I briefly met perhaps six other relatives on our father's side
of the family, and two on our mother's. We spent a few days with
other relatives in Europe when I was eleven. I felt a real connection
with my mother's father and my father's mother, somewhat less with
my maternal grandmother, and little or none with other relatives.

I was therefore surprised when one of Debi's first letters for her
family history project was to someone I had never heard of, and not
even a direct ancestor. In going through Ida's handwritten memoir,
Debi was hooked by a few paragraphs about Ida's youngest sister,
Hattie Judd. Ida had attached a small photo of Hattie that was an
apt metaphor for Ida's words—compelling but providing no details of
Hattie's complicated and, in many ways tragic, life. For over a year,
Debi poured tremendous energy into learning about Hattie. She has
since described some of her forays into our family as "going down a
rabbit hole"—a perfect description in this case.

Contrary to my skepticism about Debi's Hattie project, she wrote
a letter that absolutely captivates me. I love it that Debi has enriched
my life with vivid knowledge about, and empathy for, another relative. Her account reads like a good detective novel, where the reader
follows her through twists and turns as she discovers new clues about
this mysterious character. Many questions are raised, and some are
answered. And there's even more: Debi also wrote a letter to Hattie's grandson, Edward, which continues the Hattie saga, including
contacts with Hattie's living descendants.

What I find most compelling about her writing here is how well it illustrates two of Debi's most admirable qualities—a love of knowledge and the ability to focus great energy on a project she loves. I think of these letters as providing two stories. The first concerns the tragic life of a woman who shared only a few percent of my DNA, together with a more positive updating of her story. Second, by looking more closely, the reader will get a glimpse into the heart of my marvelous sister.

—Webb

The meaning of things lies not in the things themselves, but in our attitude towards them.

—Antoine de Saint-Exupery

The grief within me has its own heartbeat. It has its own life, its own song. Part of me wants to resist the rhythms of my grief, yet as I surrender to the song, I learn to listen deep within myself.

— Alan Wolfelt

September 2013

Dear Aunt Hattie,

I don't know if your sister Ida ever mentioned her Walla Walla great-grandchildren in a letter, but she never told Gretchen, Webb and me about you. How I wish she had and that I would have seen that striking picture of you as a young girl. I wish, too, that Mother would have driven me to Colorado to meet you when there was still time. Missing that one chance to know you, to hug you, is one of my biggest regrets. The more I discovered about your life, the more certain I became that I had to write to you, telling you what I learned and how much I longed to go back and rescue you when your sister Anna failed. But I'm getting ahead of myself . . .

Most of my life, I thought about you only as my great-grandmother Ida's younger sister by fifteen years, the last of nine children, and the only one born in Missouri. I also had a few photographs of you and your family. Then, eight months ago you slipped into my life through the pages of Ida's handwritten memoir. That was just the beginning. Soon, following several phone calls, email exchanges, and trips to Colorado and Missouri, I had a wealth of documents that told me the layers of tragedy you experienced during the last several decades of your life.

On March 24, 1950, Ida wrote, "I have a letter [from Hattie] in today's mail, wishing she had my ability at sewing—I would have had that too—for it was [a] natural gift." In telling Ida that you were envious of her skill with needle and thread, you seemed to be reaching out to her, hoping somehow to reconnect as sisters. Her comment that she had a gift for sewing tells me that she was flattered, but nothing in it suggests that she admired your musical talent in return. Instead, she claimed that, although your parents paid for your piano lessons—something they never did for her—you "never made any use of" your musical training. I bristled when I read that. Even at the age of ninety, Ida still resented what she saw as your special treatment. How could she focus on that and have nothing to say about your confinement in a mental hospital for almost three decades? I wanted to go back in time and defend you.

Hattie, age 16.

My favorite image of you is a bad photocopy—the original is lost—that Ida had attached to a page in her memoir. You at sixteen, looking pensively away from the camera lens, the soft curls spilling

onto your forehead. Maybe you were thinking about the man of
your dreams, one who would suit you as lovingly as did the dress
tailored for you by Ida, the seamstress of the family. She had made
that dress for you during a visit home, taking one of your mother's
old dresses and tailoring the heavy fabric to fit your youthful frame.
I would love to have eavesdropped on your conversation as she was
working. What advice from an older sister might she have given you?

Left to right: Randall S. Judd, Howard, Hattie.

I see a different side of you when I look at the photo of your father,
your baby nephew Howard [Ida's son] and you at thirteen. Your
impassive face reveals nothing, as if you agreed to have your picture
taken while denying so much as a peek at your personality. The
twenty velvet-covered buttons, each individually fastened, may have
served, along with Victorian customs, to keep your thoughts hidden.

That brief mention of you in Ida's memoir was interesting. But
what turned out to be much more significant is a paper my mother
wrote in 1938 for biology class, titled "Genetics." In it, she included a family tree on which she noted some physical and personality
characteristics of several persons. Three bear the label "insane." You

were one of them. In her paper, Mother speculated on possible explanations for your being so labeled, including "extreme nervousness," "tragic" marital life, and the death of both your children. (She wasn't counting your infant son who died.)

I first learned about your status of resident—inmate—of the Colorado State Hospital in Pueblo by looking online at the 1930 U.S. Census. I stared at the word "insane" and imagined it tattooed in big letters on your forehead—a label that would almost certainly have closed future doors for you in the unlikely event of your release. I hoped desperately that you had gotten out sometime that decade or the next. But you were to remain locked up for the rest of your life—more than twenty-eight years. For 10,289 days, to be precise.

In part because of my background in counseling, I was eager to learn as much as I could about you. More, I wanted to make you a real person, someone I could talk to, write to. To imagine what your life was like.

I wanted to know how you got there and whose decision it was to keep you there. How the staff treated you. What contact you had with your family during your incarceration. For instance, who might have told you how disappointed they were with how you turned out? Was it your father who, according to Ida, found little in life that met with his approval? If he sought to father children who could live up to his demands for perfection, you would have been just another grim reminder that none of his nine children could provide the parental reverence he deserved. That's just a guess.

I knew what I needed to turn Ida's casual reference to you into the story of a real person to whom tragic things happened, to reconstitute you out of the bits and pieces I had—legal documents, photos, doctors' notes. But I felt inadequate to the task, as if I were digging a hole without any skills in grave digging. I wanted somehow to do justice to your life by providing a loving burial place, cushioned for your long rest.

By consulting genealogy links on the Internet and emailing individuals with whom I had common ancestors, I learned that you had been involved in a 1913 probate case in Carthage. To learn more, I contacted archivist Steve Welden at the Jasper County Records Department. Steve and his team of volunteer historians found the probate record and also unearthed at least a dozen related items that shed light on your time in Missouri. As Steve combed through the files, he became intrigued. Sensing his interest, I sent him your photo along with my early reflections. The innocence and gentleness he saw in your face moved him deeply. His generosity helped fuel my quest to understand you and piece together your life story.

After Chris discovered [on Findagrave.com] where you lay buried, we linked those details to a 1953 letter in the family history that reported your death and funeral. At the time of your death, your Colorado nephew arranged for your memorial, shopping for a suitable dress for you and choosing a floral piece for your casket. Your niece Helen Pile reflected in a letter to my grandmother, "I am so glad that some of her own people could be there to look after her." I was consoled by her words, knowing that your family had helped bring closure to those long Pueblo years.

Thinking about the mortician sliding your body into a one-size-fits-all gown, I'm reminded of the scene in which Ida tailored a hand-me-down dress to fit your lithe frame. The mortician's work was a macabre echo of Ida's. To him, you were part of his business, an object to show his skill at making you look lifelike. I shuddered as I imagined this unsentimental preening before the cemetery workers lowered your casket into the ground. For Ida, you were a lively sister for whom she cared enough to do her best work, so that you would both be pleased with the result.

Hattie, I have learned a lot about your life before they took you to Pueblo—heart-wrenching details that smash any remaining shards of my belief that life might somehow be fair.

You were twenty-seven years old when you and Abe Mink married. I can picture you slipping your arm through his as you repeated your till-death pledges to each other, tacit assurance that love would carry you through thick and thin. And things looked good: you and

Abe celebrated the new year with new life, the birth of your daughter Emma. Then came a son, Eddie, in 1903. In just four years your family doubled in size. With a husband and two healthy children, the new century looked good.

But the thick part of "thick and thin" was not to be. A third child, known only as Baby Mink, was born and buried in 1905, followed two years later by Abe's untimely death in 1907.

Final Judd Family Portrait (about 1907)
Standing L to R: Unknown, Samuel Judd (oldest brother), Ida Judd Hilton (oldest sister), Randall Judd (older brother), Unknown
Seated L to R: Anna Judd Howard (older sister), Randall Stoddard Judd (Hattie's father), Hattie, Maria Tompkins Judd (Hattie's mother), George Judd (older brother).

About the time of Abe's death, your parents asked you and your siblings to assemble for a family photo. Ida's stance directly behind you shows the steel that would carry her for decades. In that photo, you seem to be turning from your father's indifferent mien toward your mother's stoical support. You could not have known that her care and love would end with her death in less than two years.

I was overwhelmed by the events that followed your mother's death. Although with sufficient healing time you might have rallied from the deaths of your husband, your infant son, and your mother, you could not have braced yourself for what followed. In November 1910, you traveled to Caldwell, Idaho, to say your final goodbye to Samuel, your dying brother. Emma and Eddie stayed behind in Missouri. By the time you reached Caldwell, Samuel was already dead and buried. Before you could grasp the reality of your brother's demise, you learned that your dear son Eddie, back home in Carthage, had died of tonsillitis at seven years of age. Your world darkened by incomprehensible grief, you returned home and placed his tombstone just a few feet southwest of his daddy's.

In 1912, your father, Randall Judd, died. Perhaps surprisingly, he had provided generously for you in his will. Just as you began to realize a sense of financial security, you were stunned by another loss. Although this did not involve a physical death, the event may have accelerated your descent into madness. E. B. Jacobs, the appointed executor of your father's will, took you to court, charging that you were "of unsound mind and unable to manage [your] properties." A twelve-member, all-male jury concurred with Jacobs' claim. Unfortunately, I was unable to find out any more details about that.

You wed and divorced Wesley Bowen before you and Emma married into the same family. In 1917, Emma and Glenn Cooper married just months before you married Glenn's father, C. J. Later that year, Emma and Glenn celebrated the birth of their son, also named Eddie, your only grandchild. In 1918 the pandemic flu swept through much of the country, sweeping up Emma along with hundreds of thousands of others during the second wave.

It seems you were asylum-bound even before you signed Emma's death certificate in December 1918. Emma had been the glue that held together the Cooper family, including your marriage to C. J.

Her death undoubtedly led to the splintering of your roles of wife, mother-in-law, and grandmother with the trio of Cooper males. Glenn remarried within a few years, and C. J. took off for Tennessee in search of a new life with a former wife. What chance did you have of staying sane?

To complement my personal questions about you, I needed some historical perspective on the state of mental illness treatment in the first half of the twentieth century. I jumped into the vat of information about mental hospitals, focusing especially on personal accounts by patients as well as nurses and doctors. Much of the writing pulled me in even as it made me cynical about early twentieth-century mental health services.

In 1887, journalist Nellie Bly was asked by her editor to infiltrate, by feigning insanity, New York's Blackwell Island Insane Asylum. Her assignment: to document what took place inside. Her narrative, *Ten Days in a Mad-House*, of her treatment during incarceration caused a sensation, breaking down the asylum doors for public scrutiny. It was an unprecedented first-hand look inside an insane asylum, which confirmed and amplified popular opinion of the terrible conditions inside and the primitive and often cruel treatment of patients. While there, Bly forged strong bonds with some of the residents, whom she regretted having to leave behind even as she was laying bare their treatment. I wish you could have read Bly's account.

I also read a *Life* magazine article, "Bedlam 1946," which showed that things hadn't improved much in sixty years. Incompetent and overworked doctors and staff contributed to poor conditions and patient abuse. The exposé grabbed readers' attention, stunning a society still shaken by World War II barbarities, calling American ethical behaviors into question. It was one thing to fathom such inhumanity steeped in Nazi influence and quite another to visualize such savagery on American turf. This widely distributed article would have caught the attention of many of your relatives. Some of them may have paused, questioning how to balance an "I'm a compassionate person" self-image with a contradictory "I'm doing nothing to help Hattie" self-awareness.

Yet another book, *Asylum* (1961), by sociologist Erving Goffman, studied the institutional structures that shape the lives of workers and inmates alike. An involuntary stay in an asylum frequently strips an individual of his or her unique self-identity. Years of daily rules, routine, and uniform, drab clothing result in both the loss of the individual self and the ability to see other patients as unique individuals. The unmistakable difference in dress between staff and inmates gives rise to two distinct communities, parallel universes as separate as layered geological strata. In that respect, it is like a prison.

Placed into hospital group living [also known as batch living], you were expected to follow rigid schedules and procedures designed for efficient facility functioning. There would have been no options to linger in a comfortable bed, to complete an activity, or to eat when you were hungry instead of at an assigned time.

While many American women were dreaming about fixing up their lives, your new Pueblo residence fixed it so that you would be stripped of incidentals that would have given your life some order. Like a tomato dipped in scalding water, you instantly molted, skinned of your personal possessions and comforts. You would have seen the same thing happening to your fellow patients, their unique personalities seemingly erased by routine and boredom.

Living during a dark period of mental health practices, you may have been exposed to insulin shock treatment, hydrotherapy, and electroconvulsive therapy. All of these therapies were administered to change individuals' behaviors, often to make them more manageable and submissive.

Paul Gruchow, writer and educator, had a label for your kind of courage: survival. He saw mental illness as something to endure rather than a roadblock to overcome, as if one's only chance to survive involved clinging to any ragged edges of life within reach. Hanging on for one day, then the next, and the next after that. Although best known for his extensive writing about nature, Gruchow turned his lens inward before taking his own life at age fifty-six. In his posthumously published *Letters to a Young Madman,* he described with stunning clarity his internal landscape, reflecting on his thoughts and experiences in ways that mental health practitioners overlooked. Despite the occasional compassionate treatment he received, he summarized the majority of interventions as mirroring cultural stigmas and professional biases, while giving mere lip service to healing.

Gruchow captured the paradox, found in much of the available treatment, of those who were labeled mentally ill and forced into subservient, inconsequential roles while being denied the therapeutic healing they could reap from providing service to others. Chained to a diagnosis! How I wish I could have offered you a conversation with this generous man before he succumbed to his own despair. Because he understood personal trauma and the complications that can come from the demise of key relationships, he might have empathized with your sweeping losses. And you in turn would have identified with the candor and lucidity with which he wrote. Reading Gruchow's vivid descriptions of electroconvulsive therapy, I could imagine myself on a table, feeling the gel being smeared on my temples in preparation for the placement of the electrodes.

Soon after learning where you were buried, I called the Records Department at the Colorado State Hospital. Before I completed my question about accessing your files, the contact person turned me down. Due to patient confidentiality regulations, the files were closed. I could access nothing. End of story. The technician suggested that I contact the hospital museum, a project that a committed group of individuals had brought to fruition in 1984. I called the museum and reached Nell Mitchell. Within minutes, Nell convinced me that Chris and I needed to come to Pueblo. Weeks later, in May 2013, we drove 800 miles to Colorado, where we were greeted by individuals who were eager to learn about you.

Museum curators Nell and Bob, along with Margie O'Leary, a retired psychiatric nurse, spent the morning guiding us through the museum, pointing out equipment, photographs, and artifacts, using you as a focus of the conversation: "Could Hattie have slept in this

Colorado State Hospital, Female Center, Wards 14, 16, & 18, from the period of Hattie's institutionalization. This and other early buildings no longer exist.

The hospital grounds with the Wet Mountains in the distance, as Hattie would have seen them.

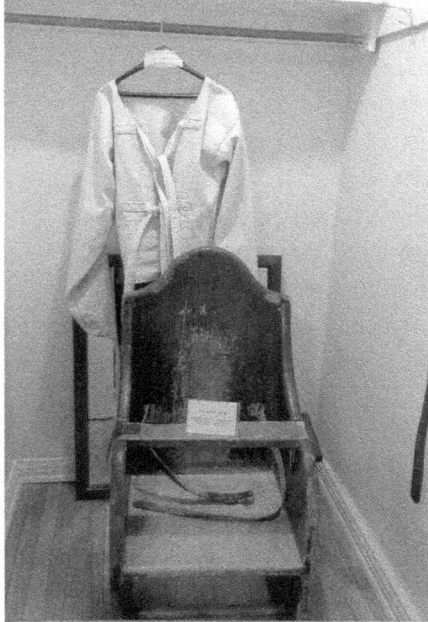

Straitjacket and restraint chair, Hospital Museum.

L to R: Margie O'Leary, psychiatric nurse who joined the staff in 1956, 3 years after Hattie's death; Nell and Bob Mitchell, museum historians, at entrance to the Hospital Museum, 2013.

dorm, met with the superintendent in this office, struggled to free herself from this restraint jacket?" I was moved by their generosity and the way they respected your humanity. In calling you by name and in acknowledging how little doctors and nurses during your time understood the human need for ongoing social and family interactions, they showed empathy for you as a human being, not a nameless, faceless mental patient. It became clear that the policies of the Colorado hospital reflected the medical and cultural beliefs of the era. One example of this was the restriction of family visits during a resident's first year, aimed at accelerating patient adjustment to institutional life. Although this strategy had obvious advantages for the institution, the benefits for residents were dubious.

When you arrived at the hospital you likely went to the office of acting superintendent Dr. Frank Zimmerman as the final step in your citizen-to-patient transition. With that single action, you gave up your name in exchange for an identification number. You became #222-429.

When I expressed my strong disappointment that I could not get your medical records, Nell suggested that I ask my physician to request them for the purpose of finding possible genetic predispositions toward mental illness. This subterfuge would enable me to learn what life was like for you inside the hospital. Was it my turn to feign insanity to get closer to you? Was I following Nellie Bly's example from more than a century before to get a foot inside the hospital door—in this case, into the medical records drawers? It felt like it, and I looked forward to hacking away at the imagined distance separating our lives. But did the hospital even have your records from sixty years ago?

I paused on the museum lawn as Chris and I left the hospital grounds and stared at the Wet Mountain Range. Did you feel drawn to those mountains as I did? While few of the hospital buildings in which you spent those years remain, the mountains persevere unchanged. Today they still stand sentinel over your last resting place.

You were buried at Mountain View Cemetery sixty years ago. We knew where to look for your grave—Lot E (East), #34, Grave: 5—but found only an unmarked plot of land. This was where we finally caught up with you. Even though your nephew had made arrangements for your burial, somehow the final act—placing a headstone over your grave—was overlooked.

On the way home, I considered how life might have been for me had you and I exchanged places—you becoming the youngest Miller, I stepping into life as the last-born Judd. Suppose some series of events resulted in my being sent to Pueblo. What might others have seen in me that appeared eccentric or problematic? Might I have been labeled manic? My overzealous laughter, my tendency to pop up and gallop meaninglessly around the room, my monotone, drone-like hum, my frequent self-interruptions, my insatiable demand for cinnamon rolls—all could be symptoms in the thinking of the time.

In September 2013, we drove to Carthage, Missouri, where I met with Steve and his volunteers at the Jasper County Records Department. That meeting brought closure to my search for Missouri documents. We also visited the Friends Cemetery in nearby Purcell, where we located the graves of Baby Mink and Eddie next to Abe's. Although records indicate that Emma's grave is there too, we could not find it.

My doctor agreed to write to Pueblo. It worked. Your medical records, totaling about 150 pages, arrived at the clinic four weeks later.

After I got home with the packet, I was apprehensive about reading the reports. Although I had for months wanted information about your life behind the hospital walls, I felt suddenly unsure, afraid of what I might learn. I was hungry to inspect the documents, yet apprehensive that I might read horrific details about you. What if the doctors gave you repeated electroshock treatments and that you died an agonizing death? What if your family truly did forget you?

Bracing myself, I opened the envelope late that Friday afternoon. As your clinical history unfolded before me, I was overwhelmed by what I saw. For the next several hours I ran the gamut from horror to hope, from moments of outrage when I thought you were treated egregiously to relief at more generic reports. I winced as I read of your repeated water treatments, worried as I read of ward altercations you initiated (of course cheering for you as you punched and pummeled), and wept as I read about the failed attempt to get you out.

You arrived in Rifle, Colorado, on November 14, 1924, at the home of Anna and George Howard, your sister and brother-in-law. Following a stressful night during which they later described your behavior as "violent," Anna and George filed a complaint with the Garfield County Court House. Your case was referred to the Lunacy Commission. On November 15, the Commission decided you were insane and ordered that you be committed to the Colorado State Hospital. On November 19, Dr. Bordner, one of the hospital physicians, interviewed you. I was struck by the clarity with which you described your trip from Missouri to Colorado. After hearing your story, he wrote, "She sold her piano for money to defray her expenses to her sister's [home] in Rifle. This was her last possession and caused her much grief to part with it." He concluded his notes:

> A white woman age fifty years, three marriages, one husband died, one divorced and one deserted her. Three children dead. Paternal grandfather was insane, one sister died in a State Hospital in Missouri.
>
> Insight, she is troubled, but not insane.
>
> Provisional Diagnosis: Manic depressive—Manic

That provisional diagnosis, for whatever reasons, was never changed during your incarceration. Although you were described on the first page of your 1953 autopsy report as "quiet, cooperative, friendly since 1935," you were buried with the diagnosis of "manic depressive psychosis."

One of the tragedies of your life was to have lived in a time when mental hospitals operated within a system where being committed was easier than getting discharged, where the entrance was wider than the exit, and where individuals in positions of authority could easily smear you with an insanity label, one nearly impossible to erase.

Although convincing others to reconsider your diagnosis was difficult, you and your sister almost pulled it off. In July 1930, Dr. Zimmerman responded to a request by Anna and George to get you paroled to their care. They made plans to drive to Pueblo, where you had already spent almost six years, and to take you back to their home [a distance of 300 miles]. Although the superintendent agreed to dismiss you, a flood washed out the road near Rifle and with it your chance of escape. When they could not rescue you from the hospital, you plunged into despair.

I agonized about what this might have meant to you. You may have suspected that it was your last chance for freedom. George had just turned seventy, and Anna was already sixty-three.

According to your hospital notes for August 10-11, 1930, "Patient very much disturbed, talkative and did not get settled down for the night until 1 A.M. At 5 A.M. [she] used profane language and was very angry. Dr. B. reports patient disappointed because her people could not come from Rifle on account of a washout. Patient disturbed, noisy, put in pack [hot or cold water] at 9:30 A.M. Patient became quieter in the afternoon." On August 12, the notes continue: "Patient very disturbed, resistive and destructive. Put in [strait]jacket at 4:15 P.M. Dr. B. reports patient in a hypomanic condition."

This was to have been no ordinary family visit, but was your chance to get out. In the end, it was your final, failed, chance. I could feel imaginary walls closing in on me, forcing the sudden expulsion of my held breath as my heartbeat raced. Oh my God, Hattie!

As I reread those pages the next morning, I realized I could not let myself become mired in your failed attempt to escape. You didn't, after all. Although you fought the system for months, even years, following that fateful day, you managed to turn your life around in the mid-1930s, finding solace and significance in your surroundings.

In January 1934, you started working for Dr. and Mrs. Fimple. I felt hopeful as I read that you were able to work in a private residence. In spite of setbacks during which this routine might have been interrupted, the records show that you worked for them until May 1947. Although I don't know the details of your relationship with the doctor and his wife, by inviting you to be their housekeeper, the Fimples offered you an environment outside the mental hospital, a place where you could restore your sense of self-worth through service to others.

I can imagine you in your self-appointed role of nurturer and person of good will during your final Pueblo years. You evolved from being a combative, demanding patient to one who was cooperative and caring toward your co-residents. In becoming a compassionate caregiver, you were among the first to put Paul Gruchow's claim about the value of providing service to others into action. [See my fictional letters between Hattie and Ida, pp. 64-70.]

November 2013

When I woke up this morning, something had changed. Rather than looking for an external you, I felt your internalized presence, an added energy as if coming from you. Your gift to me.

I have longed to understand you as you would have wanted to be known, a longing fulfilled in part as I added more of your life's details to my Hattie file. As I became swept up in your life events, I made inferences about how you gave meaning to those turning points. Imagining your life as I might have lived it, I wove my own experiences and assumptions into my incomplete portrait of you. Although I got rather good at plunking myself into your story while hanging onto my self-identity, I realized that by taking this shortcut I missed what I most craved: a glimpse of how you might have narrated your own journey. It was as if I were trying to force selected puzzle pieces from my life into yours, shoving them where they didn't belong, the edges of the pieces bent and distorted.

Even as I was aware of this tendency to miss the essence of you by viewing your experience through my eyes, I nevertheless thought I caught a glimpse of the "real" you.

I feel most poignantly connected to you as a mother and grandmother. You gave birth to three infants between 1902 and 1905. One died at birth, one during childhood, and one when still a young adolescent, barely old enough to mother your only grandson. How did you endure this triad of death which wiped out your motherhood roles?

Beyond the physical deaths was an even greater loss: the severed psychological cords between each one of them and you, the invisible connective tissue that could nurture and sustain you as they grew up, as you aged. What memories did you grasp as each relationship turned into loss, clutching those mental images until your cells absorbed them, as a dye penetrates fabric?

But here's the question: What evidence do I have to support the Hattie of my imagination? Do three photographs that reveal little about you, a trio of reflections from relatives, plus a handful of legal and medical records do justice to the real you? Other than you, who might have been in a position to narrate your life? I'm aware that you may have a large number of great-grandnieces and -nephews, sharing generational threads to you and your siblings, descendants I will never meet. What might they know about you, have heard about you, or wonder about you? Each one, fueled by a sense of curiosity would use the documents to write a different narrative about you. Same subject, same details, yet a differently narrated life. So, which is the real you? What parts of you have I conjured up, and what elements would you recognize?

You have more than enough incidental chroniclers of your tragic life story, the telling of which springs from casual interest, the crossing of paths, or records kept in dusty hospital file cabinets. Staff members at the Colorado State Hospital tracked your movement and behavior for years. As the focus of their note-keeping was on finding evidence of pathology rather than on signs of mental health, they were trained to identify certain problematic actions—ones that the hospital rules dictated some type of intervention. I would love to interview some of your former caregivers, to probe into their unrecorded observations, to mine their memories for examples of your behaviors that didn't conform to the criteria of mental illness.

As I processed the details in the hospital accounts, most often told in legal and clinical language, I couldn't hear your voice. But don't think for a minute that I only heard the stuffy, wooden reports your captors scribbled on their charts. Beyond the noise, beyond the limb-flailing that you exhibited, I got what was going on. I understood your craving for understanding from someone willing to listen to you and focus on the immense ocean of losses in which you had treaded water for years.

In addition to the gift of knowing much more about you than I did eleven months ago, I have become aware of a yearning to connect with you that will remain unrequited. Even though I knew from the beginning of this search that that was impossible, my craving has grown into an insatiable hunger, which can never be fully satisfied, although I will be looking for a glimpse of you in people I meet or while crowd-scanning. I wonder what you searched for on others' faces as you probed to know, to understand, or to connect with the memories of your unforgotten loves.

The final years of hospital notes include multiple reports of times you spent reading letters and writing to relatives. How fitting, then, that I started to write my letter to you before I found out that you and I shared a passion for letter writing. Perhaps writing gave you, as it has given me, greater self-awareness as well as a means of reaching out to others. Three years before your death you wrote a letter to your sister Ida in which you lamented not inheriting the same seamstress gifts your sister had. Clearly, you were thinking even in your final years about how things might have been, skills you could have developed, other paths you might have followed.

Although I missed you by sixty years, learning about you more than a half century after your death, the timing was serendipitous in that I was able to learn important details about your life in Missouri and Colorado. If I had waited a few years to search for you, I might have come up empty handed. It was as if you found your way to me. All I had to do was pause and tune into the details of your sister's memoir and my mother's college paper. And to take on the search.

I have searched for ways that I could tap into the flesh-and-blood you, who lies beneath what others observed and speculated about you. I have peeled back the notes, largely medical in nature, in order to grasp something tangible, a clearer sense of you, your thoughts, and your reactions. Your *words*. However, rather than unearthing your specific words, I have found I have my own thoughts and sentiments that I wanted to share with you. I have stitched my wishes for your could-have-been life into the reality in which you lived, hoping for a glimpse into your private, forever unknown thoughts. I have taken what I know of you and merged it with ways you may have tried to make sense of your life. I have woven your poignant story into mine. Different subjects, different details, yet two lives now conjoined.

Even as I near the end of my year of rooting, I remain troubled by the secrecy and silence surrounding your name in the family. It is as if a strong wind gust scattered memories of you along with the ashes of your life, leaving only dust particles. No kin who knew more than rumors of you is alive to answer my questions about you. Despite the stillness that surrounds your grave, your story pulls people to you.

When I mention you even with the barest of details, others tune in, eager to know more. Curiosity turns to incredulity as listeners struggle to fathom thirty years in an asylum. You now have a band of followers, a tribe of Hattie enthusiasts, reaching across the distance from the Southwest to the Northwest and to the Northeast. Those awaiting your story will be moved by your rewriting of your own legacy, shedding the psychological restraints that harnessed your imagination during your early Colorado years. Although never dismissed from the hospital, you made the shift from despondency to finding meaning in simple acts of kindness. You, however, no longer need to reside within the memory of those walls. You now have a chorus of support who are calling your name, reaching out to embrace, and then to release, you.

Chris and I ordered a headstone for your Colorado grave. Although you should have been buried in Missouri adjacent to your children, your grave lies 600 miles from theirs, separated by more than the width of Kansas.

HATTIE JUDD COOPER
OCTOBER 11, 1874
JANUARY 16, 1953

Hattie's Headstone, Mountain View Cemetery, Pueblo, Colorado, placed November 6, 2013.

I have tucked my favorite picture of you inside of a silver locket; the gentle pressure on my neck reminds me that you are close. As I open the clasp to see your sweet face, I can almost detect your sideward glance shifting due east. Toward your children. Toward home.

Deep love to you, Aunt Hattie

Debi

April 2020

Dear Edward,

In 2013, your grandmother Hattie appeared in my life. Her oldest sister was my great-grandmother Ida, whom I knew as Nanmy. As I read between the lines of her memoirs, I caught a passing glimpse of the little sister she seemed to judge. Intrigued, I was eager to learn more about this person. I spent a year searching for details of her daily life, for evidence that would make her a real person in my mind. I was unprepared for what I found: a vast swath of loss and death across her midlife years, followed by her tragic, protracted incarceration in a mental hospital. She must have felt so much anguish and despair.

While searching for clues, I found one ray of hope: a grandson—you. But by the end of my 2013 search, I had located only your birth date and that of your death—Edward J. Cooper: November 24, 1917–June 9, 2006. Much of your life remained a mystery. You lived to be eighty-eight years old, a poignant footnote to Hattie's life and that of her daughter Emma. And that was it. For the next seven years, my search went cold.

When my brother Webb read my letter to Hattie in early 2020, her story pulled him in, just as I had been years earlier. He immediately insisted that we dust off our "cold case"—the pursuit of Hattie's descendants—with the help of Ancestry.com. He first uncovered the date of your marriage to Rita Hansford in June 1950. With that detail in hand, Chris rejoined the search and headed for Facebook. Within seconds of his typing "Rita Hansford Cooper" into the search field, her name popped up. I breathlessly typed a message: "I am looking for connections to Edward J. Cooper, Emma Mink Cooper's son."

Even though many of my earlier Internet searches had led nowhere, I felt cautiously hopeful.

Within hours, Rita responded, "Yes, you have the right Edward Cooper." That simple reply set off an explosion of thoughts: Could Rita really be Emma's daughter-in-law, Hattie's granddaughter-in-law? Had Edward forgotten about his grandmother? What had the Coopers told Rita about Emma and Hattie? Did Rita have any pictures of Emma?

Rita turned out to be the missing human link in our story. Her generosity made my learning about you—and thus this letter—possible.

You and I are second cousins once removed. We share the same great-great-grandparents: Maria Tompkins and Randall Stoddard Judd. Their oldest daughter was my great-grandmother, and their youngest daughter was your grandmother. My mother, Emma Jane Kirsch, was a passionate family historian, researching many generations back in the Judd, Emigh, and Stoddard lines. Beyond the on-paper connections, she especially loved meeting and talking with relatives. Had my mother's genealogical research led to you as Hattie's only living descendant, Chris and I could easily have met you and Rita. Unfortunately for mother, you and Rita did not move to Kansas until 1990, the year she died. Driving to eastern Kansas to meet you would have been a memorable and life-changing event for us.

Although she did not go into great detail about it, Mother was familiar with your grandmother's tragic life, having written about Hattie in her 1938 genetics paper her senior year at Whitman College.

Rita and I began an enthusiastic exchange of messages in which she generously answered my many questions, providing details and insight about you. Her account of your distress, when you discovered where your grandmother had been a psychiatric patient and that she had already died before you could visit her, moved me deeply. It reminded me of Hattie's own experience of taking the train from Missouri to Idaho to visit her sick brother Samuel, who died while she was en route. You likely knew little of Hattie's whereabouts after 1924, and I doubt anyone encouraged her to write to you during her hospital years. You had a reason to reach out to her, perhaps newly curious about your family history. But by the time you felt ready to reconnect, she was already gone. A painful realization for you, perhaps made even more heartrending because you understood what such a reunion would have meant to her.

Your birth gave your mother and grandmother a hope for the future similar to what your grandparents felt when your mother was born. That hope died the next year with your mother's death during the pandemic.

You were only seven years old when your grandmother Hattie left Missouri, looking for a place to settle after her marriage to your grandfather, Coy Cooper, fell apart. She must have asked her sister Anna, who lived in Rifle, Colorado, if she could stay with her until she found a place of her own.

During your grandmother's long years in Pueblo, she never stopped thinking about you, never ceased looking for you, never relaxed her hope that one day she would see you. I know this is true because I, too, am a grandmother.

In an outdoor photo from 1918, your father Glenn and grandfather Coy are holding your hands as if about to swing you back and forth. Your mother stands behind you, her smile trusting, her demeanor calm. She is lovely.

(L.) Coy Cooper (Hattie's third husband), Emma, Glenn, Baby Edward. (R.) Young exuberant Edward

Seeing Emma's muted smile—even out-of-focus—allows me to imagine her mother's smile, an expression absent from the few formal portraits I have located of Hattie. She undoubtedly took this picture. I can imagine her smiling at your willingness to hang, as if preparing for the time when you would take your first steps. You look trusting, content.

Rita Hansford and Edward Cooper, wedding, June 1950 and in later years.

In your wedding photo, I see your joy and anticipation of a long life together. They might have resembled pictures taken of Hattie and Abe Mink marrying a half century earlier, their lives equally full of promise.

Rita, Webb, and I ordered a monument to be placed on your mother's unmarked grave. Next to your uncle Edward's grave, next to your grandfather Abe's. Your name is on her gravestone, as Emma would have welcomed, evidence that the Judd-Mink-Cooper line would continue.

Emma's headstone.

Although I didn't imagine there might be other essential players in the Hattie story, I found Rita, whose own story and reflections could coexist parallel to mine. It is a story with a different perspective on a family borne of tragedy, but transformed into one of hope for the future. Rita, along with her sister Carol, welcomed us into her world, and yours, with generosity and grace. When Rita told Carol that I had contacted her, Carol enthusiastically responded, "If you're a new relative of Debi's, so am I."

I am extremely grateful that Rita has brought me a sense of peace at the end of Hattie's story.

Love to you,
Debi

Postscript, September 2023

I was so very excited to meet Rita! From the minute we connected in early 2020, I looked forward to seeing her in person and learning more about your life together, including your children and grandchildren. The pandemic—similar to the virus a century ago that ended your mother's life—interrupted our initial plans for a visit. Before Chris and I returned to Nebraska in September 2022, Rita confirmed a date we could drive down to Kansas from Omaha. But as we were packing for our flight to Nebraska, your daughter, Pat Cooper, called to say that Rita had died. Even though I was sad that I never got to meet her in person, she added richness to my life. I know her stable influence and encouragement gave you the grounding your mother and grandmother could not provide for you. I can imagine the sense of loss Pat and her siblings Ben Cooper and Tom Boxley continue to feel after Rita's death. And yours.

Chris's discovery of Rita on Facebook helped me to understand that Hattie's legacy did not die with her in 1953. Think how happy Hattie would have been to know that you so wanted see her and that you had found a life with Rita. If only you had known where she was, you could have reunited in Pueblo, Colorado.

It is crucial to connect with family members, especially during times of geographic and emotional separation. My research has led to discovering previously unknown members of my family who are alive today. I'm thrilled to have met Pat as I continue to weave your story into our family history. At last, a living connection to Hattie!

Third cousins meet, Kansas City, Kansas, September 2023. Pat Cooper and Debi.

3

Ida

You cannot do a kindness too soon, for you never know how soon it will be too late.

—Ralph Waldo Emerson

Ida Judd at 16.

June 2016

Dear Nanmy,

I finally completed the task Mother assigned me fifty-three years ago. Reading and transcribing your memoirs has allowed me to know you as I never did during the nine years our lives overlapped. But first I need to go back to the beginning.

My memory of you started with a crayon. I was four or five, sitting on the carpet in Honeychile and Grammie's Seattle living room near where Grammie sat by the window facing Puget Sound. The only leftie in the family, I was working my way through a new coloring book, crayon held confidently in my left hand. You entered through the doorway at the opposite end of the room. Suddenly, conscious of your stare—which seemed focused on only my left hand—I lifted the crayon and waved it about in an arc as if to say, "You can't get me here!" I remember the joy of taunting you in the safety of an adult who would stick up for me.

The dining room was another place where things could get problematic between us. Sometimes if you and I were alone at the table, you would make a comment about my holding a fork or spoon in my left hand. With anyone else present, you would merely give me a look of disapproval. I just remember that I was having none of it. Years later I would learn of the stigma against left-handedness and the "logic" of forcing kids to become right-handed. You were the only one who made a fuss about my being left-handed and likely thought it mattered in both manners and brain development.

Four generations of Hiltons: Howard, Howard Jr., Nelson, and Nanmy.

In 1963, I was out of high school and had some time on my hands. Mother had a job for me: to type up your handwritten "Memoirs," which you had written as a gift to your grandson Howard Jr. In assigning this task, she was inviting me to be more curious about our family history. Mother had only a poor photocopy, with many pages missing the final line of writing, which she had added in the margins in her own hand. At the age of ninety, you felt compelled to write down for him some reflections of your childhood experiences, along with a few confessions related to your unrequited love. Even though I knew that you had penned these stories in the early 1950s, I couldn't connect with you, a relative with whom I had spent limited time. From my adolescent point of view, the story Mother gave to me might as well have been written by a total stranger.

In the days that followed, I began halfheartedly to type your manuscript. I devoted only a few hours, laboriously correcting my many mistakes with whiteout, watching the clock, waiting for something to motivate me. You were looking back at nine decades of your life, but I paid no attention to the content of your story. My main concern was how much this was inconveniencing me. How long would it take to make even a dent in these ramblings? What is the minimum amount of time I would have to spend in order to satisfy Mother? Even picking strawberries at Klicker's would be better—that at least was good outdoor work!

In spite of my lack of interest at the time, the project planted a seed in me, which germinated in 1986 when I helped Mother move out of our family home at 1019 Alvarado Terrace. It grew further in 2007 when I organized the family history into boxes. After joining my writing group in 2012, I thought often about your memoirs. I've looked through those pages many times, without an urge to tackle typing your story. Until now.

Once I started transcribing, I felt a strong need to type on, to learn what you had chosen to write about, to understand your passions and reflections. With no need of parental encouragement, I completed the project, twenty-one pages long, single-spaced.

You began your memoir in the summer of 1949 from the desk in your upstairs room in your daughter's home in Seattle. It was a pleasant workspace. Out your window, you could have looked beyond the broad, shining expanse of Puget Sound to Agate Point in the distance. You chose your son Howard's sixty-third birthday as the moment to launch your writing, describing your sense of parental responsibility and joy in watching him become "a man full of promise, worth, and value." In addition to graduating from the Colorado State School of Mines and serving in World War I, Howard had "made his way alone" [without his father, who died in 1909]. Despite challenges such as working with "dishonest partners, against adversity, then starting over again," he remained focused on fairness and justice.

The positive qualities you identified in Howard parallel the characteristics evident in your narrative: a strong inner drive and a determination to succeed while fulfilling your responsibilities, both chosen and acquired.

You wanted your grandson to know something about his male ancestors whom you had known as a child. Stoddard Judd, your grandfather, was a politician who had served in the New York State Assembly from 1835–37 and in the Wisconsin State Senate in 1866 and 1867. Reflecting on your childhood fear of him, you wrote, "Had I to live those years over, I should love him a lot." You had no such kind words for your father, Randall Stoddard Judd, however. Even forty years after he died, he remained in your eyes a cold, demanding, and temperamental parent—bad to the bone.

> Today [is] cloudy & dismal, & associates in memories of my father—even in my early childhood—I have no happy memory.
>
> I should be sorry to relate some of the memories I recall—& do not forget in my 90 years.

You reported but a single incident in which your father came to your aid by killing a snake that you barely missed stepping on in the watermelon patch. Your shriek brought him running. Although you depicted him at that moment as playing the role of the good guy, the incident was not enough to earn him your compassion. You saw no reason to soften your view of him decades later.

From what were surely many similar stories, you chose to tell the following:

> I had suitors a-plenty—some drifting along in the line of entertainment—& this sort of thing held—even after I was engaged & Mr. [John] Hilton a 1000 miles away—My engagement was known—but my company was sought after—[at] a Milliner shop one summer vacation I had employment at Norborne, Missouri—a town 8 miles south of the farm.
>
> One evening a fellow (I would say of 30 years) who clerked in a clothing store—near my location, invited me to attend a lecture—& my dad was mad about it—because I went. There was also another chap—of the same age I should judge (a very fine partner in a "ball room")—He too sought my company during the summer—on several occasions. He hired a livery & took me on a drive—camp meeting & one or two picnics.

One beautiful day in fall—after my return home to the farm (a Sunday)—he came out & invited me for a drive—If I lived 1,000 years, I never could forget the beautiful day—& apart from many others—(He knew I was engaged)—When we reached home—It was near the "Dinner Hour"—& Dad was on one of his "tantrums" & Hell was loose. He told Mother if she spread a table damask [cloth] on the table he would jerk it off—"dishes, food—& all"—& she knew he would do it—I have regretted a thousand times—I failed to prepare some sandwiches & a pitcher of milk—& invite him out to the carriage [for] a short explanation—& a pleasant lunch & let him drive off—It was the last time I ever saw him—He soon after took [a] clerkship in a large clothing firm in "St. Joseph" Missouri—I had two or more friendly letters—It was soon following my marriage—I had a wedding gift from him.

That dinner hour was one "sad Hellion" in my life—& one everlasting regret—I failed to have the wisdom to think of sandwiches—I will say here— This one of many like instances I went through in my life—I have decided not to report any more on this line—This is a fair sample—of many—& yet I am here at 91 years.

I can almost sense the ease with which you pulled up those feelings of embarrassment and horror, at your father's threatened behavior and also in your failure to follow decorum and offer to fix a small meal for your friend.

Your father clearly had decided that once you were engaged, you should have no other male friendships.

How did your father's behavior, both exhibited and feared, impact your relationship with men throughout your life? As a child you would not have had the wherewithal to stand up to him during his tirades directed at your siblings and others. Although he might have softened as he aged, you describe the continuation of his uncouth behaviors after your parents moved from Wisconsin to Missouri. You wrote:

But kindness should stand out a Motto in every place & everywhere—

Instead of this he neglected his common every day interests in general affairs—after the move to Missouri & spent day after day—week after week sitting smoking & reading the Bible—& [arguing] with anyone who would give him time to listen—Sometimes the war with the South—sometimes politics—but always—contentious.

Interestingly, you wrote about ordering calling cards: Miss Ida F. (Frances) Judd, which you liked enough to attach to your memoirs.

This is a card of my girlhood days—I married in October 1880—that would be 70 years ago this fall. My first two initials—spell the one great

little word "If"—& this one word stands out in my life—of many very important leads of my life's—experiences—

The reference to "If" (had you read Kipling, I wonder?) is a recurring motif in your story, suggesting that you often speculated on how your

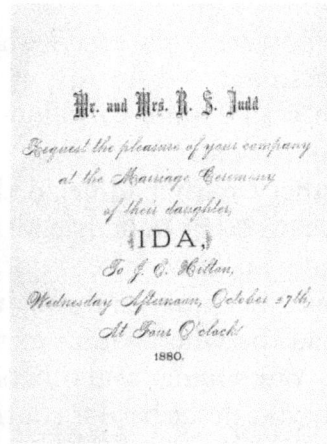

Ida and John and their wedding invitation. You were "not allowed" to be married by a preacher but instead by a Justice of the Peace.

life would have turned out differently if you had made other decisions. This comes across most strongly in the accounts of two men: your husband and an unnamed, mysterious person.

You no doubt decided that the person you married would be cut from a different cloth than your father, that any partner of yours would be, among other things, kind. You found out, however, that mere kindness wasn't enough.

John Hilton proposed while you were teaching in a district schoolhouse. Your delayed response came as you wrestled with the idea of whether a marriage could be built on mere tepid feelings for your partner. As you wrote:

> . . . I finally gave my answer in the affirmative—But stipulated I should never be willing to live on a farm. I didn't love him—He loved me—But he had such a huge selfish disposition—It just about blotted out all good points—understanding is one necessity of a successful marriage. I understood him perfectly—but he did not understand me a-tall [*sic*]. He was kind, we never quarreled—but his understanding wasn't any more than a 10-year-old boy's.
>
> Not any use to give examples or illustrations—Had I set out to try teaching him I might have succeeded, but I have my doubts—when we had been married 18 1/2 years—one beautiful summer day—I told him how I felt—& for the reason of our marriage & why—At 25 years, I asked him for my release—He gave it to me without a quarrel—Because he was grand. If he had wisely expressed 1/3 of his love, I think I could have held to the end—
>
> We lived apart mostly for ten years—He at the Mines—united only by a point of law.
>
> Never to this hour have I regretted the divorce.

Then along came the love—albeit unrequited—of your life. During the years you and John Hilton were separated, he in Leadville, Colorado, and you in Denver, you met a man who became your only true love you experienced in your ninety years. You saw him only six brief times during the decade after you met, and shared but a single kiss.

You devoted several pages of your memoir to describing the evolution of your relationship with your mystery man: your initially intense feelings for him, your subsequent suspicion that he might be married—which was confirmed—and your struggle with your decision not to see him again.

> During these years of separation—I met a man by chance—at Mont Rose, Colorado, at a change of trains—(It is at a junction.) His office for a short time was in Denver. Soon after (moved to Des Moines)—He stopped off in Denver & called me by phone—& would be at the Albany—the third time

I had met him—We had a delightful hour on the balcony & I asked him "Why such a man as he was a bachelor"—(That's the hour love came—)

If I lived 1,000 years, I am sure I never could love the same again—

There is no control—outwardly yes, but within the soul (NO)—

This friendship went on for a space of 10 years—& in those 10 years I saw him face to face just 6 times.

From the one time I met him at Mont Rose—on a return trip from Illinois via way of Chicago—I stopped over on train at Des Moines—I have forgotten name of hotel—In the morning I called by phone & he said be over in an hour—I think perhaps his call was about 3/4 of an hour—Somehow I was impressed—that he was not at ease—I have regrets to this day—that I did not engage a detective to look him up—I wrote him to the address of P.O. Box #610—& left with a very complex feeling—all that however does not touch love such as I had—

He was a traveling man—but educated for a doctor—knew a cousin of mine in Chicago—a friend of his—that & the fact that he was an advanced mason—gave me a feeling of security—our day—not in a thousand times would it by chance happen. I ran on to him coming out of the store on the corner of Larimer and 16th Street. I saw him at the Albany...

At one point in your writing, you included his reaction when he learned you knew he was married: "Now, you know me as I am."

You continued:

. . . Loss of confidence does not destroy love. But it changes the status of things mightily. The many tears that fell in those 10 years & the struggle I had with myself to be able to write a goodbye letter and never drop a tear. I have reached the place where I know I should be as unhappy with you as I am without you. I love you but my dream of your worth is shattered—all that you could be—all that you could be—all that you should be & yet you are not—so this is my last goodbye.

I never had heard of him since—& as I look back—I am glad I said goodbye. This is over 30 years ago—He was my age—doubtful if he is living today.

My middle name is Frances—I asked him to call me "Frank"—He often used the term (to be frank, and frankly speaking, etc., etc.)

Nanmy, although I have searched through your memorabilia (of course!) for the mystery man's name, his letters, or a photograph of him, I found nothing. You apparently wanted it that way. Although you may have saved a few letters at the time of your writing, none remained with your documents at the time of your death.

You wrote:

> I couldn't destroy his letters—left a few envelopes for dates—two or three letters in his writing & the rest I tore up very patiently into squares of confetti—mixed in kapok & stuffed into couch pillows—it is more than he is worthy of—but that is what I did. His dishonesty I couldn't forgive.

Not to make light of your despair, but I loved this section! I imagined you snipping the mystery man's letters into a pile and stuffing them into cushions. I would love to have seen even a photo of those pillows crammed full of his love-letter confetti! As I searched unsuccessfully for evidence of who this person was, I felt like you were taunting *me*, getting even for the crayon flailing I did in front of you when I was a kid. Where did you hide the saved letters and envelopes? When did you decide to toss them? I don't suppose you could have guessed I would one day transcribe your memoirs, let alone write my version of the family history.

Of course, it was not your writing that stunned me. It was your sewing! The crazy quilt Mother showed me in 1986 captured me just as Picasso's "The Old Guitarist" had the second I saw it. Both stand out in my memory as moments that instantly raised my estimate of both Picasso and you.

In your memoir you described how your sewing art

> was a success for me and also a comfort—and a help in the needs of many places—a help to buy a lot of things I wanted independent of any other sources. However, in the early years I took it up to help get a start and a footing in business interest. Your grandfather was past 32 years of age at the date of our marriage and had borrowed money from his father to get married. I shed tears when I learned of the fact.

Nanmy, for you, sewing was initially a means of making money, but quickly evolved into a life-saving connection with the women who hired you to design and make clothes for them. You benefited from your sewing expertise as well, designing attire for your mother and siblings, as well as yourself.

After your death in Seattle in 1953, Grammie gave many of your designed dresses and suits to Mother. Seeing the exquisite care you gave to your sewing, she donated many pieces to the Walla Walla Historical Society. When Chris and I made an appointment to visit the museum in 2020, one of the archivists had pulled out a rack of your items to show us. I had fun ogling your art, assessing the exquisite work and attention that went into them. At one point I asked if I could try on a fur coat (one of the few things you had not made), and the woman working with us denied my request with a smile. I understood her need to protect the museum artifacts, but being your great-granddaughter I also felt a bit possessive of them.

Your quintessential work of art, to me, is the quilt Mother first showed me in 1986. [See p. xiii.] I am thrilled to have the quilt in our home. It's a treasure. A masterpiece.

You were an extraordinary seamstress. In your endless creative patterns you created a harmony that you often missed in your own life.

"What we do see depends mainly on what we look for."

—John Lubbock

November 2016

A few days ago, I contacted the records department of the Pueblo hospital a second time to ask if they had copies of any personal letters Hattie sent, or received from, you. Today I learned the records department kept no personal mail belonging to the former residents. I know you wrote to each other from your memoirs and the hospital notes about Hattie. You also wrote at least once to the institution asking about her release.

The hospital's response was included in the Hattie V. Cooper documentation packet I received in September 2013 from the Medical

Records of Department of the Colorado Mental Health Institute in Pueblo. I was disturbed and annoyed by what I read.

February 14, 1942

Mrs. J. J. Hilton
Seattle, Washington

Dear Madam:

Your communication in regard to Hattie V. Cooper is acknowledged.

This patient has been getting along quite well for several years. Her physical condition is fairly good for one of her age and her only illnesses in the past few years have been from colds which were not of a serious nature. She works for an employee who lives on the grounds.

In regard to her leaving the hospital, we do not think it would be advisable as she is subject to periodic recurrences of her mental trouble, although for the past few years her condition has been unusually good.

Very truly yours,

F. H. Zimmerman, M.D.

Superintendent

How could the superintendent suggest that it was not a good idea for Hattie to leave the hospital, even though she had done well for the previous several years? My God, Nanmy, although the message in that 1942 letter was that it was not the time to talk about her getting out, the implication was that there might never be a good time for her to get out. In hindsight, we know that's exactly what happened. That's the moment I wished you, Grammie, and Mother would have headed for Colorado to demand Hattie's release. Three generations of assertive females might have succeeded.

Nanmy, I have felt bad about how I've judged your action on Hattie's behalf. I needed to find a way to reframe my view of your behavior. Knowing that you both found letter writing therapeutic, I thought: Why not write some imagined exchanges of letters between you two? It might help me to empathize with your point of view. So I took the liberty of composing some fictional correspondence between you and Hattie in connection with two events: her failed release in 1930 from the Pueblo State Hospital and your 1942 letter asking about her getting out, which I mentioned above. My writing draws from Hattie's hospital "Continued Notes" and details from your memoirs, as well as my own recollections of you. The Fimples' dog, however, I made up.

Although no such letters exist, I can imagine Hattie writing you something like the following fictional letter before her planned release from the hospital, along with your [equally imagined] reply.

Tuesday July 15, 1930

Dear Ida,

Thank you for your June letter. I was glad to hear from you. Anna's letter came yesterday and she and George are finally coming to take me away from this dreadful place. I have been waiting for this moment since they sent me away from their home six years ago, almost immediately after I arrived in Rifle.

I don't know what got into me when I first got to Anna's, but I couldn't stop weeping. I think everything just caught up with me. No one could console me. When Anna arranged for me to be taken away, she said my crying and carrying on was too much for her. However, she promised that she and George would come to get me, wherever I was, as soon as I settled down. But no one seemed to understand that I couldn't settle down when I didn't know how long I would be kept here.

When I first got to Pueblo, I felt like I had been sealed in a small metal box and could scarcely breathe. It was as if the air was rationed out along with the cotton gowns, moth-eaten sweaters, and ratty slippers that I had to wear. Those slippers were so loose that they flapped off of my heals and scraped along the floor wherever I walked.

Now I will finally be leaving Pueblo with Anna and George and returning with them to Rifle. For the first time in years I can look forward to seeing beyond the walls surrounding this place.

I don't yet know what day they will come to Pueblo, but they will be here in August. I will write to you as soon as I am settled in Rifle. My new home. Maybe I can see you again!

Ida, I'm so very happy.

Your sister,

Hattie

Friday, July 25, 1930

Dear Hattie,

I have received your letter with your good news and am very happy for you. I look forward to your first letter—even a post card—from Rifle.

I'm sorry that your release has taken so long. Safe travels.

Your sister,

Ida

In 1930 George and Anna Howard wrote to the hospital concerning Hattie's release. In his reply, Dr. Zimmerman agreed that the hospital would parole Hattie for a two-year trial period during which time they could return her to Pueblo if their relationship with her became "unpleasant." On August 10 they left Rifle for the 300-mile drive to Pueblo.

They never made it. A flash flood had washed out a section of the highway, making it impossible for George and Anna to go any farther. When Hattie received the news that she could not leave that day, she wept uncontrollably. That failed rescue attempt set the stage for Hattie to spend the rest of her life—another twenty-two years—in the Pueblo facility.

A further fictional exchange with Hattie after her failed release might have gone like this:

Sunday, October 5, 1930

Oh Ida,

I feel like I'm going mad... I cannot wake up from this hospital nightmare. Am I doomed to stay here for the rest of my life?

Whatever can I do?

It seems like every time I get upset, the nurse calls for the doctor to come and then they give me a shot that makes me black out, or they put me in a jacket restraint, or in a hot bath for hours. The hot baths are the worst. I feel like I'm suffocating in that water that's up to my neck. Can you imagine being forced to be still in a bath or bed until someone else decided to untie you?

Since Abe and my children died, everyone seems to want to shut me up. Sometimes I have to shriek and howl.

I can't live here, Ida. Please help me!

Hattie

Wednesday, October 22, 1930

Dear Hattie,

I wish I could imagine how upset you might have been when they couldn't come—but I can't.

Please try to be patient until they can work out another plan to pick you up before long. If they could make the arrangements one time, they should be able to do it again. George is just a few months younger than I am. Anna is having problems with her eyes, so may find it difficult to drive long distances. But as long as George can drive, they should be able to get you.

Your sister,

Ida

I have written two more hypothetical exchanges between the sisters sixteen years into Hattie's hospital stay. In Hattie's letters, I tried to express her acceptance of her fate and her marvelous ability to adjust to her life of incarceration.

Thursday June 26, 1941

Dear Ida,

I have not written for several weeks, although I'm not sure just how long it has been. I wrote you before that I have been working for Dr. and Mrs. Fimple for a couple of years. Their apartment is not far from where I live and I can walk there the days when I go to help clean and to feed their dog, Gretel. They just got her before Christmas. Gretel and I hit it off right away. In fact, I think she likes to climb up on the back of their davenport and watch out the window for me to arrive.

Mrs. Fimple has been very kind to me since I started working for them. In the beginning she would take me to town to go with her on a few errands, then after a few months she asked if I wanted to stop and have a chocolate milkshake at Woolworth's. I did.

Today she asked if I wanted to see the film "The Grapes of Wrath." I said yes and she took me to the Pueblo Movie Theater. I love movies. This one made me think about lots of things. When I said that to Mrs. Fimple, she took me to the library where she checked out the novel so that I could read it. She's thoughtful like that.

Most of the time Mrs. Fimple and I don't talk about my life, but today we did. As we walked around Woolworth's looking at some of the fabrics, she spotted a bolt of white cotton with black polka-dots that she wanted to buy to make a blouse for her daughter who lives somewhere in California. She asked me if I had learned to sew when I was young. Of course I never did, but I told her how well you sew and that you once made a dress for me when I was 16. I've never forgotten that dress.

All of a sudden she asked me if I had any children. She seemed taken aback by her own question and I wonder if she thought it was out of place. I told her that I had three children and that every one of them died. Mrs. Fimple cried when I told her that one son died at birth, Eddie died when he was 7, and Emma was 16 and already a mother when she died of influenza. Then I started to cry. We cried together as if we were friends.

Mrs. Fimple thanked me for telling her about my children. I thanked her for listening.

During my free time I usually read. But this week my mind is wandering when I sit in my room holding *The Grapes of Wrath*. Since Monday I've been wondering what Eddie and Emma would be like if they had lived. Emma would be 38 and Eddie 37. If Eddie and Emma were still alive, I don't think I would be in Pueblo. Do you?

Your sister,

Hattie

Wednesday August 27, 1941

Dear Hattie,

Your letter arrived in the post a few weeks ago and I didn't feel up to writing until today. Sometimes my arthritis hurts so bad in my hands and feet that I can barely get out of bed.

I'm not sure I even knew that you had a son who died at birth. Of course I remembered that Eddie died when he was only a boy. I think it happened while you were on the train to Caldwell, Idaho, to see brother Samuel when he was so ill. You saw death everywhere you looked—your husband, infant son and Eddie, and our parents. They all died within a few years.

On another note, I've never understood why you didn't pursue your piano after the lessons and training you had. I desperately wanted to study piano and wish I had been forthright about asking Uncle Jess for financial help. He would have loaned me the money and I would have paid him back. When I was in Leadville I finally bought a piano, which I moved to Denver and then Seattle. Emma Jane took to it when she was young.

Someone in the family should write down memories of our childhood days. Howard [Ida's son] and Howard Junior [grandson] have asked me if I would record some of my recollections. What can you remember from your childhood living in Missouri? Looking back, it seems as if you and I were born into different families.

I have absolutely no happy memories of living with Dad, who seemed only to grow more cantankerous as he aged. By the time we moved to Missouri, he seemed eager to offend anyone who approached him. I don't know how Mother stood to live with him all of those years.

Your sister,

Ida

Friday, October 24, 1941

Dear Ida,

I returned from the Fimples' home to find your letter waiting for me today. I saw snow on the mountains, which means winter is coming.

Mrs. Fimple fixed me a cup of tea today before I left. She asked how I was getting along. I said fine. She said I looked a little sad and wondered if something had happened. I couldn't speak for a moment. Finally I said I had been thinking a lot about my grandson, Edward. I told her Edward was born just a year before his mother, Emma, died in 1918. You knew about that, of course. I told Mrs. Fimple that Edward was 7 when I last saw him, when I left Missouri for Colorado. He was such a loving little boy. I miss him so much. He will turn 24 next month. I would love to know what he is like today, what he has made of his life. I feel like he might be thinking about me, too. I pray that one day he will reach out to me, maybe even visit me. Is that too much to hope for? I know you understand because you have your own granddaughter. Imagine what it would be like if you lost contact with Emma Jane. If I could only see Edward again, I would be more at peace with life here in Pueblo.

You asked what I remember from my childhood. I mainly recall Mother's good nature and happy disposition. I think Dad was beginning to soften by the time I was born. After all, I arrived when you were 15. I remember some of the stories that you, Samuel, and George told me about living in Wisconsin when Dad was a tyrant.

I met Abe a few months before we were married. He was so very kind. In fact, he was the kindest person I ever knew. That's one of the reasons I enjoy Mrs. Fimple. She's kind like Abe was. I was not unhappy at home, but when Abe asked me to marry him, it was easy to say yes. Emma and Eddie gave Abe and me a new focus and we were filled with hope for their futures as well as our own.

I enjoyed playing the piano and even taught lessons to some neighbor girls who lived close to the farm. I played less often after the children were born. When they all died, I couldn't bear to play for years. Even though I couldn't play, I found comfort in just having the piano. It held many memories of my early life as a mother. When I left Missouri for Colorado in 1924 to be with Anna, I had to sell my piano in order to pay for a train ticket. It felt like I had lost not only my piano, but also my memories of my past.

I didn't know you wanted to learn to play the piano. You wanted to study music and I wanted to learn how to sew.

Your sister,

Hattie

Thursday, November 13, 1941

Dear Hattie,

My arthritis has improved some and I was able to walk down to see neighbors Lillian and Arthur Sears a couple of days ago. Arthur has a beautiful garden with colors as vivid as some of the fabric swatches I've used in making quilts. Lillian is one of the kindest women I have ever met. I think you would like them. They have been fine neighbors for years.

I married John Hilton in 1880 to get away from home, and agreed to move to Leadville, Colorado, a place I'd never seen. He worked in a silver mine and I sewed for many residents. If only I could have been happy with John. It felt like I had married a boy who had little to offer. I thought kindness was the most important quality for a marriage. But it turns out that it is only one of the key conditions. Each person must have a generous disposition and there must also be mutual understanding. John was kind enough, but he thought only of himself. After eighteen years of marriage, I couldn't take it any longer. I envy your loving marriage to Abe. I never had that with John. Or with anyone.

I haven't admitted to you—and surely not to myself before now—that I wanted to help you when you moved to Colorado. I didn't offer for you to come to stay with me in Denver because I was already 65 years old and didn't know how I could support both of us. Anna offered to have you go to Rifle. She had a husband, which meant there were two of them. After Anna and George called for help and you were sent to Pueblo, Anna and I agreed that we would work to get you released from the hospital. We never thought you would have to stay there all these years.

I will write Dr. Zimmerman again to ask if they will release you. There must be some way that you can get out of the institution.

In the meantime, I am glad that you have found work with Mrs. Fimple.

> Your sister,
>
> Ida

Nanmy, I hope that I have treated both you and Hattie fairly in my imagined letter exchanges.

You concluded your handwritten memoirs with the following reflections.

> . . . So I have had a splendid Happy Life with you grandchildren & now the great-grandchildren. What a happy day we had when we went to city to buy you a suit & later, I had the wisdom to see you when you needed help. You have paid great returns by always doing your best & I feel you will wisely continue to do so to the end. Make a companion of your son Howard Nelson & guide him with love and care. Help him to understand fulfillment of his life.
>
> Much love,
>
> Nanmy

Nanmy, at the risk of sounding like a scold, I must say your final paragraph sounds a bit disingenuous to me in light of what you wrote earlier about your dissatisfaction with individuals and what you thought about treating others compassionately:

> First of all it is a very grand thing in every child's life to have a happy memory of home—& I will add I consider it one every child that lives [deserves] even if poor—there can be kindness & happiness in every day—a thank you & a consideration in questions and answers—a memory is a reflex—that builds on more & it lives on down through the years.

In relating to your sister Hattie, you seemed unable to reach out with that empathy as you neared your own death, fewer than four months after hers. I have written a hypothetical alternate ending to your reflections, one which shows a more empathic side of you. I like to think you might have died more contentedly had you included the following postscript to your memoirs.

Sunday, January 18, 1953

Hattie died two days ago and was buried today in Pueblo at the Mountain View Cemetery. Relatives Roy and Myrtle Howard [Anna's nephew and wife] drove from Paonia to Pueblo to make arrangements for the funeral and burial.

I hope Dr. and Mrs. Fimple were able to attend the memorial. Hattie was very grateful for their care and kindness.

The Colorado ground was frozen so they could only bury Hattie and did not arrange to have a headstone put on her grave. I wonder if someone in the family will remember to do that later.

My body refuses to move quickly these days. After all, I am 93 years old, so I can't expect to. But my mind has been very active since Anna called me two days ago with the news of Hattie's death.

I'm haunted by the fact that Hattie had to die alone at the asylum. As I near my own death, I'm aware of how important it has been to have Ruth and Frank here with me, to tend to my needs until the very end.

As I conclude my memoirs, I write that it is only by the greatness of the all merciful God that I was able to avoid being sent to a hospital as sisters Mary and Hattie were. After I left John and met the love of my life—my unrequited love—there were times when I wasn't sure I could go on. My nerves drowned out my sense of reason and I had trouble making any decisions during those days. Had my children died—even had they been taken from me—I could have had a breakdown similar to what Hattie had. I can now see that clearly.

Grandfather Judd, who was a brilliant statesman, developed a similar condition of extreme nervousness late in his life. Mother later told me that he had gone insane. I never knew the details of his illness as he stayed in Wisconsin. But because he had a wife who cared for him, he was able to avoid going to an institution. This condition was, I am certain, what caused Hattie and Mary to be sent away.

I wonder why no one thought Dad had mental problems. He had—especially during the last few years of his life—a deep agitation and hostility toward most everyone around. Why is it that he got away with having problems without being called on it?

So, you see, Howard, each one of in the family has this condition of debilitating nervousness—whether it is buried somewhere deep or near the surface.

Hattie had the most tragic life of any of my siblings. I deeply regret not stepping up to help her when I was still in Denver. I try not to think about that. Had she been with me, she might have been able to enjoy some of the things I had, like the Olympia music box, elegant hand-painted china, sterling silver pieces, even the feel of fine fabric that she loved as a young girl.

If I could live my life over, I would make many of the same decisions. I would, however, change three things. I would love Grandfather Judd a lot and maybe I could have made a difference in his life as he got old. I would have been more tolerant of John, knowing how much he loved our children. Most of all, I would have been a more responsible sister to Hattie. She deserved so much love and kindness in the final thirty years of her long life.

Above all, be kind, Howard, to those in your family—especially to those who cannot care for themselves.

Much love,

Nanmy

Fiction, yes. After Webb read my alternate postscript to your memoirs—the one that I wish you had written—he described it as me "resolving issues about [my] feelings toward [you]." Exactly! Based on what I have learned, it is what I might have written had I been in your place. Hattie's story moved me deeply. I truly wish I had some evidence that you had more empathy for her and had worked harder to secure her release from Pueblo. Writing my own postscript was self-therapy, a letting-go of my judgment of your apparent inaction. Were we able to talk, perhaps I could come to empathize with your point of view. I'm grateful that I can appreciate your sewing art and that you were inspired to your write your memoir. Most of all, I am glad to have found a way to make sense of your apparent emotional distance from Hattie through my imaginary letters between the two of you.

Love to you, Nanmy.

Debi

Ida J. Hilton in front of Denver home, c. 1924.

One of Ida's elegant satin suits.

The stunning crazy quilt made by Nanmy.

*"1884" and "Ruth" embroidered
near one of the corners.*

Stitching detail.

The Judd Sisters

Ida F. Judd (b. March 9, 1859).

Mary E. Judd (b. October 27, 1860).

Anna M. Judd (b. February 11, 1869).

Hattie V. Judd (b. October 11, 1874).

4

Ruth

*Grandmothers are a gift not to be taken lightly. So
many lose them, before they are old enough to know
their magic.*

—Nikita Gill

Baby Ruth, 1892.

March 2017

Dear Grammie,

For forty years I have kept a small oval picture on my dresser of you
as a young child. Recently I have been looking at that image, wanting
to know more about that little girl.

Sandwiched between a strong-willed mother and an assertive
daughter, you found your place in softness. That's how I remember
you. I saw you as a gentle soul with generously padded arms that
could wrap Gretchen, Webb, and me up in an impenetrable cloak.
The world felt safe when you held us. I wondered where you learned
to hug like that, despite never having experienced that same warmth
from your own mother. Could it have come from one of your grandmothers—Maria Tompkins Judd or Deborah Slack Hilton? I will never

know, as their love and warmth are hidden behind inscrutable faces in old family photographs. Although you snuggled with each of us at different times, I bet you could just as easily have folded your arms around the trio all at once.

We three had our own colorful memories of you, your delicious food, and your matter-of-fact way of dealing with certain wild and domestic critters.

Gretchen told of spotting slugs adjacent to the house, often on your driveway, and debating whether to report the sightings to you. When she did, you would grab a container of salt along with a pair of garden scissors and, after lavishly sprinkling the midnight black slugs with the white death, you would effortlessly deliver the coup de grace, snipping the "little buggers" in half. According to Gretchen, you showed no hesitation or repugnance when seeing the slugs or finishing them off.

Webb recently furnished this memory of you, the disgust factor of which may have surpassed Gretchen's:

> I remember walking out of her back door, then diagonally across the parking area to the front of her little barn. She grabbed a chicken, held it over a chopping block, cut off its head, and let the body flap around on the ground. She took it into the kitchen, got me to sit in a chair, and started removing the offal. When she found a "pre-egg"—shell-less, dark colored with some green, larger than a marble and elongated–she offered it to me, then popped it into her mouth. I was so traumatized by the whole experience that I remember it vividly after around sixty-five years.

My own favorite moments, from when I was six or seven, were less traumatic. Before breakfast, I would pad behind you as you headed straight out the back door to the berry patch. Examining the bushes as you walked, you would utter "Hmmmmm!" whenever you eyed a nice ripe clump of berries. You would sweep your hand among the branches, guided by your practiced eye toward the perfect just-ripened berries. You knew exactly which raspberries were ready to willingly drop right into your fingers as you lightly brushed the leaves aside. My job was to hold the bowl for your picked berries. But as you drifted down the row, I would become impatient with the process of selecting only the best candidates and try to pick ones that were not quite ripe. I remember tiring of the task and plopping down in the middle of the row, waiting for you to come back and take back the bowl and relieve me of further duty.

When I could see the mound of berries peeking over the rim of your bowl, I would start to salivate. Returning to the house, you would place the bowl of berries on your large dark cherry wood table in the dining room and carefully spoon servings of juicy raspberries into shallow pastel bowls.

Placing a single berry on my tongue, I would squash it against the roof of my mouth, giving me a raspberry rush. To this day I cannot eat a raspberry without being transported back to that Seattle dining room. Raspberries remain my favorite fruit, a symbol of your kindness—the memory of which continues to nurture me even after more than half a century.

Deviled eggs were another favorite food from our visits to see you and Gramps. You knew how to ease the weight of saying goodbye. As the Miller family made ready to drive the station wagon southeast across Washington to Walla Walla, you would pack a picnic lunch in the same red plastic sandwich cases from the Stanley picnic set we had brought with us to Seattle. The tuna salad you prepared for the triangle-shaped sandwiches may have been Dad's favorite, but I adored your deviled eggs. You would fix ten eggs, just enough so that we could each have two. Your unusual method of slicing the hard-boiled eggs across the center allowed the eggs to better hold their shape during the car ride to Vantage, a favorite rest area and viewpoint overlooking the Columbia River. You mashed the egg yolks and mixed the yellowish pulp with a bit of salt and mayonnaise. Carefully placing the two halves together, you would center the egg on a square of waxed paper, roll it up diagonally, and twist each end like a party favor. Sometimes we arrived home with a leftover sandwich or two for another day of lunching. But we never had a surplus of deviled eggs.

While I always felt safe and comfortable around you, it is strange, even with these indelible memories, that I seem to know so little about your inner life. To better understand you as a young person, I have turned to a surprising source: letters that your father, John Hilton, wrote to you when you were a teenager. Through them I have discovered aspects of his personality that contradicted the impressions I formed when reading your mother's memoirs. For example, when I first started to transcribe those pages, I simply accepted Nanmy's opinion that he was immature, shallow, and self-centered. But I came to see him in a different light when I recently read his letters to you.

John E. Hilton, taken in his late 50s.

Ruth Maria Hilton, age 17.

They tell of a man who loved you and missed you deeply during those years of separation after your mother divorced him. He sometimes wrote soon after receiving a letter from you, and although I have none of your letters to him, many of his responses come as replies to your thoughts. For example, he assured you that he wanted to spend the 1907 Christmas holiday with you even though it was out of the question. He planted a seed of hope in suggesting that things might be different in the coming year. In a note of tenderness, he—using the word you had likely intentionally misspelled in your letter—invited you to look up the correct spelling of the word "awful."

At times, he wrote of feeling "blue," lonely for you and your brother Howard. It was as if he had opened an imaginary kitchen curtain so that if you ever got close enough, you could peek through the window to check how he was doing. His writing was never maudlin in tone,

Ruth, 12, sent this postcard made of leather to her father.

Leaf-adorned photo of Ruth at two and a half years old with the cuff pin she was wearing on her collar in the picture.

"This pin is the one you had on when the picture was taken. You were 2½ years old. Your father has had this picture for at least 25 years. Zella [relative] said, 'I think Ruth ought to have this.' This pin was worn by my mother & is all of 50 years old. It was a cuff pin of hers and she gave it to you— so it will be of value to Emma Jane. The kerchief [not included] is one your mother Kirsch lent me. I still have another, but I thought it would be a nice keepsake for you. With Love, Mother" [Nanmy]

The note Nanmy wrote to Ruth about the photo and the cuff pin.

but appeared merely to report on his condition without inviting blame from you. He repeatedly told you that his life would be better if you and he lived close to each other, that one day he hoped you would.

Your father wrote to you in mid-October 1909. A few days later, on November 2, he died. You had not seen him for three years. Your mother noted in her memoirs that she received a telegram from Seattle sent by an undertaker with news of your father's sudden death from pneumonia-related complications. Paying for everything, she ordered a "beautiful casket" to be shipped to Abilene in a steel case. She traveled by train to Kansas for the burial. You were stuck at home in Denver.

I wish I could ask you the same questions that I posed to Gretchen and Webb, ones I have reflected on for more than thirty years about the death of our own father.

What was it like to learn that not only had your father died, but that you could not attend his funeral? How did you reconcile the finality of his death with your years of merely living apart from him? How did your father's death impact your decision to marry Frank Kirsch a year and a half later, when you were just nineteen?

I'm also wondering, for the first time, what it was like for you to be in Walla Walla with Gretchen, Webb and me when Dad was in the hospital in Seattle. You answered the phone when Mother called with the devastating news of Dad's death. You had to tell Gretchen and Webb, who knew his death was imminent, and me, who was clueless. In what ways did that experience throw you back forty-seven years in your own life, to the time of your own father's death?

Having sorted through hundreds of photographs from four generations of family history, I have not found a single image of you with your father. Did one ever exist? I imagine you would have kept such a picture on your own dresser throughout your life. Then, Mother— keeper of the family treasures—would have tucked it into a box along with your letters.

For several days, I have been imagining what thoughts you, as a teenager, might have written to your father during your years of separation. Your father's letters to you (written in his beautifully legible penmanship!) give me a clue as he responds to your comments. Using the clues contained in them, I have attempted to reconstruct one of your lost letters to him. I have tried to put myself in your place as you alternated between staying in Abilene, Kansas, with your father's relatives, and with your mother in Denver. You likely loved the time with Uncle George's family. His behaviors and mannerisms may well have reminded you of your Papa. Here I am imagining myself as you:

1907

Dear Father,

Thank you for your letter. Please keep writing and I will, too. How I wish I could hear from you every day. It's awfull not knowing when I will see you again. I remember when I was a little girl and would crawl into bed, knowing that if I woke up before the sun rose, I might see you as you went off to the mine. Your warm hugs made me feel safe. And so loved. Do you remember that, too?

It's hard for me to live apart from you. It sounds like it's hard for you, too. Do you know that it's easier for me to talk to you than it is to Momma? She expects a lot, especially in my piano studies and in helping her with tasks. She also gets annoyed if I am unhappy. I get blue sometimes just like you do. Just think how much better it would be for both of us if we could be together.

I enjoy school sometimes, even my piano lessons, but my favorite time is coming to stay with Aunt Alice and Uncle George in Abilene because Momma lets me stay here by myself for weeks at a time. As you know, they have a farm and a horse named Prince. I can ride most any time I want. Aunt Alice doesn't ask me to help as much as Momma does. I'm trying to teach my cousin Edna to play the piano. But she doesn't listen to what I tell her and can't remember anything I teach her from one day to another.

In January, Momma and I took the train to Missouri to visit Momma's parents and her brothers and sisters. In fact, Grandma Judd insisted that the family gather to have a portrait taken. I wasn't in the picture, and wouldn't have wanted to be. They were all too serious, and, I thought, some of them looked frumpy. For the occasion Momma sewed herself a dress, the pattern of which reminded me of something she sewed for a friend in

Denver. Momma does make beautiful dresses and quilts. My favorite quilt is the one she made with my name embroidered in one of the corners. She used to sew more of my clothes before she decided to rent out an apartment. Now that keeps her busy.

In Carthage, we stayed with Uncle Abe and Aunt Hattie. You should hear Aunt Hattie play the piano. I hope that I can sound like her one day. One of the best things about being there is spending time with Eddie, now three, and Emma, who is four. They are such sweet children and look up to me as a big sister. Of course, I love that. And, I love the name "Emma." In fact, if have a girl one day, I may name her that. But with my luck, I'll probably have boys.

One more thing—I have met a couple of boys who seem nice. Howard has warned me about not allowing boys to be "funny" and I think I understand what he means. He's just being a good brother and looking out for me.

However, there is one boy I met who is different. His name is Frank and his parents know Uncle George and Aunt Alice. He is part of a traveling show that plays around the Midwest, sometimes in Abilene and in other states. When I read his letters, I can almost hear him talking. He calls me "Ruthy" and his "girlie" and tells me that he wishes I would hurry up and finish school. I'm glad that I can tell you these things. I hope you can meet him sometime. I think you would like his sense of humor. Momma, on the other hand, probably won't be keen on my friendship with him. I haven't told her anything yet about this Frank Kirsch.

Please write soon, Papa. I think of you every day and miss you very much.

With much love,

Your Ruth

From the surviving letters that your father wrote to you in 1907, I have pulled several passages that illustrate his devotion to you and his advice for living a good life.

January 10, 1907

My dear daughter:

Your letter came today and I was surely pleased to get it, and I hope you will have time to write many more. I am glad that you are having so good a time and I trust you help Aunt Hattie all that you can. That will make your visit pleasant to her as well as yourself and the best way to be happy is to try and make others happy. You will find it pays every time.

Of course, I hope you will have lots of good weather and that you and Momma both will have a good visit. It is nice to see all your uncles and aunts at the same time, and you must remember me to them most kindly. I should very much like to see them.

Do you play any on the piano for your uncles and aunts? I hope you do the best possible for them. If I know you have pleased them, it will please me too. So, give a good report of yourself the next time. Also, tell your grandmother and father that I would like to see them again very much and hope that someday I will. I am feeling quite well most of the time, but I get the blues once in a while. A good letter will drive that away most any time.

March 13, 1907

My dear Ruth:

Your last letter came some days ago, but as I had one on the way, I did not write at once. I thought about you on your birthday [March 5] and wondered if you got your present in time. Howard was to send it. Let me know how you like it and what it was, as I do not know.

Yes, you can get the waistcoat if you have the money, but don't go in debt.

Am sorry to hear about your Uncle Abe being so ill, and truly hope he will get well soon. I have not heard from Uncle Ran [one of Ida's brothers] for some time, so will have to depend upon you to keep me posted.

April 26, 1907

My dear Ruth:

Your letter rec'd, and was very good to have a letter from you, and I hope you will not forget me.

Like you, I do not have much news this time as things go about the same one day as another. I would like very much to see all of you and get to a lower place [from Camp Bird, Colorado, altitude 7,800 feet], but a place like I have, you can't leave when you want to so I must stay until I get done, and then quit for good. Yes, if I go to Seattle I would be glad to have you along.

All I want is for you to use good judgment in all things and make your money go as far as you can. And when you run out let me know—and I trust you will help Aunt Alice all that you can and always be your father's sweet darling girl. And remember that you are but a very young girl yet, and don't waste too much time thinking about any boy. I hope that you will always choose from your friends and acquaintances nice and good people, but at your age, you should not think much of, or go often with, any young man or boy.

There are so many things that you should acquire and store your mind with, to fit yourself for the future in life, and youth is the time in which to lay the foundation for a noble and useful life. Self-denial is one of the things that we should learn early, for unless we learn to deny ourselves many things that at the time seem necessary to our comfort and happiness, we will never know what true living is. And the satisfaction we get is by trying to make others happy. Always remember, little sweetheart, that your father will always love you, and wishes you a happy, joyous life, and [will] help you all that he can.

May 1, 1907

My dear daughter:

Yes, I suppose lots of things come up to trouble you, but do you think it a good plan to let them bother you? You will find that as you get older, more and more things come along that will worry us if we will let them. But if we won't let them get a hold of us in the first place, after a while, they won't trouble us half so much. Of course, we must do the best we can at all times to avoid trouble and be agreeable to things and in situations.

It is likely that Edna does not know as much about music as you do. So, you should have a good deal of patience. Don't you think it takes a lot of patience to start anyone in music, even when you are used to it? And you have not had any practice yet. And then, my dear, you are some older than Edna and are supposed to have control over yourself and that is a good thing always to have. Not that you will not as times get provoked at others, but do not let the other person know it.

But, my dear Ruth, this sort of advice will get tiresome and I don't want to do that. But always do the best you can under the circumstances, and I will feel satisfied with you. Learn all you can about housework from your aunt. It is the first good chance you have had and it is always a good thing to acquire knowledge when you have time and opportunity.

The secret of all contentment is to keep busy. That may not seem true to you now, but you will find it true as you get older. That does not mean always at work, for you are generally busy when you are having a good time. Remember me most kindly to all the folks. By the way, have you got the pen that I gave you some time ago? The pearl handled one? If not, will send you another, also one to Edna.

3/2 – .09

Dear Daughter :–
      Your letter of the 25th came
to day and as I was sending a line
to Brother, will add a few to you too
Am very glad to know that your
marking was so good, and hope you
will try for No.1. Had a letter from
Brother to day, and you have probably
had one ere this, but he is very busy.
I like to have you write with ink,
indeed you should always write with
ink when you can, and always do
your best. I should love to hear
you play. It would drive a way the
blues. And I would be much pleased if
I could only visit you for a while,
and see how you have grown the past
2½ years Never mind Sweetheart better
times will come by and by.
I have not got one of Howards new
picture yet though he said he would send
one. I wish I could have a new one
of you too, and see if you have changed
                                                any.

I will send you some cards when I
see some nice ones, but out here in the
hills I do not see any.
      Ask your Uncle Geo. where Uncle
Charly Hilton, is and tell me when
you write the next time.
This time you forgot to tell me Mr Howards,
street No, in Ballard, Wash.
As I have other letters to write will close
for this time
            Lovingly your father, x x x x
                  J. E. Hilton

*Letter from John E. Hilton to daughter Ruth in
1909, showing his exquisite penmanship.*

Dec. 10, 1907

My dear Ruth,

Your letter came in last evening and will reply at once. In this find an order for $1.00. Sorry, sweetheart, that it is so that I cannot send more at this time, but have not received any money from outside yet, but am ready to leave here just as soon as I do.

Yes, dear, I wish I could be with you on Christmas, but it is out of the question this time. But if everything goes right this coming year, it will be different I hope. Look up how awful is spelled.

Goodbye, Sweetheart,

Lovingly, your father XXXX

John E. Hilton

Since I learned from reading your Father's letters that you spent time with your Aunt Hattie and Uncle Abe in 1907, I have been trying to imagine how you made sense of the wave of deaths between 1907 and 1910, which likely wiped out any sense of normalcy Hattie had in her life. In the brief span of three years, several key people in her world died: her husband, her mother, a brother, and her seven-year-old son. You may have found some small comfort in writing her a letter in which you offered your condolences. If you wrote, you may have written something like this fictitious letter:

November 20, 1910

Dear Aunt Hattie,

I haven't stopped thinking about you since Uncle Randall called Wednesday with the tragic news that dear little Eddie died that very day. It's sad enough that Eddie got sick after you got on the train to travel to see Uncle Samuel, and even sadder that tuberculosis took his life while you were on your way to Idaho. Life can be so unfair.

I'm also thinking about Emma. She and Eddie were so close and they played so well together.

I remember your telling me during our last visit that you wanted your children to stay close in the same way that you and your brother Samuel had. It didn't matter that he was 21 years older than you, he had looked out for you since you were a little girl. I always liked the idea that of all your siblings, you and Samuel seemed to be the closest.

When you learned that Samuel was very ill and might not survive, you surely wanted to go to be with him. You were his favorite sister and I know it meant a lot to him to know that you were on your way to Idaho to see him. Sadly, he could not hold on until you arrived to say goodbye.

The saddest thing for me has been thinking about you making the trip home to Carthage, alone, with your broken heart. I'm sorry that I couldn't be with you during the long ride home.

Much love, Aunt Hattie,

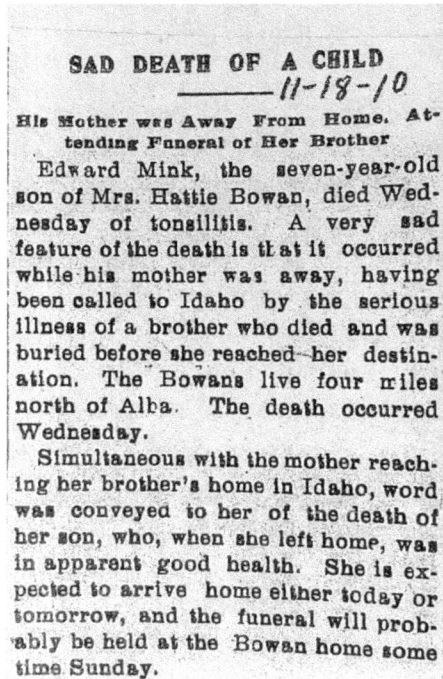

Ruth

SAD DEATH OF A CHILD
—— 11-18-10

His Mother was Away From Home. Attending Funeral of Her Brother

Edward Mink, the seven-year-old son of Mrs. Hattie Bowan, died Wednesday of tonsilitis. A very sad feature of the death is that it occurred while his mother was away, having been called to Idaho by the serious illness of a brother who died and was buried before she reached her destination. The Bowans live four miles north of Alba. The death occurred Wednesday.

Simultaneous with the mother reaching her brother's home in Idaho, word was conveyed to her of the death of her son, who, when she left home, was in apparent good health. She is expected to arrive home either today or tomorrow, and the funeral will probably be held at the Bowan home some time Sunday.

Death Announcement from the November 18, 1910, edition of the local newspaper, Carthage, Missouri (located by a volunteer historian at the Jasper County Records Department during our September 2013 visit).

[In the spring of 1909, two years after the death of Hattie's husband Abe, she married Wesley Bowen. At some point, the marriage turned sour, and Hattie filed for divorce in 1917, claiming that Bowen subjected her to repeated verbal abuse and disappeared for months at a time.]

You may have looked to Aunt Hattie for guidance, viewing her marriage to Abe Mink as a model on which to base your own romantic aspirations. Perhaps you wanted to check with her before saying yes to Frank Kirsch, your adventurous suitor. I will never know whether that was the case. What I do know is that Frank definitely had marriage in mind.

His letter of April 27, 1911 is playful, insistent, and could be summed up in two sentences: "Ruthy, I am counting on you say yes to my proposal and get right over here to Nebraska. Will you?"

Handwritten note by Ruth Kirsch identifying the letter Frank Kirsch wrote to her in late April 1911. "This letter your Daddy wrote me before the marriage. May 16th, 1911."

April 27, 1911

To Ruthy Dearest;

Say Honey as this is after the parade, thought would write you a few lines, if you have no objections, just to ask you for the last time to day if I can expect to see the dear little girlie in Nebr. Well, say something Can I? Please say SURE. You know what I am going to do Sunday. All the little brown eyed girlie and myself, all I expect to live for. Dearie, I am going to fix up here next week so be ready, WILL YOU? Gee, it sure is awful lonesome around here. How long must it be? You must remember it is all up to you after Sunday. The sooner the better for me. Don't you believe me? Say Sure. Sure expect a letter from my girlie tomorrow and then can see if she

LEWIS AND CLARK'S GREAT WESTERN SHOW

SPECIAL TRAIN OF PULLMAN CARS BAND AND ORCHESTRA 50 PEOPLE 50

THE LARGEST AND MOST COMPLETE ORGANIZATION OF IT'S KIND EXTANT

F. L. KIRSCH MGR.

EN ROUTE _Apr. 27,_ 191_4_

To Ruthy Dearest;

        Say Honey as this is after the perade thought would
write you a few lines if you have no objections justto ask you for the
last time to day if I can expect to see the dear little girlie in Nebr.
Well, sy something Can I? Please say SURE. You know what I am going to
to do sunday All for the Little brown eyed girlie and myself all I expect
to live for. Dearie I am going to fix up here next week so be ready
WILL YOU? Gee, It sure is awful lonesome around here How long must it be?
You must remember it is all up to you after sunday the sooner the better
for me Dont you believe me? Say Sure. Sure expect to have a letter from
my girlie tomorrow and then can see if she intends to meet me befor such
an awful long while. Well, say something, You little Dickens. You have met
the bunch here and know you are as welcome as you ever could be anywhere.
Dont you? We will give the big doings right here to the bunchYou know a
big feed for them and a few toasts is the program, That all right? Well,
say No or Yes, Gee, Sweetheart I am awful anxious to hear from you. Why
shouldnt I be thats what I'd like to knowWe will be in Nebr. a week from
Saturday and you in Denver Oh such an awfull distance to be from that one
that is mine, Ruthy Dear listen here Do you think that , that dream of mine
can ever come true?You don't understand,Do you Honey? You better say YES
Or I will lick you right on that double chin.Well its a pity you couldnt
write once in a while at least. Your letter to Wakeeney left Abilene the
2Ist and arrived in Oakley the No,I mean Wakeeney the23rd on the train
that comes through Abilene at 3.24 So you see if it had taken you that
long to get to Oakley I would have been in an awful state of mine to
let you be there and I up on this branch but if you would hurry you
could catch us here at that Are you going to hurry?Find enclose the corrected route so I can be sure of gettting a letter once in awhile anyway
Ruthy You Dearest, please write often Will you?Regards to Your Mother
                                 From yours forever
                                          Frank.

Junction City Kansas MayIst
Manhattan   "   " 2nd
Blue Rapids   "   " 3Rd
Marysville   "   " 4th
Wymore   Nebr.   " 5th
See Sweetheart we will be in Nebr and you WHERE?
The ice will be broken Sunday
Kiss me.

intends to meet me before such an awful long wait. Well, say something, you little Dickens. You have met the bunch here and know you are as welcome as you ever could be anywhere. Don't you? We will give the big doings right here to the bunch. You know, a big feed for them and a few toasts is the program, is that all right? Well, say No or Yes. Gee, Sweetheart, I am awful anxious to hear from you. Why shouldn't I be? That's what I'd like to know. We will be in Nebr. a week from Saturday and you in Denver. Oh such an awful distance to be from that one that is mine. Ruthie Dear, listen here. Do you think that dream of mine can ever come true? You don't understand, do you Honey? You better say YES or I will lick you right on that double chin. Well it's a pity you couldn't write once in a while at least. Your letter to WaKeeney left Abilene the 21st and arrived in Oakley the No I mean WaKeeney the 23rd on the train—that comes through Abilene at 3:24. So you see if it has taken that long to get to Oakley I would have been in an awful state of mind to let you be there and I up on this branch. But if you would hurry you could catch us here at that. Are you in a hurry? Find enclosed the corrected route so I can be sure of getting a letter once in awhile anyway.

Ruthy, You Dearest, please write often, will you? Regards to your mother.

From yours forever
Frank.

Junction City, Kansas May 1st

Manhattan Kansas May 2nd

Blye Rapids, Kansas May 3rd

Marysville, Kansas May 4th

Wymore, Nebraska May 5th

See Sweetheart we will be in Nebraska and you WHERE? The ice will be broken Sunday.

Kiss me [penciled in Grammie's handwriting].

I have no idea what you and your mother discussed about Frank, or what she might have told you about the letters she wrote to him questioning his intention to marry you. I can, however, imagine that by the time you received this letter, you would have been eager to have a conversation with your Aunt Hattie. Perhaps it would have been something like this fictitious version:

April 30, 1911

Dear Aunt Hattie,

I wish you and I lived closer together because I would like some advice from you.

I talked to you about Frank Kirsch before. He's from Abilene and that's where we met a few years ago. He is the manager of a traveling show and spends much of the year on the road. You would like him.

Frank has asked me to marry him, but Mother isn't too keen on the idea. She hasn't even met him but thinks he and I would not be a good match.

In fact she has threatened to write him a letter if I don't tell him no.

The sad thing is that I know Father would have liked him. And I'm sure Abe would have too. Like Frank, they could be playful and funny. And both wait to judge a man until they get to know him. Mother, as you know, forms strong opinions of others even before she meets them. She's like Grandfather Judd that way.

I think Mother is picky about people because she was never happy with Father. She doesn't say much about it to me, but I think she saw him as childish and doesn't want me to make the same mistake.

Frank sometimes calls me "Ruthy," a name I love. Mother doesn't.

Just writing to you, I can tell I am ready to give Frank my answer. I want to say Yes. Even though this letter has been a one-sided conversation, I can feel your support for my decision. I hope that you and Frank can meet one day.

Much love,
Ruth

Ruth and Frank's marriage license.

Ruth Hilton and Frank Kirsch Wedding photo, 1911.

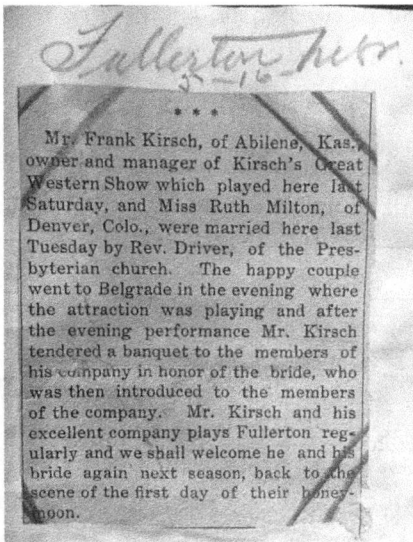

* * *

Mr. Frank Kirsch, of Abilene, Kas., owner and manager of Kirsch's Great Western Show which played here last Saturday, and Miss Ruth Milton, of Denver, Colo., were married here last Tuesday by Rev. Driver, of the Presbyterian church. The happy couple went to Belgrade in the evening where the attraction was playing and after the evening performance Mr. Kirsch tendered a banquet to the members of his company in honor of the bride, who was then introduced to the members of the company. Mr. Kirsch and his excellent company plays Fullerton regularly and we shall welcome he and his bride again next season, back to the scene of the first day of their honeymoon.

(L.) Fullerton Nebraska Newspaper marriage announcement. (R.) Ruth Kirsch and King, traveling show dog. Your name was misspelled "Milton."

You and Frank were married on May 16, 1911, in Fullerton, Nebraska.

I remember the feelings of comfort and safety your Seattle home gave me, akin to the sense of belonging I felt when at the circus with Honeychile. You created warmth at home and among your relatives and friends. Like your daughter, you found great strength through friends. Those friendships surely helped during the time Frank was on the road.

I wish I had been more curious about how you and your mother got along. I don't imagine it was through conversation. Perhaps you bonded through sewing and needlework. She was a skilled seamstress; you quilted and embroidered intricate designs on bedspreads, pillowcases, and towels. As a young girl, I especially loved the fabric dogs with embroidered faces you made from many different patterned fabrics, some donated by your friends and neighbors. I loved watching you make those soft-sculpture pooches: choosing the fabric and pinning the paper pattern over the cloth, cutting out the rounded-edged pieces, stitching them together on your sewing machine, finally stuffing them with cotton. No two were alike. I of course wanted to collect them all. My strategy was to ask for one periodically, trying not to sound as greedy as I felt. In return, you indulged me with one every time I visited you.

Your life was characterized by a lively interest in others, which naturally drew others to you. For example, Dad's letters to you, filled with playful asides and tongue-in-cheek humor, clearly show how comfortable he was with you as his mother-in-law. He could let go of editorial formalities and know that you would receive his lighthearted words in the spirit he intended.

In early May 1959, you and Frank were driving home from Walla Walla after hearing a lecture by your new son-in-law, Walter Brattain. About thirty miles from Seattle, near the town of North Bend, a front-tire blowout sent the car out of control and over an embankment. Mother and Gretchen rushed to the hospital as soon as they got the news. They agreed with the doctors, who at first thought you were in better shape than Frank. But within a day or two it became clear that you had suffered internal injuries that would prove fatal. When you died on May 6, you took a part of Honeychile with you. He never fully rallied from your death. After forty-seven years together, he had lost his life companion, the grounding force behind your marriage.

Although your death was a huge loss for all of us, you remain, after more than sixty years, a model of kindness and patience for me. I love and miss you!

Debi

Grammie as I remember her.

Grammie, Gramps, and Webb, ca. 1958.

5

Roland

I. Young Roland Miller

Many of our deepest motives come, not from an adult logic of how things work in the world, but out of something that is frozen from childhood.

—Kazuo Ishiguro

Roland Miller—"Roly" to his friends and business acquaintances—was born into a family with two sisters, one older by eleven years, the other by six. He lived at home in St. Louis for almost all of his first twenty-three years, mostly at 3843 Cleveland Avenue (still standing), just a few blocks from the Missouri Botanical Garden.

Roly's parents had graduated from the University of Michigan, his father, Armand, in chemistry and his mother, Pearl, in mathematics. Armand was a public-school educator, at various times serving as the principal at McKinley High School and Professor in the Department of Physical Sciences at Stowe Teachers College. Seven years before Roly's birth, Pearl obtained a Master of Arts in mathematics from Stanford University. From the time Roly was six until he left St. Louis, she taught mathematics at Washington University in St. Louis.

Roly prepared a table summarizing his early life, including progress in school and summer trips to the West with his family, starting when he was just a year or two old. These trips, in a homemade camping vehicle, seemed idyllic to me. I vividly recall seeing movies taken on some of those junkets, with views of lakes below soaring mountains.

In an interview about Roly's life, conducted after he died, our mother described the vacations in more detail:

> Of course, his family did a lot with his dad's being available to go in the summer. His mother also would be free in the summer. They went for two- or three-month vacations—toured the West—in a pre-luxury trailer. It was something his dad constructed that they called "the Ark." I guess it was "fearful and wonderful" (Roly's description). Roly also loved his experiences at camp in the Ozarks.

Roly and his mother on a summer vacation.

After public schools, Roly received a Bachelor of Arts degree from Washington University in St. Louis at age nineteen, where he served as editor of the university newspaper. He then spent a year at Harvard Business School. Despite passing courses with "distinction," he was forced to return home for financial reasons. (Recall that this was during the Great Depression.) After a summer job working for a newspaper in Walla Walla, Washington, he returned to St. Louis and

Roly's summary of his first twenty-three years.

Year	Winter	Summer
1912	Born in Milton-Freewater, OR; moved to Webster Groves (106 Bompart), a suburb of St. Louis	Webster
1913	Webster	Silver City, NM, and Long Beach, CA
1914	Webster	Boulder, CO, by train
1915	Webster	ditto
1916	Webster	Boulder -- drove out in Ford and trailer
1917	Webster	ditto
1918	Webster	started in 2nd Grade
1919	St. Louis (2848 Accomac) in April	to ranch with Dad and Ray (adopted brother)
1920	St. Louis, Charles School	ditto
1921	Charles School	Camp River Cliff, Bourbon MO
1922	Charles School	Camp River Cliff and Boulder
1923	St. Louis (3843 Cleveland) in May, graduated grade school	Camp River Cliff
1924	Cleveland High	Camp Niangua, Lynn Creek MO
1925	to Roosevelt High mid-year	Camp Niangua
1926	Roosevelt High	Camp Niangua
1927	Roosevelt High	summer school, Colo. U. for geology; Camp Chief Ouray, Granby
1928	graduated Roosevelt in June	to Colorado in bus on Ford chassis, in Estes and Boulder
1929	Washington U.	Camp Chief Ouray as councilor
1930	Washington U.	summer school in Boulder geography and sociology
1931	Washington U, A.B. in June	tour CA and west coast in bus, now on Chev. chassis
1932	Harvard Grad. Bus. School	loafing in St. Louis
1933	Walla Walla Bulletin till Nov. '32 then back to Wash. U. to complete M.A. in June	played to Europe in ship's orchestra; traveled there for 1 month with father
1934	Wash. U. under fellowship	

earned a Master of Arts in economics from his alma mater, followed by two years pursuing a doctoral degree in political science.

By 1935 it was clear that his fellowship from the university was not enough to cover all expenses, and he was forced to pick a career from among three possibilities: music, continued education leading to a Ph.D. and a job in academia, or newspapers. A chance encounter with an elevator operator influenced his decision: Roly discovered, to his consternation, that the fellow was a Ph.D. The implications of

Young Roland in the summer. I smile whenever I look at it.

this sank in; when his uncle, who owned the Walla Walla newspaper, offered him an entry-level job, he accepted. He moved to Walla Walla, met and romanced Emma Jane Kirsch, married in 1938, had three children, and split his time among three loves: family, music, and the newspaper.

Earning a Ph.D. was one of the few goals he did not attain, instead leaving it to each of his three children to join his parents in serving on college or university faculties.

I remember Dad telling me a few details of his early life, and love the summary of it that he left me. However, the only person from that period that I was able to meet was his mother. His father died a year before I was born, and though I recall that other household members were mentioned, I never met them or heard much about them.

One of my primary interests in joining Debi's family-history project was to learn what I could about these shadowy characters from my father's childhood, and perhaps understand how they contributed to his life. One source of information was the trove of documents left by my mother; another was the Internet, primarily Ancestry.com and Newspapers.com. The first things I noticed in Debi's collection were photographs of his sisters Dorothy and Elsa.

L to R: Roly's sisters, Elsa and Dorothy, from before his birth.

Studio portrait of Dorothy Pearl Miller (born April 23, 1900) from roughly the time of Roly's birth.

L to R: Dorothy, Roly, and Pearl, perhaps taken on a summer trip around 1930.

Dorothy died on April 3, 1931, a few weeks before her thirty-first birthday. According to her Missouri State Board of Health death certificate, she had an appendectomy on March 24, but succumbed to postoperative acute peritonitis and other complications. At the time of her hospitalization, she was an unemployed stenographer, living with her parents on Cleveland Avenue.

Debi and I inherited a photo from around 1913, taken from an envelope with the following handwritten notes. "106 Bompart Place, Webster Grove, Mo., a suburb of St. Louis. Grandmother Colby is there also. This is your Aunt Pearl and Uncle Armand R. Miller, cousin Elsa and Buster, otherwise Roland Eugene Miller. Send them back to me." On the back is written, "Elsa is the one who has been sick so long." I'm guessing that Pearl's mother, Ellen Colby, was living with the family, and her daughter, Clara Colby (see p. 111), sent this to Clara's son. Then it somehow got passed down to Roly, and eventually to Debi. Elsa would have been about seven in the photo.

L to R: Buster, Armand, Pearl, Elsa, ca. 1913.

Elsa Laura Miller, age eleven years and ten months, died on March 30, 1917, as reported on page 10 of the March 31 *St. Louis Post-Dispatch* (cause not stated). A service took place on April 1 at her home on Bompart Avenue, after which she was cremated. I can't help but wonder how her illness and death affected the five-year-old Roly. He definitely went on to live his life as if there was no time to waste. Who starts Harvard graduate school at age nineteen, after years of enjoying extensive summer vacations?

On September 18, 1917, Roly's parents adopted Marion Anderson, who was just a few months younger than Roly, and her brother Frank Raymond Anderson, who was two years younger. Quite possibly this was done to ease the pain of losing Elsa. At the time of the adoption, their names were formally changed to Marion Eleanor Miller and Raymond Frank Miller.

L to R: Roland (age 6), Raymond (3) and Marion (5), taken Easter 1918, six months after the two were adopted.

Seated, L to R: Roly, Marion and Raymond with mother Pearl.

The family records told me almost nothing about Marion and Raymond. On January 5, 1957, just before Roly's death, Marion sent a warm letter from Windsor, California, under the name Mrs. Fred M. Clemens; she signed her name "Marian." From a kind letter that

Raymond sent on February 28, 1957, after hearing of Roly's death, and a 1956 Christmas card from his wife, Josephine, I learned that they lived in San Antonio, Texas.

Using only the Internet, I was unable to confidently identify Marion and Raymond's biological parents. I did find an Ida Anderson (the name on the adoption papers) living in St. Louis around the appropriate time, but there was no record or public family tree at Ancestry that connected the two children with that particular Ida.

Fortunately, the Internet turned out to be much more helpful when I searched for Raymond and Marion's descendants. My hope was to learn more about Marion and Raymond and possibly even contact some of their living descendants to ask for photographs or information about their time in the Miller household.

Raymond proved the easier of the two to track. He was a corporal in the U.S. Army during World War II. Later he lived at 321 W. Dickson St., San Antonio for many years. His obituary (page 38 of the July 24, 1969, *San Antonio Express*) says that he was survived by wife Josephine C. Miller and son Bruce Miller. I found a public family tree at Ancestry that includes Raymond's son Bruce. I contacted the owner, who turned out to be Ethan Miller, Bruce's grandson. I learned from Ethan that Bruce died in 2021. (Oh, don't I wish I had pursued this when I first worked on this document!) Bruce had a single son, Isaac, Ethan's father. Unfortunately, there was no overlap between Raymond (died 1969) and Isaac (born 1974), so Isaac has no direct view into Raymond's (and my father's) childhood.

Noting Raymond's lifelong interest in music (both a 1941 marriage—not to Bruce's mother—and his 1969 death certification list his occupation as "musician"), Ethan asked about musicians in my family. Both Ethan (cello, guitar, bass, drums) and his older sister Alyssa (guitar, piano, violin) are quite musically talented. Unfortunately, after a few exchanges, Ethan stopped answering my questions. However, before then, Ethan sent me a photo of Raymond as an adult.

Searching for information about Marion took more time, but was ultimately more fruitful. She married Dr. H. H. Rodin in 1932, when he was in his last year of medical school and she was around

Raymond with baby
Bruce, ca. 1952.

twenty years old. He went on to be a professor of dermatology at Northwestern University and was a president of the Indiana Dermatology Society. They had a daughter, Virginia, in 1935, and a second, Donna, in 1938, but divorced after approximately ten years of marriage. According to the 1940 census, Marion completed three years of college (probably nursing school). She later married Fred M. Clemens, and had a third daughter, Marianna, in 1945; they lived in California. The 1950 census data showed that Virginia and Donna were living with Fred, Marion and Marianna.

L to R: Marion's daughters Marianna Clemens, Donna Rodin and Virginia Rodin.

The Ancestry website didn't divulge much information about the three daughters or their descendants. The good news, however, was that I stumbled upon a public family tree that included Marion and indicated that Virginia and Donna were still living, and that Virginia had a son and a granddaughter. (Ancestry hides the specifics of the living.) The owner of the tree graciously agreed to try contacting Virginia and perhaps others of Marion's descendants.

Before long, I heard from Virginia and her son, Tim. In a telephone call, multiple email messages, and a package, Virginia related what she knew of Marion's childhood. Importantly, she identified the biological parents; the mother's maiden name was Ida Marion Omohundro. Ida had put Marion and two older siblings in an orphanage after the death of their biological father, Seley Edgar Anderson, in 1915 from pneumonia. (The 1920 census data indicate that the three oldest Anderson children were then living with Ida and her second husband, Albert R. Tullock.) Also, Virginia recalled that after Pearl moved to Los Angeles, she visited Marion and her three daughters in Baldwin Park, California, when Virginia was a sophomore in high school. (Virginia added that Pearl's attempts to teach her mathematics largely failed.) The package from Virginia contained a low-quality photograph of Marion. Virginia predicted that her youngest sister, Marianna, would be my best source of information, and thus it was.

Raymond at age 12.　　　Marian at age 16.　　　Marian and
　　　　　　　　　　　　　　　　　　　　　　　　　Marianna (age 5).

Marianna sent me a number of photographs, including the three shown on the previous page. Most critically, her photos brought Raymond and especially Marion to life. The moment I saw the photo of an adult Marion (her childhood name), she became Marian (her later preferred name) in my mind, as my mental image of her, as a child in 1918, was replaced by a woman in 1950.

My understanding of Marian was made particularly vivid by a brief summary of her life that Marian wrote (and Marianna typed) in 1983. I love this window into my father's childhood.

> . . . One year after father's death, mother had to let four of us go. Charlie, at age twelve, could bring in enough selling papers and doing odd jobs to keep them. Mother did sewing. Orrin, Cecelia, and I were put in the orphanage in Webster Groves, very near Wellston [a suburb of St. Louis]. Frank Raymond was taken in by my mother's brother, Uncle Arthur, his wife Aunt Cecelia, and their only child, Hazel. Uncle Art was a laborer too, and so really could ill afford another mouth to feed, but he did. We knew them and saw them at various times until I was seventeen—really loving people. . . . One time, Ray and I were left with them for a week when we were about eight and ten. Then, when Hazel was married, all of us Millers went to the wedding. We had them for Thanksgiving or Christmas dinner a time or two. The last time I saw them was after I was married. They invited us all to a Thanksgiving dinner when I visited my folks. These were my only contacts with my blood relatives. . . .

> . . . [A]ll was ready for the adoption. They [the Millers] would come on Sundays and take me for a ride in their Maxwell Phaeton. I had never been in a car before. Well, when all was set, my three-year-old brother, Frank Raymond, was visiting me one Sunday afternoon. We were sitting on the porch of the Orphanage when the Millers drove up. Dad saw this adorable tiny redheaded doll and fell for him. He took him with me on the ride, and Dad decided he wanted that boy. Mom was all set on a girl, so they took us both. . . . Dad and I became thick as thieves, while Mom and Ray were closer than I ever was with Mom until I was married. . . . Roland, the Millers' own son, was a perfect brother and accepted us without any jealousy. We were good friends as long as he lived. . . . When my mother died, the Millers gave her a good funeral. I didn't know this until after the funeral. I'm sorry now I did not have more interest in my blood family. Uncle Art could have told me about my father as well as my mother. I was so much a Miller, I had no interest in the others.

Another tremendously valuable document contained Marianna's

recollections of conversations with Marian, prepared specifically for me.

> Roland . . . immediately embraced the new children as playmates. Perhaps their arrival helped him with the death of his beautiful sister, Elsa. The three children played together as a threesome in the attic, their designated play area. Many hours were filled happily. . . . In their teen years they had a common bond through their love of music. . . .
>
> . . .
>
> A very important member in the Miller household was Lou. She was an African-American who rode a bus daily to manage the house. . . . From her, Mom learned to iron clothes as an art form, wash laundry, dry, clean, and manage to put dinner on the table at precisely six every night. . . . I wish I could have known all the Millers and personally thanked them and Lou. I had a mother with exceptional housekeeping skills. . . .
>
> . . .
>
> The Millers recognized an artistic talent in Mom and sent her on Saturdays by bus to an Art Institute in St. Louis. . . . The Millers sent Mom to nursing school but she married Dr. Rodin before completion. . . .
>
> . . .
>
> . . . [S]he always wished I'd known "Dad Miller" as she called him. He was so kind and warm that Mom could come to him to talk. . . . In later years, Mom and Mother Miller corresponded and Mom found solace in Mother Miller's concern for her.
>
> . . .
>
> . . . Due to Mom's birth mother's willingness to give her up, and the Millers' influence, Mom enjoyed attending cultural events with my father. They shared a love for opera, orchestral concerts, good literature, and theater. . . . Her early training in housekeeping and cooking blossomed to enhance my father's life and my own.

Marianna also recalled that upon reaching a low point in her life, Marian left her older daughters with relatives and "went to Los Angeles to stay with her Aunt Elsa, Mother Miller's sister. At an opera one night, they sat next to Fred Clemens, who later became my father." She also mentioned on the phone that a couple of years after Pearl taught me to read, she did the same for Marianna, who is about two years younger than me.

If my father had lived longer, I would have met my aunt and cousins, which compounds my deep sense of loss; before this year, I missed out on knowing any such close relatives. I'm left with the unanswered question of how I reached seventy-plus years before discovering four living cousins. Still, fleshing out this branch of my family tree and contacting Marian's daughters was definitely one of the most exciting and gratifying rewards of joining Debi to plunge into the family thicket.

There was another household member that I'm convinced had a profound impact on my family. Clara Colby Thoms was my grandmother Pearl's oldest sister and a highly regarded pianist and opera singer. She lived with Roly in 1920. He was eight and she was sixty, teaching music. She no doubt interacted with Roly over a long period, because her mother lived with the Millers when Roly was born (1912), and at the time of her death (1924). Roly came away from the interaction an accomplished musician.

Much earlier, Clara had married William Mann Thoms; they went on to gain prominent positions in New York City artistic circles. Their only child, William F. Thoms, had three children and multiple grandchildren. I located Ancestry tree owners that appear to know some of Clara's living descendants (in one case the descendant herself, in another an ex-husband). I hoped to hear back from those people, and perhaps to obtain photos of Clara and/or more information about her times in St. Louis. One of them did reply and helped me as much as she could but unfortunately added little to what I already knew.

In any case, I owe my existence to my musical great-aunt, Clara Colby Thoms. Dad's love of music clearly was influenced by Clara. Although his parents were science-oriented, they saw that he had perfect pitch (probably inherited from his mother) and supported his musical training, to which Clara contributed.

Music brought my parents together. Mother, who was studying education and music in college, had been a music enthusiast since her elementary school days in Seattle. According to her diary, she met Roly in late October, 1936, through friends they had in common. You will learn much more about their courtship in Chapter 9, "Emma

Jane." The following diary extracts are a teaser. (We love the first one so much we quoted it twice!)

Nov. 5–Thursday
My first date with Roly Miller—nothing too awfully exciting.

Then, after they had another date:

Saturday—My what a day—6th & 7th
... He's been places and done things—Europe. Aka from Washington University in St. Louis, etc.

Mother was still dating other guys, for example:

In the evening had a date with Clint Ryun—God, may I never have such a miserable time again!

Encouraged by the growing success, Roly brought out the big guns.

Thursday Nov. 19th—
A perfectly grand evening—Roly & I were up to the Kelly's [sic]—Quiet but so restful ... Heard Debussy, Stravinsky, & Benny Goodman—Watched a fire (what magic there is in it). He [Roly] plays jazz superbly.

("The Kellys" refers to John and Martha Kelly, Roly's Uncle and Aunt, and Roly's employer for fourteen months at that point. Their home was at 1019 Alvarado Terrace, which was to be our home starting around 1946, and Mother's home for another forty years.)

That grand evening was the end of Mother's dating other guys. My father's love of music and his piano virtuosity had "sealed the deal." I'm immensely grateful that Clara guided my father toward a love of, and accomplishment with, music, steering him away from his mother's example of teaching university mathematics. I know, from personal experience, that wouldn't have made him what is nowadays called a "chick magnet." I note in passing that Debi has an even greater reason than I do for acknowledging the wonderful influence of Clara Colby Thoms, since there is a direct line from Dad's love of music and the cello to her existence, experiences, and loves.

While my father grew up in a household with two or sometimes three adults and four other children, I met only his mother. It is my own fault for never asking either of my parents for more information about his siblings. It wasn't until I was retired from work and in my seventies that I became intensely interested in my father's childhood. After the passage of a century, details have been difficult to discover; this report gives basically everything I learned. The rewards for me from the search included deeper connections with my father (from what I learned) and with my younger sister (from sharing in the search), plus friendships with cousins I knew nothing about. Of the pieces I have written for our family-history project, this is my favorite.

—Webb Colby Miller, February/March 2023

II. Webb's Letter

My father didn't tell me how to live. He lived and let me watch him do it.

—Clarence Budington Kelland

Roland Eugene Miller, 1912-1957.

Dear Dad,

This is just a note to "cherry-pick" events from my life that I think might interest you, in chronological order. First, I want you to know what comes to mind when I reflect on our time together. Second, I'll tell you about my struggle to cope with your death and how I eventually overcame that despair. Third, I'll recount aspects of my professional life that I believe you will appreciate. In a real sense, you and Mom guided my most consequential choices. Also, there is a deeper motive here: the discussion leads me to a whole raft of questions for you. Though they could not be answered even if you magically appeared, they are a major component of my thoughts about you. Fourth, I describe a paramount interest in my retirement years, which is directly related to you. Along with these four subjects, I will point out a few of the many topics not covered in detail, for a variety of reasons including a self-imposed page limit. Finally, I close with notes about the future of our family-history project.

I recently wrote about your childhood—facts known to you that I was just starting to glimpse. The only parts that were new to you concerned machinations (such as the Internet) and twists and turns that led to discoveries about your life. Here I'm going to "flip the script" and talk about things I understand but you don't, because they happened after you died. The first, brief topic is the only exception to the rule; I include it because, though I'm sure I often thanked you for my wonderful childhood, I no doubt didn't thank you enough.

My memories of the thirteen years of my life known to you are heavenly. I relished our many family outings—skiing, boating, rockhounding, and the summer in Europe, among other events. I particularly appreciate the times I got you all to myself, for instance fishing or camping. These rich experiences showed me many possibilities for my later life, and your love and support left all of my options open. When I had children of my own, I became acutely aware of what a phenomenal job you did, finding the time and energy for these activities. Thank you, thank you, thank you for the gift of a dream childhood.

My only negative comment (and I mean this humorously, although it is true) is that because I never sensed even the slightest tension between you and Mom, I was unprepared for marriage. I had no experience guiding how to respond either when my wife expressed anger about me, or I felt anger about her.

Like most kids, I had some concerns. They weren't caused by you, nor did they seriously disrupt my life then or later. Also, I don't sense that you experienced them in your childhood. Thus, they've been relegated to a letter that I wrote to my younger self. [See p. xlvii.]

The family skiing in 1951.

You in your second boat, Presto. Mom on shore with our dear family friend, Dorothy Robinson.

*Gretchen on a rock-hounding trip, looking for
opals above the Snake River in Idaho.*

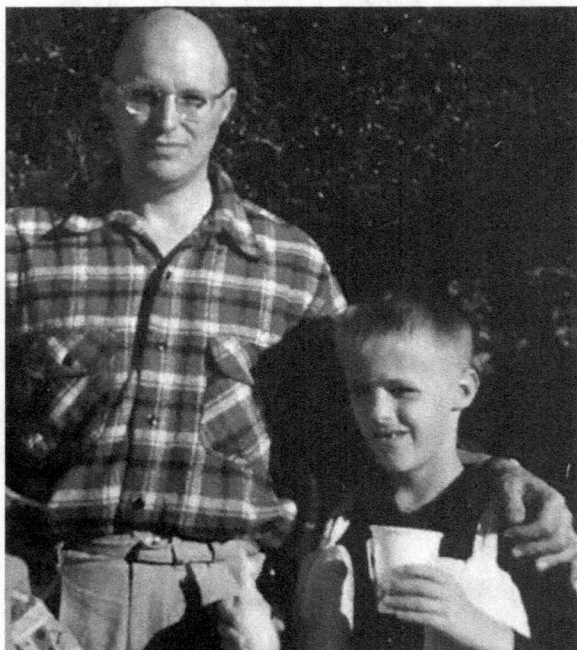

*I loved my times outdoors with you. Notice the deviled egg wrapped in
waxed paper in my right hand, as described in Debi's letter to Grammie.*

And what kid wouldn't love a bedroom that looked like a cruise ship?

My idyllic childhood came to an end when you fell ill. In the months surrounding your death, I experienced almost the full range of human emotions. In an attempt to cope with my runaway feelings, I reinvented myself by becoming a serious student and physical fitness nut. Debi has beautifully described the events surrounding your death. The writing is so exquisite and so faithful to my memories of you that I haven't attempted to cover that ground again.

I acutely mourned your death for many years, feeling that holding onto my pain was how I could express my love and loyalty. Unfortunately, I also interpreted your death as proof that if I loved someone too much, they would leave me, inflicting soul-numbing pain. I believe that Mom was a victim of this inference for thirty years, while I held her at arm's length rather than run the risk of feeling so much pain again. Roughly thirty-five years ago, around 1987, encouraged by my wife Nan, I decided that retaining and indeed treasuring this pain could and should be set aside. That way, I could throw off the shackling fear about loving another person. Besides, I doubted that you would want me to hold on to you that way. (My life was changing in other important ways at that time; more about that later.) I am eternally grateful that I mended my ways and had a wonderful relationship with Mom toward the end of her life.

My professional life fits neatly into two periods: a melding of mathematics and computer science in the period roughly 1968 to 1987 (ages 25 to 44), then a focus on biology from 1988 to 2013 (ages 45 to 70).

You know better than most people how arcane and divorced from real-world applications mathematical research typically is. How many years would it have taken you to understand your mother's master's thesis? Would that effort have changed your life afterwards? You see my point. My work in mathematics and computers was similar, and not even of interest to very many others in the field. On the plus side, I developed a perhaps unusual modus operandi: I required that my research questions be relatively unstudied, rather than already being pursued by a crowd. With my first choices, it turned out that others were wise to focus elsewhere, and I won't describe details of that work, unless you request it. (I'm not holding my breath.)

My career before age forty-five was successful by some measures; I had been a full professor at respectable universities (Santa Barbara, Arizona and Penn State) for ten years, but my professional and domestic lives were in flux. I periodically shifted my research focus and changed where I lived even more often: four years in State College, then four in Santa Barbara, then four in Tucson, then back to State College. This wanderlust was motivated by a perceived choice between (Plan A) stay in the same place, doing much the same things, get old, and die, or (Plan B) move to a completely different environment and reinvent my life. Indeed, between ages thirteen and forty-four, I never lived more than four consecutive years in the same location. It took me that long to become comfortable with knowing the outline of the rest of my life.

Then, around age forty-five, several aspects of my life almost simultaneously metamorphosed. (One could speculate about causal relationships between marrying Nan, putting down roots, and switching academic discipline, but I don't have any insights to offer here.) One change was that my physical wanderlust evaporated; I've lived in State College for over thirty-five years, moving only once, a distance of about five miles.

While I was contemplating how to spend the rest of my working life, Mom was sending me newspaper clippings about a forthcoming, huge project in biology, namely determining the complete human genetic makeup (consistent with Mom's longstanding fascination with genetics). Despite never having taken a course in biology, I decided to try my hand at identifying and solving some relatively unstudied problem that would eventually be widely recognized as important. After a year of trying to understand enough about the current state of biology that I could find the right topic, I picked my focus, put my head down and my tail up, and beavered away for the next twenty years.

The problem I selected assumed the availability of complete genetic information—the "genome"—for humans and another mammal, where the goal is to identify the similarities and differences between the two species, and use that information to help discover how the genome sculpts living animals, as well as how accurately a specific laboratory animal can model human disease. I assumed that the human and mouse genomes would be available before I retired. Fortunately, that assumption turned out to be pessimistic, and I got to apply the approach I developed to a number of animals: mouse, rat, rhesus macaque, platypus and chicken, among others. Each of those projects involved many other scientists. Recently (2023), ten years after my retirement, I saw a collection of papers published in the top-tier journal Science comparing the genomes of 241 mammals, so my chosen research focus no longer counts as "relatively unstudied."

Throughout my development and use of computer methods to compare DNA sequences between species, it was important to me that the same approach could be used to compare one human genome to another, thereby to better understand some genetic disease, or to compare normal and malignant genomes from the same individual, so as to better understand, and eventually treat, cancer. Cancer has of course interested me ever since your death, and, as I discuss during my office visits for prostate cancer, it is inevitable that intra-individual DNA comparisons will become a regular part of cancer treatment.

After the large projects comparing the genome of humans with that of another species, I worked on smaller projects with a collaborator at Penn State, Stephan Schuster, who developed the capability to sequence genomes. Much of our effort focused on the genomes of endangered species, like the Tasmanian Devil and the California Condor. In addition, we were the first group to sequence individuals from southern Africa, including several bushmen and Archbishop Desmond Tutu. To celebrate completion of that project, your grandson Andrew and I flew to Namibia and met those folks.

Webb with Ngubi, whose genome we determined and analyzed, taken the same week as the next photograph. The "N" is pronounced with a specific click sound. He was amazingly fit for a 70-year-old. Though pictured here in traditional garb, he is widely traveled; his musical group has performed in a number of countries.

Archbishop Desmond Tutu, a Nobel Peace Prize winner, with Webb and Andrew, 2010.

I heard disapproval of this project from the National Human Genome Research Institute (NHGRI), a branch of the NIH, that funded my research for a number of years. They sounded annoyed that I wasn't working on the research I had proposed some years earlier, namely interspecies genome comparisons. Shortly thereafter, I noticed that the NHGRI website had a page listing the Institute's recent accomplishments, which included the project. Another story about that project concerns how my collaborators reacted when I discovered that the Archbishop's mitochondrial lineage (*i.e.*, his mother's mother's mother's . . . mother, at some undetermined time in the past) was a Bushman. They were concerned he wouldn't want to learn of his descent from such a lowly group. I replied that I felt he would be thrilled, especially given his apparent desire to speak for all black Africans. He confirmed my expectation when I asked him. Later, Eric Green, the head of NHGRI, told me he had met the Archbishop and asked him what he found most interesting about his genome; the answer was his Bushman ancestry.

My reputation among biologists centers on two papers on which I worked early on, that is, by 1995. They describe a family of computer programs called "Blast." Each paper has been cited in the reference lists of at least 80,000 papers. In other words, at least that many biology publications stated that Blast played an important role in their success.

On the other hand, my stature among my family members rests on a paper, published in 2008 with me as the first author, about the woolly mammoth genome. Our goal was to show that ancient DNA samples can be sequenced to the same accuracy as modern samples. We used the woolly mammoth because a sample was available for a couple hundred dollars on eBay, much more readily than ancient human samples (which would have been more interesting to me). It was surprising that this analysis could be performed on 20,000-year-old hair, so surprising that my collaborator Stephan Schuster and I were named to the 2009 Time 100 Most Important People.

This paper has made me famous with Debi. In 2019, we and our spouses went to the annual gem show in Tucson. Whenever we came across a fossil dealer, Debi embarrassed me by mentioning that her brother had "sequenced the woolly mammoth." When I bought a mammoth tooth on the spur of the moment, she wanted to have one, too. The years of work leading to that paper were thereby validated.

Webb and Chris with the woolly mammoth teeth.

This summary of my research successes leads to the above-mentioned raft of questions that I have for you. You died days before your forty-fifth birthday. From my personal experience, life before age forty-five may be a poor predictor of life thereafter, which greatly raises my curiosity about your unrealized later years. Clearly, the analogy between us breaks down because your years twenty-five to forty-four played out in one location, but mine in many, and my shifting job focus was perhaps more extreme than yours (though you did work in numerous newspaper departments). Still, noting your extensive childhood travels, I may have inherited some of my wanderlust from you. In any case, I'm left pondering the real possibility that you might have wanted to upend your own life, say, after your children were safely away. Do you think you would have wanted to leave Walla Walla? I know you felt drawn to working at a top-tier newspaper, but was the attraction strong enough that you would leave your friends in Walla Walla? Also, is it possible that you would have switched careers, perhaps to become a full-time musician or finish your Ph.D. and become an academic? Or what about becoming an architect? In an interview covering your many accomplishments that Mom gave twenty years after your death, Mom said, "If there was one thing he was frustrated about, he would have loved to be an architect." She told how you helped Mabel Groseclose redesign her apartment, and how fascinated you were with the design of Dorothy and Clyde Robinson's house. At the very least, you could have vicariously experienced becoming an architect alongside your granddaughter Megan and her husband, Jim. There were so many exciting avenues open to you, and it is a tragedy that you and I never got to see how your life unfolded.

I've been retired for about ten years. Nan and I moved to a farm, where much of the year is spent working outdoors, mostly gardening. But that would interest Mom more than you, I think. However, something else has been afoot that directly concerns you; I think you'll love hearing about it, especially how effectively it brought two of your children together. It even gave Debi and me some cousins (your nieces) to treasure.

A few years ago, Debi began to focus on the family history. She had inherited over a dozen large boxes with thousands of family documents, diaries and photographs. Finally, she could no longer ignore those ancestral voices, and I felt a magnetic pull toward her project, especially after I saw how much it enriched her life. Yearly pilgrimages to Nevada became a wonderful part of the collaboration, during which we immersed ourselves in learning about our ancestors.

One item that I found in Debi's boxes took me back to the time of your death—a letter from me dated January 2, 1957, after you had gone to the hospital in Seattle for the last time. I wrote:

> Dear Mom & Dad
>
> Happy New Year!
>
> Saturday I went to the show with Dee.
>
> Sunday I went hunting with Art. We didn't get to [sic] much (in fact —)
>
> Monday I was sick.
>
> Tuesday I did some work around the house.
>
> And today; back to the salt mines.
>
> Now — so much for my latest activities.
>
> I hope you (Mom) can find a special nurse so you can spend some time relaxing.
>
> We all send our best love and hopes for a speedy recovery.
>
> Webb

Apparently, I was so invested in creating an alternate, tolerable, reality that I wrote such a detached note. I trust that you immediately saw through to the underlying grief.

My strongest goal for the family-history project has been to learn about and connect with your childhood as best I can. I was immediately drawn to photographs. The first to capture me was a studio portrait of your second sister, Elsa, taken when she was around ten. Of all the photos I have seen of my ancestors, I find hers far and away the most compelling, other than yours. Her face mesmerizes me; she was clearly a person that would have greatly enriched my life to have known, and seeing her photograph I am aware of tremendous loss. What a tragedy for you, your parents and me that she died before

Elsa Laura Miller, May 15, 1905–March 30, 1917.

her twelfth birthday. All that I will ever know about Elsa are the few facts I could find in the family records and on the Internet. Though I strongly regret that death claimed your father and oldest sister, Dorothy, before I could meet them, it is little Elsa that hurts me most.

This leads to more questions I have for you. I would love to hear about your sisters and adopted siblings, and anything you can tell me about your childhood and adolescence would delight me. Please tell me how the loss of Elsa affected your parents. You were only five when she died, but do you have any memories of her? And what about your oldest sister Dorothy, who died just three weeks shy of age thirty-one when you were nineteen? Do you think it is a coincidence or perhaps a dark genetic tragedy that your father's sister Laura died young (age nineteen), back in 1895? Or do you think that all this family misery was just from a lack of modern medicine?

I was also drawn in by several photographs of you as a toddler and a few from your student years. Any concern I had about having lost my deep connection to you immediately vanished. It has been

Roland Miller at age 20.

years, indeed decades, since I shed tears over losing you, but I cried as I looked at your eyes and ached for the additional time together that was ripped from us.

Just a few months ago, I returned to learning more about your adopted siblings, Raymond and Marian. (You no doubt knew that she preferred that spelling to the original "Marion.") It turned out that I just barely missed my chance to meet Marian about twenty years after your death, as Debi discovered quite recently; Debi is the appropriate person to tell that story.

You must have heard about your mother visiting Marian and her three daughters. Did you meet any of the three? I don't remember any mention of them, and it took some detective work on my part to establish contact with two of Marian's three daughters, which I finally did a couple of months ago. The youngest, Marianna, has welcomed Debi and me, and become the cousin we always wanted. She has a strong interest in family history, but has until now been limited to studying her paternal ancestry. I hoped that the method I used to locate Marian's daughters would work to identify living descendants of Marian's older siblings, providing Marianna with a new universe of blood relatives and me with what Art Carey called "shoestring relatives." [Art, who was mentioned above in my bumbling letter, was one of my surrogate fathers, along with Clyde Robinson and Walter Brattain, who helped guide me through adolescence. Being married to the adopted daughter Laura of John and Martha Kelly, Art was himself my shoestring relative.]

I was also motivated by a desire for those descendants to learn about their relationship to Marian, and to welcome her into their family tree. I felt certain that you and Mom would want me to attempt this. This was the only time I can remember making a decision based on what I thought you would want. Among Marian and Raymond's descendants, only Marianna and her sons, Erik and Karl, encouraged me to proceed. While I initially wondered if it was any of my business, all doubts vanished when I sensed your approval. It turned out that at least four of the siblings' descendants were sufficiently interested in genealogy to create family trees using the same computer resource that I use, though none of them included Marian or Raymond among their relatives. One of the four displayed a huge family tree (over 11,000 individuals) and referred to herself as "Family Historian by day, Registered Nurse by night." I wrote her, ending with this: "No trees at Ancestry acknowledge that Marion and Frank were biological children of Seley and Ida Anderson, and I'm hoping to find someone who will fix that. Are you interested in learning more?" Her reply began with: "Heck, yeah! To the nth degree!" This woman, named J'Anette, is married to a grandson of Marian's older sister, Cecelia, who died at age thirty-five and left behind a daughter. The daughter thought she remembered her mother mentioning a red-haired sister who had become a doctor, which became family lore only tangentially related to reality. However, J'Anette had been unsuccessful at locating the mystery sister. It turns out that Marian's prolific middle brother, Oren, had nine children, and I have perhaps thirty living shoestring relatives. The new relationships are beginning to unfold as I write this.

Debi and I will continue to explore family history even after completion of our book. For one example, the flip side of identifying descendants of Marian's older sister and brothers, as already described, is to learn about her parent's ancestry, that is, going backward in time from Seley Anderson and Ida Omohundro, instead of forward. J'Anette has traced the Andersons back to the 1700s in Canada. The Omohundros in North America are said by some to all descend from Richard Omohundro, who came from England to Virginia around 1670, though J'Anette hasn't traced Ida's paternal lineage back that far. Chris remembered once seeing a book about Omohundro genealogy. Indeed, a 1287-page book called *The Omohundro Genealogical Record* claims to trace Richard Omohundro's descendants for seven generations. Fortunately, it can be read on the Internet, and may provide hours of entertainment for me one day. Also, overcome by a case of genealogy fever, I discovered how Marianna's husband Willi (Wilfred W. Waak) can learn about ancestors of his parents, who came from Germany; a German woman that I found on Ancestry has answers. I foresee many enjoyable hours of interaction with Marianna, learning about her relatives and my shoestring relatives.

Also, there are a multitude of blood relatives Debi and I could learn about, write about, or write to. For me, the first order of business is to learn more about your father. Just last week I enjoyed my first real sense of connection with him. In his diary from a trip to Europe in the summer of 1933, after spending July traveling with you, he wrote of traveling alone in August and the joy of solo hikes in Switzerland's Lauterbrunnen Valley. I remember taking solo hikes there in 1988

Photo from Armand's diary, apparently him at the Matterhorn, August 1933.

while on my honeymoon with Nan. (Thank you, by the way; I would never have gone there if you hadn't introduced me to that region in 1955.) [See photo at the bottom of page 183.] I wonder if I inherited my love of solo hikes from your dad. [See pp. 311-313.]

Another option is to write follow-up letters about new topics. For instance, I'm confident you would be interested to hear about my children, and I could write about them and their offspring at great length. Here is the briefest summary: I provided you with five grandchildren, all leading happy and admirable lives. I'll add just one snippet. Your grandson Andrew wrote a guest opinion piece (editorial?) about global warming that made the front page "above the fold" of the New York Times, November 19, 2021, in the international regular edition and November 23 in the domestic print edition. I remember one of your newspaper colleagues asking me if I had any printer's ink in my veins. Maybe it skipped a generation.

Roland Miller (at the piano) with The Yellowjackets.

I'm confident that surprises await as Debi and I press forward with family history, both newly discovered relatives and surprising facets of known relatives. An example of the latter is that I knew you could play jazz, but I didn't know that you did so in public. Digging through the family cornucopia, I came across a photo—which I absolutely love—of you playing in a band. It appears to date from your time in Walla Walla. What other surprises about you are in store for me?

Front and back of a family document that leads to a mystery.

Without a doubt, Debi and I will be left with unanswered questions. For example, we still don't understand how you came to be born in a tiny Oregon town. Another mystery concerns an old document from Mom's collection of treasures; I think I remember her saying that it is the baptismal record of your grandfather, John Jakob Mueller. The mystery here is the document's date of 1821, though Jakob was born in 1840. An expert in old German documents at Ancestry kindly translated the hand-written portion as follows. "Thus wishes your most faithful godmother Anna Müller née Bolliger, of Gontenschweil, and from your beloved godfather Joh. Jakob Müller of Unter Kulm, since you were born in the afternoon of the 24th day of December in the year 1821, and baptized on the 30th day in the church in Kulm." The reverse side says "Baptismal certificate, J. Jakob, 1821." I'm left feeling puzzled. However, the ever-present realization that a particular family-history effort may lead to a dead end has the bright side that surprise discoveries are all the more satisfying.

As Debi and I work to understand more about our family's history, you will remain a central figure, and my love for you will only continue to grow.

—Webb, April 2023

III. Debi's Response to Webb

I vividly recall Webb's 2016 visit to Henderson, Nevada, when he began his real search into the family-history trove, especially Dad's box of photos and documents. It wasn't long before he pulled out a photograph of Elsa Miller, Dad's sister who died at age eleven. I saw immediately how the photograph impacted Webb. Young Elsa could have been his daughter. Her look, calm but knowing, suggests a life maturity and awareness in which she will not challenge her fate.

Her sweet face triggered a deep and universal feeling in Webb, one that brought to mind his father's untimely death. Perhaps our sister Gretchen, upon learning of the assassination of Robert Kennedy, whom she idolized and may have seen as a kind of father figure, had had a similar reaction. These moments triggered the emotional well of grief that exists in all of us who have experienced the death of someone key to our lives.

Today I found myself responding to a photo Webb added to his "Young Roland" piece, made all the more compelling by new information he has recently learned. (See p. 105.) It is of Roland, Marian, and Raymond, taken a year after Elsa's death, and a few months after the latter pair's adoption into the Miller family. Sitting together on a large rattan porch chair, each is fancily dressed for Easter, holding a woven basket. Roland is the oldest at six. In their expressions I see longing. For Roland it is a sibling, for Marian and Ray, their birth family, and especially for their mother, who made the agonizing decision to "let them go." I wish I could ask each what he or she saw when looking back at that picture.

Webb writes touchingly of his having recently located Raymond's great-grandson and Marion's daughters and getting key information from them about that early time in their lives—I loved hearing about his search and the elation as he heard back from each. He was moved by Marianna's account of her mother's memories, written in 1983, in which she reported her own mother's painful decision to place some of her children in an adoption agency and of the serendipity of the Millers adopting both siblings. Without Marianna's willingness to share the account, we would never have known of the poignancy of that moment, nor of the special bond each developed with one of the parents. She described Raymond and adoptive mother Pearl, and Marian and adoptive father Armand, becoming "as thick as thieves." (Raymond died in 1969; Marian in 1998.)

Of course Webb wondered how six-year-old Roland would have responded to the change in family dynamics brought about by these new Millers. Marianna's report was positive! Roland proved himself to be an endearing young version of the father we so loved. In tears, I read about the young threesome playing together in the attic and finding a bond through music as teens. It's as if Marianna has given us another piece of the Dad puzzle, filling in details of his very young life as a sibling about which we knew nothing. I was also moved by Marian's late-in-life realization that she missed the chance to better know her blood relatives, having settled so comfortably into her life in her adopted family. "I was so much a Miller, I had no interest in the others." What a gift this is for us to know a bit about Marian's life reflections!

For Webb, a "bombshell" moment occurred when I called to tell him about my first phone conversation with Marianna. As she was describing the years she and her husband Willi Waak lived in Santa Barbara in the 1970s, I interrupted, "Of course, Webb lived there during that same time." She paused, then continued, "Yes, I remember well when my mother visited us with news from Emma Jane that Webb was in Santa Barbara. In fact, he lived just blocks from where we were. Mom and I were eager to meet him, to bridge this long silence in our family history." According to what Marian had written in a letter to Mother, she regretted not being able to see her adoptive brother again before his death in 1957 and would have been delighted at the possibility of meeting his son. Marianna described her phone call to Webb's number and the brief conversation with a female who answered. (At that point, Webb and Trudy were separated, and when asked, Trudy would likely have said she wasn't interested in meeting them.) Unfortunately, Webb never learned of the call and thus missed this extraordinary opportunity to meet Dad's adopted sister and niece, who could have provided a longed-for link to Dad. Marianna suggested to me she hadn't told Webb about the phone call as she didn't want him to feel bad. "Au contraire," I said. "I think Webb would be thrilled to know that you wanted to connect with him almost fifty years ago." I was right. Webb's word was "gobsmacked." Here was a moment in his past when this craved-for cousin or aunt/uncle connection was just blocks away in Santa Barbara. He would have loved the opportunity to meet the woman who had known Dad as a child and had her own memories of their St. Louis childhood.

Dad would be jubilant knowing of Webb's curiosity about family history and his craving to learn more about his siblings. He might have wept reading Webb's writeup.

Along with my early discovery about Hattie, this lovely piece perfectly bookends our work on the family history project. Whereas with Hattie I had to imagine her state of mind at critical times in her life, the new information Webb obtained about Dad's childhood has added rich factual detail to his brief but intensely productive years. Gretchen and Mother would also have been thrilled.

Thank you, Webb!

—Debi, April 2023

IV. Debi's Letter

I believe that what we become depends on what our fathers teach us at odd moments, when they aren't trying to teach us. We are formed by little scraps of wisdom.

—Umberto Eco

Dad!

You almost got me in trouble by dying, you know.

It all started when you took off for Seattle on the eve of your October 1956 surgery to remove a cancerous kidney. The follow-up treatment was radiation, which would also be done in Seattle. Between treatments you were in Walla Walla. Gretchen, Webb, and I learned little about your prognosis. As the youngest (age eleven), I was kept mostly in the dark.

Between appointments you spent considerable time at home sequestered in your bedroom. I stared longingly at that ecru door, thinking of ways I might sneak in, sit down in your emerald-green chair, and keep watch over you as you slept. But what held me back was my fear that I might learn the awful truth. With you tucked away inside, I convinced myself that you would get better if we just let you rest.

By December your medical team told you and Mom that your disease would be fatal. I learned this only years later. Behind our backs, they had come up with a plan to make you as comfortable as possible for your remaining weeks.

You had spent some of December in the hospital in Seattle, but wanted to be home for Christmas. Friends Mabel and Bob Groseclose drove you and Mom to Walla Walla on December 23. We stood in the kitchen around the black wrought-iron table while you sat on one of the vinyl chair cushions that seemed too cheerful for the occasion. About the time that your pain overwhelmed you, someone suggested we give you your presents early. I kept my emotions in check while standing a safe distance from you. But you really threw me a curve when you asked me to open a ribbon-tied package containing a classical record set you wanted. With my guard down and your eyes locked on mine, I read in your expression that this might be your final request of me. I took one look at you and bolted from the room and up the stairs, throwing myself on the bed. But nothing could hide me from the frightful reality that grabbed onto me in the kitchen as I looked into your eyes. Somehow I knew I was looking death in the face.

Hours later, you left for Seattle. That was the last time Gretchen, Webb, and I saw you. I can't remember anything else from that day or the following days or weeks, until January 21, 1957. Late that afternoon I returned to Green Park Grade School to get my violin. After I grabbed it and was leaving the building, I noticed the light on in the office and went in. Mr. Doak, my sixth grade teacher, was talking with the principal, Mr. Beard. I joined their conversation and suddenly the three of us were laughing loudly—I was loving the moment of hilarity during the otherwise somber month. Glancing at the time, I saw it was straight up five o'clock.

Soon after I returned home, Mom called from your Seattle bedside at the Virginia Mason Hospital. She said you died at 5 P.M.

In the weeks and months that followed I was in some frozen emotional state. My life as I had known it had gone away. I lost my appetite for music, school, and friends. The only time I focused on the present was when I crawled into bed. All day I dreamed of dreaming about you. My dreams were the antidote against an unbearable reality. For months, I would fall asleep and return to the sewing room. Just down the hall from my bedroom, that room was a universe away from the reality in which you no longer existed. I raced down the hall in my dreams and found you casually waiting for me to show up. You stayed in that room for months, but never let me find you during the day. I told myself that our night meetings were our secret, yours and mine. No one else would understand. After all, I was your youngest child and deserved a few more months with you.

It was as if my sole Christmas gift in 1956 was a roll of invisible "grief coupons" that I had to redeem in order to move on with my life. They came without inscription, without directions or expiration date, and no promise of reward. There was no jolly carousel ride in my future. To admit or show grief was taboo in the 1950s, especially for kids. Mom thought she could spare us from intense sadness and potential psychological problems by remaining stoic. She worked to keep us focused on school and daily living. The irony of the situation was that we kids were expected to work through our grief on our own, which was impossible. I remember crying alone, longing to be held.

Sixteen months later, Mom had remarried and hauled Webb and me to Chatham, New Jersey (Gretchen stayed behind to attend Whitman College). Mom's new husband was a scientist at the Bell Labs, and we moved into the house in which he and his son, Bill, lived. I felt like I was in a foreign land. Once there, however, I saw my chance to redeem some of my "grief coupons." On misbehavior.

I knew of no handbook on teenage mischief, so I played it by ear. I sought friends from the fringe crowd. Mother balked when scrawny Dieter showed up at the house with his greaser hairstyle piled up into a wave you could surf on. To her, he was the quintessential East Coast hood. Dieter and I laughed about Mother's initial reaction to him. Mom worried that I was headed for trouble with a capital P: promiscuity and pregnancy.

Dieter and his laid-back friends saved me from having to confront myself. Nobody asked me any questions. We just rode around, listening to loud music and smoking. We never talked about our personal pasts or wondered about the future. We lived in the moment. Luckily for me, they were good kids who chose to goof off and act cool. Had they been otherwise, I could have gotten into real trouble and thereby confirmed Mom's suspicions. But in reality I was a lousy pseudo-delinquent whose primary joy was exasperating her with my posturing. I touted my bleached bangs, painted my fingernails red, and acquired an East Coast accent, of which I was especially proud. I managed to flunk P.E. one semester, which baffled even the gym teacher. I cannot recall what I did to earn that F, but I clearly remember the perverse joy I felt when I received the first failing grade in the history of the Miller family. I suppose I thought an F was a merit badge to a delinquent.

Dad, as a child I knew and loved you as the great father you were before you left us. Knowing that you were no longer in my life, I didn't love you any less, but I think I wanted just to hold on to my childish image of you, like a keepsake hidden away, perhaps.

My childhood memories of you are tableaus, frozen in time. I want to expand them to include the Roly Miller who was born in Milton, Oregon. Your writing may provide answers to some of my questions and will fuel my search through your letters, journals, and editorials. Some of my questions are: What questions drove your thinking as a young person? How did your sister Elsa's death and your parents' decision to adopt siblings Marian and Ray change you? Where did you learn about fair-mindedness, especially in journalism? What was it about Mom that snagged you so quickly? As you and Mom braced for your death, in what ways did you encourage her to live?

For two decades after your death, I felt troubled by my inability to talk about you without a giant lump forming in my throat or tears streaming internally, if not down my cheeks. I could not remember you without an unappeasable longing. But in the end, it was the healing power of music that led me back to you. While living in Idaho Falls in the mid-1970s, I attended a symphony concert and felt the lure to play my violin, silent since your death. Although I had kept the violin during those years, it lay undisturbed in its case. In the garage. Those were brutal conditions for any hand-crafted fiddle. The day after the concert, I tuned my violin and cautiously tucked it under my chin. The chin rest felt uncomfortable, yet familiar, next to my skin.

And with that act, I began the journey of mourning. Through my reconnection with my violin, through writing, and through conversation, I learned what I needed to do to put your life and death in perspective. I finally was able to remember the joy of loving you to complement the unshakable pain of your loss.

There was almost a fifty-year interim between those early reunion dreams, from which I never wanted to awaken, and my most memorable dream. Two years ago, you reappeared in a dream in which I learned that you were alive and could be found at a nearby meeting. I rushed to the spot and instantly recognized your tan raincoat and beige Fedora before I caught sight of your face. I was incredulous: you were still in your forties, yet I was old enough to be your mother. Although you didn't recognize me, we chatted for a few minutes until you paused and asked who I was. As I haltingly told you my name, you searched my face and queried, "Oh! You're not my little Debi... are you?"

Even though that "exchange" took place in a dream, I began, from that point on, to see you from a different perspective. Before that dream, I saw you only as my dad, the father who died too young. Following the dream, I was able to step out from behind my self-absorbed orientation in order to peer at the world via the lens through which you might have viewed your life. I could imagine some of your

experiences and decisions, even some of the questions that fueled
your thinking. As I awoke from that dream, my cravings for private
reunions with you had changed into an intense desire to know you.

As I began my research, I soon learned that you were a hard act to
follow—academically, musically, and professionally. You graduated
from Washington University when you were barely nineteen. Following a year at Harvard, you returned to St. Louis to complete an
M.A. in economics and political science. As if that weren't enough,
you were a musical whiz on cello and piano. You truly struggled with
your decision whether to pursue a career in music or accept your
uncle's invitation to work at his newspaper in southeast Washington.
Luckily for Walla Walla, you chose the latter and made quite a name
for yourself. In addition to working your way up to become editor
and publisher of the *Walla Walla Union-Bulletin*, you served the
community as president of multiple organizations. And you kept on
making music. As principal cellist with the Walla Walla Symphony,
you rarely missed a concert in twenty years until your illness.

Hearing of your relentless pace, one might infer that you slighted
your family. Au contraire, you shared some of your most creative
moments with us. You orchestrated trips to the Oregon Coast, led
arrowhead searches along the Columbia River, and organized family
musical ensembles that included all of us. Your infectious sense of
humor energized bedtime marches as your young trio followed you
single-file up and down the stairs. One at a time, we fell out of the
queue and into bed as the remainder clipped rhythmically on until
each had turned in.

Many people in the community looked to you as a role model.
Upon your death, the abrupt termination of that crucial and sought-af-
ter inspiration dazed all of us. Your death triggered a dramatic sense
of loss in others. In addition to mourning you, your acquaintances and
friends were bereft of a future in which you would challenge them to
look beyond their natural biases to consider multiple points of view.

Many saw you as a man of great promise. Some compared you to
William Allen White, who at the time was described as "America's

most famous small-town newspaperman." Your fair-minded editorials
received both regional recognition and awards.

Part of your memorial eulogy captures the way many saw you:

> "The typewriter on Roly's desk was more than a tool to him. It was a part
> of a newspaper—a part in the process of bringing the truth to people—a
> factor in the essential practice of the human art of communication. Roly
> Miller's typewriter was to him a sacred instrument."

Your typewriter likely helped you capture Mom's heart as well.
You wrote her nearly every day in August of 1937. I bet the Seattle
mail carrier even recognized the sparkling-eyed girl standing on 8th
Avenue NW as she waited for another typed envelope. You wrote "R
Miller" just below the "Bulletin Printing Company" return address.

You probably never saw the journal Mom kept during the year
you two met. She wrote that you won her over in just a few days.
Previously, she had quite a male following, evident in the letters from
Victor, Bob, Clifford, and George she likely stashed and forgot. After
your first date, Mom wrote that the outing was "nothing very exciting."
But then, following a several-day hiatus from writing, she confessed
to her journal: "There are so many things that can't be placed here.
Everything seems so worthless beside this one thing now."

She dropped her former beaus, and you became the victor. In
her journal, Mom described some of the ways you electrified her
life. Even her penmanship changed. The formerly nondescript letter
"h" morphed into an elongated arch that almost sailed off the page.
Every "h" in her entries from December 7–12, 1936, spoke of the
exhilaration she felt after you swept into her life. [See pages 336–338.]

It is a pathetic thought. We struggle, we rise, we
tower in the zenith a brief and gorgeous moment, with
the adoring eyes of the nations upon us, then the lights
go out, oblivion closes around us, our glory fades
and vanishes, a few generations drift by, and naught
remains but a mystery and a name.

—Mark Twain

Dad, I have to tell you a story. In early 2015, Gretchen and I happened to be talking about your career at the paper. Afterward, wanting to know more, I went to the *Union-Bulletin*'s website, where I read about John G. Kelly's forty-five-year tenure as editor and publisher. The article noted that he had retired as publisher in 1955 and was followed by Frank Mitchell. But I knew that you had been editor and assistant publisher beginning in 1948 and became publisher in 1955. It was only in 1957 that Frank became the publisher. There was no evidence on the website that you had ever worked at the paper! I couldn't let this omission stand. I immediately emailed the managing editor, Alasdair Stewart:

February 16, 2015

Dear Mr. Stewart,

Having read the online history of the *Walla Walla Union-Bulletin* today, I anticipated seeing my father's name—Roland Eugene Miller—included as publisher from 1955 until his death in January 1957. He had served in a number of positions, from sports editor to assistant publisher and editor (1948), prior to John Kelly's invitation to succeed him as publisher in 1955.

I'm sure this was an oversight, an error that John Kelly would have wanted to be corrected. I would be happy to supply additional information. The 1981 publication, *John G. Kelly: His Life and Legacy*, includes a comprehensive review of my father's contributions to both the newspaper and to the community.

I hope to see his name added to the list of former publishers.

Thank you,
Debi Miller Bonds
Henderson, NV

A response arrived the following day:

February 17, 2015

Hello Ms. Bonds,

Thank you very much for the note. I just read your dad's obituary, and I'll update the history page on our site shortly. It's always neat to learn new things, so today that mission's accomplished.

All the best,
Alasdair Stewart
U-B managing editor

When I revisited the WWUB website hours later, your name was there. You're welcome!

I continued my quest to keep your memory alive. In July 2017 Chris and I stopped by our old home on Alvarado Terrace. Standing in silence before the blue-gray house with its wide, welcoming steps and giant maple tree shading all from the summer sun, I thought about how you had lived there just eleven years. A brief time for you, but a lifetime for me up to that point. I thought of what you accomplished in that time—your commitment to our family, your community service, your music, the creative ideas you expressed in your writing. I suddenly needed to visit the *Union-Bulletin*, an urge I hadn't had for at least fifty years. I had to see the office where you wrote your thought-provoking articles.

As we walked through the front door of the newspaper the next morning, I felt something shift inside me. It was as if I had stepped back in time and become a child again. I knew this building very well.

The young woman at the counter asked, "How can I help you?"

"Thank you, but I would just like to walk around," I said.

"I'm sorry, you can't do that. We don't allow people to just walk around on their own," she replied.

Dad, I wanted her to know I wasn't just any person off the street, that I had a good reason for being there. I wanted to tell your whole story, how this building used to be your second home, that this was where you spent over twenty years roaming and writing, working your way up from lowly staff to publisher.

Instead I answered, "Oh! My father used to be the publisher and editor of the paper. I just wanted to look around . . ."

She looked at me, wondering how to handle this, then excused herself and returned with a man who I guessed was about to convince me that I couldn't just buzz around like the boss's daughter.

He greeted us warmly, introducing himself as Brian Hunt, the publisher. No, he had not heard of you, but was eager to know something about you.

Mr. Hunt gave us a tour of the building, much of which had been extensively renovated. We saw the press in action and the staircase where I fell down and broke my arm when I was six. He took us to a large conference room near the entrance that he thought might once have been your office. Yes! I remembered coming into this room. You usually kept your door open but were rarely at your desk, preferring instead to roam the building, carrying in hand some copy for the next issue. As we entered, I noticed a bookshelf along the wall to my left. I immediately spotted the same book I had mentioned in my email to the managing editor—*John G. Kelly: His Life and Legacy.*

"Oh look! There's the Kelly book," I said, grabbing it from the shelf. I flipped to the page with the photo of you with a shovel, breaking ground for the construction of the *Union-Bulletin* building in 1947. Here was proof that you really had been here, that you were important to the paper and to the city was well as to your family. I showed Brian the picture, as if to say "See? That's Dad right there!" (I learned later that The Seattle Times Company bought the *Union-Bulletin* in 1971, which might explain why no one at the paper knew your name.)

Having walked again where you walked—especially parts of the building that were pretty much unchanged, like the press room—I knew it was time for me to get to know you better, to solve the mystery in my mind of who you were as a writer and thinker. As soon as we got home, I would begin by exploring some of your documents in the family history containers.

I discovered a very intriguing letter from Columbia University, dated January 1950, informing you that your 1949 editorials had been nominated for a Pulitzer Prize and asking you for a photograph and "biographical data." That sounded important. I emailed Columbia University requesting more information about the selection process. I attached a copy of the letter you had received. I wanted to know some things about the nomination process. First, was it the newspaper, a select team of journalists, or you yourself who had been nominated? That didn't seem clear. I also wanted to know how the nomination process itself worked. Did a person or committee read editorials? If so, how did they know you wrote them?

Almost immediately, Mr. Sean Murphy from the Pulitzer Prize organization responded:

Hi Deborah,

Thanks for reaching out! Prior to 1980, all Pulitzer Prize entrants were designated as "nominees." As many used this (possibly unknowingly, possibly with duplicity) as a professional distinction in a manner analogous to the Academy Award or Grammy processes, the Pulitzer Prize Board introduced the current system whereby each jury chooses three nominated finalists that are subsequently considered by the Board.

Your father's case (and it was his work that was entered by all indications—as most editorials are unsigned, the jury had probably heard through the proverbial grapevine that it was his work) does reflect a very brief interlude in Prize history where the journalism juries were chosen by the American Society of Newspaper Editors to ensure a more geographically diverse pool of winners. In part, this was precipitated by the Columbia Journalism School's then-dean (Carl Ackerman) taking less of an interest in Prize affairs as he struggled with a combination of depression and agoraphobia; accordingly, our records from this period are very spotty. What this letter suggests is that the ASNE-era journalism juries operated in a manner akin to the letters, drama and music juries, which often request entries that were not in the applicant pool. (One presumes that they were able to obtain the articles, which is why they only requested the headshot and bio for the press packet.) Conversely, the post-ASNE journalism juries operate in a very compressed window (about a month from the entry deadline to the three-day jury meetings at Columbia where the finalists are chosen) and are essentially precluded from requesting additional entries due to the short window.

Please feel free to contact us if you have any additional questions.

> Best,
> Sean Murphy
> Digital Content Manager
> Office of the Administrator
> The Pulitzer Prizes

I also asked Brian Hunt about the authorship of the 1949 editorials. He responded:

As to the editorials, I think it's a safe assumption that your father either wrote them or was very involved in their writing. We have an editorial writer here now, though everything flows through my desk. At that time—larger newsrooms, for one, and a different structure—it'd make sense to me that he would have led that process.

Best,
Brian

I decided after reading those emails that I would assume you to have authored every 1949 editorial. After all, you were Mr. Responsible and took the craft of journalism seriously from your first assignment as a sports reporter through your years as editor and publisher. You would have known when you had written something that met your standards for succinctness. You pointed out some of those early pieces to Mother, who in turn clipped them from the paper and enclosed them in letters to her parents. She often penciled "Roly's best" or "Roly thought this was a good one" on the clippings.

Although Mother kept several of your editorials, she had only one from your nomination year. But I found all 344 of the available editorials from 1949 forward on an online newspaper archive. I scanned each for readability and common themes and printed 136 of them. Combining the editorials, your personal and professional letters, and the papers you presented, I now have a sizable collection of your writing.

I sometimes daydream about stringing every sentence—each word—you wrote into a single line of text and printing it onto a ribbon stretching the one-mile distance from 1019 Alvarado Terrace to the newspaper building on First Avenue. Walking back and forth along its length, I run my finger over your words, like a needle on a phonograph record, hearing you read them to me. "Roly's Philosophy." Out of the counterpoint of that stream of words flows your passion for music, learning, and community, grounded in your fair-minded reasoning and enlivened by your playful prose.

Mother talked about your love of language, as did many others at the time of your death. You must have fallen in love with words at a young age. Your need to write was a grand way to give shape to ideas, to mine the ore of your imagination.

Your parents, both educators, nurtured your love of language,

Walla Walla and Union-Bulletin *memories.*

Dad and Claude Gray in the Newsroom.

Receiving the 1951 Washington State Press Award.

A moment of levity at the Chamber of Commerce Luncheon, 1952. [L to R]: Jerry Cundiff, Jr., Richard Baxter, Roland Miller.

Runner-up in the Purple Cow Milking Contest, June 1952.

*Roland (AKA Buster), November 1913. Already, at 22
months, surveying the world for his first story.*

especially writing. For example, your mother would have supervised
the development of your spelling and impressive cursive skills. I can
infer this from a letter you wrote to your father when you were six and
a half. In only forty words, you told a story of generosity, your wide-
eyed amazement at the quantity of food, an afternoon of childhood
fun with a sibling, and the call to dinner. It is a complete narrative.
Moreover, you already showed an intuitive grasp of leading with the
most important story items. My favorite word in the short missive

is "mess." It's as if you worked so hard up to that point to sound mature, then caved and used a catch-all word that was not only fun to write but also fun to read.

Dear Papa:

Fischers [neighbors?] gave us some string beans and a head of cabbage. They gave us such a big mess that it will last us for three days. Baby [Raymond] and I had a lot of fun. I must stop now and have dinner.

Lovingly,
Roland M.

You discovered your talent for language as a member of the St. Louis High School debate team and as a writer for the *Record*, the Washington University publication. By the time you moved to southeastern Washington to work for the local newspaper, you realized that you could use a print format in creative ways. You could even use a front-page layout to announce your upcoming wedding.

It was an ingenious plan: At Mom's Delta Delta Delta spring

*The original front page,
April 24, 1938* Union-Bulletin *banner:
HOOVER FIGHTS RECESSION IN MORALS.*

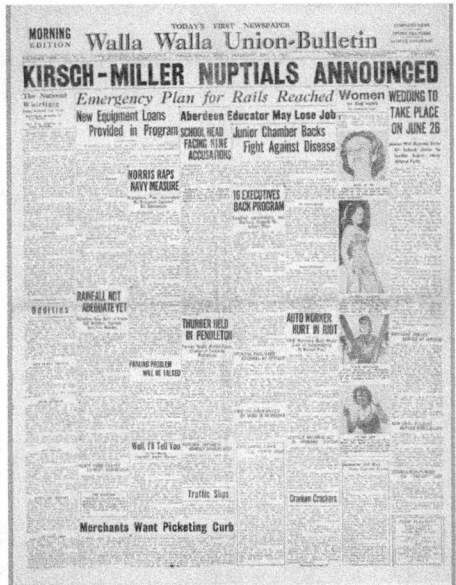

*May 7, 1938 Dad's "Special Edition" banner:
KIRSCH-MILLER NUPTIALS ANNOUNCED.*

formal on May 7, 1938, newsboys would distribute to attendees a "special edition" of the *Walla Walla Union-Bulletin* with the banner "KIRSCH-MILLER NUPTIALS ANNOUNCED."

To create your custom edition, you would need a front page the typesetter crew had already type set, with a banner and story about the same length as yours. You found a suitable layout on Wednesday, April 27, 1938, eleven days before the Tri Delta banquet. You asked the typesetters to reset the letters for your story and printed the full front page to get the effect you wanted. I would love to have seen your expression as you anticipated how the banquet guests would react to the souvenir page.

I can almost hear the newsboys, chanting as they walked among the banquet tables, "Get your news right here! Read the top story! Newspaper writer snags popular co-ed!"

The story reads:

KIRSCH-MILLER NUPTIALS ANNOUNCED
WEDDING TO TAKE PLACE ON JUNE 26
Senior will become bride of Roland Miller in Seattle event; many attend party

Friends of Miss Emma Jane Kirsch, Whitman college [*sic*] senior, were surprised to learn [on] May 7th of her approaching marriage to Roland Eugene Miller, Walla Walla newspaperman. The date of the event has been set for June 26, according to Miss Kirsch, who ought to know.

Announcement of the forthcoming nuptials was made at the annual spring formal dinner dance of Delta Delta Delta, Whitman college [*sic*] sorority of which Miss K. has been president during the past year or so. Newsboys distributed copies of the announcement to the assembled guests, it was hoped.

It was all a big surprise to those present, who had been given no reason to suspect any such developments. Several people when interviewed stated: "We had no idea they were serious."

Miss Kirsch is the daughter of Mr. and Mrs. Frank L. Kirsch of Seattle. Her mother was present Saturday evening.

The prospective bride is prominent in college activities of various sorts, being president of this-a, that-a, and those-a. A veteran office-collector, she

Roland and Emma Jane's wedding photo from June 26, 1938.

heads Mortar Board, the three Deltas, and a host of sundry items which do an effective job of interfering with her private life.

Mr. Miller, whose parents failed to come West from St. Louis for the party, is a writer for the Walla Walla *Union-Bulletin* and nobody cared to hear anything about him anyway.

The marriage will take place in Seattle.

The following day, May 8, a Seattle newspaper published a brief announcement:

Wedding: Emma Jane Kirsch and Roland Eugene Miller

Unitarian Chapel Seattle, Washington

June 26, 1938, 4 o'clock in the afternoon

Your editorials demonstrated your eloquence and fair-mindedness, delivered in the professional tone required of an advocate for the community and region. When writing to family and friends, you set all that aside and allowed your unbuttoned, playful and often irreverent side to come out. This was not a Jekyll-Hyde transformation—rather, it showed that you were a master of tailoring your writing to your audience.

For example, when you and Mom traveled to St. Louis in 1949, leaving your three children with Grammie and Gramps in Seattle, you wrote to us about a morning outing to the zoo. The letter seems perfectly composed to place its readers young and old on the scene, with just enough detail to keep it interesting. In just over 300 words you managed to describe the weather, the scene, your activities, and your feelings. You pointed out a similarity of monkey behavior to children squabbling. You told us you were sending a gift. Always the educator, in your account of visiting the shoe factory, you made an essential point: the things that make our lives easier, like shoes, have a history. They are made. And of course you end by encouraging us to behave!

June 3, 1949

Dearest Family:

St. Louis has turned quite hot—and also humid, so it is quite sticky, but not too much for us yet. We've had more rain but it didn't cool things off for very long.

Yesterday we went to the St. Louis Zoo and had a wonderful time. There are a good many animal shows of various kinds—elephants, seals, lions, and others—but we had time for only one, so we went to the monkey show. It was really surprising. The monkeys, or chimps, rode on bicycles, played (!) musical instruments like the piano and trombone (just like Daddy & Gramps), rode horses, walked on high stilts, did tricks on bars & ropes & large rubber balls, and acted like a bunch of children at school or playing out in the back yard. In fact, they seemed to resemble children in everything they did, but especially when they started to quarrel and scream at each other.

We bought a very nice book that tells all about the zoo and all its animals, and are going to mail it to you tomorrow if we can get to a post office. If not, we will do it Monday.

There are so many things to do that we just can't find time to do them all in only 8 days. I have many friends from the time I used to live here, and just to see them all once is a real problem. Then they want us to see them again and are mad when we can't do it. But it is lots of fun seeing people again after all these years of being away and I am enjoying it very much.

Today, while going downtown, we stopped at a shoe factory and saw how Johansen shoes are made. It was very interesting and takes a lot of time and trouble.

Hope all the children are behaving themselves & helping Grammy.

Love to all for now,
Daddy

You wrote some of your most endearing letters to your mother-in-law. Your letters to her are evidence that the two of you had quickly developed a warm connection. From the beginning, you saw her as an excellent and empathic listener, with whom you could banter playfully as well as bare your soul. You perhaps found that you could be more yourself with her, through your exchange of letters, than with your associates in Walla Walla.

January 10, 1937

My dear Mrs. Kirsch:

I must apologize for my negligence in not writing sooner . . . As you might guess, I am rushed considerably in my present job at all times, and it seemed as though this was one of the worst weeks on record. I do manage to get away for a couple of hours in the evening to see Emma Jane, but it seems like just a minute before she is due in at the dorm and I have to come back to knock out a couple of more stories before going to bed. Fortunately, this schedule will last only until June after which I hope to get back to something like normal living.

I wanted to thank you again for your extreme kindness to me during my stay in your house. It is a rare faculty to be able to make a person who is more or less a stranger feel so completely at ease, and you may believe that it was appreciated by me. Of course, I felt as though I ought to know you already, from things your daughter had told me, but first meetings are apt to be a little strained, the more particularly when it suddenly dawns on you that your only girl is bringing home a boy for you to cast the eagle eye upon. Well, I can only say that I have never enjoyed any visit more, and that I hope to be able to continue our grand friendship for a long time. (Yes, Mrs. K., I AM crazy about your daughter. Is it a surprise?)

This is probably the most improper thank you note ever written, but I'm not very good at writing prim and proper epistles. Besides, this isn't a

conventional and meaningless communication but a sincere appreciation
for everything you did for me while I was in Seattle. I shudder to think
how completely I made myself at home, but I trust you will understand
and regard it as a compliment.

I assure you Emma Jane is in good hands here. Of course, I could wish
that she didn't have quite as much time left in school, before she graduates,
and that I could see her more than I do at the present time, but I understand
that passive acceptance of the situation is good for one's soul.

Meanwhile my very best regards both to you and Mr. Kirsch, and
again, gracias.

Yours,
Roland

By November you were addressing your letters to "Moms and Pops,"
having divested yourself of the last trace of formality.

You also let them in on a little secret: you found certain gatherings
unbearably boring, even though you accompanied Mother, at her
urging, to some of them. You described becoming restless in church,
singling out the music, which bothered you "something fierce." Being
a classically trained musician with perfect pitch, you might well have
found the congregation's singing jarring and off-key, the music lame
and superficial. While you could easily have made suggestions to
the music director about future repertoire, I think it was rather the
totality of the church experience that got to you—the music, the Bible
readings, the homilies, the organ perhaps in need of tuning, the stuffy
air itself. The faint sarcasm of becoming "pillars of the church" after
only two appearances suggests that they were happier to have nabbed
you than you were to be there. Reverend Palmer's sermons may have
been "the best in town," but they weren't enough to offset the rest of
it. I wonder what it really was that made you squirm. Could it have
been that you didn't see the reason, the purpose, for going to church?
Somehow, I think you might have been more comfortable sitting in
a sanctuary of ideas.

By the way, Mother told me another story about how you avoided
boredom at Miss Hanna's piano recitals. You would find a seat in the
rear of the hall and, making sure no one was looking, slip an Earle
Stanley Gardner mystery out of your jacket and read while students

A few early Miller family memories.

Millers' living room about 1948.

Debi, Gretchen, and Webb at the Highbergs' in northwest Washington.

Dad pulling the "Presto" in a July 4th parade with the three kids on the boat.

who did not share your genes labored through their pieces, setting the book aside only to watch Gretchen perform.

Monday November 6, 1938

Dear Moms and Pops:

I'm still on this screwball schedule whereby I work at night and am free during the daylight hours, which has one advantage so far as getting things done around the house but which mostly is a pain in the neck.... The chief trouble is that Ejay says I get underfoot around the house, so that she can't get her work done, but I won't see her at all unless I'm home during my off hours. What a life! . . .

We are rapidly becoming pillars of the Congregational Church, having attended for two Sundays in a row. All this religion likes to lay me out. . . . Rev. Palmer has given quite good sermons both times, and we feel he is by far the best here in town, but I generally get restless in church if only because the music bores me something fierce. Emma Jane, having somewhat more of a conscience in such matters, is the guiding force behind our attendance, or I fear I wouldn't get there much more than about twice a year. . . .

Yours,
Roland

If you prize your memories as they are, by all means avoid—eschew—writing a memoir. Because it is a certain way to lose them. You can't put together a memoir without cannibalizing your own life for parts. The work battens on your memories. And it replaces them.

Annie Dillard, "To Fashion a Text" (1987)

Dad, I finally figured out how to connect to you. In daydreams since I began this letter in 2012, I have imagined walking down a hall, around a corner or even finding you at the top of some stairway. You show up in my dreams at night. My memories of you are like faded, grainy home movies that never change on replay. Photographs capture you frozen in moments of time. Your letters and editorials are a window into your thoughts and desires. But, while all these things helped in their own way, they weren't enough. Just reading your words wasn't sufficient, neither were stories about you. I decided to try my luck writing to you again. But nothing I wrote satisfied my craving. What I had needed all along was a way to collaborate with you.

When I was a first grader at Green Park School, I decided to enter a poetry contest. My teacher, Mrs. Lincoln, told the class: "This is a competition open to all of you. Just write a poem—even a short one—and give it to me by the end of the week." Somehow it turned out that you and I worked on it together. (I would love to know how you remember it.) Maybe you asked me what I wanted to write about, and I said, "A bunny!" You might have asked, "Okay! What is that bunny doing? Did it make you want to laugh?" Working together at the kitchen table with paper and pencil, we produced something original. Seventeen words that earned me first prize in the first-grade poetry contest—and a dollar!

> Funny little bunny,
> As funny as can be,
> Wrinkles up his little nose
> For everyone to see.

There you have it, our collaboration. If only you had stuck around, there would have been many more chances for us to write stuff together. It would be decades before I would realize that or fully appreciate your gift for language.

Early on, you figured out how you used words to lure, to incite, to entertain. Mother knew it, as did her parents, your parents, your readers, your friends, your colleagues. Gretchen and Webb knew it.

I—the youngest, emotionally the neediest of your children—knew it least of all. You talked with Gretchen and shared moments together in the symphony, you had conversations with Webb while fishing, the two of you planning and preparing for those outings then heading out together on another adventure. I remember staring at you.

I watched you from a slight emotional distance, waiting to grow into the relationship with you that awaited me, the companionship that I knew was coming. It wasn't that I saw myself as unworthy, rather that I felt unprepared, unready. The relationship with you needed to wait until I had matured enough to have true time with you, as if I had a limited number of coupons, a restricted amount of time, never wanting to use it up, to exhaust the possibility, to drain the fuel tank.

I was always good at saving things for an undetermined future date. I did that with my favorite outfits, such as the azure shorts and top set, made of a soft silky fabric of the most gentle blue I had ever seen. I loved the combination as much as any I had ever chosen. I used to try it on, turning in front of the hall mirror while imagining going out in the attire. But at the last minute I would change into something I'd worn many times. I wanted to save it for a special occasion. It was as if I did the same thing with you. Save up your "Dad time" until you're ready, I would think. . .

Meanwhile, I just needed to know that you were somewhere where I could get to you if I needed to. As a second grader, I learned that life was fragile. Mrs. Doschadis (our teacher) announced to the class one day that my good friend Beverly Joseph would not be in school that day because her father died the day before. That meant parents could die at any time! Even before she finished telling us what few details she had, I swung my head around to look at my classmates, wondering whose dad would be next. None of my peers looked as panicky as I felt. Would it be Jack's dad? Or GG's, Nancy's, or Sigrid's? Or would it be mine? Would you be next? I don't remember sharing my fears with you or Mom, but I worried a lot during the weeks after Mr. Joseph's death. I remained anxious about leaving you for the rest of your life.

In a letter to your mother-in-law, you observed and described my agitation on that day when our family left without you for Europe with the Walla Walla tour. You stayed behind for business reasons and would meet us in Germany a few weeks later.

June 7, 1955

Dear Mom,

Debbie was the only one who broke down during the day—she had "butterflies" all day, finally cried a lot about leaving me, but braced up and presented a brave front at the time the plane took off. But I fear there were more tears in the offing.

Roly

You couldn't know that my sobs at the airport as Mother, Gretchen, Webb, and I departed for Europe while you stayed behind temporarily would set me up for a life of longing, despite your assurances that you would see me soon. In a mere year and a half, we would all learn what your leaving—death—would mean to our lives.

While Annie Dillard's aim was "to fashion a text," understanding that in doing so, the written work has effectively replaced her memories—those phantoms in the mind—my goal in writing about you is to restore, renew, and revise my connection to you. Through the watering of my seeds of such history as I can recall, you emerge as the person I knew but yet didn't. I would have to look at your life more deeply to catch a glimpse of the vast experiences you had physically and psychologically.

I, as well as Gretchen and Webb, remembered you as a kind of saint. You were the perfect dad, organizing outings for us, educating us, and above all being a role model for success in life. How could we ever hope to reach your heights? To change that saintly image, I must bring you back to life in my mind as a fallible human.

I have said many times that there was only one time I can remember getting angry with you. In the 1950s, Webb and I had a favorite half-hour weekly TV show that we would watch down in the basement. There being no way to record a show to watch later, we had one chance to watch it. On this occasion you had called the family into the living room so that you could read to us something important. It may have been an article about the life of ants. Normally I would have been fine with it. But not when *Ramar of the Jungle* was on! I sat there stone-faced with ears closed. I was missing my favorite show!

I was looking for something to add to that memory, a stronger corrective to your flawless image. Well, I found it! When reading one of your editorials from 1953, about the Rosenbergs' trial, I thought, "No way! Dad couldn't have written this!" My image of you as fair-minded and empathic was crumbling. I had to find a way to work through that on my own, imagining how you might help from this distance of time and space. And I did.

*[It was] as if a society turned its magnifying lens
on these people until they caught fire and were burned
alive.*

—E. L. Doctorow, *The Book of Daniel*

In 1951, Julius and Ethel Rosenberg, American citizens, were arrested, tried in federal court, and convicted of conspiracy to commit espionage for the Soviet Union. They were executed at Sing Sing in 1953. This was front-page news across the country, and you needed to weigh in on it. And you did, in an editorial from the *Walla Walla Union-Bulletin* of June 24, 1953, just five days after the execution. Let's take a look at it:

Full Protection of Law

Sob sisters with a pinko leaning will doubtless use the Rosenberg execution for years to sound off against the American method of doing things. But if one were to analyze the history of the Rosenberg case closely, he would find that it presents the strongest possible contrast between U.S. and Soviet ideas of justice in dealing with spies, with all of the odds on our side.

Julius and Ethel Rosenberg denied to the finish that they had acted as spies for Communist Russia in atomic secrets, but they were found guilty by a jury trial and no judge or court has subsequently questioned the correctness of that decision. The only question, at any time, has been over legal technicalities.

In Russia, for persons convicted of acting as spies for a foreign country, punishment would be quick and effective, requiring only a matter of days at most. Yet it took more than two years for the Rosenbergs to exhaust their legal protections of the democratic process of justice.

Six appeals for stays, retrial or clemency went to the U.S. district court during the long legal battle. Changes in the date of execution, originally set for the week of May 21, 1951, were permitted to give the upper courts ample opportunity to study the case.

Seven times the case was before the U.S. circuit court of appeals. In each case the circuit court held that the trial judge had acted properly. On one point only, the court suggested that the Supreme Court might look into the point of law involved.

Seven times the case went before the Supreme Court with requests for review. Generally, the ground was that the Rosenbergs had been tried for treason without proper safeguards. Some members of the court dissented on every occasion, but a majority always held that no action should be taken to change the verdict of the lower courts.

In addition to all of these legal stays and appeals, the case went repeatedly to the White House. President Eisenhower found it waiting for him when he took office, Truman having held the matter over for his successor. After a detailed study, the President found no reason to intervene.

It is difficult to see how anyone could contend that the Rosenbergs were denied their full measure of justice—especially when one knows that in their favored Soviet Russia the whole subject would have been closed more than two years ago, without any opportunity for review, public discussion, or criticism of the course of action.

Your opening line took my breath away. "Sob sisters?" "Pinko leaning?" Those heavily loaded words put me immediately on the defensive. Suddenly I was seeing another, unfamiliar, side of you, one in which you enlisted your narrative skills in the service of condemnation. I have reread your editorial many times, trying to understand why you would have supported the Rosenbergs' death sentence. You are saying that "pinkos" should understand that the trial was a perfect example of American justice in action, especially when compared to how the Soviet Union would have handled it. The Rosenbergs got a fair trial, went through all their legal appeals and delays including multiple appeals to the White House, but did not manage to escape execution. In short, the system worked and justice prevailed. That should be clear to all the "sob sisters."

In brief, the American justice system insures that people get what they deserve.

It seemed impossible that my own father—the epitome of the fair-minded editor—would endorse something that I considered so unjust. For the first time in over thirty years of rifling through your documents, I was judging you. I had to find a way to resolve this.

I reminded myself that in the early 1950s America was very caught up in the Cold War, and there was great fear of the nuclear capability of the Soviet Union. There was much popular support for the death penalty for selling our weapons research to hostile countries.

Your editorial perspective seemed in line with the many newspapers endorsing Judge Kaufman's death sentence, including the *St. Louis Post-Dispatch*, one of your favorites.

I needed to know more about your logic and also that of the press in general. What did journalists really think about this case?

Although you knew the details of Julius and Ethel Rosenberg's arrest and execution—U.S. citizens convicted of conspiracy to commit espionage—you could not have known of events that surfaced in the years following their deaths. Details uncovered decades later confirmed Julius's involvement in passing secret nuclear documents to the Soviet Union, but little support remained for charging Ethel Rosenberg with any crime, let alone electrocuting her.

New York Times journalist Sam Roberts had trailed David Greenglass for years, looking to interview him about his testimony that had sent his sister to her death. In 1993, he finally began to talk. Greenglass told Roberts that he had been a spy and, crucially, that it was his wife Ruth, not Ethel Rosenberg, who had helped him type up his notes. He also suggested that Ruth had fabricated the plan to accuse Ethel of typing David's notes. "Her testimony forced me to revise mine. I [initially] told the FBI the story and left Ethel out of it, right? But my wife put her in it. So what am I gonna do, call my wife a liar? My wife is more important to me than my sister. And she was the mother of my children."

What might you have done with this information?

On April 6, 1951, Judge Kaufman handed down his sentence: death in the electric chair.

Julius and Ethel were immediately placed in separate cells in the court house basement. Each serenaded the other. Julius sang "The Battle Hymn of the Republic" to Ethel.

Ethel, the singer, chose one of the most famous and best-loved arias in the operatic repertoire: "Un Bel Di" ("One Fine Day") from *Madama Butterfly* by Giacomo Puccini, the emotionally wrenching aria of a wife awaiting the return of her husband.

In the aria, Butterfly imagines a reunion one fine day with her

American husband. His ship will enter the harbor with great fanfare. She, standing on a hilltop, sees him, a "tiny speck" making his way up the hill. He calls to her from a distance, but she doesn't answer right away, as she says, "partly to tease him and partly" (here her voice rises with emotion) "so as not to die at the first meeting." He will call up: "My dear little wife, fragrance of verbena!"—names he called her when he first came there. She concludes by singing to her personal maid Suzuki, with great emotion: "And this will happen, I promise you. Keep your fears [if you must]; with unalterable faith I shall wait for him." Puccini's music perfectly captures Butterfly's tragic hope, full of tenderness and longing.

I can almost hear Ethel's loving musical farewell to her husband. Gretchen and I—your own "sob sisters"—are weeping.

Dad, can you hear us?

Dad, now it's time for the two of us. Curious about your thinking in 1953, I would like to be able to travel back in time to sit with you as you wrote your piece, looking for details that contributed to your conclusions. What sources of information did you use as you sat at your typewriter?

During these many years since the Rosenberg trial, you have been unable to add a postscript to your 1953 editorial. Thus, I am stuck with that being your final word on their guilt and execution. Following much reading and reflection, I have come to believe that, given the evidence that I have seen in recent months, you would have found it as persuasive as I did. I wish you and I could discuss the trial—the dramatic accusations of the prosecution along with the perjured testimonies by David and Ruth, both of whom were as convincing as fine stage actors.

Most of all, I would love to team up with you to co-write an editorial. Sitting at adjacent keyboards, we—father and daughter—could tell the Rosenberg story Miller-style, considering the legal and humanitarian aspects of the case. We would draw back the curtain on the propagandistic efforts of the Truman and Eisenhower administrations to frame the case as a blow to freedom and democracy, revealing what it really was: a tragic trial that fueled a hateful national judgment. This would be our chance to team up as writers committed to fair-mindedness and compassion.

Dad, I can't wait.

In 2002 I received a note from your friend Vance Orchard, whose thirty-year career at the *Union-Bulletin* began in the early 1950s, during your most productive years. He had enclosed an article he wrote for the *Waitsburg Times*, a heartfelt remembrance of you—forty-five years later—that eloquently describes the loss your untimely death meant for Walla Walla and beyond.

I revisited Vance's piece several times over the next few years during my early work on the family history project, wondering how I might incorporate it into my writing about you. Then in 2017, I noticed something. (You know how that goes—in your favorite mystery stories the detective enters a room looking for anything that might shed light on the murder. Suddenly his eye fixes on something that proves crucial to solving the case.) It turns out that Al McVay had interviewed several individuals in connection with a book about John G. Kelly. He donated the interview tapes to the archives of the Whitman College library, "where they are available for research by historians." That was my "aha!" moment.

Here's how the recording happened: In July 1978, Al McVay drove to Alvarado Terrace to talk to Mom about you. He had spoken with many Walla Wallans about Kelly, gathering information for the book *John G. Kelly: His Life and Legacy*. The five individuals collaborating on the project were close colleagues of yours at the *Union-Bulletin*: Iris Meyers, Claude Gray, Vance, Jim Hutcheson, and Al himself. They had all worked closely with you two decades earlier. In the book, they devoted an entire chapter to you: "A Profile of Roland E. Miller." Just listen to the introduction:

> For two decades the community and the region shared an outstanding spokesman with above average vision for advanced development of natural and human resources. The paper also had an articulate and brilliant leader and journalistic craftsman as its helm until cancer terminated his career at 44.

Pretty impressive, don't you think? The accolades went on for thirteen pages. Those tributes echoed throughout the community for years, as Mom recounted in her conversation with Al. Of course I also remember hearing rave comments about you in Walla Walla decades after your death. "Oh, you're Roly Miller's daughter. His death was a huge loss to everyone in the Pacific Northwest," an observation that never failed to take my breath away. You wouldn't believe the legacy you left.

But back to Al McVay's visit with Mom: His goal in interviewing Mom was to explore your life and influences, to learn details that could add depth and substance to the book. Knowing her well, he would have written down questions that would tap into Mom's extraordinary memory. Her mental acuity and delightful storytelling skills, he knew, would provide a lively exchange.

I'm having a heartening fantasy in which you and I could listen in on that summer 1978 exchange. It would be so much more fun to have you join me. Of course, Mom and Al would be sitting on the twin dusty-blue loveseats, and you and I could perch on the silk emerald and ivory striped sofa. (Remember those cushions with the compressed filling following years of use? Not as comfortable as the love seats, but okay for our purposes.) I would be listening to them while watching your reaction to Mom's comments.

Al wanted to know your reasons for moving to Walla Walla in the mid-1930s to work for John Kelly, about your diverse influences on the newspaper and community, and your role as a father. In her responses, Mother would often interrupt her own train of thought, injecting a scenario that perfectly captured the crux of an earlier question. Her phenomenal memory for details allowed this. It's as if while talking, she was scanning through old Rolodex files for incidents that could momentarily bring you back, in a way. She sounds a bit like Colombo, the detective played by Peter Falk, who, when leaving a scene, would turn and add, "Just one more thing." Mother's narrative was a multicolored crazy quilt, dizzying at first but in which every swatch of fabric is an integral part of the whole. Many of those snippets were more relevant to portraying you than were her responses to specific questions.

And her voice! I hear it now so differently than I did years ago. I always remembered it as pleasant. But listening closely to the fifty-minute recording today, I hear the musicality in it, its resonant tones, and fluctuating pitches. I imagine that her voice grabbed you subconsciously if not visibly when you first met. Like an intoxicating melody, her speech might have conjured for you the vision of a mezzo-soprano rehearsing her aria offstage.

Even her "no" responses had a musical quality, giving a pleasant percussive tap rather than an insistent gong one often voices when disagreeing.

But it was her laugh—a youthful giggle that I found most moving, drawing Al into the moments when they could remember the essence of you. Shared delight. As I listen to the conversation, your form begins to emerge from the mist of years, still and forever 44 years young. Dad and Debi, eavesdropping together.

Just after Mom died in 1990, I announced to Gretchen and the hospice worker that you and Mom would have lunch together that day. I found comfort imagining the two of you having your own reunion. Ultimately I would join you as well. I have reflected on that hypothetical meetup, an afterlife, for years. I no longer find this postscript to life credible, rather I am drawn to a more plausible explanation. I find comfort in imagining that some of your carbon atoms have blended with Mom's in the earth's atmosphere and will continue to circulate as long as the universe exists.

Imagine! Some of the particles that formed the physical and psychological you, borrowed from the universe, may be the same substances that nurtured the Oregon spruce of my young violin. After your deaths, you and Mom returned those life-generating atoms to the atmosphere and are all around me.

In addition to giving us life, you gave Gretchen, Webb, and me unconditional love while modeling how to live with curiosity and focus. Gretchen, your fourteen-year-old daughter, learned an important insight by watching you. In an exchange with Mother about why you died, Gretchen said, "This is just as puzzling as to ask why we live in the first place. It is more important to pay attention to how we live."

Although I can't know where your atoms are circulating, your words live on in what you wrote, even in what I am writing. When your descendants read your words, I bet many will demand, "How could you have left that out of the family history?" Bottom line: Webb and I could easily do a Dad book: *Roly Miller: A Man of His Word.*

Care to collaborate?

A lifetime of love,
Your Debi

P.S. I put you back on your pedestal. Although I knocked you off during a spat between my 2020 certainty about Ethel Rosenberg and your 1953 logic about justice, you are back in place. Forever the family saint.

Oh, wait . . . There are two more things I want to tell you about:

First, I want to recall two gatherings that took place ten years apart. The first, in August 1946, took place just four months after you and Mother moved from a small house on North Clinton Street to spacious 1019 Alvarado Terrace. This festive get-together, celebrating the visit of your close friends Bob and Helen Hubbard, may have been one of your first major parties at "Ten-nineteen," the beginning of a decade of lavish entertaining and holiday gatherings for friends and family—occasions filled with possibility and promise. As the *Walla Walla Union-Bulletin* recorded the event in its society pages, "Hubbards Are Being Feted: The arrival of Mr. and Mrs. C. R. Hubbard and their son, Gordon, in Walla Walla this past week to renew friendships with Walla Wallans has inspired a round of informal entertaining in their honor. Visiting from San Marino, California, the Hubbards have been house guests of Mr. and Mrs. Roland Miller during their stay. In their honor the Millers hosted an alfresco supper in the garden at their home Thursday evening for two dozen guests."

By the summer of 1956, the Hubbards had moved again, this time to Albuquerque, New Mexico. On August 14, Bob wrote you a letter and included copies of "special editions" about stores he had recently opened. He noted the "wonderful" invitations to visit Walla Walla from the Stevenses, the Beavers, and you. He added, "We hope that we can, some of these days, accept your invitation. But right at the moment, we are trying to dig out from under and it doesn't look like it will be possible this summer at all. Please let me know what is going on in the Miller family."

In late fall, everything at 1019 Alvarado Terrace changed. Word spread quickly among your friends.

Forward to late November 1956 for the second party. The Hubbards, along with their son, Gordon, returned to SE Washington to see you. Several couples in your social circle joined together to celebrate your years of deep friendship: Bunnie and Ralph Stevens, Millicent and Nat Beaver, Mabel and Bob Groseclose, Frances and Bruce Casper, and Iris and Bob Myers.

Beneath the "festive" air of the evening, however, lay a deep sense of melancholy. In September, Dr. Nat Beaver paid a visit to Mother. His voice had a sense of urgency as he mentioned his deep concerns after seeing the preliminary test results and suggested she take you immediately to Seattle for a thorough medical evaluation. The Virginia Mason Hospital medical team soon determined that you had a malignant kidney and removed it. But surgery wasn't enough; your cancer had metastasized. The chemotherapy, still relatively new, wasn't working. The Seattle doctors told Mother your prognosis was dire, and your friends knew the importance of getting together while you still had the energy.

In the 1956 photo, Bob Hubbard is sitting on the sofa to Mother's right. Mabel is sandwiched between the two of you, with Helen Hubbard to your left. Young Gordon is standing on the far right of the photograph behind Dr. Beaver. Everyone looks serious.

Just left of center in the picture, you are looking to one side, your face a sober mask as you momentarily withdraw into yourself. Listening to the voices of your friends—as familiar and comforting as

Bob Hubbard's visit, November 1956.

one of your favorite string quartets—you are caught off guard. How could you not be? You were cushioned, physically and psychologically, within this group of individuals who loved you, sharing lively conversation and pleasant memories. It could have been just another fun evening in the middle of your years of socializing. But fear for your life had spread among your friends. In their love for you and urgency to keep you with them, they seemingly gathered around you as a bulwark against death. You were glad they were there, but in that moment it seems as if you knew this might be the last time you would enjoy their company. You may also have felt the injustice of dying just as your best years were beginning.

Dad, did you know? Could you sense that the treatment wasn't working, that this could be one of your final social gatherings? I wonder what your friends talked about after saying goodnight to you and Mom, what you were thinking about as you crawled into bed.

I have glanced at this picture many times over the years, picked it up briefly as I thumbed through documents from your files. But today I see something different, more intimate. The Stevenses, likely hosts of the evening, stand off to the side, having made sure everyone else was visible from the camera angle. They and their guests surely cherished that November moment, a celebration of your life that you were still able to attend—almost like being at your own wake. Their hearts full, recalling your energy that inspired them in countless personal, social, and musical experiences over the years. Their minds heavy with the knowledge of your ephemeral future.

The second thing, which I waited until last to write in the hope that I would find documents that would bring it to life, is about your music. I wanted to do more than list your many accomplishments such as playing with the Walla Walla Symphony Orchestra for two decades, frequent chamber group performances, serving as symphony board president, and on and on. Just yesterday, I found what I could use! Writing a bit about our final family musical outing would be a good place to start. But first a little background.

From the time you were born, you were surrounded by music. Although I don't know when you began cello lessons, your exposure to piano came early in your St. Louis home. It wasn't long before your parents noticed that, as soon as you had learned the names of the notes on the piano, you were able to identify each one by its pitch, without looking at the keyboard. If you were asked to sing a C, you could do it instantly. You could do that for any note. You were born with perfect pitch!

But there was a problem.

What if the piano was lying to you? Suppose the A wasn't really an A. Your father, who tuned the family piano on his own, for some reason tuned it a half step lower than it should have been. Every note was a half-step flat. When you heard the pitch you learned to identify as A, you were actually hearing an A-flat. Your father didn't realize that his faulty tuning of the piano would have lifelong implications for your sense of pitch.

In her 1978 interview with Al McVay, Mother described your auditory handicap. When tuning your cello, you would initially whistle the A-flat pitch you had in your memory before adjusting the note a half step up from that. Once you shifted the pitch to where it should be, you were okay.

After college, you were on track to become a professional musician, having, along with other gigs, played keyboard in an ensemble on a boat to Europe the summer of 1931. You played piano—including jazz—and cello splendidly. Mother said that you could have played in the St. Louis Symphony Orchestra had you stayed in Missouri.

And now, back to a memory that stands out for me from December 11, 1956, the opening concert for the Walla Walla Symphony. We five Millers climbed into our Ford station wagon for the short drive to Walla Walla High School. Gretchen, who had recently successfully auditioned for the orchestra, was in formal black, toting her flute. Once at the school, Gretchen headed to the rehearsal room to leave her case and coat while the rest of us settled into the rounded-back fold-down seats in the center section of the auditorium, under the balcony. I felt claustrophobic, but Webb and I liked being able to sit wherever we wanted—we felt grown-up. You and Mom likely sat a couple of rows in front of us. I remember nothing else of that concert beyond being there, but have just read your review of the program that appeared in the December 12th *Union-Bulletin*.

Suddenly, something feels terribly wrong. I'm jarred by the thought of how things should have been that evening over six decades ago. It could have been a pleasant musical experience listening to Gretchen as part of the symphony backing the guest soloist, violinist David Abel. But you belonged in the principal cellist chair instead of sitting with us in the audience—which you never before had done for a symphony concert. Although on some level I would have known that you belonged on stage, I was too young to process the implications of your disease. You would normally have been sitting just a few feet away from Mr. Abel. Mesmerized by the rich music pouring from his violin, you would have glanced at him and wondered how a kid of twenty-one could play with such vitality and maturity. You could recognize exquisite playing instantly.

In the interview with Al McVay about your life, Mother shared the following.

> The soloist David Abel came in December, the time that Roly was really quite ill and we went to the concert. It was very unnerving for Roly to

have to sit in the audience and listen to it because he wanted it to go so well and he wasn't feeling up to par. It was quite an emotional experience.

Such restrained reflections from Mom. You were in the audience because cancer had compromised your body and you could not play, let alone sit on stage. There you were, watching your older daughter play from a distance instead separated by a few music stands. But you had a job to do that night: to concentrate on the soloist and the orchestra's performance in order to write a review for the next day's newspaper.

Had I any idea at the time of the poignancy of that moment—your final musical experience where you had to be a stalwart observer and write a review that would capture the audience's mood in that auditorium—my keening would have drowned out the orchestra.

*The Walla Walla Symphony Orchestra, William Bailey,
conductor, Roland Miller principal cellist, circa 1951.*

And what about the emotional currents between you and Mom at that moment, your realization that this could be your final time to sit together in the same auditorium where you had innocently sat side by side for a musical performance in November 1936—where Mother knew more about the pieces than you did? That would have grabbed you. You two had only twenty years together!

Your December 12, 1956, review for the *Union-Bulletin*:

The Walla Walla Symphony Orchestra opened its 1956-57 season at the high school auditorium in more than satisfying style, presenting a program which by all standards must be rated the finest in the 49-year history of the local musical organization.

High point of the concert was the appearance of David Abel, young San Francisco violinist, in the Beethoven Concerto in D. This was an electrifying performance, a thrilling and skillful blending of brilliant technique, beautiful tone quality and authoritative and understanding musicianship. And he was given magnificent support, especially in the first and third movements, by the orchestra itself.

The Beethoven concerto is, of course, one of the truly great works in the entire literature for violin and orchestra. Only the mature performer can hope to make it more than just a collection of notes on the printed score. It is to the real credit of both the artist and his fellow players that the composition emerged as a cohesive entity, full-bodied as Beethoven wanted it, tender and lyrical where it should be, but with the driving and unifying force that sets it apart from the merely adequate.

Abel is a young man with all the equipment for a top-flight violinist, and it was obvious Tuesday night that he was not only thoroughly at home in the music but capable of meeting any demands, whether they be artistic or technical. He has a rich, full tone, complete precision in his playing, great facility and accuracy in the fastest and most demanding passages, and a sure bowing technique. His phrasing was never stilted, but he did not permit the luxury of over-interpretation or excessive variations in tempo. Everything was in extreme good taste, and the overall effect was completely gratifying.

The orchestra seemed inspired by the artist. The opening allegro movement was virtually flawless, both in its responsiveness to requirements of dynamics and its sureness of intonation. And the concluding sections of the work were a masterpiece of sensitivity and movement.

. . .

One could not avoid being aware that something special was going on, and the audience response confirmed this view. The storm of applause that greeted the conclusion of the evening was far from perfunctory; the listeners were genuinely excited and thrilled. It was an evening to be remembered, and one which marked another substantial step forward in the development of our orchestra music in the past several years.—R.M.

You wrote in the last sentence about progress "in the development of our orchestral music in the past several years." In your mind, you were still a part of the musical voice of Walla Walla.

Driving home after the concert, with Gretchen likely high on her experience as a fourteen-year-old in the orchestra to which you had introduced her, how did you hold it together? How did Mom control herself? This had to be another huge farewell moment for the two of you, knowing that the symphony would go on into the future but without your encouragement and exquisite cello voice.

6

Europe Extravaganza 1955

No better way to spend your money, whether you have it or not, than a trip abroad. My personal recommendation: Don't put it off too long and decide maybe you'll do it in ten or fifteen years. We talked it over and concluded that too many things can intervene—war, depression, illness, etc. So we simply closed our eyes to the cost and took off. And if it takes ten years to pay off the trip, we'll figure it was well worth it.

—Roland Miller, 1955

March 2018

I can almost remember the moment Dad and Mom told us kids we were going to Europe for two and a half months. I paid the closest attention to the plans about Dad. As editor of the *Walla Walla Union-Bulletin*, he could not be gone all summer. He would join us for those last weeks when we would drive around parts of Europe. On June 6, several friends gave us a wonderful send-off at the airport as the four of us boarded the plane for the East Coast. After a few days in Washington, D.C., we continued on to New York City, where we met with the other tour members and—gulp—boarded a giant Italian ocean liner, the SS *Conte Biancamano*, for a week-long voyage, destination Gibraltar. I remember decadent eating, exploring the ship, and hanging out in the pool area with a few adults and kids—especially Webb—grateful for his putting up with me. Gretchen, who turned thirteen on the boat, was already gravitating toward the more mature conversations.

Back on solid ground, we traveled at breakneck speed through parts of Spain, Italy, Germany, Austria, and Switzerland, before we reunited with Dad in Paris on July 31st.

I remember how excited I was when he landed in Paris and may even have galloped toward him in the Paris restaurant. Together at last.

Time enough to visit Dad's Paris relative, Genevieve Monod, before flying to London for a few days, during which we said farewell to the tour group. Then off again to Frankfurt, where we rented a Volkswagen bus for the final three weeks of our stay. I can almost hear Dad grumbling in disbelief as he crammed our bags and souvenirs into the vehicle. "Emma Jane, isn't it time to send a trunk of treasures home?"

The Kullmans, distant relatives (see p. 181) whom we visited in Frankfurt, had a teenage son, Norbert. We invited him to travel with us for several days in Germany and Switzerland. There was room for one more in the van, and Gretchen, Webb, and I loved having another kid along. Norbert entertained us with his English (which was far better than our German) and was a great help as we asked about accommodations and what to order when dining. But there was more to Norbert than met the eye. On one occasion, when he and Webb were alone in their hotel room, he pulled a knife from his suitcase and waved it in front of Webb saying, "I *keel* you!" Although Norbert likely meant no harm, it nevertheless shook Webb up.

In 1982, twenty-five years after that trip, Mom put together a generous album for each of us of European pictures and writing to keep that summer alive in our memories. After she sorted through hundreds of slides, made dozens of prints, labeled and numbered each by location, she secured them in the albums. She filled plastic sleeves with her many different written perspectives: letters to and from Dad, pages from her European journal she typed to include, Iris Myers's travel notes, and Dad's notes for a travel talk he gave to the Kiwanis Club. He called it "Innocents Abroad." The final product became a perfect example of how I might organize the family history around individuals and events. What a treasure that turned out to be!

I'm including snippets from Mom's letters to Dad from the East Coast and Europe along with notes from her travel diary—with parenthetical comments she added in 1982. Dad's commentary on her letters and reports on his activities in Walla Walla are a fun partial round-robin, his tone both playful and confessional as he lets Grammie in on his thoughts. Grammie saved all of the writing, which ended up with Mom, in a way, completing the round-robin circuit.

June 13, 1955

Dear Mom:

Thought you might be interested in reading two letters from Emma Jane, written in Washington, D.C., as well as one from Debby which was written on their plane trip east.

Things very quiet around the house, as you can imagine. But they weren't quiet the first few days. Bingo [the family cocker spaniel] got me up every morning at 5 A.M., then finally went on a tear Thursday night, getting me up four times to let him out, let him in, and still barking half the night. I got about three hours sleep and I fear the neighbors were equally unhappy, so we parted company. He is now boarded out at the vet's. I guess Bingo just was too much at loose ends with the family gone.

Went sailing yesterday, and although it was a little too windy for my taste—being just an amateur in the business—I had a good time. Managed to acquire a bit of sunburn in the process.

Hope you're feeling better. Take care of yourself.

Roly

July 9

Dear Mom,

. . .

Too many invitations out to dinner for me—the first week E.J. was gone, I managed to take off six pounds, but am having trouble keeping it off. But I'm making out fine, and time is passing rapidly before my takeoff to join the family. It will be most welcome.

Best of everything,

Roly

July 20

Dearest Mom:

Here's Emma Jane's latest letter—it may be the last that I'll send over to you. Everything sounds fine except for the finances, but I guess one doesn't go to Europe very often and I can always hock the Crown Jewels if necessary.

Best love,
Roly

Excerpts from Mom's letters to Dad (She wrote grand narratives to him during the weeks between our departure and the end-of-July Paris reunion):

June 8–9, 1955

Dearest Roly—

Just a short note—but Webb just got up and said, "What time is it—where am I—what's the name of this ____?" Guess he's confused.

For dinner we went to the S & W Cafeteria and then walked to the Washington Memorial. Debby and Webb said, "Let's go to the Lincoln Memorial." Gretchen put up quite a fuss, but we walked.

June 10

Hard to get everyone underway today. But, hurrah, there's sunshine for the first time! So today we'll go to the Capitol and Library. Glad we're not attempting to do this all in two days. Yesterday morning we walked to the White House and went through that. Then the children saw the squirrels in Lafayette Square, and we hoped to get back to feed them.

In the afternoon, the children wanted "to do" the Washington Monument again. I said I'd take the elevator, got to the top, and waited and waited. Never did see the 3, so since the elevator finally had broken down, I decided they didn't make it, so walked down. When I saw the guard, he said, "Are you looking for the Miller children?" Anyway, they were not in sight. I knew they had I.D. cards and hoped they'd be all right. Guess they were, since they had walked back and arrived. I did call as soon as I got to a phone and left a message. Then walked back to the Annapolis Hotel from there. Anyway, we're getting in shape! Or should be.

While I was standing in line to go up the elevator, the woman behind me asked where I was from. When I said Washington State, she said, "California," and then when I remarked, "Walla Walla," she asked, "Do you know the Tompkins?" She said her husband worked with Paul and he had flown in yesterday for some meeting. Her name, incidentally, was the same and she seemed to know most of the Tompkins clan. [It was so typical of Mother to run into people she knew or recognized from home during her world travels.]

Love,
Emma Jane

From Iris's notes from the *Conte Biancamano*:

Saturday June 18 (boarding the boat)

Much excitement. Hundreds of passengers and visitors milling around ship. Seems a perfect maze but may get used to it.

Up on deck for departure. Stayed out until we'd sailed past the Statue of Liberty, darkly silhouetted against sunset. Then down for a rest before dinner. All 15 of us eat at one large table. Dinner a little disorganized. Webb amazed by his potato salad—plate of sliced potatoes—nothing else. Slept like a log. Very smooth sailing.

June 20

In the evening saw part of an Italian movie. Later on deck talked about bullfights with Foster Radford and Gretchen. Ship rolled quite a bit through night.

June 22

Took a few movies while on deck. At lunch, Webb proved the daring one and ordered both squid and eel.

From Mom's letters to Dad:

June 22–25, 1955 (Shipboard)

Dearest Roly,

We did get off all right, although it was a push at the last, since I couldn't get the kids organized to go in various directions, the elevators were the slowest in history at the Victoria [Hotel].

One thing none of us was prepared for was the complete foreign nature of the ship and crew. No one speaks English well and only a few seem to have a few words of intelligible English and many none—difficult. We have had a pleasant trip so far, though. Our cabin is quite commodious and we do have air with an outside porthole, which was covered yesterday. We were in the gulf stream and it is rougher there, we're told.

Our food has been good—rather different—but none the less enjoyable. Sunday night was the gala dinner with wine and champagne and filet mignon—extra good. Tomorrow night for Gretchen's birthday we'll arrange festivities and of those I'll write later. Breakfast is from 7:30–9:30, lunch at 12:30, tea at 4, then dinner at 7:30.

Debby is really set up, since she played Bingo last night and won $9.50.

She first won $5, then a third of another winning. She remarked, "I guess I'll not play again."

Webb's friend Leo Wallenburg, (who has made 8 trips to Europe and is Webb's age [11], took Webb along yesterday to get his hair cut just like Webb's. [I had a huge crush on Leo on the trip, and let everyone know. I even named a hamster Leo after our return. Leo, however, was not smitten by me.]

Sunday June 26, Rock Hotel, Gibraltar.

Gibraltar is delightful and although the weather is not extremely clear, it is beautiful and the view certainly magnificent. The hotel reminds me of some old lady I saw in the lobby—rather elegant appointments [furnishings], but a bit out of date. But the brass knobs, railings, etc., do shine.

Webb's living in his walking shorts now. The laundry is piling up, so we'll really look forward to Madrid for that reason.

Love,

Emma Jane

June 26 from Iris's diary in Gibraltar—

Up at 5:30, had breakfast and then to first-class lounge to await boarding officials. Steamed into harbor of Gibraltar. Vendors in small boats selling stuff as *Conte Biancamano* anchored in bay. Passengers taken off on small boat.

We have a large room with balcony at the Rock Hotel. Webb and Foster took occasion to dash up and down hall visiting all our rooms. Bursting into ours and with eyes wide, Webb said, "B-b-be careful of the toilet paper. It's slick on both sides." He was right.

More of Mom's letters to Dad:

Córdoba, Spain, July 1, 1955

Dearest Roly:

I'm surely neglecting you, but life is very busy these days, more than you can imagine. When I stop to think that it was only last Sunday I wrote from the Rock [Gibraltar hotel], and it's now three stops [Cadiz, Seville, Córdoba] later—I'm breathless. Spain is fascinating and I only wish I could go to almost any street corner and sit (or stand) with my camera. It would be wonderful. What would I see? First, an older (but not always) woman entirely in black—dress, hose, shoes and veil—then a military person in olive drab with a small red tassel on his cap, a priest with a wonderfully shaped hat like a bowler with a larger brim, a boy on a bicycle with a load of wooden racks or jugs of wine or water, then a small donkey carrying an unbelievable heavy load of coal, perhaps, or twigs or rocks (if a road is being built nearby.) I can't begin to tell you all that would go by.

Webb pulled quite a stunt last night in Seville. He bolted the inside of the door and Debby had stayed down in the lobby with me while I played bridge. No telephoning (rang at least two minutes), no calling, no knocking at the door could possibly awaken him. So (with no Spanish) I charaded (new word) to the desk man that the bathroom windows opened into one another across about a 40-inch square opening going down three stories or so. He got a ladder and crawled through (fortunately both windows were open) into their bath and unbolted the door! I told Webb he could return me the 50 pesetas I paid the man for a tip. What an experience and no Spanish, either.

Love,

Emma Jane

Madrid, July 4, 1955

Dearest Roly:

Madrid is a big city and many of the endearing experiences of our earlier stops in Spain are missing here. For the first time, at this hotel there is a line of demarcation in the dining room—we're definitely "el grupo"; no choice, long waits, complete ignoring of our simplest wants. Tonight, I want to try Restaurant Horcher, if it's possible.

Yesterday morning (Sunday) we were taken to El Escorial, about 25 miles away from here, to the burial site of the kings, and had lunch at the Victoria Palace. The crypts were most interesting, as well as the massive simplicity of the whole building.

Then we were back here an hour, ready to leave to go to the bull fight. Hope my pictures turn out well—one bullfighter and six events yesterday. The color of the crowd (the place holds 25,000) as well as the various fighters is exceptional. It's run off with amazing precision and the crowd reacts as a single unit, as if they were led by a yell leader. It was gory, but everyone seemed to have survived the experience all right.

Every day I'm asked about how many more days until Daddy comes. So, we'll be really glad to see you.

Best love to all,

Emma Jane

P.S. The accident to the epergne [an ornate tiered centerpiece, often glass] (R.M. Note—I broke it!) doesn't seem fatal. Maybe I can find something in Venice. Somehow—although I like it—others are more precious to me.

> Hotel de Rome
> Florence, Italy
> July 14, 1955

Dearest Roly:

Florence (or Firenze) has much to offer in the shops—the leather work is fine, the jewelry especially beautiful, the linen and blouse work exquisite... but all at a price, most of them too high to be much good this trip. Anything of lapis lazuli that I'd like is out of the question and malachite of any decent size is high. I did buy a silver bracelet at Peruzzi's yesterday for $26–but I guess that seemed moderate after pricing gold baubles in Rome which began at $40 for just one. Beautiful cloths for 12 with tags of 75,000 lire (over $120.) I bought a couple pairs of gloves and two bags (one of which Gretchen can use for carrying her purchases, conveniently) at the Straw Market. I've also looked for cuff links for you of silver but haven't seen a thing—scarcely a cuff link anywhere.

Our drive from Rome to Florence was warm—very—but nevertheless most enjoyable. The scope of vistas and the greenness of the countryside is wonderful. I'm sorry we never stopped so I could get a picture of the oxen (white) at work. We'd see one field being worked by oxen and the one across being ploughed by a tractor.

Webb told Pedro [guide] he would work on an anti-Pedro campaign if he didn't produce some mail from you.

The children are counting the days now till your arrival. I guess we are thinking it will be nice to have you around.

> Best love,
>
> Emma Jane

> Hotel Cavalletto & Doge Orseolo
> Bad Reichenhall, Germany
> July 19, 1955

Dearest Roly:

Although it's late (after midnight), we will have no early morning deadline such as today's 6 A.M. or the 6:30 in Venice, so I'll start a letter. We don't have anything scheduled until 2:30 in the afternoon when we go into

Salzburg. We're assured that everything in Salzburg is booked solid, even to bathtubs, so we are staying here in Germany about 15 miles away.

Fenton Radford [tour member] and I were joking about smells of Venice and we concluded it should be bottled and sold as Canal No. 5.

Thanks for your sending my letters on—I've found so little time to write except to you, even post cards.

Love,

Emma Jane

These excerpts from Mom's travel diary she typed in 1982, include thoughts twenty-five years after the trip:

July 20

By the time we arrived [in Salzburg], it was a real downpour and it was our day to shop. We did find a Lanz store and Gretchen and Debby both have new dirndls and Webb, lederhosen. (I resisted buying a dirndl, but I remember Webb thought it looked so good on me.) I did find a blue wool Lanz dress I liked and bought. Had dinner at Peterskeller Restaurant and then went to see the famous marionettes in Mozart's Magic Flute.

July 21 Salzburg

(1982: I still think our descent into the salt mine—and the things we saw under the earth—was one of the top experiences of the trip.)

July 26 Heidelberg to Frankfurt/Main

Arrived at the Frankfurter Hof (excellent hotel) and before dinner called Erich Kullman. We saw them all in the evening except Norbert who is in the mountains. They live in good-sized apartment and pleasant surroundings. Lots of war damage evident. Mary Kullman (Erich's mother was my grandfather's niece. She had visited in Abilene when a young child with her mother, my grandfather's sister Klara) actually speaks a few words of English, but no one else, so lucky I can speak some German.

July 27

Erich and Mary Anne took us to the zoo—wonderful collection of animals (I remember that the zoo had been almost destroyed during the war).

(L.) Gretchen, Webb, and Debby, Washington D.C., U.S. Capitol Building June 1955.
(R.) Ocean Liner SS Conte Biancamano, *June 19-26, New York City to Gibraltar.*

June 23, 1955, Gretchen's 13th Birthday Dinner at
sea, Gretchen in center wearing striped hat.

Gretchen and Webb at the
Colosseum, July 11, 1955.

Train into the Salt Mine near
Salzburg, Austria, July 21, 1955.

Gretchen, Debby, Norbert Kullman (relative, about 15), and Webb, in Rothenburg, Germany, girls in dirndls, guys in lederhosen, August 11, 1955.

Gretchen and Dad, Grindelwald, Switzerland, August 19, 1955.

Erich Kullman and Dad, Mother, Webb (in hat covered with pins),
Gretchen, Debby (sitting), August 26, 1955, just before our send-off.

Debby, Mother, Webb, and Gretchen boarding the plane in
Frankfurt, heading for Amsterdam, Vancouver, B.C., a stop in
Seattle to see Grammie and Gramps, and home to Walla Walla.

July 31, Paris and Roly

Waited in hotel (others went on a tour) since we expected Roly to join us any time from 11:30 on (it was 1 o'clock before he did arrive). Then we were all together for lunch and then afternoon tour around Montmartre (artist area), Sacre Coeur and saw a procession with music and then to Napoleon's Tomb (Les Invalides).

In the evening we went to see Genevieve Monod and her family. Delightful evening and Debby had a hilarious time with Laurence [also about 10 years of age] and their non-understanding exchange.

August 1 Paris to Manchester, England

Our flight to Manchester was all in order. (1982: Debi's classic comment, "What language do they speak here?" George Holder was on hand to meet us. We had corresponded as pen pals starting about 1933 and then lost contact during WWII. He wrote again about 1947 and so we had kept in touch.)

August 3 Blackpool from Preston

Left not too early, since the three were all tired, but headed for Blackpool. Debby and Webb seemed to have a wonderful time on all the various rides.

August 7 London

Went to Madame Tussaud's Wax works. Webb and I took off on our own and saw Tower of London and Crown Jewels and then had 15 minutes (!) to go to the British Museum, since it was closing so soon.

August 8 London to Frankfurt

Got off to a bad start because the porter did not answer our call to help with luggage in order to get to airport. I thought Roly might have a heart attack, he was so worked up! We had to get all of our luggage down to first floor and then into taxi and to airport, took some doing with limited time. Flew into Holland and then on to Frankfurt.

August 9 Frankfurt

Roly packed up the Volkswagen bus we'll have for three weeks. Stopped by Kullman's and then off to city.

August 10 Frankfurt

Norbert was asked to go with us, but there was some question since high school had already started, but some arrangements were made so he could go. We hope he will have a good time.

August 14 St. Gallen, Switzerland

Started from Fussen about the usual time (9 A.M.) and to cross the border into Austria and decided to have lunch at Hotel Central, Greganez in the garden and then into another country (Switzerland). Passed Lake Constance, but I was asleep part of the way.

August 18 Lauterbrunnen

Roly and Norbert left early to take the Jungfrau trip—felt he should and it was as perfect a weather-wise day as we have had.

August 23

Off to Freiburg.

Left Solothurn after breakfast and had a stop at Olton to visit friends. After Olton we started for Unter Kulm, where Roly's ancestors came from. We went into the small Evangelical Lutheran church and stood to see the organ that his great-great-grandfather played and searched the graveyard for possibility of names. Lots of Muller and even Muller–Muller combinations but nothing we could recognize.

August 26 Frankfurt

Spent a hectic last day attempting to collect all of our displaced items... never found Webb's glasses. We're to leave airport at 7:45 P.M.—all Kullmans were there to send us on our way—flowers, etc.

August 27 Amsterdam

Took bus, after taxi, to terminal and arrived at airport at about 10 P.M., but plane did not leave until nearly midnight. (1982: Does anyone else remember that we had to put everything on the scales, with a small allowance for each of us—we were well loaded at the end of the trip and paid nearly 100 dollars in excess baggage?)

August 28–29 On way to Vancouver, B.C.

One can easily lose track of time—9 hours of time change. Landed at Vancouver, B.C. 2 hours late. Rocky Mountains were just beautiful as we flew over.

Met by Grammie and Gramps and celebrated my 40th birthday in Seattle.

It was a memorable trip and nothing can ever quite replace the first trip abroad.

Iris wrote a grand summary of the highlights of the Whitman tour for the August 21, 1955, *Walla Walla Union Bulletin*:

How Did We Find Europe? By Shoving Tourists Aside
By Iris Myers
U-B Woman's Editor

Half a million Americans—give or take a few—swarmed over Europe this summer. Chances are if you had been swooped up bodily from Walla Walla, Kalamazoo, or Binghamton and plopped down at random at any one spot of the continent you would have landed on the aching, blistered feet of a fellow American.

With 14 others, your reporter traveled for 55 days by boat, bus, train, river steamer and plane, not forgetting the miles of marble-corridored museums and stone-floored cathedrals trudged on foot, through eight European countries (ten if you count an hour's stop in Scotland for a spot of tea and a change of trains in Belgium).

Fifteen in Party

We were 15 Americans (out of approximately half million), all from the Pacific Northwest, ranging in age from 10 to five times 10.

From the time we landed on a sunny morning June 26 at Gibraltar, after an eight-day crossing on the Italian liner, SS *Conte Biancamano*, we were "the group" shepherded by an amiable young Spanish-born Parisian named Pedro. It was Pedro who eased us through customs and immigration, interpreted our wants to waiters in Spanish, Italian, French or German, got us to railway stations on time, saw to the transporting of our 25 separate pieces of luggage and helped us fathom the mysteries of lire, francs, pesetas, marks, and groschen.

We sweltered in 120-plus heat in Spain, shivered in snow and ice near the top of Switzerland's majestic Jungfrau, got drenched in a downpour in Austria, watched floating icebergs off the coast of Labrador and reveled in perfect weather in Paris.

European Cuisine

We ate eel in Madrid, wild strawberries with meringue and cream in Seville, Wiener schnitzel in Frankfurt, rare roast beef and Yorkshire pudding in London, fondue in Lucerne, crepe suzettes in Nice and hamburgers in Rome.

We listened to a symphony concert in the courtyard of the Pitti Palace in Florence, saw the Folies Berger [*sic*] in their native habitat, laughed at Falstaff's antics in the Shakespearean theater at Stratford-on-Avon, sat open-mouthed as one matador killed six bulls in the Madrid bullring and marveled at the artistry and staging of the Salzburg Marionettes.

We spent exactly 20 minutes in the Louvre to gape at the Venus de Milo, the Winged Victory and the Mona Lisa, loped through Del Prada in the wake of a college professor-turned guide, peered at age-dimmed Murillos in the half light of a Spanish convent and found the perfect museum building in Amsterdam where daylight, not artificial lighting, illuminates the old Dutch masters.

We skirted the azure blue Mediterranean of the French and Italian Riviera by train and bus, crossed the Dolomites and the Alps by spectacu-larly curving roads, dodged motor scooters in Rome, taxi cabs in Paris and bicycles in Amsterdam.

Shopping Spree

We—or some of us, at least—bought dueling swords in Madrid's Flea Market, leather goods in Rome, perfume in Grasse, glassware in Venice, silks in Florence, watches in Switzerland, binoculars in Germany, gloves in Paris, gin in Amsterdam and tweeds in London. But we window-shopped more than we bought.

We snapped pictures of monuments, of churches, of museums, of bridges, of castles, of palaces and of people.

In Spain we saw road workers pounding up rock with hand mallets for 22 cents a day, watched doe-eyed soft-spoken hotel maids on their hands and knees scrubbing tile floors and marble stairways, sensed the friendly curiosity of the natives in smaller, more remote villages and just outside a church where we'd been shown a fortune in jewels resting in a locked case, we felt a small boy's hand tugging at our sleeve and a wisp of a voice begging for a peseta. Some place along the way we were told, somewhat sadly, that "Spain is occupied by its own army." And in every village from one end of the country to the other, Franco's men were in evidence.

Bomb Damage

We saw literally hundreds of new apartment houses being built—in Italy, in Germany, in France, in England. We viewed bomb damage in Frankfurt,

Heidelberg and Cologne with a feeling akin to shame and had that feeling erased when we saw the same thing—and worse—in London.

We saw headquarters for American Forces in Austria, at Salzburg, soon to be dismantled and moved out in accordance with terms of treaty agreements. We saw a tremendous swimming pool and playground there, the gift of American soldiers to the children of Salzburg, and heard an Austrian woman say of the impending removal of American troops, "It is not good." We listened to a former German soldier in Heidelberg as he shrugged his shoulders and commented, "All occupation soldiers act alike . . . I know, I was one in France."

From the vantage point of home and familiar surrounding we can look back upon the two months as one of the most interesting experiences of a lifetime.

I've pulled a few remarks from Dad's several pages of typed notes prepared for his Kiwanis Club talk, which contains suggestions about how to get the most out of a trip to Europe.

Although his recommended topic was governments and trends of foreign countries visited, he opted to talk about what he did and saw on his travels during the three weeks abroad. "Everyone is traveling now," he reported.

He compared conveniences and costs of traveling with a guided tour and choosing one's own route and schedule and encouraged voracious reading of guidebooks before traveling.

A purely personal observation: Before you leave, collect all the names of possible contacts with people who live abroad you can get your hands on— and I'm talking primarily not about Americans living abroad in the armed services, but of natives. Before we were through with our trip, our youngsters were saying that every town we got to, we were calling and seeing either a second cousin or the great-aunt of a friend or even a casual acquaintance of a casual acquaintance, and there was some truth in the claim. But it made a tremendous difference in our tour. Instead of spending all our time visiting the usual palaces and museums and glaciers and night clubs, and talking chiefly to other American tourists we went into the homes of the English and French and German and Swiss, saw how they lived, what they did, tasted the foods they ate, and in general came away with a far better appreciation of life in Europe than did most of our fellow travelers.

We found that even in cases where the contact was a very casual one, the people were just as delighted to meet and know us as we were to meet and know them. They opened up their homes to us, invited us to dinner, we reciprocated by taking them out to dinner, so it sort of evened up on the hospitality score and we had the pleasure of making firm friends with some very fine people. Even relatives. In some cases, we wrote ahead, in others just called when we got to the town, but it worked out very well either way. We had some language difficulties but managed to get across some ideas and conversation despite this. I feel we got a great deal more out of the trip than if we had merely followed the usual tourist tracks and spent our evenings in the bars with fellow Americans.

Reflecting on Dad's concluding comments years later, I found his suggestion to splurge, not scrimp, on family travel poignant and timely. None of us—especially Dad—could have guessed that we would never again have the chance to indulge in such a trip with him.

The summer of 1955 was a truly magical time for all of us. Webb and I are including this segment for two reasons. One, thanks to Mom, the trip is the most thoroughly documented slice of Miller Family life we have from that period. The surviving letters illustrate the state of interactions among our five family members. I can imagine all of us sitting around the kitchen at 1019 Alvarado reminiscing about the trip. Second, we see this as the second-most, albeit distant, formative event of our childhoods, behind Dad's death less than 18 months later. We felt hopeful and optimistic about the future and had no reason to worry about what lay ahead.

7

Bridging Lives

"It takes a village to raise a child."

—African proverb

I. Washington Childhood

As young children in the Walla Walla community, Gretchen, Webb, and I won the "it-takes-a-village" lottery. Our unearned bonanza arrived in the form of a lifetime of nurturing and inclusivity extending outward from our parents to their friends, many of whom had children of their own. But two childless couples stood out from the rest. Dorothy and Clyde Robinson, along with Mabel and Bob Groseclose, were our "bonus" parents. They were so natural at cosseting their friends' children that we all got it: they were born to be parents. But they weren't. When young, we Millers put a different spin on their situation. We were sure they would have struggled to tend to any would-be offspring. After all, they gave away so much affection, how much would have been left over for their own kids? Looking back on those years, it's hard to believe that the two couples could have been as active as they were in Walla Walla society and still have time for us, but they did. And after Dad died, they became an even more important part of our extended family.

Mabel and Bob operated the Groseclose Funeral Home in Walla Walla, a successful business about which Mabel sometimes joked, "People are dying to get through our doors." Bob held offices in many business and civic organizations as well. Mabel also taught elementary school, accruing many devoted graduates who kept in touch with her for decades. When she wanted to impress someone with her prowess as an educator, Mabel would say, "Well . . . I was Batman's first-grade teacher." And she was. Her most famous student, William West Anderson, changed his name to Adam West before 20th Century Fox cast him as the original Batman in the 1960s television series. Dad and Mabel had also worked together in the development of a planning commission for the city of Walla Walla.

Clyde Robinson was chief of electrical engineering for the U.S. Army Corps of Engineers in Walla Walla. Over the course of his career he worked on the electrical systems of eight major dams in the Northwest. Dorothy was a trained nutritionist who taught classes in food preparation and had been the food manager at a prominent restaurant in Portland, Oregon. After World War II ended, she learned the secrets of Italian and French cookery while Clyde was working with the Corps repairing war-damaged overseas airports. In Walla Walla she held "legendary" parties and served meals worthy of a Julia Child Award. She never lost her passion for preparing and serving exquisitely palatable dinners. Mother and she collaborated on many meals and were forever on the hunt for new and decadent recipes. (Dorothy's maiden name was Judd, which must have sparked some interesting conversations with Mother. Apparently they determined that they were indeed distantly related.)

Our family spent many afternoons and evenings on Circle Drive at the Robinsons' home. They had designed their kitchen with two sliding doors at right angles—useful in closing off the kitchen from the adjacent living room. Webb and I found them even more suitable for playing elevator. At age eight, he was already a savvy operator. "What floor today?" "Oh, how about the 59th?"

The Robinsons and the Grosecloses were our guests at 1019 Alvarado Terrace for most Thanksgiving and Christmas Eve meals. These feasts took place in our dining room. A large curved window overlooked a brick terrace, next to which rose a huge maple whose branches spread shade across the side lawn in summer. In the center was a Japanese birdbath and tulip tree, beyond which stood a backdrop of evergreens. Our dinner guests would queue up to serve themselves at a curved mahogany table, which held Mother's entrees, side dishes, and accoutrements along with her Rosenthal china. (That crescent-shaped table, made by the Imperial Furniture Company, is the only piece of the original dining room set that I have. Looking at it today takes me back to those festive parties.)

Begun in the late 1940s, those memorable meals remained an uninterrupted tradition until Christmas Eve 1956, when the order of our family life was blown apart.

Years after Dad's death, Dorothy recalled to me his plea the last time Clyde and she saw him: "Promise me you will look after the children." They kept their word. And when Mom died three decades later, they remained close to us for the rest of their lives.

A year after Clyde's retirement in 1968, he and Dorothy moved to Cape George Colony, a private residential community on the Olympic Peninsula, a few miles from Port Townsend, Washington. Clyde had collaborated with architect Kenneth Richardson on the design of both their Walla Walla house and their new home, built on a cliff overlooking Discovery Bay, from which one can see nearby Protection Island and the San Juans in the distance to the north. It was a perfect setting: Clyde could play golf and walk to his heart's content, and together they drove their boat around Discovery Bay and the Strait of Juan de Fuca. Mother knew Clyde was a rock and gem enthusiast and had given him some of Dad's rock cutting and polishing equipment. Clyde generously shared pieces with us, including a bolo tie he gave to Chris.

In summers, Chris and I would visit them in their peaceful retirement home, often taking the Edmonds–Kingston ferry. The sunsets, sea breeze, and Dorothy's dinners were unsurpassed.

For the last decade of her life, Dorothy and I talked on the phone almost every Sunday. Even during our last visit, after Clyde's death, Dorothy, then ninety years old, showed me a recipe for overnight breakfast strata that she had wanted to prepare. "Next time," she said. Dorothy died on a Friday in September 2004.

I recently read letters Dorothy and Mabel wrote to Mom during Dad's final month in the Seattle hospital. I am struck by how confidently they made themselves a part of our daily routines of school, extracurricular activities, and grocery shopping. They knew what we needed without being asked. They recorded their observations and, in their writing, offered assurances that we three were holding up well.

What Mabel and Dorothy inferred about our states of mind was consistent with the cultural norms of the 1950s. Dealing with the death of a loved one had to come from within. Self-reliance was thought to build strength of character. Diversion was a common strategy that could reduce brooding about one's loss. If kids isolated themselves from others and didn't talk, it was their choice and should be respected. Bereft individuals were expected to work through their anguish alone.

Reading their letters, I see their devotion to Mom and Dad and how they understood the ways our maturity, or lack thereof, had already begun to guide our behavior. Gretchen, less than three years older than Webb and me, already faced Dad's demise realistically and comprehensively, asking Dorothy how our lives would change. Webb helped out with household tasks and saw to our guests' needs. He reached out to Clyde by giving him a book on Einstein to read.

I withdrew into myself.

Each of us children had different memories of that time after Dad died. During one of the last conversations Gretchen and I had about his death, she described going to Dorothy and Clyde's home on Circle Drive. Their home and warmth offered an inviting and healing space for her to spend time away from 1019 Alvarado Terrace.

Webb recently described two memories from the months after Dad died involving Bob and the Robinsons. Bob caught Webb by surprise when he gave him his prized collection of "bird points"—tiny arrowheads—he had collected years earlier along the Clearwater River in Idaho. Overwhelmed with emotion, Webb wept. In what was probably the summer after Dad's death, Dorothy and Clyde took Webb to Salt Spring Island (located in the Strait of Georgia between British Columbia and Vancouver, Canada). He remembers Clyde introducing him to Christopher, a boy about his age, who took him fishing a short way offshore in a rowboat, to catch ling cod.

Beyond the attention and presence of others, I remember almost nothing from those weeks and months following Dad's death. Whatever others said to me about his demise went right over my head. By tuning out those reports, perhaps I could keep some part of him alive. Over the years, Dorothy and Mabel talked with me about Dad's death.

Those conversations helped me make sense of my earlier behavior. Mabel acknowledged that, by interacting with family members of the deceased in their funeral business, she had learned how to listen and empathize. In retrospect, it seems clear that connecting with others would become my central driving force. For me, living is about finding and nurturing bonds. These women, in the company of Mother, modeled how to develop and maintain lifelong connections.

From Mabel Groseclose:

January 18, 1957

Dear Emma Jane:

When you come home, I am sure your children will seem very young and helpless to you—and rightly so—for they are very young and they will be turning to you for protection from frightening realities. But as I saw them last night, they were dignified adults, gentle with each other, so appreciative of their grandmother and so considerate of their callers.

Frank Elliott [minister] came while I was there. Webb cut and served me a piece of chocolate cake, then asked me if I would like a glass of milk, which I did.

While Frank ate a piece of banana cream pie, I went downstairs to watch T.V. with Debbie—I didn't talk to her, feeling that I might be intruding on her heartaches.

Your children are showing the same strength of character you and Roly have shown. You have given them a rich heritage. Your mother, too, is an inspiration to know—she is so kind and generous and has treated the children as real people, strong enough to face up to realities, but at the same time recognizing that no one can do anything for an aching heart, that each individual must carry by himself.

Everyone here sends their kindest thoughts and wish we were not so helpless to do more.

Lovingly,

Mabel

From Dorothy Robinson:

January 8, 1957

My Dearest Friend,

Here I am sitting out in front of the Engineers waiting for Clyde. No pen in my purse but your mother gave me this stationery this morning as we were shopping. I have meant to write since Saturday when we talked, and so many other times, but when there was a minute the pen wouldn't write. Little prayers and loving, protecting thoughts to you all day—and to Roly, and our wishes for the best for his sake.

Wednesday—Just got back from taking Gretchen and Webb to school. We had several inches of snow last night.

I know Gretchen and Webb understand and are trying with all their will to be brave and not do anything that will upset their Grammie. Webb goes off and cries alone a little, and it breaks our hearts, but we respect his independence and try to help him in other ways. I told Webb this morning to help Clyde by asking him for help, as nothing would please him more. Webb jumps out of bed and comes and helps his Grammie and this morning was out shoveling the snow off the porch, steps, walk, and sidewalk. He has grown into a man, and I think he must be treated and consulted that way.

Gretchen is so sweet and it almost seems as though she was comforting us.

Debbie, I don't know—I don't think she faces it but I may be wrong. Your mother and I feel that all they can do and want to do is diverting, helping with the heavy weight of their thinking. Mrs. Smith, Wilbur's mother, seems to have given wonderful comfort to Gretchen with a good philosophy. We try, but your young-uns have wonderful grit. I wish they could write what they are thinking, but I can't write my own thoughts, but I am with you in every way I can be.

Later—Had a chance to let Gretchen talk a little bit—she understands, but had so many things that bothered her—"Would they all get to stay together at this house"—'Would Mother have to work"—"How long"—"Would they bring her daddy home." Your mother and I reassured her completely, I think. Grammie and Gretchen both know that Debbie has the knowledge but doesn't want to face it and Grammie thinks it's better not to force it. Mr. Elliott visited Mrs. Kirsch [Grammie] and they had a comforting talk.

I'll just mail this long overdue letter.

I hope you know how we ache for you and love you—

Just ask anything!

Dorothy

Dorothy's message "just ask anything!" turned out to be a promise of lifelong support to us. After Dad's death, the Robinsons' and Grosecloses' loving presence in our lives helped us survive this time of loss. When we were unable to grieve collectively as a family, they

Some Robinson and Groseclose memories.

Holiday dinner, 1019 Alvarado. Bob is facing camera, in front of Clyde, who is looking at the camera.

Mabel and Dorothy (in paper dresses) host paper-themed bridal shower for Debi, 1967.

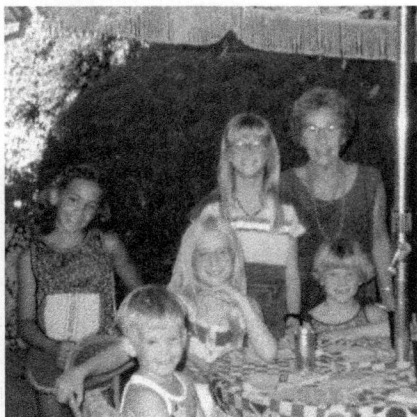

Mabel's patio party for Emma Jane's visiting grandchildren, 1979.

Gretchen, Dorothy, Emma Jane at Robinson's 50th anniversary party, Cape George Colony, 1987.

Dorothy and Clyde attending reunion at Gretchen's beach house, Arch Cape, Oregon, 1990.

Webb and Dorothy at Gretchen's Portland condo, 1990.

Gretchen's 50th birthday celebration (including Dorothy and Clyde, Lucca, Italy, 1992.

Chris and Clyde, Cremona, Italy, 1992. The Robinsons drove here with Chris and Debi to see the Stradivari Museum, 1992.

reached out to each one of us in those months of sadness and, during the coming years, remained our most devoted friends. I am especially moved by the ease with which they were able to offer their support to Mom during her grief and transition to life with Walter, while at the same time nurturing the three of us kids, accepting us where we were psychologically. Their generosity remains a model of friendship for all of us to follow in our own lives.

For our first Christmas after Dad's death, Mabel personalized her invitation to their open house (an annual event for their close friends and their children) to our family. The envelope included stick figures representing Honeychile, Grammie, Mom, Gretchen, Webb, and me. Mabel knew our grandparents would spend the holidays in Walla Walla. Looking at it now, I am struck by her thoughtfulness in including them in her drawing of our family.

"THE TRUE GIFT IS A PORTION OF THINESELF"
--Emerson
Our gift to you this Christmas Season
with pots and pans
and spices too
with loving hands we'll create for you
your BREAKFAST, BRUNCH or LUNCH
Call it what you will—but COME
Anytime between 11 a.m. and 2 p.m.
SUNDAY, DECEMBER 22

For the PORTION OF THINESELF to us
Out of shiny paper or last year's Christmas cards
Cut and paste a cone, cube or tube—each of you
To hang on our O SO BARE CHRISTMAS TREE
Inside tuck a slip of paper (this is for next year's party)
On it write your name and your BIRTH MONTH AND DAY
No year—Ages do not count at
THE GROSECLOSES

II. Two Lives

"Sometimes I think I have lived two lives."

—Emma Jane Miller Brattain

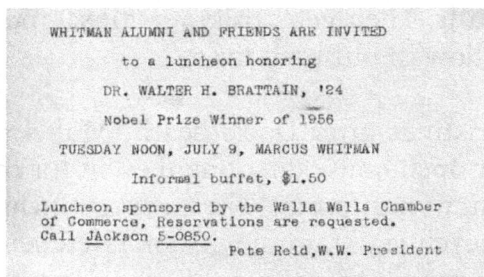

> WHITMAN ALUMNI AND FRIENDS ARE INVITED
>
> to a luncheon honoring
>
> DR. WALTER H. BRATTAIN, '24
>
> Nobel Prize Winner of 1956
>
> TUESDAY NOON, JULY 9, MARCUS WHITMAN
>
> Informal buffet, $1.50
>
> Luncheon sponsored by the Walla Walla Chamber
> of Commerce, Reservations are requested.
> Call JAckson 5-0850.
>   Pete Reid, W.W. President

Mother's postcard invitation to the Walla Walla Chamber of Commerce
Luncheon honoring 1956 Nobel Prize winner Walter Brattain.

Both newly widowed, Mother and Walter Brattain first met in New York at a Whitman College reunion dinner. Walter had graduated in 1924, Mother in 1938. In the late spring of 1957, only a few months after Dad's death, Mother traveled with Dorothy Robinson to the East Coast to attend a meeting of the League of Women Voters. Walter's wife, Keren, had died only a couple of weeks before the dinner, and he may have been seeking solace in the company of his Whitman colleagues. Because of Walter's fame, Mother likely had taken note of Keren's obituary, which had been published in the *Walla Walla Union-Bulletin* on April 12.

Perhaps there was a moment during their brief conversation in New York when they felt the rawness of each other's loss.

After returning to Walla Walla, Mother sent Walter a sympathy note along with a book recommendation she thought he might find meaningful. On July 1st, a week before he was scheduled to visit Walla Walla, Walter responded. He would be in southeastern Washington on July 9th, the featured guest at a Chamber of Commerce luncheon. He said would call her if he could find time. He did.

Walter returned to the East Coast, and they began exchanging pleasantries. As their letters continued, they found they had much more to say. Although Mother's letters are absent from the family history, Walter's writing reflects his initial loneliness, his growing affection for Mother, and—following his December 1957 visit to Walla Walla—his hopes for their future together.

4011 East Mercer
Mercer Island, Wash
July 1, 1957

Dear Mrs. Miller,

Thank you very much for your note. It was some time before I was able to get a copy of [Joshua Liebman's] *Peace of Mind*. I have read the chapter in question ["Grief's Slow Wisdom"] and it does help to make one see that one's problem is as old as the ages. Things still hurt, however, and I guess only time will solve that.

I am visiting my parents here in Seattle. Expect to be in Walla Walla Monday and Tuesday July 8th and 9th. I will be a guest of the Chamber of Commerce and may be quite tied down, but will try to give you a ring if I can.

Sincerely,

Walter Brattain

August 14, 1957

Dear Mrs. Miller,

It is high time that I write and thank you for the good time I had with you in Walla Walla and for your courtesy in sending me the clippings. I was, by the way, very pleased with the handling of the story in the Bulletin. The subtitle to the picture should have mentioned the Bell Telephone Laboratories.

I just got back to N.J. a couple of days ago after quite a trip, most of it unplanned. My son is still out there. I seem to have brought some decent weather to the East with me, so that the transition was not too painful.

Speaking of transitions, was your comment on transistors from vacuums a play on this? Anyway, if transitions in space were only easier, we might see more of each other.

Sincerely,

Walter Brattain

Dec. 30, 1957

Dearest Emma Jane,

Just a note to let you know that I arrived safely 20 minutes ahead of time. Clear as a bell—beautiful view from Mt. Baker in the north on past Mt. Hood to the next peak in Oregon on the South. Never saw it prettier.

Sat quietly all the way over and thought about us. Realized that there is really a fairly simple solution which I will save to tell you at a more convenient time, preferably after we have had a chance to absorb all that has happened in our very eventful weekend.

May I thank you from the bottom of my heart for all you did to make it so pleasant.

When I arrived here I had, of course, to give my father and mother a blow by blow account of both business and pleasure. Succeeded in completing this with only one or two minor squabbles and interruptions regarding stories that concerned people I had met—Mother telling Dad to hush, which, of course, is all that is needed to egg him on.

It occurs to me that it will be nice to call you occasionally and that from New Jersey I can very well do so without disturbance to the household if I know about when you usually wake in the morning. I will, of course, have the advantage over you. To wake me up, at say 7 A.M., you would have to make the call at 4 A.M.

Love, Walter

Jan. 2, 1958

Dearest Emma Jane,

It was sweet of you to call last night. I was hoping that you would. It does seem a shame that tomorrow or the next day Bill [Walter's son] and I must fly back to New Jersey, and that we will not see each other again before this. However, any future plans with or "without strings attached" depend somewhat on my continuing to earn a living and the place where I do that is presently in New Jersey.

You will be amused to know that the day after I came back to Seattle, my mother promoted the idea of Bill having a chance to get acquainted with Gretchen, Webb and Debbie. She thought it would do him good to have brothers and sisters, etc., just as if it [our marriage] were all decided. Where she got that idea, I wonder! Maybe it is all decided, except that as Marcus Whitman said, "Our plans require time and distance."

Of course, you realize that I have not really proposed to you yet. Somehow I have a feeling that it is not necessary. Hope you won't have to wait until the next leap year. Hope you realize that the last is in fun, my dear. I will take care of that little matter in due course. Don't want to attach the strings too soon.

Really there are many things I should write and discuss with you but have the feeling that these can wait a while. That for a while it is just fun to think about you and to anticipate the fun it is going to be (and is) to know that we have been lucky enough to meet and that in this time of sorrow, we may and, no doubt, will find comfort and joy together, which in a way will be a tribute to the ones we mourn.

I worry, however, a little that you may be building me up in your mind far beyond reality.

I am really quite an ordinary individual and somewhat selfish with my share of bad habits, some of which are sure to annoy you when you get to know them better. Such will be the real land mines, as you so aptly expressed it "no strings attached." That best of love and companionship between man and woman is that, that exists without any feeling of confinement, just joy in knowing the other is there.

As you can easily see, I am really quite insane! The pink cloud we are riding on is sure to evaporate, but I feel that when it does, we will be there and it will still be fun.

Of course, it would be unfair to Webb to offer him any bite, but we might try to interest him with a trip through the Bell Labs. My son is forever after me to go again. I will be on the watch for some appropriate pamphlets that may stir his interest. I do hope Webb and Bill will hit it off.

Can I really add anything more to this letter? I feel as if I have written from the depths of my being. Only hope you can decipher my atrocious handwriting.

Love and kisses,

Walter

Letters from Mother's parents capture their cautious support of her rapidly evolving romance. Reading and rereading the letters, I am flooded with compassion for all of them.

Extract from a letter of Grammie's to Mother:

April 29, 1958

Dearest EJay and children,

Well the week is flying by and I hope you are accomplishing a lot.

Had a letter from Walter yesterday—written on Sunday after he talked to you. He didn't ask for your hand! Ha! Ha!

I called the Brattains on Tuesday to give a progress report. Talked to Mari as Mrs. B was in the yard.

Love,
Mother

From Gramps (Honeychile):

January 3/58

Dear Emma Jane and the Kiddies:

Well, no doubt you are all busy as the bees and so are we at this time. Now in regard to your decision, we do not want to criticize you in any way, as you are on your own and know the ways of life, and have in the past made a good report. As to regards to Walter, I think he is a man of the world, and a good scout, in the language of the circus: reliable in band and sober in orchestra. Of course I think you are further along than we think. Of course there will be some jealousy by some of your friends. So far, the only thing I would criticize you on is the fact that the children have not been to the last resting place of their father. And I do think that important for them to know. As there will be days that they should be able to go there and see and feel the ending of our time as their Daddy has. Of course Roly had a funny way in regard to the end and made some of the statements in the past regarding some which you would not approve. But I do think that you have to respect them just the same.

BESTEST TO ALL, from Your Dad

In March 1958, Mother wrote to John and Martha Kelly. Written with great deliberation, her message illustrates the depth and insight of her thinking about her future with Walter while reflecting Dad's final wish that she remarry. Although Mother was not one who typically wrote drafts of letters, I can imagine her laboring over this one. She knew Dad had been like a son to John and Martha, and that his death had quashed the Kellys' dreams for the newspaper, which had begun soon after Dad's arrival. Mother knew that it was a big deal for her to be flirting with remarrying so soon. It was possible that the Kellys might see her marrying again so quickly as a slap in the face. She would have to choose her words carefully.

March 9, 1958

Dear Aunt Martha and Uncle John,

I'm wondering if you have heard from someone else that I'm going East this month? I would prefer to tell you myself. I have the reservations for the children and myself to leave the 19th of this month and return April 1. During the week between Christmas and New Year's, Walter Brattain, who is from New Jersey, was in Walla Walla. We naturally saw as much of each other as possible, since to see me was one of the two reasons he was here. The other was the Brown Fund for Whitman College. We had met in New York last spring at the Whitman alumni dinner; I saw him briefly when he was here in July and then a correspondence started in the fall and continued.

Perhaps I never told you that as Roly went to surgery, he remarked to me that if the thing was happening to me instead of him, that he would be terrified, and said that if anything happened he wanted me to remarry, but that he knew it wouldn't be easy with three children. Trying to keep the moment of such heartbreak as light as possible, I said the only thing I could think of and that was that if it were to ever be, I'd be most particular. My close friends expressed a concern that they didn't know anyone who could ever slightly interest me and so when they knew of Walter's coming to add some brightness to a very sorrowful period (remembering a year ago), it eased the situation into one of anticipation, rather than great sadness. Not that that part can ever be obliterated and often a work or some sound conjures up some of the terminal things that if one allowed oneself to dwell more than a fleeting moment, it would be no good.

Perhaps one of the close bonds between Walter and me is that we both have shared the same kind of sorrow and personal defeat. I can think of no other way to express it than it will be just another plateau, but I do know that a chance to have complete happiness again is more important than some of the incidental details that can be thwarting. That is one of the main reasons for my going East with the children; he, too, has Bill, who is soon to be 14. Since it was impossible to work out vacation time for them here, we will be there when Bill is on vacation.

As you know, there are no quickie rules to follow, no book of instructions to read, that one must follow as best he can his head and the dictates of his heart in such matters. We both, after happy marriages, can be aware of what it takes to make another, I assure you. I've attempted to keep so busy this past year that I scarcely had time to think, haven't whimpered, haven't asked "Why?" And have gone on as well as I could, but I do know that I had not expected anything to come about at this time, but I also know that I am lucky to have someone interested in me as a person. I've been aware of those much older than I am who are alone and the kind of life they have. Frankly, it doesn't appeal to me after being happily married once.

Please know that if there were just the two of us, we would find it a simple matter, but with four children, we want to work it out satisfactorily for them as well as for us.

I do hope that you can share with us the happiness that we are thinking would be in store for us. Personally, I can't help but feel that Roly would approve. You know he was a really great person. And somehow Walter and I have discussed that to make a second marriage work, when we think it can be worked out to ours and the children's satisfaction, would be a tribute to both Keren and Roly.

This was the most naturally happening event I believe and for that we can both be very thankful. One certainly can't put time clocks on anything and to fight something that has happened is much worse.

I hope that you can be happy for us and I do hope that I am the first to have told you.

My love to you both,
Emma Jane

Honeymoon letters to Mother from Gretchen, Webb, and Debbi, mailed on May 18, 1958:

Hello Mom,

Well, here it is almost 10 & I'm the last one to add my message. I'm almost the last one many times in many things, it seems.

I am sitting here feeling very sore and I am as red as a lobster. Yesterday after the parade I went to Susan Baker's & spent the afternoon in the pool. I just tanned then but today I went to the river & wow! I'm pure red, red, red!

I've really been on the go a lot lately but I'll be settling down now for finals start a week from Tuesday.

Mrs. Riess just said for me to tell you that we'll write every Sunday, but I'll sure try to get letters off more often than that.

I better get busy with some oil or something before I melt away.

Much love to you both.
Gretchen

Dear Mom,

Hi! Having fun. And/or?

Guess I'll tell you what I've been doing. Friday night I went on a hayride. Saturday I went (was forced to go) to the horse show and parade. At night Clyde and I went to the Tucannon to go fishing. I just got back.

From what I hear, my grades are 2nd highest in the 9th grade.

Say hi to Ph.D. & F., W.H.B. [Webb's humor: Walter's doctorate, and Father, Walter Houser Brattain]

Love, Webb

Dear Mom,

I hope you are having a wonderful time. The days are going very fast. I received some information about camp yesterday. Mrs. Smethurst sent for 3 applications because Dorothy Santler is going also. I hope it is still alright. We are having our final science test Tuesday and I have been studying very hard.

Sun. Night

It's about 9:20 and I'm awful tired, so I guess I'll go to bed. I'm going to sleep downstairs. This afternoon about 3:00 the Smethursts took me up to the 7-mile bridge. We had fried chicken. It was very good. We also went wading. Aunt Martha called at 7:45 this morning. Everybody said to tell you hello. We all miss you.

Please tell Father Brattain hello. [Hello to Father Brattain! What was I thinking?]

Love, Debbi

P.S. Please write soon.

Of the three Miller kids, Gretchen was the most mature, fair-minded, and accepting of Mother and Walter's marriage. Webb and I were more skeptical about it and remained so for years. How our feelings about Dad, Mom, and Walter evolved over the years runs throughout this book.

I regret that I never asked Bill Brattain to write about what it was like to have Webb and me invade his space when we arrived in New Jersey. Walter had even asked Bill to give up his room so that I could have the largest of the three extra rooms upstairs. Imagine! I never even thought to thank him.

I've often wondered what it was like for Bill to have two more grieving teenagers under his roof. He was not an open book. While he seemed to accept warmly Mother's marrying his dad, it was hard to know how he felt about Webb and me. Were we welcome in his home, or were we interlopers?

I wish Mother had taken a picture of Bill, Webb, and me—similar to that image of Dad with his adopted siblings—after we showed up at 7 Williams Road in Chatham, New Jersey. Webb and I moved into Bill's house just as Marian and Raymond moved into Dad's. Of course, we were teenagers on the cusp between childhood and adulthood, not small children. But it is still interesting and perhaps significant that Dad and Bill were in somewhat the same position. It is another connection to think about as we look back on our lives in the Judd-Kirsch-Miller-Brattain extended family.

8

Walter

Here in the corner attic of America, two hours' drive from a rain forest, a desert, a foreign country, an empty island, a hidden fjord, a raging river, a glacier, and a volcano is a place where the inhabitants sense they can do no better, nor do they want to.

—Timothy Egan (*The Good Rain: Across Time & Terrain in the Pacific Northwest*)

Painting of young Walter by his aunt, Bertha Houser.

I. Young Walter Brattain

Walter Houser Brattain (1902–1987), our stepfather, came from a pioneer family, and he believed this upbringing was critical for his later successes. In a 1964 interview, he said:

> . . . I think as far as my meager competence as a physicist is concerned, it is significant that my maternal grandfather was a flour miller by trade, that my paternal great grandfather, Andrew McCalley was also a flour miller by trade, [that] I spent considerable of my youth—a lot of years of high school and while I was at college—in a flour mill run by my father . . . and that I could take a Dodge engine of that vintage apart and put it together.

. . .

I also think it significant that both my grandfathers crossed the plains, one in 1852 and one in 1854. They were pioneers. My mother and father were born in the Territory of Washington. And, of course, I think it's also significant that they both had a college education. In the case of my father, he worked his way through high school in Spokane as a photographer's helper, then worked his way through college, threshing in the wheat fields and one summer running a pack train for the USGS that surveyed the Idaho–Montana line in the Bitterroot Mountains.

To dig deeper into Walter's family background, anyone sharing Webb's need for words to be accompanied by graphics may find it useful to have pictures showing the main familial relationships (see also p. 454) and locations.

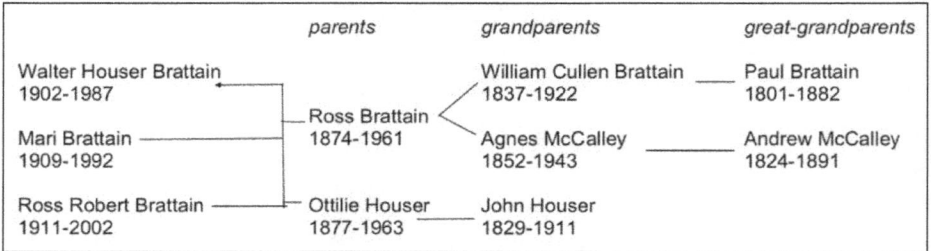

Family tree of Walter's relatives discussed here.

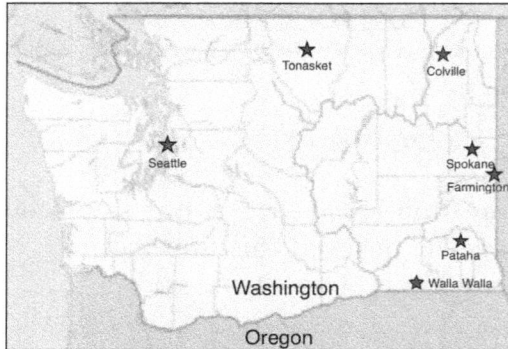

Brattain family locations discussed here.

Historical context is important for interpreting Walter's remarks. The first large party traveled the Oregon Trail in 1843, even though sovereignty of the United States over Oregon wasn't established until 1846. These were times of intense conflict with Native Americans, no doubt driven by their unfair treatment by settlers and the U. S. government. In 1847, Indians massacred thirteen people at a mission established in 1834 by the Reverend Marcus Whitman and his wife, Narcissa, located ten miles west of current Walla Walla. Also, there were several "Indian wars" in what are now Washington and Oregon, between 1855 and 1858. Indeed, Walter's paternal grandfather, William Cullen Brattain, served in the so-called Rogue River (Oregon) Indian War of 1855, as did William's uncle, Benjamin Brattain.

Another of Walter's ancestors, his maternal grandfather John Houser, suffered a disastrous encounter with Indians while coming west in 1854 with a party of emigrants. The wagon train was attacked and only thirteen of the entire party of thirty-three escaped with their lives, traveling five days and nights without food. They made their way to Salt Lake City, and from there to the California gold fields.

By the early 1850s, much of the best Oregon farmland had been claimed by the many thousand families that had made the journey. Pressure on available lands continued to increase as more settlers arrived and often had large families that grew up to want their own farms. Eventually, some of the more adventurous settlers moved north looking for available land. The case of Andrew McCalley, the father of Walter's paternal grandmother, is illustrative. Andrew was born in Scotland in 1824. In the summer of 1850 he sailed to Prince Edward Island, Canada, and was joined thereafter by his wife and two daughters. Over the next four years, while still in Canada, another daughter (Walter's grandmother Agnes) and son were born. The family then immigrated to Illinois, and later to Iowa; three sons were born during that period. In 1858, the McCalley family, five other families, and six young unmarried men left Peoria, Illinois, arriving in Salem, Oregon on September 15, where a daughter and two sons were eventually born. Around 1871, Andrew left Oregon and established a flour mill at what is now the center of Walla Walla. He remained there until his death in 1891. Of his children, two spent the remainder of their lives in Oregon, three stayed in Walla Walla, and the others, including Agnes, scattered to various locations in Washington.

Another Oregon pioneer who eventually went to the Territory of Washington was Walter's paternal grandfather, William Cullen Brattain. He came to Oregon in 1852 with his father, Paul Brattain, six brothers and three sisters. Two uncles preceded them there, Jonathan (1845) and Benjamin (1846). Walter's grandfather was the only one of the family to leave Oregon.

As a young man, William left for the gold fields in Idaho. Walter's brother Ross Robert Brattain (universally called "Bob") has written extensively about the rugged times that William faced, including encounters with cougars and grizzlies, and once seeing nine men get hanged in Elk City, Idaho, charged with killing miners to get their gold. Bob writes:

> In 1867, when he was past thirty, Granddad reviewed his position and decided it was time for him to leave the rough life. The more he thought about it, the more the peace and quiet of the Willamette valley stood out in sharp contrast to the rough and ready mines. He wanted a real life and family so he bought a mule, a saddle and an outfit and started for Lewistown. He planned to follow the main trail through eastern Oregon to the Willamette.
>
> My Grandfather and Grandmother got married in Springfield [Oregon] Nov. 30th, 1870. In some ways they were an odd pair: Grandfather was 6 feet 3 and weighed 190 pounds, and his bride Agnes McCalley probably never weighed 100 dripping wet with a flatiron in her brassier . . . She may have been small, but she knew that her clan lived by the motto "Come home with your shield or on it." [Count on R. R. Brattain to eschew tired phrases like "do or die."]
>
> They had two children in Springfield, Uncle Leslie and Aunt Francis, and then moved to a log cabin on the Idaho–Washington border close to Farmington. Grandfather was the assessor for the surrounding territory and had to ride around and collect taxes. . . . They lived a long happy life together, and the first child born in that log cabin was my father.

While not as rugged as life in the Idaho gold fields, things were still difficult. Whereas Oregon became a state in 1859, Washington didn't join the union until 1889. Walter's father, Ross, recalled (*Walla Walla Union-Bulletin*, June 14, 1957, page 28) the following events.

> In the spring of 1877 we were on the Father DeSmet trail above our Farmington homestead cutting trees for rail fences (no barbed wire in those days)

when we learned that Chief Joseph was on the warpath. He had been ordered by the U.S. government to take his band out of the Wallowas to a reservation near Lapwai, and his young men were in a bitter, massacring mood.

So Papa led a string of wagons to Fort Walla Walla, then went back to help build a fort at Farmington. The first letter Mama got from him said that Old Man Ritchie had been killed by three Indians sent to find out whether the Coeur d'Alenes would let the Nez Perce go through their territory.

I played under the locust trees at Grandfather Andrew McCalley's mill until fall, when the war was over and it was safe to return to Farmington. A few years later, my family sold our ranch to Fred Hayfield and moved to Spokane, so us youngsters could have good schooling.

Years later, Ross wrote an autobiographical sketch, which includes a description of his father's opinion of Chief Joseph.

It would be unjust to a great character even though at this time he was a greatly feared enemy, if there was not something said about who was to blame for Joseph's war. Though our family came very close to being one of the casualties, my Father always felt that Joseph was justified in his stand.

The Nez Perce had acted with honor ever since meeting Lewis and Clark, while Whites had repeatedly broken treaties.

Flour millers also populated Walter's maternal side of the family. After running a mill in Colville, north of Spokane, his maternal grandfather, John Houser, built an imposing flour mill at Pataha, a seventy-five-minute drive northeast of Walla Walla, in 1878. (The mill closed in 1940 but is currently a restaurant.)

Walter's mother, Ottilie Houser Brattain, was born in Colville on April 12, 1877. She was baptized by the Reverend Cushing Eells, founder of Whitman College, named in honor of his fellow missionary Marcus Whitman.

Ross graduated from Whitman College in 1901. Ottilie, a gifted mathematician, attended Whitman and graduated from Mills College in Oakland, California. They married on May 7, 1901, at the Houser family home in Pataha. The college granted Ross's request for early graduation in order that he could accept a government position in Amoy, China, as assistant principal of the Tung Wen Institute. The president of Whitman, Stephen Penrose, officiated at the marriage ceremony. Immediately, Ross and Ottilie caught a train to Spokane to visit her relatives and his parents. Then on to Seattle and Tacoma.

The English ship they were to board, the *Glenogle*, had lost a propeller entering the Strait of Juan De Fuca. It would take a month for a replacement vessel to arrive from the Glen Line Company. While they waited, the company paid for the newlyweds' stay at the Tacoma Hotel. In mid-June, Ross and Ottilie boarded the *Glenesk* out of Tacoma, the start of a 6,500-mile journey across the Pacific. Ross's account, "Marriage and China," documents their travels to and return from Amoy.

The Tung Wen Institute was founded in 1898 by Mr. A. Burlingame Johnson, United States Consul at Amoy, along with six wealthy Chinese merchants. Three educational goals guided the instruction: Providing Chinese boys with a solid education in English, business, basic math and science.

Having arrived in Amoy (today called Xiamen), a port on the South China Sea in Fujian Province, Ross and Ottilie settled into a brick house, and Ross began his administrative and teaching duties at the English school for Chinese boys.

Ross wrote "It was in many ways a wonderful life. It was a small community. No pretense, just be yourself."

Ross and Baby Walter, Amoy 1902.

Ottilie and Baby Walter, 1902 Christening Day.

The China experience proved to be short-lived. Ottilie returned to Washington in 1903 with baby Walter in tow. Ross had been offered a potentially lucrative position selling insurance to the Chinese but ultimately decided that he needed to be with his family and returned to Washington as well in January of 1904.

Both Ottilie's willingness to set aside her academic aspirations to accompany Ross to China and Ross's decision to turn down a career in China to rejoin his growing family testify to their need to place family above career choices.

Walter about five years of age with his mother, Ottilie Houser Brattain.

Ottilie Brattain with son Walter, age 7, and baby daughter, Mari near Spokane in 1909.

Walter and his parents spent seven years in Spokane, where Ross worked for a stockbroker specializing in mining companies. The Brattain family talked often of having "wagon-wheel blood in its veins," a trait that no doubt made working in an office in a growing city like Spokane unpalatable for Ross. He was eager to strike out on his own, as many of his family had done before him. After Ottilie and Ross lost two infant girls, Walter's sister, Mari, was born in 1909 and his brother Robert in 1911.

In 1911, the family moved 150 miles northwest to a valley near the Okanogan River, which flows south out of Canada and is a major tributary of the mighty Columbia. Ross's father and older brother had settled there several years earlier. Ross purchased land and cattle, plowed the rich loess soil in the spring, and harvested corn during the summer months. After a few years, Ross built a flour mill. Bob tells a story that gives insights about the man who raised them:

Just before we moved to Seattle, Dad obtained a lucrative contract which required a specific milling regime. Unable to reach our Czech miller on the phone, Dad phoned Mother, who was in charge as a company officer. When he returned he discovered that our macho miller had refused to accept instructions from a woman, and that not a bushel had been milled. Next morning Dad headed for the mill to straighten things out, and I secretly followed. The first discussion took place in the little office under which I hid. As I had suspected, the miller remained true to his macho creed, and Dad said that he would have to fire him. However, he climbed the 80 ft. to the top floor and started to help the miller transfer his tools into his tool chest. As they were packing the many tools a miller has, the miller lost his head and got a beautiful handmade hunting knife out of a drawer and started for Dad. He was small, so Dad just grabbed him, held him out the window 80 ft. above the ground and calmly said, "Drop the knife or I will have to drop you." He complied and Dad helped him finish packing, helped carrying the heavy chest down and gave him a check for two weeks. No hard feelings, just don't threaten me. The knife was stolen from me in graduate school.

Even at age eight or nine, Walter had a professional demeanor.

Walter had begun his education in Spokane at Roosevelt School. Now, in the Okanogan River valley, Walter rode five miles on horseback to attend grade school in Tonasket (2010 population 1,032), a journey that suited his adventurous temperament. He must have smiled when he awoke on rainy mornings, knowing that instead of riding his horse to school, he would be chauffeured to school by his father in the brand-new Ford. In school, he showed great skill in arithmetic, for which his teacher allowed him to skip a grade.

Devoted to providing the best possible education for her children, Walter's mother decided Seattle might be a good place for him to begin serious studies. The Alaska Gold Rush in the 1900s had exploded Seattle's population from about 80,000 to 237,000. High school enrollment grew even faster, from about 700 to 4,500 between 1900 and 1910. The city surely offered more opportunities for educational and social development than would a rural setting. Queen Anne High School, built in 1908 on the highest hill overlooking Puget Sound, became a classic architectural landmark. Bertha, Ottilie's older sister, offered to let him, his brother Bob and their mother, live with her for his freshman year. Although the school—its teachers and students alike—may have been congenial enough, Walter intensely disliked the urban environment. He preferred the outdoors and found city living confining, much as his father had when working in Spokane. He yearned for the wide-open spaces of eastern Washington.

His parents got the message.

After one year in Seattle, Walter, Bob and Ottilie rejoined Ross and Mari in Tonasket, where Walter enrolled in school. In the middle of his third year of high school, he dropped out to work the fields alongside his father. This turned out to be a memorable year for both of them. For Ross, it was a chance to see his son as a committed and responsible partner, almost a colleague. For Walter, it was a time to observe the diverse farming skills his father had honed, to become part of a team, and to fine-tune his inference skills about what tasks needed to be done. These abilities would serve him well in his professional and personal life.

Interviewed in February 1993 for the book *Crystal Fire: The Birth*

Walter walking behind the plow on the farm near Tonasket, about 1917.

of the Information Age by Lillian Hoddeson and Michael Riordan, Walter's brother Bob shared a couple of wonderful stories from their days on the Okanogan ranch:

> The summer Walter was fifteen was the first summer we lived up on the range. We put our cattle up on the forest service range, where they charge so much a head. Walter lived up on the range, where we took supplies to him about every ten days. He was just a kid. Out there, he lived alone, was in charge of the cattle, and kept two to three horses with him at a time. If there was any cattle roundup, he'd have plenty of help.
>
> I remember one time that Walter was out with the corn cutter and going, a meteor came over, came over close, scared the devil out of the horses and they cut loose and ran. And there was the damndest pattern cut in the corn field you've ever seen. We didn't know where it landed. The next day, with our father's permission, Walter and I got on horses and rode to see if we could locate the meteor. But we never found it.

Sometime in those solitary hours plowing his father's fields, Walter formed a clearer idea of his future: he wanted to return to school and, following in his parents' footsteps, attend Whitman College. However, he would have to make up some lost time as a result of his farm work. His parents learned that the Moran School for Boys, on Bainbridge Island near Seattle, would enable him to finish high school in time to attend Whitman. But there was another problem: Moran was expensive. As he was only the first of three siblings interested in an education, it was hard to justify the investment. Ottilie may have mentioned the financial hurdle to her sister. Just as Aunt Bertha had given them a place to live while Walter attended Queen Anne High School, she again stepped in to assist by paying his tuition at Moran.

The Moran School for Boys was founded in 1914 by Frank Moran, son of a prominent shipbuilder. The location was close enough to Seattle to allow for visits home for students from the Seattle area, yet isolated near woods, water, and mountains. Instead of a traditional course of study, the curriculum featured individual tutoring. Each teacher was assigned two to three students per term, which allowed for close supervision and instruction. In reflecting on Moran, Walter wrote:

> It may be of interest that two of my teachers at Moran were graduates of Whitman College, Stanley Yates, a Rhodes Scholar, taught English and Cecil Yates, Physics. Each student at Moran had a job and mine was to run the Diesel engine that generated the power for the electric lighting system at the school under the supervision of Cecil Yates.

Walter's educational opportunities relied heavily on support of his Aunt Bertha, who came to the rescue once more when it became time for him to attend college. But her story extends well beyond those acts of generosity, and a little of it is worth telling here.

Bertha Houser (known as "Aunt Botsell") was quite a character, not at all what one might expect of a small-town girl from the Wild West. (Pomeroy, the larger town next to Pataha, had a population of 1,425 in the 2010 census.) Both of her parents (Walter's maternal grandparents) came from Germany, and they took Bertha back to Europe to study art. Later, she lived in far-flung places including Boston, Paris and Honolulu, and traveled extensively in Europe, Mexico and Central America while continuing her art education.

The website for Washington Rural Heritage includes copies of many letters to Bertha from a suitor, John Bertram Brady, who went to Paris to propose to her, unsuccessfully. Unfortunately, he died in 1912 on the *Titanic*.

Bertha Houser in her pongee dress, Paris, France, circa 1903-4. The soft-woven silk fabric for Bertha's dress likely came from China, from her sister Ottilie.

Walter's siblings, Mari and Bob Brattain, benefited from growing up in the same environment. Mari graduated from the University of Washington and enjoyed a career in advertising in Seattle. Bob also graduated from there and went on to study physics at Princeton University. Among Bob's more noteworthy achievements was introducing his close Princeton friend, John Bardeen, to Walter. One is left to speculate how much this affected Walter and John sharing a Nobel Prize two decades later. Bob was so successful as one of the first molecular spectroscopists that "Robert Brattain" has an extensive Wikipedia page (though not as long as Walter's, as one might expect).

Walter's siblings Bob (born 1911) and Mari (1909) provided a close-knit network during years in Tonasket and beyond.

Young Walter received an impressively wide range of experiences before finishing high school, from backbreaking farm labor to education by a Rhodes Scholar. He then attended Whitman College in Walla Walla, graduating in 1924 with a degree in physics. He went on to attain a level of fame that few possess. Although people were often ready to give him special treatment, he never demanded it, but remained humble and hardworking—true to his pioneer heritage.

One of many examples of Walter's humility that we witnessed took place around 1975, when Walter visited Webb and Walter's friend, the physicist Brickwidde, at Penn State. Twice, at a reception at the Brickwidde house and again after Walter's colloquium, another physicist said to Walter, "It must have been nice to work in physics back when it was so easy." Walter's response was no different than if the man had expressed pleasure at their meeting. Walter, your mamma raised you right.

—Debi and Webb, May 2023

II. Webb's Letter

*If I have seen further it is by standing
on the shoulders of Giants.*

—Isaac Newton

Dear Walter,

The project with Debi to delve into our family history and write to our loved ones has made me much more aware of the similarities of my life decisions to yours; I want to tell you what I've come to understand. In addition to my many memories of you, this letter draws on the two long interviews you did for The American Institute of Physics Oral History, one in 1964 at Bell Labs and one in 1974 at Whitman College, which are easily found on the Internet. No doubt those interviews have been treasure troves for everyone interested in the golden age of solid-state physics, but occasionally you described aspects of your personal life, and those remarks gave me new insights about you.

While I don't recall feeling overt resentment toward you when my life was upended by the move to New Jersey to live with you, the new surroundings were difficult for me, and I was motivated to downplay your importance because my father had reached mythological stature for me (and remains there).

Of course, my move to your house also disrupted your life, and I wonder how you felt about that. The main hints I've found so far are statements in your 1974 interview:

> . . . My first wife died in the spring of '57, from cancer . . . at an alumni meeting shortly thereafter in New York, I was introduced to my present wife, with the comment that "You're both in the same position." She had just lost her husband from cancer. Her husband was managing editor of the *Walla Walla Union-Bulletin*. . . . My wife came out of course to New Jersey. The oldest daughter was here [Walla Walla] in college, but she brought the younger daughter and the boy with her. There turned out to be problems with raising, particularly the daughter, in this region where she [Emma Jane] didn't know the families of the boys that the daughter had dates with. And she finally made the decision that she was going to have to take them back to Walla Walla.

Blended family from around 1962. Bottom: Bingo, our beloved cocker spaniel. Front row: Gretchen, Mom, Debi, Walter. Back row: Gretchen's husband Stephen Kafoury, Webb, Bill.

Please accept sincere apologies from "the boy" (not the boys Debi dated) for adding stress to your life. (But don't blame me for Mom moving back to Walla Walla; I didn't want it. I was going to start attending Whitman College that August, and was anticipating having access to an empty house one block from campus.) For my part, I don't have any unpleasant memories about you from that period (or indeed ever). You did a fine job of treating me as your son, despite my weak showing at making you my father. Your goal of creating a harmonious stepfamily was largely successful, notwithstanding my incomplete commitment to that project.

You and my biological father of course shared a central part of your lives—marriage to my mother. But in other respects, your lives, especially your early years, were quite different (though it seems like remarkable coincidences that each of your mothers had a degree in mathematics, and each of you had two sisters that died at an early age). My life has been in most ways more like yours than his. Some of the ways are evident; our childhoods in eastern Washington state, attending Whitman College, careers in a quantitative science with a final switch to biology. While it is possible I was simply preordained to follow in your footsteps, I believe that your example was instrumental in many of my most fortunate choices.

Now, over sixty years later, I see that shortly after we met, one of my experiences bore a notable similarity to one of yours. I realized this when, as I started work on this letter, I saw a photo [see p. 219] of you walking behind a team of three horses plowing a wheat field in eastern Washington. Indeed, we both started farm work earlier, me driving a truck in pea harvest at age thirteen. About forty years later, and at close to the same age (perhaps sixteen), I would be sitting on a Caterpillar D–6 plowing a wheat field in eastern Washington. I'll bet we had the same experiences of doing our best to keep the rows straight and coming in after fifteen hours of work with our eyes the only parts of our faces not completely buried under dust. However, I should note that the similarity ends there, since my experience of work as a teenager fell far short of yours. You reported in the 1974 interview, ". . . when I went through my senior year at high school . . .

I had spent one whole year . . . herding cattle in the mountains, with a rifle, my own camp. I only saw my family on occasional weekends and saw practically no other individual outside of my mother and father and brother and sister." That wasn't the last time that my life, though similar in some ways, bore a rather pale resemblance to yours.

Some of my most pleasant memories of the two years I lived with you are of a backpacking trip into the Okanogan Wilderness that you orchestrated, and the time we dangled bait over the minuscule Idaho stream and caught the tiny, starving trout as they jumped for it. I was pleased to see how John Bardeen, your closest friend, characterized part of your later life: "He played golf regularly at the local country club, and he resumed fishing in rugged surroundings." Golf (which John greatly enjoyed) and wilderness fishing (which I suspect he would never try) in the same sentence! That proves to me that you loved trips like ours. The seed you planted in me didn't bloom for 30 years, but eventually solitary wilderness adventures became a major satisfaction for me. I have tried to expose two of my children to the

Bill and Webb on a trip to the Okanogan Wilderness.

lure of such trips; maybe in 30 years Andrew or Kathleen will take up the family tradition.

More connections in our professional lives are evident to me. I loved the following quotation from your brother Robert from page 101 of *Broken Genius: the Rise and Fall of William Shockley* by Joel N. Shurkin: "Now Walter couldn't carry Bardeen's jock strap as far as being a mathematician, but he wasn't bad or stupid." Perhaps unlike many people, I'm satisfied, probably even glad, that I'm not particularly smart. But look how far we got! A rich person should be prouder if none of the money was bequeathed by their parents, like scientific accomplishment without a huge amount of inherited intelligence, right? Of course, my accomplishments don't hold a candle to yours. I didn't win a Nobel Prize or take my wife to the White House, but I did take Nan to a nifty banquet for the Time 100 Most Influential People of 2009.

It is immensely helpful that you placed so much emphasis on producing a clear record of your life as a scientist, apart from technical publications. A prime example is your meticulous and charming "Saga of an Expedition to Stockholm, Sweden, December 1956" about your tour of Scandinavia including the Nobel festivities. When book authors describe the interactions leading up to the invention of the transistor, or the resulting Nobel ceremony, they frequently use your words. I imagine this is because Bardeen was too modest to record those events, and Shockley's huge ego distorted them.

I'm a bit jealous that your fellow physicists appreciate the importance of your observations and make them freely available. No doubt that is partly because semiconductor physics between 1930 and 1970 is currently a heck of a lot more interesting than early bioinformatics. (This ugly word refers to producing or using computer programs to analyze biological data, particularly from genomes.) In 2009, I received the Senior Scientist Award from the International Society for Computational Biology (incidentally, for which I attended a conference in Stockholm), and, though I wasn't explicitly aware of your two interviews mentioned above, I decided to contribute by starting a tradition that recipients would record their observations from "the early days."

It is unfortunate, at least in my opinion, that the tradition didn't stick; as far as I know, others from the early days of this field haven't recorded their impressions. (Nowadays, the "target audience" for my writings is much smaller—just you and my other family members.)

A guiding principle of your professional life was to remain a laboratory scientist and avoid, at all costs, becoming a manager of other scientists, as illustrated by the following remarks from the American Institute of Physics Oral History Interviews.

> There was a period under Fletcher—when Fletcher, back in the late 1930s became director of research—in which I was told by Fletcher that there were opportunities out in the Labs where they had jobs for men. It meant a rise in the organization chart and it meant of course an increase in salary. And I told him very definitely that I wanted to be a research physicist. I of course wanted to get paid what I was worth—I probably told this very softly to him, because Fletcher was a very nice individual. Fletcher reported this to Kelly, who was next in line in the organization at the time. Kelly didn't accept this and called me up into his office and we had a long discussion. I told him, Kelly talked strongly and the way to get along with Kelly was to talk back to him. I told him very strongly that if I couldn't be a research physicist in the Bell Telephone Laboratories, I'd have to find another job. And, of course, if I'd accepted one of these opportunities for advancement, I wouldn't be sitting here now.

I absolutely shared with you the distaste for "moving up" to managerial duties, and I wonder how much I learned of it from you or gravitated towards it because of shared teenage experiences of pride in working alone. My piece about "the early days" written for my Senior Scientist Award, mentioned above, says this: "A bioinformatics leader about half my age once expressed amazement that I still write programs . . . . My approach to staying excited about research is to mix long-term projects, which provide the continuity that Ph.D. students need, with novel, short-term projects where I am a main programmer and sometimes the only Penn State participant . . . . Without the latter kind of project, *i.e.*, if I were simply managing other programmers, I would find it much more difficult to get out of bed in the morning."

One result of my current family-history project with Debi is a heightened awareness of how earlier decisions in my life echoed some of your choices, as just mentioned. However, the project itself represents a similarity between us that is only now developing. Through my work on the project I am becoming more aware of how much I have been shaped by my ancestors, among which I now count you. Clearly, you had a very strong sense of family continuity that I am only now coming to mirror. Near the end your 1964 interview, conducted when you were fifteen years younger than I am now, you were asked who deserves credit for your accomplishments as a physicist. Instead of citing the scientific colleagues who contributed to discovery of the transistor, whom you profusely thank on other occasions, you acknowledge the role of family history. You said, "I think as far as my meager competence as a physicist is concerned, it is significant that... both my grandfathers crossed the plains, one in 1852 and one in 1854. They were pioneers."

It is only recently, as a result of my ongoing project with Debi, that I might well cite family history if asked who deserves credit for my accomplishments. Perhaps I would include a comment like "I think as far as my meager competence as a scientist is concerned, it is significant that I got to spend a lot of time with Walter Brattain." In my appreciation of my forebears I, once again, find my life mirroring yours.

The similarities between your life and mine give me confidence that you were as happy with your life as I am with mine. This conclusion is supported by statements you made at the end of your 1974 interview, answering a question about the most personally pleasurable period of your life:

> Really all of it's been very satisfying, even . . . herding cattle starting in the summers when I was fourteen years old. But I did not like following three horses and a harrow in the dust. My chief impression is that I was always fortunate by being many times in the right place at the right time. . . . My favorite statement is that I've been indeed fortunate to spend my life trying to understand how things happen. To be able to earn my living this way.

I find that your last few sentences definitely apply to me, though I enjoyed my time pulling a plow with a tractor in the dust.

Both Debi and I understand and appreciate you far more as a result of our recent explorations of family history. The transformation of Debi's impressions of you has been particularly delightful to witness.

And I've become clear about the extent of my debt to you for many life lessons.

I doubt I was genetically preordained to follow my career path. Instead, similarities in our early lives, plus the appeal of your professional standards, led me ultimately to an extremely enjoyable professional life. Perhaps "nurture" won out over "nature." Also, I can only hope to have shown others the kindness you exhibited by unconditional acceptance of "the boy"—me—as your son. I love you, Walter Brattain.

III. Debi's Letter

You know, my dear, that I like your children. I can
only hope if our luck continues to run, that they can
accept me and that I can, in some small part, replace
their loss.

—Walter to Mother Jan 11, 1958, from a 24-page handwritten letter.

May 2019

Dear Walter,

This morning I went for a walk down Amador Lane, as I often do, past the post office, fire station, and Mormon church. It is a pleasant walk, the street lined with mesquite, palo verde, and pine trees interspersed with Tuscan blue rosemary and red yucca, whose stiff, pinkish flower stalks jut out rudely across my path. Most days I just turn off my thoughts and enjoy the air and sun. But today, memories of you flooded my brain. I was glad to leave those floral distractions behind as my pace quickened and, shifting into autopilot, I could focus on you.

Two images almost twenty-five years apart flashed before my mind's eye like a split-screen video. I realized they were bookends to the story of our evolving relationship as stepfather and stepdaughter.

In both scenes I was staring at the back of your head. The first, from 1957, shows you and Mother sitting together in the living room of our family home. In the second, twenty-five years later, you were at the kitchen table in my rented house in Walla Walla.

The story between the two is about my attempts to come to terms with our relationship.

Image one: 1957. I first met you in late December. You had flown from Chatham, New Jersey, to Walla Walla to meet with faculty at Whitman College. You had also set aside time to spend with Mother, who planned a small open house for you the first night. On your last evening, the two of you spent a couple of hours alone together. Although you may have thought you were *à deux*, someone was watching. . .

Very soon after you arrived at the house, it became clear that Gretchen (15), Webb (14), and I (13) were to vamoose. We headed upstairs to our separate bedrooms. I made a point of noisily shutting my door. Then I snuck soundlessly back down into the kitchen. I pushed open the swinging door just enough to see past the dining room to where the two of you were sitting coyly on the dusty-blue love seat, your backs toward me. It was as if I were watching a drama starring Mother and you, wondering where this was leading.

She had put on a classical record—perhaps Tchaikovsky's *Serenade for Strings*—to set the mood and serve as filler during the early, awkward moments of conversation. I stood two rooms away, my left hand on the cool white tile of the counter top inches away from a big slab of carrot cake. But I was too focused on the scene unfolding on the sofa to distract myself with food. I could think of nothing but eavesdropping.

Suddenly, you and Mom leaned closer together. I almost choked on my fear that you had come to take something that didn't belong to you: Mother's heart.

I saw you as the villain in this drama, a threat to her need for grieving, which I expected would extend into the coming year and beyond. Surely any man who could tempt her away from my barely dead father represented trouble. I couldn't accept that Mother might find happiness with some guy while I felt so lost. I rationalized then that I was thinking of her welfare. But I see now that I expected that Mother and I would be partners in grief. If she were to hook up with

you, I would be left to suffer alone. And you, Walter—the usurper—
were threatening my chances of survival.

Five months later, following a flurry of letters, phone calls, and a
trip (Mother, Gretchen, Webb and I) to Chatham, New Jersey, to visit
you and meet Bill, you and Mother were married in nearby Summit
on May 10, 1958. We Miller kids were at home in Walla Walla.

Image two: 1982. A quarter of a century later, I had divorced, moved
from Idaho Falls to Walla Walla, and rented a small house near you
and Mother. Brenda (8), Scott (5), and I lived in our "little red barn"
on Valencia Street. Although you might easily have walked the few
blocks to the Whitman campus, you preferred to drive the tan Kar-
mann–Ghia convertible. You fell into the habit of stopping by on your
way home. On one occasion, you stayed for dinner. As you sat down
on a bright yellow wrought-iron chair with a back scroll that reminded
me of a treble clef, one of your belt loops got caught on the end of
the back scroll. Unable to move, you panicked, twisting in your chair.

I, too, felt a sense of panic. I could see that Alzheimer's already
held you in its grip, a spiral of dementia that was upending—and
would ultimately end—your life. Suddenly I saw your future as a road
dead-ending in a thicket of weeds, along which control of your world
would slip relentlessly away over time. You would be deprived of your
last deal of cards that should have been death by heart attack on the
18th hole of the Walla Walla Country Club golf course. My God, if
anyone had earned the right to a fair and lightning-quick demise, you
had. At that moment, we both could see how this disease would erase
you, Walter, leaving only a physical shell.

On that evening, I realized that I had missed out—due to my own
selfishness—on truly knowing you. Flooded with regret, I would
watch you slip inexorably away, along with my hope of feeling close
to you, loving you.

Two disquieting memories, burned into my brain.

You and I got off to a rocky start. For one thing, I didn't know what
I was supposed to call you. "Doctor" was my first name for you, one

which made you uncomfortable. I can see why. For months I avoided referring to you by your name. But by the time you and Mother were married, I knew I had to call you something. After you headed for Paris on your honeymoon, I wrote a "Dear Mom" letter. At the end I penciled, "Please say hello to Father Brattain." Father Brattain. Good grief!

I came up with my brattiest way of referring to you in New Jersey when talking with my immature friends. You became "the man who sleeps with my mother." I later settled on "the man who married my mother." When speaking directly to you, I said "Walter."

As you might have guessed, I thought of my dad in mythical, almost supernatural terms. But you wouldn't have known that I held onto my near-perfect image of him for fifty years. Even then, I was only able to chip away a small corner of the frame protecting my fantasy. But it was through writing about my father that I finally would come to know him in the larger context of his rich, albeit brief, life.

And it has paved the way for me to know you.

I hope that by writing to you I can replace those troubling vignettes with an expanded sense of the richness of your life. I knew that you had lived a fascinating and impressive life. My challenge was to set aside my judgment of you so that I could move beyond the resentment I had nurtured for so many years.

Each relative I have included in my work on family history has his or her own story, and I have had to present each in the way I thought worked the best for that person. In writing to other family members, for example, I felt comfortable reading their letters and related documents, then weaving my own thoughts into the details of their lives.

In your case, I needed a biographer. My own recollections and minimal understanding of your momentous research, even when coupled with the saved documents, left a huge gap in the story I wanted to tell. I had to consult outside sources to fill them. In September 2018, Chris and I spent a day at the Whitman College Library Archives in Walla Walla, Washington, sifting through files from the forty-five boxes—thirty-five linear feet—of scientific and personal documents in the Walter Brattain Family Papers. Aided by archivist Dana Bronson, we combed through a small portion of your papers, documents, and awards, including your Nobel Prize medal, and selected several photos, letters, and articles to copy and add to our documents.

In one file, we found a detailed *Washington Post* article about the 1962 Nobel Laureates White House dinner, hosted by President and Mrs. John F. Kennedy in celebration of the United States's achievements in science, literature, and world peace. We also found photographs from that dinner. I was transfixed by an image of Mother and you, taken just as you entered the White House banquet hall. Your faces shone with the awareness of being present at a historic and momentous celebration. I wanted to be there, sharing with you the brilliance of the hall, the sound of cultured conversation, the electricity generated by dozens of great minds mingling.

In early May 2019, I searched online for details of the gala. As if it were my kismet, I came across a 2018 book by Joseph Esposito: *Dinner in Camelot: The Night America's Greatest Scientists, Writers, and Scholars Partied at the Kennedy White House*, a remarkable study of a unique event. After I read the book, I wrote to Mr. Esposito about his masterful handling of the material and of my connection to the gathering. He responded quickly, apologizing for not having included more details about the scientists present. I loved his line, "So many Nobel laureates and so little space." [I have a lot more to say about that dinner in Chapter 9.]

I'm grateful to have worked on this project long enough to understand that you belong in the family history. With Webb's encouragement and Joseph Esposito's timely book (which includes a marvelous picture of you standing behind Jacqueline Kennedy), I now have a new image taking center stage in my mind, one that is pushing farther away the memories that have haunted me for years. But I'm getting ahead of myself, eager to tell you what I have learned and how it has changed my view of you.

You can observe a lot by watching.

—Yogi Berra

You were a born observer and grew up watching nature, individuals, surfaces. Later, as a scientist with a supreme ability to notice experimental details, you quickly figured out how to pick out key phenomena. You recorded your observations with precision.

I can see that now.

It is extraordinary that when reflecting on the past we often notice—for the first time—what may have been there all along. Above all, it was Webb's letter to you that jarred me out of my complacency about you. In it he reflected on his immense admiration for your integrity as a scientist and his memories of being with you in the Idaho wilderness and at a colloquium at Penn State University. Webb saw you in ways that, until this year, I could not.

Oh! What things I am noticing: your lifelong passion for learning and science, your deep gratitude for individuals who helped and taught you, your commitment to give back to Whitman College in memory of those who served as your role models. I see your dedication to community both in work and in life, your pursuit of understanding, your brilliance as an experimenter, your insistence on sharing the credit for your scientific accomplishments. I am in awe of your love for Mother and your acceptance of us, her wary teenage trio.

During the past several months I have examined documents and letters written by you, about you. Some I have read before. Many more were unfamiliar. But all were new in the sense that I was reading each one from a fresh point of view. I now feel connected to you.

I'm very excited to write to you about what I am learning. For example, in 1999, Michael Riordan and Lillian Hoddeson wrote *Crystal Fire: The Invention of the Transistor and the Birth of the Information Age*, a fascinating book that, coupled with the PBS documentary "Transistorized!," details the history, decisions, and personalities that drove your semiconductor research.

Some of my favorite findings are from your story "The Saga of an Expedition to Stockholm, Sweden, December 1956," a firsthand account of when you, John Bardeen, and William Shockley received the Nobel Prize in physics. In it you highlighted noteworthy experiences, memorable events I have not read about in other sources.

There is something haunting in the light of the moon;
it has all the dispassionateness of a disembodied soul,
and something of its inconceivable mystery.

—Joseph Conrad

When I stare at the moon, I think about the ways it has shone in my past with you.

Right after your visit to Walla Walla in late December 1957, Mother must have written in a note to you that I had looked up at the sky one January evening and exclaimed that you could see the same moon from New Jersey.

You wrote in your next letter to Mother, "A kiss to Debby for thinking the moon was also shining here. . . ."

Brenda and Bopa, Christmas 1973, the year before they read Goodnight Moon.

A few weeks before you and Mother were married, you wrote this poem about her and your hope for the two of you:

> A little girl should not be battered
> About the moon and its phase,
> Since these problems should be easy to face
> With the man that really mattered.

You then added: "Not so good, but you, I trust, get the point."

One holiday in the mid-1970s, you and Mother came to Idaho Falls, Idaho, for Christmas. Brenda, two-and-a-half years old, toddled over to you with her copy of *Goodnight Moon* and held it out for you to read to her. When you finished the story, she hopped down, ready to head for another activity. But you weren't quite finished with the moon. With no encouragement, you launched into an explanation of the moon's rotation around the Earth and its influence on ocean tides. Facing you, she stood rapt, not because she understood, but likely because no one had spoken to her in that manner before. At some point you realized that your message might be a bit over her head and said, "That is enough for now." Walking away, she turned her head a few times to look back at you.

Your funeral took place at the Congregational Church in Walla Walla on Monday, October 18, 1987. The evening before, Joan Baez gave a concert at Cordiner Hall, which Mother, Gretchen, and I attended. In addition to some of her well-known songs, she sang "The Moon's a Harsh Mistress." The melody and words moved me deeply. I've recently been listening to various recordings of that Jimmy Webb song.

I think you would especially like Renee Fleming's operatic, almost elegiac, interpretation. Although the message is a bit cryptic, I love the phrase "See her how she flies / Golden sails across the sky / Close enough to touch / But careful if you try. . . ."

You were buried in Pomeroy, Washington, where several of your Houser relatives lived. Your brother, Bob, read the poem "Do Not Stand at My Grave and Weep" attributed to Mary Elizabeth Frye:

Do not stand at my grave and weep,
I am not there, I do not sleep.
I am a thousand winds that blow,
I am the softly falling snow.
I am the gentle showers of rain.
I am the fields of ripening grain.
I am in the morning hush,
I am in the graceful rush
Of beautiful birds in circling flight,
I am the star shine of the night.
I am in the flowers that bloom,
I am in a quiet room.
I am in the birds that sing.
I am in each lovely thing.
Do not stand at my grave and cry,
I am not there. I do not die.

Although I did not weep for you when you died, Renee Fleming's song about the moon reminds me how easy it is to remember you through tears. I miss you.

Fun facts: Light takes about 1.3 seconds to reach Earth from the Moon. So, when you and I were viewing it from opposite coasts, moonlight was reaching both of us at the same time. But we weren't seeing the Moon as it was at that instant! And to put things in perspective, as I write today, there is a star in the constellation Pisces, known only as HD217107—a star like our own sun. The light that left it about the time you were courting Mother is still on its way to me, scheduled to arrive sometime in 2023. You and I are connected by astrophysics.

I was stunned when I read in a long letter to Mother that you liked Gretchen, Webb, and me from the start and hoped that we would come to accept you.

At last, I see you. As I stare at your picture, I wish you could look back at me.

I no longer wonder what to call you. I will call you by your name.

In the past I would often pronounce your name with a harshness that aired judgment, almost as if I could hear the word "wall" in your name. When Mother, Webb, and I moved into 7 Williams Road with you and Bill in 1959, I brought along my own "wall," a psychological barrier that became somewhat porous over time, but which only recently has crumbled.

For decades I believed that calling you by a different name would magically change my image of you. But I had it backwards. It wasn't your name that needed changing. The "wall" I had built had to come down. When I let go of "*Wall*-ter," I realized that Walter had been there all along. Your name is perfect.

When I say it now, it is often with a slight catch in my voice. With the initial release of air following the soft circular formation of my mouth, I can feel the great affection I now have for you.

Walter holding Scott, 1019 Alvarado, ca. 1979.

It is at a surface where many of our most interesting and useful phenomena occur. We live for example on the surface of a planet . . . it is essentially at a surface of a plant where sunlight is converted to a sugar . . . much of biology is concerned with reactions at a surface.

—From Walter's 1956 Nobel lecture in Stockholm, Sweden

Infant Walter Brattain , Amoy, China, early 1903.

Look at you, the young scientist! I see you are eager to offer your first insights into surface properties, a lifelong focus that culminated in your lecture fifty-three years later when you received the Nobel Prize in physics. Your parents, equally observant, would have smiled when seeing this picture, understanding your wordless narrative.

What fun I have had expanding my understanding of you. Above all, it is your consistency that informed all your relationships and accomplishments. You remained grounded in family and mentors, to forebears, and the scientific method. I was moved by your commitment to your family and colleagues, your sense of equality, your longtime friendship to John Bardeen, which led to your discovery of the transistor effect and beyond. But it's the playful episodes—those unexpected moments when nonsense rules— that I love most. In this letter, I'll remind you of three of those: a final exam at Whitman, a letter about pecans, and a stunning conclusion to the Nobel celebration.

Talk about unexpected!

John Bardeen's biographical memoir, written after your death, includes key details about your undergraduate years beginning in 1920. The following story about the final exam in Professor Brown's class includes a great "gotcha" moment, the kind that could only take place between friends who have great respect for one another:

> With financial help from an aunt [likely Bertha], Walter followed his parents and attended Whitman College. He was stimulated to study physics by an outstanding teacher, Benjamin H. Brown, who had many students who went on to successful careers. The physics majors in 1924 in addition to Brattain were Walker Bleakney (professor at Princeton), Vladimir Rojansky (professor at Union and Harvey Mudd colleges), and E. John Workman (president, New Mexico School of Mines), all of whom had distinguished careers. The members of this famous class were known as the "four horsemen of physics."

> Bleakney tells an anecdote about Brattain's student days that illustrates the determination in response to a challenge that he showed in later years:

> Once he asked Professor Brown about a problem, and Brown said we could not solve it because we had not yet studied the necessary tools. But Walter persisted, and Brown said to him, "If you solve it, I will excuse you from the final exam and give you a grade of 90." Of course, Walter rose to the challenge and in a few days he did achieve the solution. Brown sheepishly admitted he had made a mistake but lived up to his promise. When the other three of us were slaving over the final exam Walter was gleefully chortling on the sideline. But we had the last laugh. When the final grades came out Walter's was the lowest in the class! You can be sure we did not let him forget that.

You reflected in several interviews on an exchange you had with your mentor Benjamin Brown:

> I asked Brown about going on [in physics]. I told him that I didn't want to go on unless I could be at least better than average. In fact, I think I asked him whether he thought I had what it took to be a good physicist. I didn't want to be a mediocre one. And he assured me that he thought I was capable of being a good physicist.

After Whitman College, you received an M.A. at the University of Oregon, then a Ph.D. At the University of Minnesota in 1929. You described choosing your major because you liked the subjects of physics and math. You found English studies and foreign language learning difficult.

Your Ph.D. thesis was titled "Efficiency of Excitation by Electron Impact and Anomalous Scattering in Mercury Vapor." You were at the right institution at the right time: J. H. Van Vleck was there, teaching one of the first courses in quantum theory in the United States. Your interest in electrons and surface states never lost traction with you.

Following your 1929 graduation, you worked several months for the Radio Division of the National Bureau of Standards, where you met Joseph Becker of Bell Labs, who had just presented a paper and was looking to hire a scientist who could think for himself. You met both criteria. While it was your nature to be respectful of others for whom you were working, you also knew when it was appropriate to speak out and speak up. If hired as a scientist, you would be willing to argue with your boss.

In 1931, you and Becker began work on copper oxide, one of the better-known semiconductors. As you explained, "The Bell System was interested in this material because of its rectifying properties and possible use as a modulator of electrical communication signals."

By 1940 you had shifted your focus to the purification of another semiconductor, silicon. Most research at Bell Labs was on hold following the December 1941 Japanese attack on Pearl Harbor. The military sent out a call for scientists to work on the magnetic detection of submarines. You quickly signed up to help. During World War II you were associated for twenty-two months with the National Defense Research Committee at Columbia University.

*The creative element in the mind of man . . . emerges
in as mysterious a fashion as those elementary particles
which leap into momentary existence in great cyclotrons,
only to vanish again like infinitesimal ghosts.*

—Loren Eiseley

*There's always a starting point, a seed. And the one
seed of technology with the most things emerging from
it is obvious: the transistor. The transistor led to the
microchip, and that led to the incredible amount of intelligence we have in the palm of our hand today. Every bit
of technology we have in our computers, smartphones,
and tablets, or in the huge computers and hard disks in
the data centers, that's all thanks to the transistor. It's
the one invention that hasn't really been replaced. (Popular Mechanics, November 17, 2014)*

—Steve Wozniak, co-founder of Apple

And now for the hard part. I've been working on my letter to you for
two years, starting with the beginning and ending segments, saving
the meat of the sandwich for last: the discovery of the transistor. I
never expected it to take this long, but I suddenly realized that I want
to hold on to this experience—like that evening in 1982 when you
came for dinner and your trousers got caught on the back of your
chair, holding you in place. So please allow me to grab hold of your
shirt collar as you head for the exit!

After he read *Crystal Fire: The Birth of the Information Age*, Webb
wrote to co-author Lillian Hoddeson, a senior research physicist at the
University of Illinois, expressing his gratitude for the research she and
Michael Riordan did into you and your colleagues' lives and careers.
In reply, Hoddeson wrote how much she admired you as a scientist
and as a human being. Webb and I both loved learning of her respect
for you and the delightful interviews she had with you.

In 2022, I also wrote Hoddeson after reading her book *True Genius:
The Life and Science of John Bardeen*, co-written with Vicki Daitch,

which contained the story of his subsequent research and second Nobel Prize in 1972. John remains the only physicist who has been awarded a Nobel Prize in physics twice. Hoddeson knew John Bardeen well and was aware of his deep affection for you as a friend and colleague. I wrote in the hope of obtaining copies of some of your and Bardeen's correspondence. Most of it, however, is held at the University of Illinois archives, which I one day hope to visit.

Broken Genius: The Rise and Fall of William Shockley, by Joel Shurkin, covers not only Shockley's childhood, his scientific genius, and career highlights, but also his eventual descent from fame to ignominy. Three major factors contributed to his fall: his unwillingness to share power and decision-making with subordinates, his beliefs that Blacks were overall less intelligent than Whites, and his promotion of eugenics. To many, he was variously a racist or an advocate of Nazi-style experiments in human selective breeding.

Your biography could well be titled *Grounded Genius: Walter Brattain's Journey from Plowman to Physicist*. It is long overdue. Who will write it?

The story of the key players in the discovery of the transistor began in Princeton, when your brother Bob introduced you to John Bardeen. John and Bob were graduate students, both physics majors, when they met in 1934, and quickly became good friends, bridge partners and bowling competitors, playing on a Princeton bowling league. One weekend Bob suggested that you join them for a two-day round of bridge playing. You all enjoyed each other so much that it became a frequent activity.

After World War II, Mervin Kelly, the president of Bell Laboratories, was eager to move forward with semiconductor research. He selected scientists to be part of a newly formed Solid-State Division, with a research focus on developing a semiconductor switch to replace the limited vacuum tube. William Shockley and Stanley O. Morgan led the team. In turn, Shockley chose you, an experimental physicist who had an uncanny ability to devise and build anything, and John Bardeen, a theoretical physicist. Also involved were Gerald Pearson, an experimental physicist, Robert Gibney, a physical chemist, and Hilbert Moore, an electrical engineer.

You later described the experience of working with that group of scientists:

> I cannot overemphasize the rapport of this group. We would meet together to discuss important steps almost on the moment of an afternoon. We would discuss things freely, one person's remarks suggesting an idea to another. We went to the heart of many things during the existence of this group and always when we got to the place where something had to be done, experimental or theoretical, there was never any question as to who was the appropriate man in the group to do it.

Shockley was intent on designing the first semiconductor amplifier. When his device failed, he asked John and you to figure out why. The larger team worked on various experiments with mixed results, looking for amplification.

Shockley often worked alone, coming up with potential designs and experimental possibilities, many of which he asked John and you to try. You and John had a marvelous time: John proposed experiments, which you then carried out, meticulously recording your observations. John interpreted the results and recommended alternative experiments.

During the "Miracle Month" from November 17 to December 23, 1947, you and John came up with one innovative idea after another. In early December, John suggested replacing silicon with germanium, which resulted in partial success. You built several devices—each one a little better than the last—and it all came together on Tuesday, December 16. Your genius idea was to place a ribbon of gold foil around a plastic triangle, cutting it through one of the points. When the point of the triangle touched the germanium, electric current entered through one gold contact and increased—amplified—as it rushed out the other. You had created the first point-contact transistor.

Although pleased with the results, Shockley was livid that he had not played an active role in the crucial experiment. His colleagues agreed that after that moment, he was never the same. Whatever sense of camaraderie he had enjoyed with the research group had been shattered.

On December 23, after days of repeating the experiment to confirm your observations, you presented your findings to the VIPs at Bell Labs. You had invented the first working solid state amplifier.

You later recalled in an interview Shockley's reaction:

> He called both Bardeen and me in separately, shortly after the demonstration, and told us that sometimes the people who do the work don't get the credit for it. He thought then that he could write a patent, starting with the field effect, on the whole damn thing, to include this. I said, "Oh hell, Shockley, there's enough glory in this for everyone!"
>
> It's only after it was found that there was a patent [from the 1930s] by [Julius] Lilienfeld that read on the field effect, that this was abandoned. I don't think this would have gotten through the Patent Department. Before our patent was written, Bardeen and I were both privately questioned as to the other's participation. Both of us said that it was a joint project.

Shockley, distraught with his role as an outsider, spent the next few weeks working in isolation, obsessively intent on figuring out an even better transistor, one for which he would not have to share credit with John and you. Aware that the point-contact transistor would be difficult to manufacture, Shockley labored over designs for a different type, the junction transistor.

The Bell Labs lawyers had their work cut out for them in writing patents for the device.

Lilienfeld's patent was for a device controlling electrical current almost identical to Shockley's original idea. As the point-contact transistor was undeniably different, the lawyers filed a patent with yours and John's names.

You and John had designed and constructed the device but had not given it a name. Calling it a "point-contact solid state amplifier" was less than snappy. You asked your colleague John Pierce, who was word-savvy (he went on to become an accomplished science fiction writer), for a suggestion. He walked through the logic of a variety of names until coming up with "transistor." "That's it!" you said.

A ballot then went out to thirty-one people—staff, executives, and members of the solid-state team asking them to indicate their top three name choices from the following:

___Semiconductor Triode

___Surface States Triode

___Crystal Triode

___Solid Triode

___Iotatron

___Transistor

___(Other Suggestion)

We know which one won.

Attorneys filed four patents on the initial solid-state amplifier. Two were based on Shockley's original design for the field-effect transistor, one was for the device you and John built, and one was for Shockley's improved version, to be called a junction transistor.

Two patents were accepted: The point-contact transistor and the junction transistor.

The point-contact transistor patent was granted on June 17, 1948, as #2,524,035, U.S. Patent Office.

The Bell Labs sent out this announcement about the transistor:

June 30, 1948

TO ALL MEMBERS OF THE LABORATORIES:

A special demonstration for members of the press is being held at the Laboratories today in preparation for the first public announcement tomorrow, July 1, of an important research discovery recently made by members of our staff. As a member of the Laboratories team, interested in all the achievements of our organization, you are being given this advance information on the discovery, which when fully developed is expected to play a highly significant role in the future of electronics and electrical communication.

What is to be demonstrated is a new device, known as a Transistor, which though wholly different in structure and principle, will perform nearly all the functions of ordinary vacuum tubes. . . . In appearance, the device is strikingly simple. In consists of a small metal cylinder, three-quarters of an inch long. Contained therein are two hair-thin wires touching a tiny piece of semi-conductor soldered to a metal base. Experiments with the Transistor in circuits have results in amplification as high as 100 to 1. Some test models have been operated as amplifiers at frequencies up to ten million cycles per second.

In today's press show a radio set constructed entirely without vacuum tubes, but using instead several of the tiny Transistors to provide amplification, will be demonstrated, as well as several important telephone uses.

An early issue of the "Bell Laboratories Record" will carry a complete story regarding the Transistor. Technical details are scheduled to appear in a forthcoming issue of "The Physical Review."

BELL TELEPHONE LABORATORIES INCORPORATED.

Soon after the announcement, you wrote a letter to your mother, in which you enclosed copies of articles from *Time* and *Newsweek* hailing the discovery.

July 10, 1948

Dear Mother,

We are glad that you are getting some enjoyment out of the recent notoriety of Bardeen and myself. It was somewhat amusing to compare the treatment we got with that given to some other discoveries in the last few years of somewhat lesser importance. That, however, is neither here nor there since the scientific publication in the July 15 issue of *Physical Review* and the future developments will be the final measure of its significance. What will probably be the best semi popular exposé will be the August 1 issue of *Electronics*.

As for the shekels, I have already gotten one above average raise and in the way of the laboratories will probably get several more. If I wanted to sell my soul for a mess of pottage, could probably do so now very easily.... To have had a share in doing something of this kind is to me worth many shekels. A little more than a year ago I would not have given two bits for my chances either. Another interesting slant is as follows: it has been suspected since about the time I graduated from college, that something of this nature should be possible. Becker and I did some thinking about it back in 1935. Before the war, Shockley raised the question again, and after the war, he continued to think about it. Actually all the ways that were thought of were patented, (including Shockley's as it turned out), but none of them worked. In spite of all this, the way the transistor works is new and the discovery was the result of not just trying to make something this way but of doing experiments to better understand the fundamentals of the electronic structure of solids. . . . It is the biggest advance in the semiconductor field since the discovery of the solid rectifier. . . . The research was not, of course, directed to this goal. That would not be research. The work was directed to the understanding of the fundamental processes.

It certainly is nice to have the work that you have been doing for 15 years crowned by such a result. One, however, has need to be very humble when one looks back and sees how many places one could have made a wrong turn. One is also humble when he thinks of others in the field doing good work and coming very close only to have somebody else come along and use the results of such work as well as our own to build up to the final result.

I would like to get a copy of the Walla Walla newspaper account if possible. One of the boys in our publicity department went to Whitman for a year and it was he who sent the news to a friend on the Walla Walla paper along with some extra info about Professor Brown, etc.

The word is "trans-istor" not "trans-itor."

Love to you all,

Walter

Official Bell Labs photo (1948) of Shockley, Bardeen, and Brattain. Walter hated this pose because it was his microscope and he thought he should be sitting there.

Walter's preferred image of Brattain and Bardeen (R) at work, with Shockley looking on.

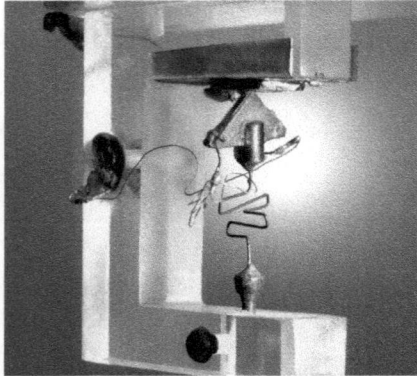

The original point contact transistor, designed on December 17, 1947 by John Bardeen and Walter Brattain. Demonstrated to the Solid State Team on December 23, 1947.

Following the June 1948 announcement of the discovery of the transistor, the research team continued to struggle. Shockley suggested experiments, such as improving the point-contact transistor, which you and John inferred would keep you busy while Shockley continued with potentially productive research.

As an attempt to salvage the research group, you wrote Shockley a letter at the end of January 1950.

January 31, '50

Dear Bill,

A few remarks from our talk of yesterday. It appears that the discovery of the transistor has ruined the best research team I ever had the privilege to work in. I have realized for some time that something was wrong but it was only last night that I saw this clearly. I see now that the publicity should have used no names. I think there was an effort in the beginning to give the credit to the group as a whole. The patent department squelched this. I know Gibney resented his treatment and I think Pearson felt left out, but the latter I don't know for sure. Anyway the milk has been spilt.

It appears to me that a great part of our misunderstanding has been caused by my misdirected and inadequate attempts to get the group back on the pre-transistor basis. I admit that I have had a selfish interest in trying to do this. I see now that my efforts are just making matters worse and jeopardizing among other things our friendship. With these remarks I intend to cease and desist.

In conclusion, let me say that I believe you have more to gain personally by trying to get the team back together than you have by concerning yourself about how you spend your time and what you personally do, etc. Please believe that I am sincere in this.

Walter

Dissatisfied with the research conditions at the Bell Labs, Bardeen accepted a position with the University of Illinois Urbana-Champaign in 1951, a decision you endorsed, but grieved for the outcome. You would be losing your closest research colleague of your career. Although you and John remained dear friends for the decades to come, and would spend time together at conferences and during personal visits, you never were able to work together again.

Between 1958 and 1980, you and Mother traveled the world meeting with members of the scientific community. These pilgrimages proved life-renewing for you both. Your need to remain connected to the research community in which you had lived for decades rekindled Mother's love of traveling and her absolute joy in meeting and forming friendships with others. Your travels included China, Japan, Korea, Russia, Iran, and Europe. Had she lived a bit longer, Mother could

Bad Schachen Hotel, Lindau, Germany, June 1965. L to R: Walter, Mother, George de Hevesy, 1943 Nobel Prize winner in Chemistry.

*Mother and Walter, likely at a conference
in Bad Schachen, Lindau, Germany, 1965.*

Walter (sitting across from Mother) toasts John Bardeen (far left) at his 60th birthday party, University of Illinois.

Walter and John at the Walla Walla Country Club, 1971.

At the 25th anniversary celebration of the transistor at Bell Labs.

*Mother and you on dusty-blue love seat (the twin sofa facing the one on which
you two sat when I spied on you from the kitchen in 1957).*

At Bell Labs.

have created a stunning saga of your travels together, weaving photographs into her journals.

> *"Brattain and Bardeen, I would say, they loved one
> another as much as two men can. They were two very
> complementary human beings. It was like Bardeen was
> the brains of this joint organism and Brattain was the
> hands."*

> —Michael Riordan, co-author, Crystal Fire

Your friendship with colleague John Bardeen remained one of your
most meaningful human connections.

Nick Holonyak, a colleague of John Bardeen at the University of
Illinois, told stories [in an interview quoted in *True Genius*] about
John's and your extraordinary friendship, which went beyond mutual
professional respect. He captured your colorful verbal exchanges as well
as the deep sentiment between you two. I was especially moved by his
telling of John's reaction upon hearing of your death. Even though you
spent your final years in Seattle's Jacobsen Nursing Home and would
have been unable to communicate with—even recognize—your dear
friend and colleague, your relationship remained, for John, every bit as
alive as it had been when you worked together at Bell Labs. Reading
this description brought me as close to you as anything I have read
about you in thirty years.

Holonyak recalled that Bardeen had phoned him on the same day
he learned of your passing. Nick instantly knew something was wrong.
Usually if Bardeen wanted to talk, he would walk over to Holonyak's
office and sit down for a while. "And I'd drop anything and everything I was doing, because however long he wanted to stay or talk, we
would talk." But upon your death, Bardeen had called instead. Nick
was aware that his wife Kay was waiting outside, but he just let John
speak. "John stayed on the phone a long time and was obviously very
upset, for Brattain had been really truly his partner." At one point
during the conversation, John whispered, "I'm next."

A good steward of your award and ensuing fame, you traveled around the world to lecture and perform positions of leadership. For example, you were chairman of the International Commission on the Physics of Semiconductors and U.S. delegate to the Assembly of the International Union of Pure and Applied Physics.

You had felt the lure to retire to the Pacific Northwest even before you and Mother married. Washington had always been a part of your core identity. The rugged outdoors and the seeds of your education held deep roots.

In 1962, President Louis B. Perry invited you to spend one week a month teaching at Whitman, continuing until you retired from the Bell Labs in 1967. You worked with senior level physics students and developed a science course for non-majors. You were quoted as saying, "I feel that no man should obtain a bachelor's degree without having some concept of how things happen in the world. The world of science is the development of concepts that give us an understanding of how things happen." Although taken before you retired from the Bell Laboratories, the photo of you at the blackboard captures you in one of your most comfortable activities: explaining science as you understood it, the joy of understanding surface properties and beyond.

To you, the measure of academic success was to have inspired even one or two students to continue studying, to do something important. Just as you had experienced the mentoring and encouragement from your teachers and professors, you wanted at some core level to influence others in that same deep way.

Today, you would be at the front lines of scientists promoting a global approach to the climate crisis. Already in the 1970s you were promoting wind power as an alternate energy source and were tuned in to the challenges facing the international economy and of feeding the world's growing population.

The Walter Houser Brattain Lectureship Fund was established at Whitman. You were a member of the board of overseers, co-founder of the Benjamin H. Brown Professorship of Physics and of the Roland E. Miller Scholarship Award in Music. The Walter H. Brattain Physics

Amphitheater, located in the Whitman Hall of Science, was completed in 1981.

November 2020

Fifty-three years later, I'm remembering this moment of your guiding me down the aisle in 1967. My hand reached under your arm as we walked together, hands connected. You were as focused on the correct path ahead as you were in the photograph with Mother as you headed to meet President and Mrs. Kennedy at the White House in 1962. As we walked together, I could see you out of the corner of my eye. Now, in my mind's eye, after years of delay, I am looking straight at your face, seeing those intent yet kind eyes. When Chris and I married in 1982, he walked me down the aisle. If I could re-do it, I would ask you to walk with me. That was one of the last times you and I were together before you moved to the Seattle care center.

The lifelong theme of my life—my essence—has been about connection to others, the timing of which I wanted to be on my own terms. What happened between you and me was that for years I shied away from forming any deep bond with you. Even as I started working on the family-history project, "Chasing Shadows," years ago, I felt little drive to write about your life.

You remained in the shadows. What has evolved during the past two years—wonderfully—is that your shadow has been chasing me. At some point I turned just enough to see you out of my peripheral vision, and, gradually, to look at you directly, closely. And now I cannot look away. The gift of finally seeing you, knowing you, and posthumously loving you, has been one of the greatest joys of my life.

I love you, Walter!

Debi

Walter walked me down the aisle at my wedding to Gary Agenbroad, 1967.

*Debi and Chris's wedding, 1982. (L to R): Walter, Jon
St. Hilaire, Chris, Debi, Gretchen, Mother.*

IV. "The Lightning Has Struck"

A Journey to Stockholm

The Nobel Prize in Physics 1956 was awarded jointly to William Bradford Shockley, John Bardeen and Walter Houser Brattain "for their researches on semiconductors and their discovery of the transistor effect."

—The Royal Swedish Academy of Sciences

Walter, before you go . . . I must return to your transistor effect discovery and what happened in November 1956. Just a year before you and I met, your world was turned on its head with the announcement that you, John Bardeen, and William Shockley had been awarded the 1956 Nobel Prize in Physics. You wrote marvelous reflections during your time in Stockholm, and I had such fun learning about you and the events surrounding the quintessential scientific accolade. Science enthusiasts and much of the world will remember you as a Nobel Prize winner. Your "Saga of an Expedition to Stockholm, Sweden" introduced me to one of my most treasured images of you.

As a complement to your moment being recognized by King Gustav VI Adolf, I was equally excited to read about something few are aware of: your induction into the Society of the Ever Smiling and Leaping Frog, or as I call it, your "Nobel Lite" award. Read on. . . .

Nineteen fifty-six. During the final days of October, you had heard rumors about a possible Nobel Prize announcement. It wasn't the first time you had been told "this could be your year" to receive the quintessential award for discovering the transistor effect. If so, would it be John Bardeen and you? Or would the prize include Shockley as well? But hearing from colleagues that you had a good chance of winning was very different from receiving a call from someone who had sure knowledge of the United Press announcement. Or better yet, receiving the official cable from the Royal Swedish Academy of Sciences. As

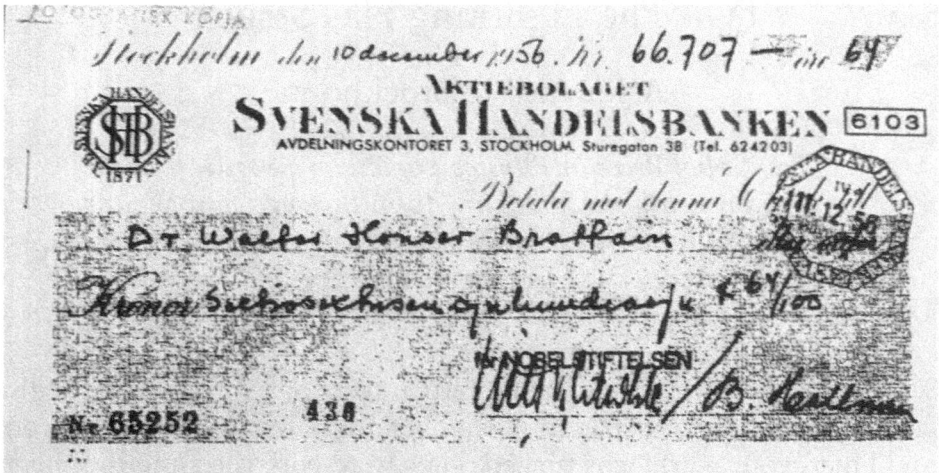

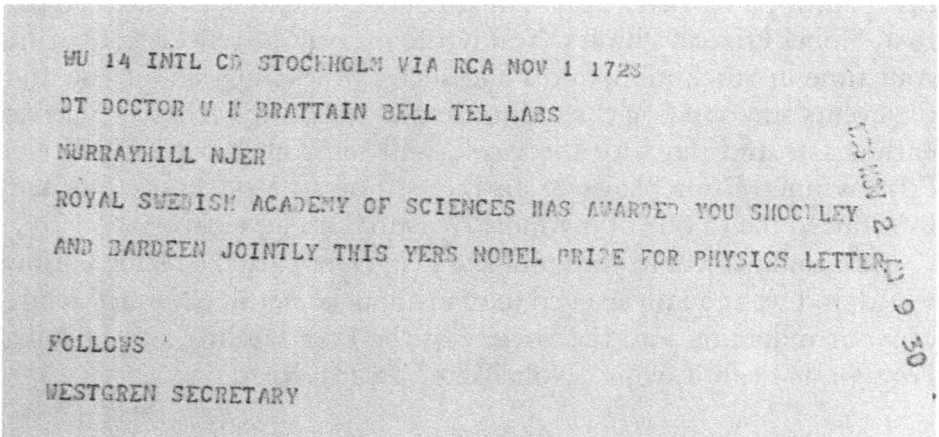

*The check for Walter's share of the prize money and the
telegram notifying him about the award, 1956.*

a skeptic, you would wait until you had seen the evidence, held the proof in your hands.

Early on the morning of November 1st, an ambitious young reporter showed up at your door at 7 Williams Road in Chatham, eager to get the story of your first reaction to receiving the Nobel Prize. But you knew better than to jump the gun by offering even tentative remarks, details that could be inaccurate, even misinterpreted. Instead, you knew the best reaction would be to profess ignorance and encourage him to call the Bell Labs for any official word. You likely closed the door and finished your breakfast as you scanned the local newspaper. You might have seen a reminder of the Chatham School Board meeting that you would attend that evening. After all, your school board committee had important information to present to the other members. Before grabbing your briefcase, you would have kissed Keren goodbye, then (I imagine) looked at her with raised eyebrows, in anticipation and incredulity at what the coming hours might bring. Dashing for the car, you would have seen the undeterred reporter still waiting. As you drove off, he followed you as you drove to the Murray Hill laboratories, still in pursuit of the big story.

Although the cable from Stockholm wouldn't reach you for another twenty-four hours, your colleagues at the Bell Labs moved ahead with an announcement.

NOBEL PRIZE AWARDED TO TRANSISTOR INVENTORS

The 1956 Nobel Prize for physics has been awarded to Walter H. Brattain of the Laboratories and John Bardeen and William Shockley, former Laboratories staff members. The trio received the award for their invention of the transistor, which was announced by Bell Laboratories in 1948. . . .

Conferred by the Swedish Royal Academy of Sciences in Stockholm, the prize is accompanied by a monetary award of $38,633 which will be divided among the three recipients. . . .

In addition to the formal announcements and acknowledgments, you saved the intimate and endearing correspondence with your parents during the days immediately following the life-changing news. As you read your father's letter, the salutation "Walter Boy" likely added an air of normalcy to the incredible happenings. To him, your win was both natural and deserved. No matter how the events of early November might change how the world saw you, you would remain, at your core, "Walter Boy." Your father's clever takedown of Shockley is worth quoting in full:

Nov 5, 1956

Dear Mother, Mari and Dad,

As you already know the lightning has struck. I am trying to write this as the telephone rings and the messages still pour in. I am of course proud and happy but very humble when I think of all that went together to make it possible. First, all that you and Dad did to bring me up and to try and knock off some of the rougher corners and also to keep me in one piece.

Then Brown and Bratton, Milne, Tate, Van Vleck [teachers] and many others. Finally Becker and all my other colleagues at the Bell Labs who really made it possible for Bardeen and I and Shockley too to do what we did. When I think of all this I realize that it is not quite fair for individuals to be singled out in such a manner. I can only hope that I can be worthy of the events to come.

I am of course extremely glad that I have at least brought honor to my family and to all my forebears.

Love, Walter

Orogrande, Idaho
Nov. 8, 1956

Dear Walter Boy:

This letter is late because confirmation of the award was very slow reaching me. Mari's message to Fielder's store, Orogrande, Idaho, reached me via W.U. to Grangeville, then relayed to Elk City on Pacific Telephone, thence over Forest Service Telephone to Max Jensen at Filber's store. The way it came was that my sister had won the Nobel Prize. Of course, I knew that was wrong, but I hoped it was, what it turned out to be.

Walter Boy, it is almost too good to be true! But it is true. The little boy that I promised Uncle Walter should be named after him, actually has grown up and his hair has grown grey, and here is to be given the prize in his life study and effort.

Of course in my feelings, there is nothing strange about the result, so far as your mother is concerned, for she gave her all to her children, and fully deserves the reward. So far as I am concerned it seems to me I have fallen far short of what she gave, except I shared with her an undying love for her and our children.

Ottilie has not told me when you go, except that you, Keren, and Bill are going.

Forget all the bickering. Let [Shockley's] conscience take care of him.

Drink deep of the joy you and John will get out of it. And if a little slops over on him, it can't be helped.

I moved down off our mountain at Gene Mulcahy's request as another snow storm would make it hard to get down without shoveling.

I will stay here until the coming of a man from Texas is resolved.

At this table it is cheaper to eat venison or elk than bacon. Bacon costs money.

Love to you, Walter Boy, to Keren and to Bill, from your father and grandfather, with all the good wishes for a grand time, and especially tell John [Bardeen] that some day Ottilie and I want to meet him and his.

Again, Love from Dad,

Ross

In September 2018, as Chris and I looked through many of your papers in the Whitman College archives, I uncovered the following letter nestled in the file of Nobel Prize correspondence.

Nov. 2, 1956

Mr. Walter H. Brattain,

Murray Hill, New Jersey.

Dear Sir:

We can offer a new crop of shelled pecans, packed in 5# cartons at $6.00 for the 5# postpaid anywheres [sic] in the United States or Alaska. These are all perfect halves, and packed in beautiful containers.

There [sic] will make ideal Thankgiven [sic] and Xmas gifts for you and your friends.

Mail check for whatever orders you care for us to fill.

Yours very truly,

NATCHEZ PECAN SHELLING CO.

Krouse

P.S. Want to congratulate you on winning the 1956 Nobel prize.

You surely saved and savored this letter for its ironic humor. It was not the only time in the glow of your Nobel prize that pomp and formality would be juxtaposed with the mundane and ridiculous. There would be another, much larger in scale, turn toward the frivolous.

As the frenetic energy around the Nobel Prize announcement settled down, John Bardeen decided that, despite his intense involvement in another research project at the University of Illinois, he wanted to go to Stockholm, and the two of you arranged to travel together. Although the Bardeens opted to leave their children at home, you and Keren chose to include Bill.

Knowing what to wear in Stockholm was a problem. Keren went into New York for a day of looking and was able to pick out what she needed, including a hat that you described as "the hat to end all hats." Almost tearfully, Keren reported her purchase, fearful that you would be angry because of how much she had spent. Rather than finding it extravagant, you were delighted she found the perfect complement to her coat. A big question for you was what to wear to the Nobel ceremony. In Chatham, you had consulted with a neighbor, Ben Pfeiffer, who happily loaned you one of his two white-tie outfits. I bet he smiled, knowing that his formal attire would stand before the king of Sweden at the Nobel ceremony.

Bardeen, Shockley, and you held conference calls as you figured out some scheduling concerns, such as the order in which you would deliver your Nobel lectures on December 11, the day after the awards ceremony. John and you wanted Shockley to speak between the two of you—where you thought he belonged—and only through some fast talking by Bardeen were you able to convince him of the rationale for that.

The evening before you flew to Sweden, your friends fêted you in New York. You wrote, ". . . [E]specially poignant to me was the thorough going-over that I received from my good friends and colleagues Pearson and Garrett. This was something I will never forget. It brought tears to my eyes. An honest man cannot but admit that the acclaim of his closest associates is sweet music indeed: a very high spot if not the highest of all."

First stop: Denmark. Upon arriving in Copenhagen, you and John were welcomed at the Niels Bohr Institute, where you were to deliver a lecture at a seminar on theoretical physics. Fearing he might miss your comments, Bohr insisted that the schedule be reordered to put you and John at the beginning, pushing back the other presentations. Ever thoughtful, you were concerned about the "poor fellow who had to wait until 4:30 to start."

This was a grand time of reconnection for you and John, as you spent most days together in Denmark and Göteborg [now Gothenburg], Sweden, before traveling together by train to Stockholm, where you and John were met on the platform by various dignitaries and introduced to your "attendants," who would be your personal assistants during your stay in Sweden. You later reported that without the help of Gunnar Lorentzon, your attendant, you would not have been able to get through those demanding days. Following introductions, you were escorted to Stockholm's Grand Hotel, where your family and the Bardeens checked into neighboring fourth-floor rooms.

December 10, the anniversary of Alfred Nobel's death, was the official Nobel Prize Day.

The "butterflies" leading up to the ceremony caused some last-minute panic. As you dressed for the event, you inventoried which parts of your attire you could claim as your own: "underwear, shoes, socks, shirt, vest, overcoat, scarf and hat." The rest were borrowed, including Phi Beta Kappa and Sigma Xi keys from your Bell Labs colleague John Hornbeck. As you were getting dressed, Bardeen phoned with an urgent request to borrow a tie and a vest. There had been "an accident" with his tie, and his vest had returned from the hotel laundry colored an unintended green. John wore one of your vests that day.

You described the Nobel Prize ceremony and banquet in wonderfully rich detail:

> The Lorentzons arrived all dressed up . . . and all five of us got into the car reserved for us, number 18, at 15:30 sharp. We were driven through the streets of Stockholm in the gathering darkness and very dense afternoon traffic—stop and go and sit—we wondered if we'd ever make it. We

Bill (R) and Ekeberg's grandson, who, although neither could understand the other, had a good time together. This photo made the front page of the Swedish newspaper the following day.

Nobel Ceremony December 19, 1956.
Front Row (L to R): Emmy and May Shockley (wife and mother), Jane Bardeen, Keren Brattain and son Bill, Unidentified.

King Gustaf VI Adolf presents the Nobel Prize to Walter Brattain.

noticed some people obviously going to the same place hurrying along on foot, making much better time than we were. Our driver, at least, was not worried. It was the 25th year he had driven Laureates to the Concert Hall. Finally we arrived. He took Keren, Bill and Mrs. Lorentzon to a cloak room where they were to wait for Lorentzon. He then took me to the anteroom and went on. There we waited until the audience was all seated and the Royal family had come in, to the fanfare of trumpets. We marched in, to more fanfare, in a double line, each with a sponsor on his left, led by two student marshals in sashes with the Swedish colors, and sat down in a V of chairs formed around the podium on the stage—the Laureates on the right and sponsors on the left arm of the V facing each other and the audience at an angle. Everybody stood as we came in. Each one as he got to his seat made a bow or reverence to the Royal family and then sat down. I forgot to flip my [coattails] up and thus sat on them. Our view of the audience was excellent. The Royal Family was seated in a row of chairs just in front of the audience. In what would be the peanut gallery in the U.S. was the orchestra. Everybody except children, even the press, was in full dress.

The first item on the program was a speech by His Excellency Ekeberg in honor of Nobel on this 60th anniversary of his death. After this the orchestra played a Serenade by Dag Wirén. Next was the speech sponsoring the physics prize winners by Prof. Rudberg. He gave his speech from memory and did very well. All speeches were in Swedish, but at the end he turned to us and extended his remarks in English, mentioning the fact that we in a sense had stood on the shoulders of all the other workers in our field to mount a summit that they had not reached. As he mentioned each of our names we stood and walked forward on the stage facing the audience, where we each made a bow, then down the steps on our right one after the other. Here we went forward to accept our prize from the King, one at a time. You bow or make a reverence to the King, listen to him as he presents the medal and scroll, accept these in your left hand, leaving the other free to shake hands with the King. You then step past the King, sideways so as to not turn your back, bow to the Queen and continue sideways until reaching the stairs on the left. The correct procedure is to then make an inside turn, mount these stairs, and at the top face the audience and bow again, finally arriving back at your seat. Shockley went first and made all his bows properly. Bardeen came next, and as he stepped past the King to make his bow to the Queen, the King stepped back and got right between him and the Queen. I observed this, so gave the King plenty of room when my turn came. You do not really hear what is being said by the King. While you are receiving the prize a fanfare is being blown for the previous Laureate and anyway you are in such a state of mind that, even if the King shouted, you probably would not hear or remember. A common question in this regard said in fun is: "What did the King say?" I tried to say, "Thank you, Your Majesty," but maybe only my lips moved. . .

I did not at first see where Keren and Bill were sitting. They were in the front row to my right somewhat back of the way we were facing on the stage. When I went down the steps, I should have seen them but was so concerned with my behavior that I did not. It was only later that I turned my head and saw where they were sitting. I am sorry that I do not have a picture of the Concert Hall from where I looked at it. It was a grand sight, with tier on tier of seats in a horseshoe around the sides all filled with people. The front of the stage was banked with yellow chrysanthemums. At each door stood student marshals at attention who were relieved about every fifteen minutes by other students. On the stage back of us sat those Nobel Laureates, present, of other years and the members of the Academies and Institutes that have the responsibility of choosing the prize winners.

After all the awards had been presented, we stood up as the Swedish National Anthem was played and the King and Royal family walked out. We congratulated each other, stood in a group for pictures and proceeded, in a sense one by one back to the anteroom. We were supposed to turn in our medals and scrolls for exhibition at the dinner that night so we took a good look at them while we might. As I walked out there was a roving photographer taking a motion picture shot of me head on. It is not easy to walk naturally towards such an obstruction blocking one's path, but I did my best. Finally, I got to the anteroom where Lorentzon was waiting for me. I picked up my hat and coat and he took me to Keren, Bill and Mrs. Lorentzon and they congratulated me. I kissed both the ladies and we piled into our car, number 18, and went back to the hotel for a quick brush-up. Remember, all this had taken place in full evening dress. We straightened our ties, had a quick drink, then got back into our car and were taken to the Stock Exchange building.

Because the Swedes were feeling very bad about the world situation in general, and the Hungarian people in particular, they had decided to hold a smaller dinner than usual. There were 175 instead of 1,000, and it was held at the Stock Exchange rather than the Town Hall.

Back at the hotel we all met more or less at random, as I remember, in the lobby about 23:00. Some of the Laureates went on to bed. Bill did likewise. As we arrived, Lorentzon went immediately to arrange for a table for four in the dining room to proceed with the celebration. The party gradually grew to include the Bardeens and our attendants, and finally at the last Shockley and his wife, who had apparently been left behind in the shuffle, came wandering into the dining room alone. So we yelled at them and they came over and joined us. The bill for champagne, which we drank this night, came to about 200 kronor. It was a grand time; we were certainly in a hilarious frame of mind. Stories were told, can't remember now where everyone sat, but a royal time was had by all.

In his book about William Shockley, author Joel Shurkin detailed some of the Nobel Prize activities. He had obtained a copy of your Stockholm reflections, referring to them as "a marvelous sixty-two-page diary of their adventures at the Nobel ceremony," which he used as a reference in his chapter about the Nobel Prize. As I read Shurkin's take on the events of the days in Stockholm, I felt compassion for Shockley, who was at that point very much an outsider. Shurkin realized quickly while reading your account how close you and John were, both physically as you traveled and psychologically as friends and colleagues. "Shockley's arrival did not change the informal social structure that had evolved. The Bardeens and Brattains stuck together, spending time with the Shockleys only when necessary. A pleasant dinner together in New York was one thing; days together, apparently, were more than the men could tolerate."

I wanted to learn how someone gets nominated for a Nobel prize. According to Nobelprize.org, "The Nomination to the Nobel Prize in Physics is by invitation only." All information about the nominations is confidential and cannot be revealed until fifty years later. Thus, nominations specifics to the 1956 Nobel Prize were not posted on the website until 2006.

You were nominated a total of seven times over a four-year span. Thus, seven individuals recommended that you be awarded a Nobel Prize. John was nominated eight times during the same period, including one year, 1955, when one F. Loomis submitted the names Bardeen and Shockley for the prize. Shockley was nominated six times, and

Walter's parents visiting Keren and him in Chatham, New Jersey, early 1957.

in 1953, was not included in the recommendation by F. Nix. As it turned out, you and John could have won a Nobel Prize in 1953, or Bardeen and Shockley could have won in 1955. You three, all key in the discovery—spread as it was over time—deserved the prize.

In 1959, you nominated Charles Townes, who had nominated you three in 1956. John Bardeen nominated three individuals, including Townes. William Shockley did not make any nominations.

According to Neil Shurkin, Shockley wrote the Academy demanding to know if rumors that someone had opposed his nomination were true. Their response in essence was that it was none of his business; the nomination process is secret and he should just enjoy the honor.

The Presentation Speech by Professor E.G. Rudberg, member of the Nobel Committee for Physics, included a charming description of the transistor effect and its discovery. I am quoting just the final paragraph of his introduction.

> Your Majesties, Your Royal Highnesses, Ladies and Gentlemen.
>
> . . .
>
> Doctor Shockley, Doctor Bardeen, Doctor Brattain. The summit of Everest was reached by a small party of ardent climbers. Working from an advance base, they succeeded. More than a generation of mountaineers had toiled to establish that base. Your assault on the semiconductor problem was likewise launched from a high-altitude camp, contributed by many scientists. Yours, too, was a supreme effort—of foresight, ingenuity and perseverance, exercised individually and as a team. Surely, supreme joy befalls the man to whom those breathtaking vistas from the summit unfold. You must have felt it, overwhelmingly. This joy is now shared by those who laboured at the base. Shared, too, is the challenge of untrodden territory, now seen for the first time, calling for a new scientific attack.
>
> Thus salutes you, Nobel Laureates, the Royal Academy of Sciences.
>
> And now, my solemn duty, nay, my treasured privilege: to invite you to receive your award from the hands of His Majesty the King.

Late in the afternoon on December 16, your first day that included extended free time, you sat down with the dictating machine that had sat untouched in your hotel room since you arrived ten days earlier, and talked into this non-interrupting machine for four hours. This narration became "The Saga of an Expedition to Stockholm, Sweden, December 1956."

On December 19, you, Keren, and Bill flew back to Idlewild and then went home just 19 days after you had left. "An overall experience the likes of which one can hardly fully appreciate or much less properly describe. In a sense we had really come back to earth for the first time since November 1, 1956."

In the photo [p. 270], Keren sits perched on a stool. Your parents look ready to burst with pride while an unidentified colleague shares the moment. This picture captures both joy and uncertainty: a shared celebration with your parents and an uncertain future for your cancer-stricken wife, who died just weeks after this memorable reunion.

V. "Nobel Lite"

On Monday, December 10, 1956, John Bardeen, William Shockley, and you walked across the stage at the Stockholm Concert Hall to receive the Nobel Prize in physics. Three days later your same trio attended a second celebration organized by a group of high-spirited science students at Stockholm University. This event, where chemistry and physics laureates were inducted into the Society of the Ever Smiling and Leaping (or Jumping) Frog, could be called "Nobel Lite." Just three and a half miles from the site where you were awarded the quintessential international prize, you met again to accept what undoubtedly is one of the more "ribbeting" awards.

The best antidote to solemnity is buffoonery.

It's not hard to imagine that, after the formality and panoply of the Nobel ceremony, that some hi-jinks involving "smiling and leaping frogs" might be in order. The Swiss psychiatrist Carl Jung coined the term *enantiodromia* to refer to the process in which some extreme point of view transforms into its opposite. In this case an excess of gravitas must be relieved by some nonsense (and in this situation, considerable amounts of alcohol), so as to restore the Nobelists' mental balance. One might also think of the smiling and leaping frog as a way of poking fun at the "serious" enterprise of science, while honoring it at the same time. Either way, it's both a celebration of genius and a tether to some possibly inflated egos.

On royal occasions, there is a certain way to do everything, down to the smallest detail, something which you learned to your chagrin when you realized (or were told) that you had been sitting on your tuxedo tails during the official award ceremony. But it was a different story at the Society of the Ever Smiling and Leaping Frog. Forget decorum. Monday's fanfare and formal welcome by the King of Sweden were replaced by Thursday's swashbuckling greeting by frog order president Sven Westman, after which you and others, following Westman's croaked commands, hopped up to stand on their chairs in the middle of the festival.

In her article "Leaping Laureates" [The-scientist.com, Oct. 1, 2009], Andrea Gawrylewski writes, "This mysterious Order got its start in the winter of 1917, when a group of students in the Stockholm University science fraternity decided, in the nature of warm-hearted ribbing, to bestow a small metal frog upon a fellow classmate during their annual Christmas party. [In Swedish, the same word can mean both 'frog' and 'blunder'.] The next year, the recipient passed along the frog to another student."

The name "Ever Smiling and Leaping Frog" comes from a famous Swedish song called "Små Grodorna" ("Little Frogs"), sung to a children's ring dance performed around the midsommar pole (a festival pole decorated with lots of flowers). The date of December 13 coincides with the St. Lucia celebration, one of the most important Swedish holidays. The tradition of initiating Nobel laureates into the Order began in 1936.

Science students at Stockholm University sent letters to Nobel Prize attendees inviting them to the December 13th event. Although I have been unable to locate the correspondence you received in November 1956, the message surely would have been similar to this invitation sent to Richard Feynman, a 1965 Nobel Prize winner in physics:

October 27, 1965

Dear Sir,

The Union of Students of Science at the Stockholm University congratulates you sincerely on your being awarded the Nobel Prize.

On December 13th, we are having our Lucia celebration, a specifically Swedish tradition commemorating the return of light to our winter's darkness, to which said occasion we have made it a tradition to invite Nobel Prize winners of science.

We should very much appreciate your attending our celebration during which you will be dubbed a knight of the Order of the Ever Smiling and Jumping Frog like formerly most Nobel Prize winners of chemistry and physics.

On your arrival to Sweden we shall have the pleasure of sending you a formal invitation and we hope that you will reserve this evening for us.

Yours sincerely,

Lars Soderstrom
President

From Walter's "Saga of an Expedition" to Stockholm, Sweden

This (Thursday) was the night of the students' party and full dress was in order. Again, Keren put on her prettiest evening dress and we went down to the lobby to wait for our taxis. For some reason taxis were very scarce this evening. Lorentzon had arranged for one for us at 18:45. Bardeen's taxi came first, then we got ours about 19:00, and when we left the Shockleys were still waiting in the lobby. They did not arrive at the party until about one-half hour after us. Again we had a card showing our seating with the ladies we each were to escort. I found out who my lady was and had her well spotted when all of a sudden she disappeared, and then it was explained to us that those who are members of the Society of the Ever Smiling and Leaping Frog would come in to dinner in a separate march and since my lady was a member I would not see her until later. There was also an unattached lady in the same predicament so I escorted her in and found her place at the table. Sven Westman, president of the student body, was host. He sat in the middle of the head table facing the rest of the dining room. Barbro Levin, secretary of the students and hostess, sat on the other side facing him with Shockley on her right, and I was on the same side as the president with a lady between us. Back of us was a stage. The members of the Society of Frogs marched in, preceded by a great big green frog with a glowing cigar in his mouth and one eye blinking. This was punctuated by a song that they were all singing in regard to said frog. The frog was put on the stage and then when everybody was at the table, a student called for some other student to start a toast; a song was sung and at the end of the sound we all stood up and lifted our glasses and drank a first toast. For another song and toast we all stood on our chairs. This was quite a scramble as we had to help the ladies as well as climb up ourselves.

This was the first occasion that Shockley undertook to use some of his magic. He got up on his chair and got the attention of the audience and pulled a flower out of the air and presented it to our hostess, and then immediately proceeded to do it again, just to show he could, all with the proper patter. This was very well received and after he was through, the students sang "For He's a Jolly Good Fellow." I decided that Shockley wasn't going to be the only one that responded, and told the story about the cat who was a consultant and the student responded as before, but I'm afraid only those that knew their English well got the point.

Toward the end of the dinner a whole troupe of girls in their Lucia costumes—all dressed in white—very beautiful—came in singing, carrying glögg (wine punch) and served it to us.

Next came the ceremony of the Ever Smiling and Leaping Frog. Three masked individuals stood on the platform, one holding a candle so another could read what was on the back of a tremendous scroll and another one was holding the emblems of the frog to be awarded. The first award was made to the host and president of the student body and then two other individuals in the student body, one a girl, were awarded the emblem and then several professors. Those already members were wearing either a green sash—color of the frog—or a green frog on a green ribbon around their necks. Finally each of the Nobel Laureates present was awarded the emblem. After the ceremony was over the students put on a skit that was exceedingly well done, in Swedish. There was an English synopsis in front of us and the story was easy to follow. The students had worked into the skit the sequel of a transistor oscillator, a calculating machine and atomic energy along with a medieval setting. The main characters were a father, a daughter, the villain, and, of course, the hero. When this was over we proceeded out and down a few flights of stairs to a general sitting room. During this time the hall upstairs was being cleared for dancing. However, it was now 24:00 and we were all pretty tired. Most of the Nobel Laureates paid their respects to the host and hostess, had taxis called for and went back to the hotel and to bed.

Prior to reading your "Saga of an Expedition to Stockholm," I knew nothing of this delightful frog affair. The thought of you "scrambling" to get onto your chair has stuck with me and has become one of my more endearing images of you. And the frog medallion, what had happened to it? Did you toss it out in Sweden, a trivial token, or had it somehow made it back to Chatham and, possibly, to Walla Walla? I had seen no evidence of the lead amphibian when sorting through family treasures with Mother or subsequent to 1990. And, if I had seen one, what would I have concluded about such a frog anyway?

In the height of my curiosity about you in late 2019, I began to wonder if, by some chance, the green critter could have ended up in Portland with Bill. When Chris and I traveled to Portland in January 2020, I asked your granddaughter, Karen, if she had heard her dad mention a frog medallion. Of course, by that time, the frog had taken on new significance to me, and I hoped it had meant enough that you would have kept it long after the Stockholm week. Karen thought she had seen it in one of her dad's drawers and found it quickly. The frog is now "on loan" to us. It is much more than a chunk of painted lead. It is a direct connection both to you and to a great story. Each time I pick it up, I imagine you leaping onto your chair in a moment of levity, and I smile. It is a treasure.

Walter, I love reading your descriptions of the Nobel Prize announcement, preparations, presentation, and postscript. Throughout your life you maintained a certain formality in your actions and relations with others. Reading what you have written and what others have written about you, I'm moved by your need to do things the right or "proper" way. You might have learned this on the farm, where you oversaw the plowing of fields and cattle roundups. You applied those same strategies to your scientific work. You had to set up your experiments and report your observations with great attention to detail. Then during the Nobel ceremony, you monitored your colleagues' behavior to make sure you were following protocol, evident as you watched John Bardeen as he approached the King. I bet you did this as well during the playful frog ceremony. You would have been searching for the proper way to scramble onto the chair.

You were a scientist married to a scientist. Scientists want to explain the world, to bring order out of chaos. It's natural that your family life would be much quieter, more "adult" than the Miller crew's was. You weren't used to goofball adolescent behavior. When we Miller kids arrived in your life, you wouldn't have known how to handle the situation or us. What I saw in you as aloofness was merely your approach to life as you had always lived it. Unfortunately, I had little empathy for your formality until it was too late. I now see from your report of the "smiling and leaping frog" event that you had this playful side, a common ground where you and I might have met. Where we are meeting today in my imagination.

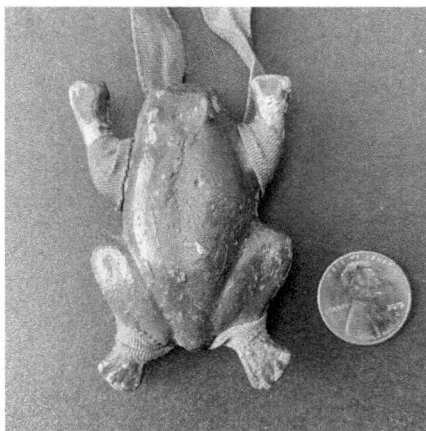

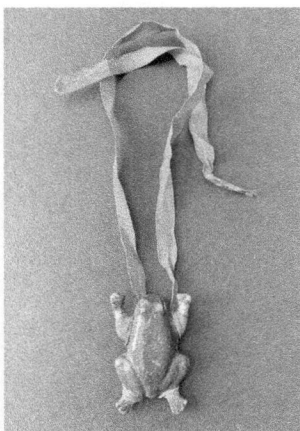

Lead frog medallion with green grosgrain ribbon, worn one playful December, 1956 evening in Stockholm.

9

Camelot: Dinner at the White House

This Nobel Prize dinner, the largest of the Kenne-dy White House years, came at a time when the United States was at the height of its power. It can be argued that the world was different for many reasons after this time. One thing is clear: there never has been a gathering of such American intellectuals at the White House since. The value that we place on the contributions of artists, writers, scientists, and thinkers was at its apogee.

—Joseph A. Esposito

Nineteen sixty-two. President John F. Kennedy knew the kind of gala he wanted to host: a dinner honoring living Nobel Prize laureates from the Western Hemisphere. Although he often left such plans to the First Lady, this night was his idea, and he was in charge of the guest list. The White House mailed invitations to hand-selected individuals on March 31. Walter Brattain, John Bardeen, and William Shockley made the cut and received their envelopes in early April, with an unambiguous return address in all capital letters. Later in the day, Walter called Mother, who was in Walla Walla, to tell her about the event. Hearing the immediate change in her voice, he knew she was elated and a bit stunned by the invitation to the White House. She had, after all, been to the country's most famous residence a year earlier as a tourist—peering into rooms off limits to the public—never imagining that she would one day walk in as an invited guest.

In letters to Mother that week, Walter provided details of the event. He also expressed some amusing concern about her dress, worried that she might ask Gretchen and me to be her personal stylists. Fortunately, she bypassed us and consulted her close friend Peggy Mantz, who had attended many formal military events in Washington, D.C., and around the world. Peggy knew whom to call: Tish Baldridge,

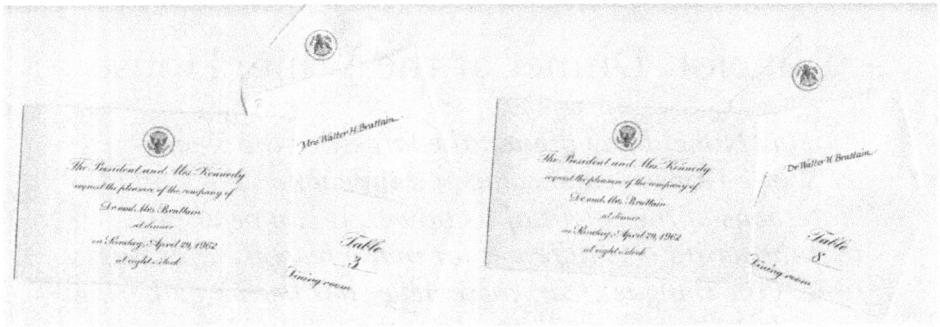

Seating assignments for Dr. and Mrs. Brattain.

*Main Dining Room Seating Plan, John F. Kennedy Presidential Library
and Museum. Mother sat at Table #3 (5:00 position); Walter sat at table #8
(10:00 position); President Kennedy sat at table #7 (12:00 position).*

The Dining Room with tables numbered.

Walter is standing below Washington's portrait, looking toward Jackie Kennedy.

Walter is in the back row, second from right.

The White House Entrance Hall—The Brattains arrive.

Jacqueline Kennedy's social secretary. Tish's recommendation of long, formal attire quickly assuaged Walter's anxiety.

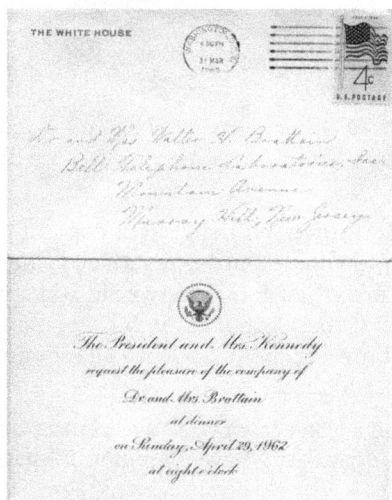

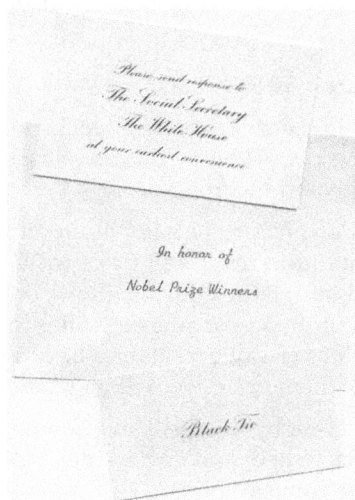

The White House invitation.

Three of Walter's early April letters to Mother referred to the White House dinner.

April 3, '62

Dearest Emma Jane,

Yesterday was a hectic day. Razanov was here from Russia. The boys were practicing their talks for the New York Academy this weekend. I have to get busy on my Gettysburg talk. This weekend John Bardeen will be my guest.

And of course the President's invitation. And the pleasure of talking to you. The invitation is for 8:00 P.M. April 29 (dinner), black tie. The National Academy [of Sciences] meets Monday, Tues, and Wed. April 23–25. The Physics Society the 23–26. I will plan to stay over Friday and Saturday I think in Washington, though we could come back to New Jersey and go down again Sunday. You work things out the best you can. It would be nice if you could be there for the Academy meetings and if we stay in Washington Friday and Saturday, you could let the Mantzes know.

If you can spare a day or two afterwards in N.Y., you could help me pick out a new suit. And, of course, I will enjoy your company as long as you can stay!! . . .

Love, Walter

April 8, '62

Dearest Sweetheart,

Just got home after seeing John off. Will write to you before I do anything else. Now to answer some of your questions, though I guess I better call you tomorrow.

Yes, it is the Nobel dinner and it is dinner. Will enclose a copy of the invitation. Yes, I will drive to Washington. Jane Bardeen is also trying to find out about wearing a long dress. I promised John you would write her any info you got and she will write you. If there is not enough time, maybe you better call her. Plan to have a telephone company car with chauffeur to pick them up so we will go to the dinner together. . . .

Went by the [Bell] labs hoping to find a letter from you. Was right. Came home to bed, and up and into N.Y. at 9:00 A.M. to serve on panel. John and I got home at 7:00.

Another letter from you and one from Mari, saying how much they enjoyed your visit to Mercer Island.

John and I got to bed by 11:00 and today played golf. Most people at the club had also seen about the White House dinner in the *Times*. . . .

Love, Walter

April 11, '62

Dearest Sweetheart,

Your good letter came today. Will return the card with this and also some other things. . . .

If the information does turn out to be "short dress," please don't make it too short! Because it does not become you, especially when you sit down! Don't listen to your daughters in this regard. If they like to show their behinds, it is something I have no control over. . . .

Much much love to you, my dear.

Walter

Each detail of the gala, from dinner seating assignments to place settings, was exquisitely prepared. To encourage lively conversation, couples were placed at different tables, most of which had ten guests.

In the Main Dining Room, Walter was seated at table #8, Mother at #3. I imagine that they might have shared a brief wave at an opportune moment.

In the photograph of them approaching the Kennedy welcome line, Mother is walking with intention toward the hosts. Cautiously, Walter trails behind, walking as if on a narrow beam which requires his attention to avoid a misstep. Cradling her elegant thin purse in her left hand, Mother looks as if she is determined to be present as best she can, considering that she spent most of the day in bed, ill with one of the worst colds of her life. Nothing was going to keep her away from this memorable moment. After all, she had outfitted herself from head to toe in the finest wear Walla Walla had to offer, had her hair coiffed and sprayed, and had flown across the country to join Walter at the White House.

May 2019. I needed to know much more about this event, and so I searched the Internet. Although I expected to find links to newspaper and magazine articles, maybe even a book about the Kennedy dinners that might refer to the 1962 festivities, I was stunned to find an entire book about that one evening, published just months earlier, titled *Dinner in Camelot: The Night America's Greatest Scientists, Writers, and Scholars Partied at the Kennedy White House*. It was like finding a hundred-dollar bill on the sidewalk! So much of my online investigation into Walter's life had resulted in pieces written more than a half a century earlier, and now I had found something that was within the span of my memory but about which I knew little.

I ordered a copy and read it straight through, penciling notes in the margins and highlighting various passages. The second I finished it, I knew I had to write to the author, Joseph Esposito. Portions of our email exchanges appear below:

Subject: Dinner in Camelot
May 16, 2019
Dear Mr. Esposito,
I recently watched the 2018 Gaithersburg Book Fair video in which you

introduced *Dinner in Camelot*. You opened with a question to the audience: "How many people are aware of this dinner that took place in 1962? The Nobel dinner. Any familiarity with it?" Alone in my Nevada living room, I enthusiastically responded yes! I could imagine being in Maryland, listening to you describe the White House dinner—the exquisite planning involved, the posh reality of the gala, and the implications of such an event in the context of this country's cultural and political history.

I had good reason to know of that dinner—it is part of my family history. Walter Brattain (who shared the 1956 Nobel Prize in Physics with John Bardeen and William Shockley for their semiconductor research along with their discovery of the transistor effect) and my mother, Emma Jane Brattain, attended the April 29th extravaganza.

Within minutes of watching your video, I ordered the book. As anyone with a connection to this event might have done, I first scanned the book's index for Walter Brattain's name, then looked at the photographs, hoping to find (which I did) a casual shot of him. I was especially delighted to see pictures of the decorated tables along with the seating plans, which immediately pulled me into the excitement of the evening. Walter sat next to Jean Kennedy Smith at table #8, and Mother sat almost directly across from Rose Styron at table #3. I easily identified the gold chair on which Mother would have sat during that extraordinary meal. Each piece of cutlery and crystal precisely placed.

In searching through family documents, I found my mother's reflections, "Nobel Laureates Dinner at the White House," which she wrote after returning home. Her descriptions, for me, complement your writing, and I would like to share a few of them with you.

In the early 1960s, Walter still spent much of his time at the Bell Laboratories in Murray Hill, New Jersey. The morning of April 2nd, he had telephoned Mother, then in Walla Walla, Washington, to ask whether she would like to go to the dinner. As you might imagine, she was flabbergasted by Walter's invitation.

One of my mother's close friends with strong ties to military protocol, called the White House social secretary, Tish Baldrige, to ask about the women's equivalent of the black-tie edict. "Preferably a long dress and gloves." Mother felt fortunate that she was able to find just the right attire locally.

. . .

She wrote of the lure of the celebrity autograph. Walter had offered to take her menu card, successfully obtaining a coveted quartet of signatures: Robert Kennedy, Jacqueline Kennedy, John Glenn, and Robert Oppenheimer.

Ever interested in putting isolated incidents into a larger context, I made inferences about a photograph in your book (the upper photo facing page

171) in which a bespectacled Walter is standing—hands behind his back— holding a card. He seems to be looking in Jacqueline Kennedy's direction, strategically planning when to approach the First Lady for her signature.

. . .

My discovery of your book came at an ideal time for me. My brother and I have been working on a family memoir project since 2012. Your book has given us new energy to write about our stepfather.

As a self-absorbed high-school junior in 1962, I had little interest in things my mother was doing that didn't directly concern me. My father's untimely death from cancer, followed jarringly soon by my mother's marriage to a Nobel laureate, had set me adrift from the moorings of my secure family, forced to chart my own course with no compass. Now, nearly thirty years after her death, reflecting on her written account, I am able to share her experience. Beyond that, I can celebrate Mother's life with Walter by continuing to tell her story.

Thank you for your extraordinary research and stunning writing.

Warmly,
Debi Bonds
Henderson, Nevada

[May 16, 2019] Subject: RE: Dinner in Camelot

Dear Ms. Bonds:

Thank you very much for the e-mail regarding the Nobel dinner, your mother and stepfather. This is great information, and I am delighted to be able to see it.

I researched your stepfather and was obviously impressed with his work. I'm sorry that I did not discuss him and a number of other Nobel laureates in depth, but I made a decision to focus on several people and, by happy coincidence, they were congregated at a half-dozen tables. I see that your mother sat next to Dr. Glenn Seaborg. He interested me a great deal, but I only gave him fleeting attention. So many Nobel laureates and so little space.

Rose Styron was a great help in piecing together the evening and, as you know, wrote the foreword to the book. I'm sure that there was lively discussion at that table, including the humorous story that Rose tells about Dr. Albert Szent-Györgyi and muscles/mussels.

Of course, the evening was a memorable one for everyone who attended. We are fortunate to have some of these accounts and now I'm thrilled to learn of your mother's perspective.

I have attached two documents which you may not have seen. The first is the RSVP to Tish Baldridge, which presumably was written by your mother. The second is Dr. Brattain's letter to President Kennedy. Both are from the Kennedy Library.

The most extensive photo account of the Nobel dinner was in the May 11, 1962, issue of *Life* magazine. My publisher bought the rights of one of those photos for the cover of *Dinner in Camelot*. I have several copies of this magazine, and if you provide me with your address, I will send you one. I will not be able to send it out until next week because I'm leaving shortly for a conference in New York and will be gone for several days; I will be talking on two panels about the putting together of *Dinner in Camelot* to an annual meeting of biographers.

Writing this book was a great joy for me. I have come into contact with many interesting people with all sorts of ties to that evening and to the Kennedy era. I am very glad to hear from you. The audio book is coming out in August and a notable professional audio-book reader is doing it. My agent is working on getting a movie or television adaptation of the book—I think the dinner is an ideal topic for the screen—but, of course, such deals are challenging to obtain.

Best wishes,
Joseph Esposito

Subject: *Life* magazine
July 2, 2019
Dear Joseph,

Thank you so very much for sending the May 11, 1962, issue of *Life* magazine. Indeed, the article—especially the photographs—captures the energy and sense of camaraderie among the guests. The coverage hints at some of what took place during that fantastical evening. Your book illuminates the event.

In one of my earlier emails to you I made inferences about Walter's activity, concluding that his immediate goal was to obtain Jackie Kennedy's autograph. Upon closer examination of the photograph, I could see that he was not holding anything behind his back. But even allowing my imagination to guide his behavior at that moment, I have felt a greater connection to the activities of the evening.

Also noted on the cover of the magazine was the birth of a 225-pound elephant (later to be given the name Packy, as in "Packy-Derm") at the Portland, Oregon Zoo. I was delighted to see a second article in the magazine that had, by coincidence, a connection to my family history. The link is that my mother's father, Frank Kirsch, owned a traveling carnival and was a circus enthusiast. Gramps (as we called him) was a close friend of Morgan Berry, who owned an elephant named Belle, who was Packy's mother. . . .

My siblings and I were elated by news of Packy's birth and visited the Oregon Zoo several times over the years. In 2016 Chris and I took four of our grandchildren to the zoo where we met with Bob Lee, the elephant curator, who referred to himself as "Bob in elephants." Sadly, Packy died in 2017 of tuberculosis. I was grateful to have made the effort to introduce my grandchildren to Packy.

Had he lived as a member of my generation, Gramps's thinking about animal captivity would have evolved to question the ethics of housing animals such as elephants in zoos. However, even for his era, he was ever committed to respectful and compassionate treatment of workers and animals.

Reflecting on her life, my mother often said she felt as if she had lived two lives. The complement of the circus and Nobel laureate connections illustrates that.

My epistolary approach to family history includes a letter to my grandfather with broad details of his history and sense of wanderlust, which he passed on to my mother. With Walter, Mother traveled the world attending various scientific gatherings.

Thank you again for sending the issue of *Life* magazine with two features relevant to my family history.

Warmly,
Debi

Subject: RE *Life* Magazine
July 2, 2019

Dear Debi:

Thank you for the e-mail and for the very interesting information on Belle/Packy. That is a fascinating story and it is quite amazing that there were two articles in this issue of *Life* which were meaningful to you. I need to confess that despite having a copy of the magazine on my desk now for more than two years, I never paid any attention to that article. Overall, *Life* really was a wonderful publication, one which richly reported on so many events, including the best photographic coverage of the Nobel dinner.

Also, thank you for the photographs. It is not often when you see an elephant getting out of a car!

Best wishes,
Joseph

Subject: News from Nevada
February 4, 2020

Dear Joseph,

Six months ago you and I exchanged emails about *Dinner in Camelot*. I wanted to share an update to the story that my mother told about the White House gala, in which she mentioned two autographed dinner menus. I had searched for them among her papers without success. I knew they were not in the Brattain papers at Whitman College and was pretty sure that Walter wouldn't have given them to anyone at the Bell Labs for safekeeping. I had pretty much resigned myself that they were lost.

Last weekend, Chris and I flew to Portland to go through family memorabilia now at my niece's. Deborah knew I was writing about Walter—including the 1962 gala. She had pulled out a brown scrapbook labeled "The Walter Brattains" that included photographs of the event. Back at our motel room, where we could peruse items at our leisure, I leafed through the notebook and discovered a plastic covered page containing various items: a matchbook cover labeled "The White House," their official invitation to the event, place cards, and a program of readings by Mr. Frederic March

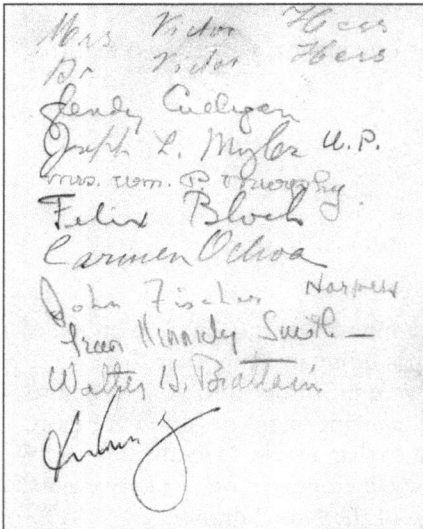

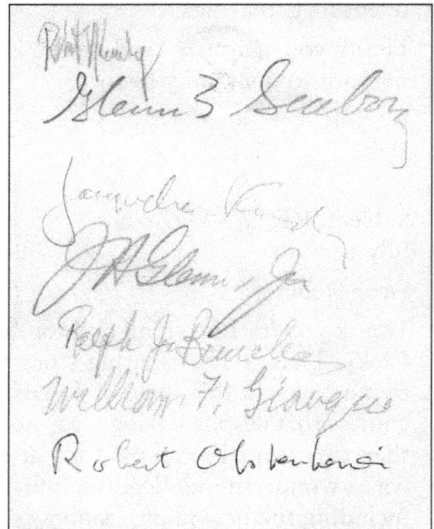

(L) Walter's Menu: Mrs. Victor Hess, Dr. Victor Hess, Glendy Culligan, Joseph L. Myler, Mrs. William P. Murphy, Felix Bloch, Carmen Ochoa, John Fisher, Jean Kennedy Smith, Walter H. Brattain, John F. Kennedy.
(R) Mother's Menu: Robert Kennedy, Glenn Seaborg, Jacqueline Kennedy, J. H. Glenn, Jr., Ralph J. Bunche, William F. Giauque, Robert Oppenheimer.

from the works of previous Nobel prize winners—Sinclair Lewis, George C. Marshall, and Ernest Hemingway. Half-hidden beneath this miscellany were two cards—the dinner menus. Quickly flipping them over, I saw the coveted autographs! Chris quickly figured out that the signature just under Walter's is John F. Kennedy's. Mother had identified several names in her reflections that I emailed to you. She didn't mention JFK, so it's possible that Walter had his menu in New Jersey at the time.

Chris and I elatedly carried them back to Nevada. I'm attaching photos. What a gift for us to find at this time. . . .

Warmly,

Debi

After returning to Washington State following her grand adventure as a guest at the White House Gala, Mother wrote her reflections on the event. In her delightful narration, she captured the speed with which the event was organized and the lifetime of memories she took away:

NOBEL LAUREATES DINNER AT THE WHITE HOUSE
April 29, 1962

To begin our story, I should go back to the morning of April 2 when Walter called me from New Jersey and asked whether I'd like to go to dinner at the White House. Perhaps, this didn't come with quite as much impact as it might have, if Mrs. Howard Baker had not mentioned (and finally sent to me) the article from a coast newspaper of a syndicated column that mentioned that if President Kennedy wished to show the superiority of American science over you-know-who that all he need do was to have the Nobel winners of science at one fell swoop at the White House. So, somehow, the whisper of such an idea had become a reality in not too long a time.

First thing in a woman's mind on such an occasion, of course, is, "What to wear?" . . . Rather than fretting very long, I decided to dispatch to Peggy Mantz the request to find out what was best since I knew she would either know or know whom to ask. So directly to the White House social secretary, Tish Baldridge, she went and had the answer, "Preferably, long dress and gloves.

Color and material optional." That was settled, then I need look
for (and to find) a long dress. Fortunately, I found one right here
in Walla Walla, but only one in my size, and all the alteration it
really needed was to be shortened. So the blush pink tricot with
softly shirred bodice and simple shoulder wide shirred straps with
a bit of heavy white lace on the front, pearled and sequined, was
my dress for the dinner. Also a pair of imported French stretchy
gloves and pink satin slippers to match and then my only jewelry
was a pair of long chandelier earrings, picking up the pearl and
highlights of the dress ornamentation. My evening coat was a
French blue brocade. I purposely mention the "French" aspect
since the evening has other such aspects, as I'll mention later.

The anticipation of the evening did mount, but I was unable
to enjoy it to the real peak that one would like to preserve for
such top times since I came down with a dreadful cold and
needed to stay in bed all day on Sunday in hopes that I could
last through the evening.

I had the feeling that since I had come nearly 3,000 miles
across the country to be at the dinner, I just had "to do or die."

Walter had arranged for the AT&T Co. to furnish a car and
driver for us and that was a luxury since the weather had been
rainy and blustery all day in the area. On leaving our hotel, the
Sheraton–Park, we stopped by the Hay Adams Hotel to pick up
Jane and John Bardeen and elderly Dr. Erlanger from St. Louis.
So we arrived almost precisely at 8 P.M., as read our invitation,
at the South entrance to the White House. This is the side with
the rounded portico and since it was still light, not raining at
the time, but somewhat overcast, one had full view of the yellow
tulips in front of the White House.

. . .

There were exchanges of introductions as we came out of
the oval reception room into the lower hall with the beautiful
red carpets. I had a fleeting moment of wondering what kind
of retinue it took just to keep these carpets in such beautiful
pristine state. We ascended the stairs to the upper floor into the

foyer where the orchestra was playing. An offered arm of an aide was extended and we stopped to pick up our names upon small, beautifully hand-lettered envelopes which gave us our table assignments. We then seemed to float into the East Room, were announced (not in the way the Brattain name is said, but rhyming with sustain) and were told to remain in somewhat the same area until we went through the receiving line. . . . Soon, with the great influx of the gathering, one name slid into another, but one snapped me to attention and that was "Col. and Mrs. John H. Glenn, Jr." In publicity later, I've read that this was their first time for dinner at the White House, too. . . .

The assembling group began to give semblance of an old home week or certainly of a gay class reunion, and this atmosphere likely contributed much to the overwhelming success of the party. By this time trays of assorted drinks were passed, and also with beautiful linen Madeira napkins. (Hope no one used them as a handy souvenir.) The East Room or ballroom is a glittering room, all creamy white and gold. A huge bouquet dominated the outside wall. I think it had lilies and lilacs, massively grouped; the crystal chandeliers were certainly sparkling, too, perhaps reflecting the brilliance of the gathering. Also there are the two tremendous portraits of Martha and George Washington on the outside wall. I also remembered that just a year ago I had gone through the White House as a tourist, BUT this was very different. One wasn't looking at, but participating in.

One could mention many people. The Linus Paulings seemed to be ubiquitous and they possibly met most everyone there. We knew that he had been picketing the White House that day before they came to dinner. I was able to find out first hand that he had Oregon connections, had actually attended Oregon State. I remarked that he and Walter were the only two that evening with Northwest "roots," and he immediately said to Walter, "But you were born in China." He had no doubt perused the lists of such individuals to know them in hopes to secure support for this campaign against nuclear testing. We had a chance to say our greetings to Pierre and Nancy Joy Salinger; Walter had attended Whitman College with Nancy's mother and I had known Nancy as a Tri Delta during her years at Whitman.

In about an hour's time (or less), the colors were presented and "Hail to the Chief" was heard, and standing in the door were our host and hostess. We were instructed that the man preceded the woman in the line and so off we went to pass in front of the Kennedys. Another instruction we had been given was that, after going through the line, the Nobel laureates would remain in this room for pictures, while the others found their places at the tables. Walter and I were not at the same table, but we both were in the dining room. There were also tables set up in the Blue Room where Mrs. Kennedy was the hostess, while the President presided in the State Dining Room. I realized that after I had gone through the line, I did not know what Mrs. Kennedy was wearing! I had shaken hands and murmured some

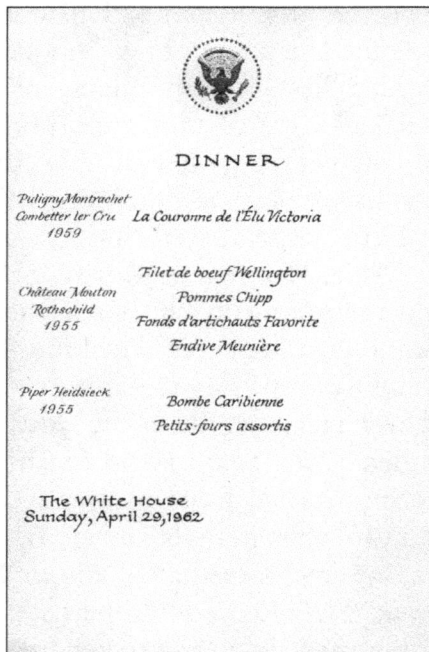

DINNER

Puligny Montrachet
Combetter 1er Cru   La Couronne de l'Élu Victoria
1959

Filet de boeuf Wellington
Château Mouton   Pommes Chipp
Rothschild   Fonds d'artichauts Favorite
1955   Endive Meunière

Piper Heidsieck
1955   Bombe Caribienne
Petits-fours assortis

The White House
Sunday, April 29, 1962

The dinner menu.

delight at the invitation, but had looked directly at them. The president's face was radiant, but Mrs. Kennedy seemed quiet toned, in contrast. Incidentally, I later saw that Mrs. Kennedy was wearing an off-shouldered Grecian style softly molded green gown and her hair was less of the brioche that was shown earlier in some other publicity.

. . . The State Dining Room was tastefully done to reflect a green feeling; we used the Truman china and I was impressed with the gold cutlery and the pearl-handled fish and entrée knives, which must have been from the late 18th century. There were about 15 tables of 10 each in the dining room. Table Number 3 was near the door, but in direct line with the president who had Mrs. Marshall sitting on one side. I think Mrs. Hemingway was on his left. I spotted Walter eventually and we waved a greeting across the room. Dr. Glenn T. Seaborg was the host at my table. At each place was our beautifully penned name card, the menu, a folder of matches which stated simply upon the cover, "The President's House." The others at Table 3 besides Dr. Seaborg and me were Dr. William Giauque (from the University of California at Berkeley, who sat on my right, then Mrs. Philip Hench, Dr. Julius Stratton (President of M.I.T.), Mrs. Edward Kendall, Mrs. Felix Bloch, and Dr. Szent–Györgyi and two more I apparently don't remember and didn't know. [Also at table #3 were Mr. Van Wyck Brooks and Rose Styron, who sat across the table from Mother, likely making it almost impossible for them to converse.]

Walter had the wonderful idea of having each one at his table autograph the back of his menu card. Mrs. Smith, his hostess, assumed greater significance when he found out she was Jean Kennedy Smith. Others at his table were Dr. And Mrs. Victor Hess, Glendy Culligan, Joseph L. Myler (United Press), Mrs. William P. Murphy, Felix Bloch, Carmen Ochoa, and John Fischer (Harper's).

When we discovered, after dinner, how much fun the autographs could be, I, with Walter's help, ended up with not only Drs. Seaborg and Giauque, but also Robert Kennedy, Jacqueline

Kennedy, John H Glenn, Jr., Ralph Bunche, and Robert Oppenheimer. (Perhaps someday I'll need to name this in my will!)

. . . The menu card might need some translation since the La Couronne de l'Élu Victoria was a hot fish mousse with creamed lobster and crab sauce. This was followed by a Filet de boeuf Wellington, a most interesting dish of tender filet encased in a bread covering served with a gravy. The "Pommes Chipp" (just plain old potato chips from any old grocery), expendable as far as I would be concerned since to serve them onto the plate with a spoon and fork was a feat. But the fascinating baked structure—possibly of latticed bread—was a work of art. There was a salad of artichoke hearts and endive. Somehow upon thinking back, I fail to remember the endive, but the lovely wines (all French) were a Puligny Montrachet Combetter le Cru (1959) and Chateau Mouton Rothschild (1955) and Piper Heidsieck (1955) which went with the Bombe Caribienne and Petits-fours assortis. This was a two-flavored ice cream bombe and the cookies were very simple ones. Coffee was served at the end, too.

Toward the end of the dinner period, a microphone was brought in and placed in front of the president, and he proposed a toast to the future, to those present, and to peace. He caused much merriment by telling that someone had named this gathering his Easter Egghead Roll and went on to say that not so much intellect had been assembled at one time in the White House since Thomas Jefferson dined there alone. This quip was much to everyone's amusement since he went on to enumerate that Jefferson "could calculate an eclipse, survey an estate, tie an artery, plan an edifice, try a case, break a horse, and dance the minuet." Was it an afterthought that he conceded that Ben Franklin might have been included, too?

. . .

After we all made a somewhat leisurely retreat back to the East Room, we found chairs had been set up for the anticipated program of reading by Frederick March; we had been given small programs which stated the selections he would read. The works were of three Nobel winners, non-living Americans. One excerpt from Sinclair Lewis's work of *Main Street*, a few short paragraphs from Gen. George Marshall's speech made at Harvard which foretold the Marshall Plan, and an as yet unpublished chapter from Ernest Hemingway's novel of non-naval warfare off the coast of Cuba.

Before this section of the program started, somehow William Shockley was at the podium and suggested that a return to the president's toast was called for, and proceeded to take care of the matter. Both Mrs. Hemingway and Mrs. Marshall were at the dinner and were given seats of honor.

After the lights came back up, we all rose and started to exit, slowly. No one seemed in much of a hurry; it was a resplendent evening and no one was in any great hurry to have it end, it seemed. It was fun to partake of it, to just look on. We seemed to be washed to the foyer and it was then approaching midnight, so we knew that the evening was nearing the end. The closing minutes were savored and it looked then as if Jane and I should get our coats, but in so starting were intercepted with the signing of the guest book. Walter had really wanted to dance and the Air Force Strolling Strings were playing that kind of music to add a gay feeling to an already star-studded evening.

Since all wonderful and good things must come to an end, this did, too. But since often the anticipation of an event is as great a thrill as the experience of the actual event itself, so is the retelling, rethinking, and remembering which will go on for all the time that is ours to enjoy. It was a wonderful experience to have had a 1/175 part in such a gala, the first of its kind to be held at the White House.

Emma Jane Brattain 1962

Stepping back to view this event in the cultural and political climate of the 2020s, I wonder when, if ever, we might enjoy a comparable level of appreciation for scientific research and the arts, as well as a sense of shared national identity and mutual respect through reasoned, fair-minded dialogue.

10

Emma Jane

*On one hot summer day late in August 1915, a
baby girl came into the world (so I'm told). This was at
Abilene, Kansas. The infant was soon named a double
name: a popular procedure at this time. The name was
derived from each of the grandmothers, thus satisfying
both sides of the family. It proved to be Emma Jane with
Kirsch added to this.*

—Emma Jane Kirsch, from a 1938 Biology–Genetics term paper.

I. Young Emma Jane Kirsch

We preface our letters to our mother with a brief account of her life
up to her college graduation. It is a prelude to our individual letters
to her, which are highly personal. Debi's letter in particular draws
upon our mother's journals and letters and serves to round out what
is only touched upon here.

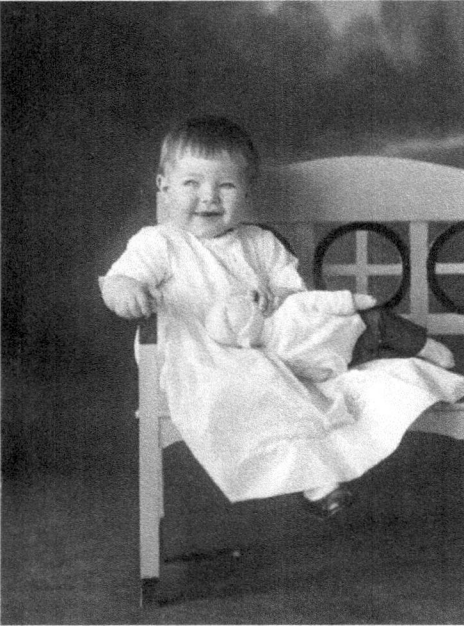

Emma Jane at about 18 months.

*Emma Jane (front right) at her
second birthday party.*

Abilene, Kansas, birthplace of Emma Jane Kirsch.

Our mother, Emma Jane Kirsch, was born on August 29, 1915 to Frank and Ruth Kirsch. She was named after Frank's mother, Emma Koerner, and her maternal great-great-grandmother, Jane Ricketson. In 1919 the family moved to Denver, Colorado, where they lived for three years before moving to Seattle in 1922.

Emma Jane in window frame of the Seattle house, built 1927-1928.

Postcard of Emma Jane, age 3.

Emma Jane, Frank, and cats
Useless and Lonesome, in front
of their first Seattle home.

In 1945, Nanmy sent the above picture postcard of three-year-old Emma Jane to Gretchen, also age three. Her message read: "Dear Gretchen—This is a picture of your mother when she was a little girl like you—Put it away and save for you & Debby—I miss you very much—Be Happy & have a lot of nice play. Your daddy has a lot of nice things for you at play time. Love, Nanmy." Along with her own memoir, begun four years later, this card seems to show that Nanmy wanted to leave something of the family history to future generations.

Emma Jane's lifelong fascination with words was evident early on. Here is a piece from a handwritten folder she titled "Short Stories I Have Written" (perhaps around ages 12–13, following a train trip to Colorado with her mother).

"The Mountains and the Puget Sound"

From my window I see the most beautiful scene. It is of the mountains and the Puget Sound.

The Mountains stand lofty with snow in their lovely, deserted valleys. The calm peaceful water in the foreground is a deep olive green. The sky is a clear azure blue dotted here and there with white fluffy clouds forming fantastic shapes and forms.

Boats large and small break the silence and peacefulness of the water.

About 5 years old.

Homemade dress for high school senior portrait.

From an early age, photographs and diary entries reveal her insatiable love of clothes—store-bought or made by her mother or grandmother.

She kept journals of her activities through four years of high school and three years of college. She wrote about friends, social life, concerts, and complaints about low grades. The day after hearing Rachmaninoff perform, she flunked an algebra exam. From the beginning, she set goals for herself, showing maturity beyond her years. She expected there would be highs and lows, joy and disappointment throughout high school, and dreamed of traveling abroad after graduation. Throughout, three defining themes emerge: activities, music, and relationships.

Emma Jane's parents strongly encouraged her love of music. While she was in high school, they purchased a Steinway piano for her. She studied with Eva Chamberlin in Seattle for several years, giving recitals as early as 1930. During her high school years, she attended many student programs and professional concerts and heard such international favorites as violinists Fritz Kreisler and Albert Spalding, and baritone Lawrence Tibbett, of whom she was especially fond. (Today, we can hear dozens of their performances on YouTube.) She filled two large scrapbooks with newspaper clippings related to classical music.

Emma Jane with her favorite cousin, Billy.

Emma Jane experienced the death of three important relatives during her high school years. Her cousin, William E. "Billy" Kirsch, who was like a brother to her, died at age twenty in a small-plane crash near Salt Lake City in 1932. Earlier that year, her grandfather Kirsch, with whom Emma Jane had practiced speaking and writing German, had died. The following year, she lost her aunt Klara, another relative who had written letters to her in German.

After her high school junior year, Emma Jane and her parents took a six-week trip to Chicago, visiting relatives and looking at colleges. One of those schools, DePauw University in Greencastle, Indiana, seemed a good fit, and so she spent her freshman year there. Although living in a rural area had limited her social activities, she took full advantage of them once she got to college. She was elected president of her pledge class in Delta Delta Delta sorority. There was no shortage of young men; social events were frothy meet-and-greets between the sexes. Emma Jane preferred men who were good with words over the ones who merely talked a good line.

Emma Jane left DePauw after her freshman year. While cost was a factor, she explained that her primary reason for leaving DePauw after one year was that her life had gotten too complicated, implying that too many boys were requesting her time. She transferred to Whitman College in Walla Walla, Washington, much closer to her parents.

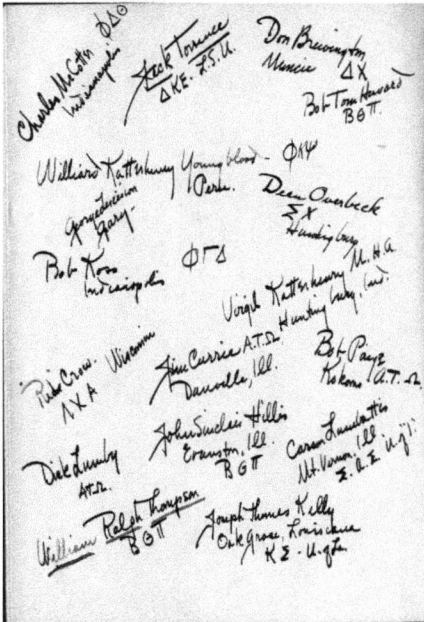

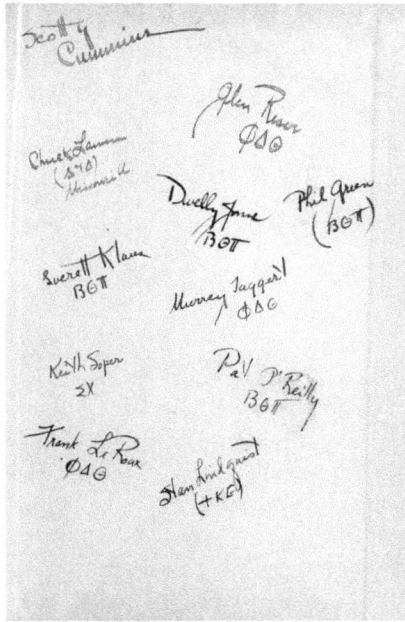

L: Freshman year, DePauw University 1934-1935. R: Sophomore year, Whitman College 1935-1936.

She kept a record of men she dated, along with their fraternities, during her freshman and sophomore years (pictured above). Her unofficial minor in boys ended late 1936 when she met Roland Miller.

Emma Jane flourished at Whitman. She was president of Mortar Board (a national honor society), president of the Delta Delta Delta sorority, a member of Mu Phi Epsilon (a co-ed international music society), and society editor for the college newspaper. She graduated in May 1938, with a major in music education.

Emma Jane's college graduation photo, 1938.

II. Webb's Letter

*All that I am, or hope to be, I owe to my angel
mother.*

—Abraham Lincoln

Dear Mom,

This is my love letter to you, by parts a thank-you, an apology,
and a celebration. I know I told you these things before your death,
but now, thirty years later, I want to revisit them with the wisdom of
hindsight. However, I can't resist starting with a bit of humor at your
expense. I hope that you, like me, can enjoy mention of your foibles,
when it comes from a position of love.

Digging through a long-forgotten stash of family photos to help
me compose this letter, I came across a picture that I just cannot
ignore. As a preface for the photo, I want to recall the time, in 1969,
when Trudy and I moved from Seattle to Pennsylvania. You took care
of our only child (others were forthcoming), Megan, age about nine
months. When we met you and Megan at the airport after the two

weeks, I was amazed at how much larger Megan looked. You said, proudly, that if you waited thirty minutes after she stopped eating, you could get her to eat some more. I probably said something snarky, like "Right—that's a contest you wouldn't want to lose."

Back to the picture I could not ignore, it was of an infant in your arms—which I wouldn't have recognized, except that on the back you wrote that it was me at four months; in contrast, I look skinny in my photos as a toddler. For much of my life I was unclear if I made you proud, but now I see that at least I started off the right way. Did your head swell?

Mom holding the gigantic four-month-old Webb,
sizing him up, after four months of upping his size.

I think of our relationship after Dad died in three phases: a close connection for the first few years, then a long period when I largely shut you out of my life, then years when we had numerous adventures together and you had a major influence on my life.

I'm frankly amazed at how strong you were right after Dad's death. You gave me permission to work in pea harvest the following June, at age thirteen, when I spent twelve hours every night driving a truck and slept during the day in a bunk house, making $1.25 an hour plus room and board. Then, when I got some time off, I asked if I could spend my salary to buy a shotgun. You gave me the go-ahead and asked family friend Bob Groseclose to help me with the choice. When my own son, Andrew, turned thirteen, I was aghast when I tried to imagine how I could cope if he wanted to work on a farm and buy a shotgun. I've never figured out how you made it work.

You always had time for me. I remember your making two 360-mile round trips to Clarno, Oregon, so I could spend two weeks at the paleontology summer camp sponsored by the Oregon Museum of Science and Industry. Also, you took me to the Snake River around Page, Washington, so I could shoot a Canada goose, which required you to sit in a cold car for hours. Another time you drove the 230-mile round trip to Moses Lake, where I could see a hypnotist who specialized in relief of stuttering. These are just a few examples of how much effort you spent to step into Dad's shoes in those formative years.

Then I started college, and at the end of my first year I reported wanting to temporarily drop out of college (where my freshman performance had been underwhelming), and travel around the country with my friend Ned Quistorff in a Volkswagen van. You consulted with my surrogate fathers, Clyde Robinson and Art Carey, and were talked into dropping resistance to the plan. This may have made it easier for me to acquiesce when my youngest daughter, Kathleen, wanted to drive around the country alone to many national parks. However, my trip was long before cell phones, and included six weeks in Mexico, completely out of touch. Fortunately, your fears that I would become a ne'er-do-well didn't materialize, and instead I returned with a dedication that I had never before felt for succeeding in school.

However, I had already entered a long period where I largely kept you out of my life. When I was in college, at least during the times you spent in Walla Walla, we lived only a few blocks apart, but I used your home mostly as a place to do my laundry. (Well, maybe that is a little harsh.) Then, through my three years in graduate school, seven initial years at Penn State, one year at IBM Labs in New York State, four years in Santa Barbara, and four years in Tucson, our contact was largely limited to your occasional visits to my family and reunions on the Oregon beach.

Your most noteworthy effort for me during this period was your heroic project taking Megan and Mari to Europe. You did an admirable

Mom photographed Sarah decorating the tree, Christmas 1972.

Mom's photo of Megan and Mari outside, Christmas 1972.

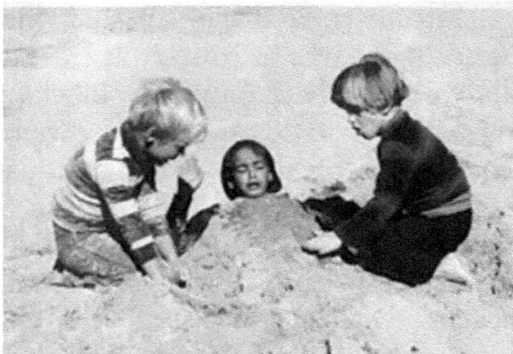

Andrew and Brenda Agenbroad bury Sarah at the Oregon beach.

job of recreating for them the experience that you and Dad gave us kids in 1955. I agree with you that it was valuable to see Europe at that age, but I was unable to provide it for them at that point in my life. Megan tells me that she probably would never have thought to go into architecture if it weren't for this trip, when she was "able to see buildings newly as more substantial and tactile places." I note, somewhat cryptically for the moment, that this was not the only time you had a substantial and positive influence on a career choice in my family.

Heidelberg Castle, June 1984. Front row: (left) Mom,
(center) Mari and Megan on either side of the guide, Chris.

I don't remember that we ever had a truly meaningful talk in all of that time. Even then, I knew that I was just insulating myself from any chance of again experiencing the devastating loss of a parent.

The reawakening of our relationship started around 1985, when I moved from Tucson back to State College. Our first adventures, or at least me taking advantage of your devotion to me, started when I settled on summer vacations consisting of three or four days in the mountains, doing my best, largely successfully, to not see another person. Frequently, I would get to Walla Walla, and you would ferry me to and from the trail-head, typically hours away. We both decided to end the tradition after I hiked in the Blue Mountains, a couple hours' drive from your home. When you were returning from dropping me off, your car broke down in the middle of nowhere, and it was several hours before you saw another vehicle. For my part, I stumbled a bit on a trail across a steep slope leading down to a river far below, and realized that I probably would not have been found for days if I had fallen. Clearly time to look for a different adventure.

Webb and Mom getting ready to drive to a trailhead, late 1980s.

We then tried a couple of multi-day wilderness rafting trips, one with Andrew on the Rogue River, then one with Nan on the Snake. You were over seventy, so I wasn't surprised when you called a halt to those trips.

Just a few weeks after your death, your final grandchild made her appearance: Kathleen Colby Miller. Your descendants gathered at Gretchen's Oregon beach house that summer, joined by your dear friends the Robinsons, to celebrate your life.

You and Kathleen would have hit it off famously. You had a lifelong love of archaeology, felt disappointment that no courses in the subject

Webb in the Wallowa Mountains of northeastern Oregon.

Mom rafting on Oregon's Rogue River, perhaps in 1989.

were available when you went to college, and enjoyed Egyptian tours of ancient sites. For her part, one of Kathleen's college majors was in Mediterranean History, and she went on a weeks-long "dig" in Egypt. These common interests might have made her the grandchild you felt closest to.

Mom's youngest child and youngest grandchild, Kathleen, summer 1990.

In three ways, you influenced my life even after your death. In two cases your effect is huge and undeniable; in another, it is more subtle but equally pervasive.

First, you played a key role in a perhaps surprising decision that positively affected me for many years. In 1987, I finished work on a book; I had written a research monograph and two obscure computer-science texts over the previous nine years (I'm not a fast writer), and I was ready for a change. Also, I was aware of being almost exactly Dad's age when he died, which heightened my sense of the importance of this decision.

I spent a year exploring subjects new to me, mostly areas of computer science, such as artificial intelligence. During that time, you started sending me clippings about something called the Human Genome Project. At the time, it seemed like a non-sequitur for my life, but it wouldn't have been such a surprise to me if I had known about your longtime interest in genetics. Why did you suspect that it would catch my fancy? Did Walter's late-career change from physics to biology have an influence? The last time I had heard a lecture about biology was in Mr. Kerns's ninth-grade general science class. Also, I don't think I had ever expressed interest in biology to you (or to anyone), at least since the paleontology summer camp.

But catch my fancy it did and, as they say, the rest is history. Unfortunately, I never got a chance to really thank you because it wasn't until a few years after your death that it became clear that your suggestion was pure genius. It is extremely unlikely that I would have moved to biology without your guidance. Instead, I probably would have frittered away my last working years in some branch of computer science.

I would have loved to share the fruits of your influence by asking you to accompany me and Nan to the dinner for the Time 100 Most Influential People of 2009. Sitting across the small table from us was John Kennedy's former advisor Ted Sorenson (previous recipients can attend the galas). You would have asked whether he attended the 1962 dinner for Nobel Prize winners, and, as JFK's main speechwriter, had he penned some of the words you heard that night? Later, we would have listened to the stirring keynote address by first lady Michelle Obama, who was only a couple of tables away. We could have searched the crowd for President Obama, who was a recipient that year, along with Hillary Clinton and Ted Kennedy. I imagine myself sitting there and looking over at you to see if you realized what a great job you had done, from guaranteeing that the baby Webb was properly nourished, to suggesting that the middle-age Webb should maybe investigate genome sequences. I think I see your head swelling just a little.

Your second, perhaps less direct, influence is that your interest in gardening has recently taken root in my life (pun intended). In the two years that the two of you overlapped in my life, did you ever talk with my wife Nan about her passion for gardening? For the last dozen years, we have lived on a farm, and her gardens now cover perhaps four acres. I don't see how to capture their glory, including an acre with several thousand daylilies blooming, in a few photos.

Nan and Webb in her one-acre daylily garden,
showing a few of the thousands of blooms.

Mom with a dahlia.

A minuscule sample of Nan's gardens.

Nan checking out Webb's tropical garden. Dahlias at lower left.

Besides her specialization with daylilies, Nan tends an unbelievable variety of plants. (This is done entirely because of her need for beauty in her life; plants are neither seen by many people nor sold.) However, it is her few dahlias that never fail to remind me of you. I have several garden areas of my own, where I tend to grow plants that don't overlap with hers. My favorite among these is my little tropical garden (in Pennsylvania, no less), focusing on banana plants, elephant ears, and cannas. I intend to always include a dahlia in a prominent place, in your memory. Do you think I would have become thus obsessed if I didn't have a residual memory of your devotion to your garden?

The third influence you had on my current life is 100 percent yours, and has been absolutely marvelous. You seem to have carried out a campaign over decades to pass the torch of family historian to Debi. You might have been concerned to see those boxes of treasures sitting untouched in her basement for many years, but then gratified when she finally ignited. The surprise (to all of us) was that I eventually burst into flame about family history. Without Debi's involvement, and by inference without your torch-passing campaign, I never in a million years would have shared your passion. You gave me years of enjoyment and a far deeper connection to my younger sister, father, and stepfather. And to you. Also, I feel like this provided me an opportunity to repay your love, if only in small part. Whereas Nan seems comfortable with the idea that her marvelous gardens cannot survive without her, I'll bet that you wanted your love of family history to percolate down the family tree. I'm doing whatever I can to facilitate your wish, by condensing family records into short letters, like this one.

I thank you for the magnificent strength you showed by pinch-hitting as my father in my formative years. Also, I apologize for the twenty-plus years when I largely kept you at arm's length out of my fear of again being devastated by loss of a parent. And I celebrate all the direct adventures we had in the years before your death, as well as the vicarious ones we had thereafter. Mom, I love you.

III. Debi's Letter

We never think that our mothers will die. It was like suddenly an abyss opened at my feet—I was standing on nothing. It was the strangest thing. Her passing away ripped the solidity out of the world.

—Ben Okri

Dear Mutti,

It was early December 1989. The reality of what could have caused your memory glitch and confusion as we took you to the Omaha airport for your flight home didn't hit me immediately. The first hint that something was amiss was when we stopped at Crossroads Mall in Omaha to avoid arriving at the airport too early. Sitting at the food court, Chris and I were taken aback when you gestured toward a pair of green art-deco sconces above an adjacent fast food counter, and spoke the only nonsensical words I ever heard you say, "Do you recall that person, Greenglass?" When Chris and I looked at you and asked what you meant, you shook your head and shrugged helplessly. After a couple minutes of silence, we resumed our conversation almost as if nothing had happened. I was still worried, but I didn't think it was a situation that needed urgent medical assistance. You seemed a little confused when checking in at United Airlines, but then rallied again. You insisted you were fine to travel. When the woman at the airport check-in desk assured me they would keep an eye on you throughout your flight, I called Jody and Bruce Poland in Walla Walla, who were to meet your plane. After your flight departed, Chris and I drove home to Wayne.

Later that evening, I called family members and friends to tell them what was going on. Their responses ranged from "It's likely nothing—I'm sure she'll be fine" to "It sounds ominous." Early the next morning I called our doctor at home and asked how worried he would be if you were his mother. Without a pause, he said, "Very worried!" I thanked him, hung up and immediately made reservations to fly to Washington. Three days later I was in Walla Walla.

The first step was to see your doctor at the Walla Walla Clinic to review the brain scan taken two days after you returned home. I remember vividly her coming into the examining room. After the usual how-are-yous, she snapped the X-ray into the film viewer on the wall, pointing to a significant mass in your brain. You and I looked at each other, stunned. As we exited the clinic, I took your hand. Your fingers felt firm, stubby, cool to the touch, life-worn. Stepping into the cool December sun, I felt the ground shifting beneath me. The mass—dark cloud—from the X-ray clouded my own vision, almost causing me to stumble. Everything I had taken for granted in my world was suddenly gone. I was now sailing uncharted waters.

During the next three weeks, we held hands a lot. It suddenly seemed natural and necessary. I wanted my life to flow from my hand to yours, giving you strength, healing you.

Days later, Gretchen met us in Seattle for your appointment with Dr. Mitchel Berger.

We knew of Dr. Berger's reputation in neuroscience. He had operated just weeks earlier on a colleague who had a malignant brain tumor. This gave us grounds for hope. Further, he seemed to care about you as a person, not just another patient. As we were leaving your initial consultation at the University of Washington Medical Center, Gretchen and I walked ahead as he escorted you into the hallway, where you cornered him, telling him in no uncertain terms that the only thing that mattered to you was quality of life. Your final years with Walter in his cognitive decline had convinced you that a life without a functioning mind was no life at all. On hearing you speak with such firm conviction, I turned back and saw Dr. Berger nodding, empathy and compassion in his eyes.

Webb flew in from Pennsylvania before your surgery, and Bill drove up from Portland. The five of us spent several hours together in your hospital room. At one point I crawled up on your bed as we thumbed through your address book noting individuals we should contact. I remember wishing I could stay right there by your side until time for your surgery. We were all anxious, yet optimistic.

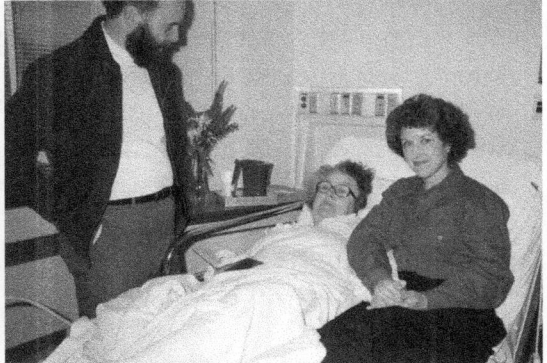

Two days before surgery at Mari's with Gretchen and Bill; Webb, newly arrived from Pennsylvania; on the eve of surgery as we gathered around Mom in her University of Washington Hospital room.

The four of us waited for updates during the several-hour procedure. A nurse came to the waiting room a few times to report the surgery was going smoothly. We knew you had to be awake to enable them to probe your brain to identify the affected areas. When Dr. Berger approached us after your operation, he described the tumor resection, adding the fateful words "I couldn't get it all." After a few silent moments, he recounted your chat about archaeology as he probed your brain. This was a first such surgical exchange for him.

How could your brain, rich in knowledge of archaeology and endless details of other topics, not provide some guarantee of your enduring stamina? I thought you were invincible, that you could withstand most any surgery. I had it wrong. Within days you were in a coma.

Christmas Eve 1989. You lay comatose in your third-floor hospital room. The tumor, which had destroyed your expressive speech center, ensured that you would never talk again. I sat with you, ambivalent—grateful to be there, yet panicked about what to do. The nurses had encouraged me to talk to you, assuring me that you could hear my voice. Yet when they left the room, I simply sat there. With the verbal ball now permanently in my court, I could not speak. I groped for words that might reflect a pretense of normalcy. None came. What could I possibly say to you on this day I had been certain would never come?

Before your seizure, I was sure that we would converse about interesting things forever. From the time of your diagnosis, we talked nonstop about each step of your treatment and prognosis. Yet here we were at the end of the line. On this late-December day, I sat mute, watching over you like a stone angel.

What kind of daughter was I, who couldn't speak when you most needed my verbal comfort? You surely would have known what to say to Dad during his own last days when you sat with him in a different Seattle hospital room. But sitting with you, I simply buckled under the pressure.

On Christmas afternoon, Peggy Mantz, a longtime family friend and Seattle resident, insisted that Aunt Mari and I join her and her daughter for Christmas dinner. As Mari and I talked about your imminent death and what it might mean to all of us, I said that I would miss most the sound of your voice, how you expressed yourself. I was grateful to have the mountain of your letters to me over the years. I could reread them, hearing your voice saying the words. I added that I knew it was in your personal writing—your journals—that you would speak most vividly and intimately. I explained how reading your journals would allow me to know you as a young girl.

Peggy did not approve. "But Debi, they are not yours to read. They belong to your mother, and I'm sure she wouldn't want you to read what she wrote privately so many years ago. If my daughters ever found diaries of mine, they would know better than to disrespect my privacy by reading them." I could tell this made sense for Peggy, and that her daughters surely understood that about their mother.

Sitting at Peggy's that Christmas afternoon on the cusp of your death, I didn't have the energy to defend my logic. I wanted to say, "Peggy, Mother all but told me to read anything she had written. We have an openness in our relationship and have a shared interest in journals. I'm not snooping on her private life in morbid curiosity. Mother saved correspondence—both hers and others'—like it was a key part of her genealogy." Your tacit permission for me to read and reflect on your journals was as obvious as anything you left me in your will.

Later that afternoon, I dropped Aunt Mari off at her condominium before returning to the hospital. I almost expected to pop into your room and find you dressed and eager to walk the half-mile distance to Meany Hall on the University of Washington campus, where you and I had heard some marvelous string ensembles a few years earlier.

Instead . . . the unfathomable. Eyes closed, supine, you lay breathing as if you were merely in a deep sleep, I felt as alone as I ever remember feeling. My God! Cancer had yanked Dad from our lives at Christmas thirty years ago and was back to make me an orphan. I couldn't bear to look at your sweet face, so I pulled the chair over to your right foot in that dim room, even then fearful that you might open your eyes and look at me only to see my overwhelming panic. I slid my fingers under the industrial-strength leggings the nurses had put on your immobile limbs. As I massaged each foot, I could feel twitches—likely involuntary—that told me there was still life in you. Oh Mutti, you and I both know that you are supposed to outlive me. The last time you were in the hospital was when I was born!

On December 28, Dr. Berger met with Gretchen and me in a conference room with an imposing wooden rectangular table. This was not a routine visit to your room. He needed to discuss the recent brain scans that showed the tumor had spread like wildfire from your left hemisphere speech center across the corpus callosum to the right hemisphere. He said it was the most aggressive form of glioblastoma he had seen in his two decades as a neurosurgeon. Leaning our heads into our arms on that solid oak table, Gretchen and I wept. Dr. Berger's unhurried compassion while delivering the grim prediction unwound us emotionally.

Gretchen insisted you spend your last days in Portland at her home on Northeast Stanton Street, under hospice care, away from the hospital. On January 1, I drove behind the unmarked ambulance in which you lay, the 180 miles to Portland on I–5, where you could lie in Deborah's room, surrounded by Mozart symphonies playing at low volume on the cassette player.

You died the following morning, January 2, 1990.

Only after twenty-nine years am I now able to tell you how horrified I was those last days of your life. I'm writing to say that I ignored Peggy's admonition and turned to your journals. I needed to know you as a young girl, to understand what you and I had in common as girls dreaming of leaving home.

I know you would understand my need to hang on to you by reconstructing your life. After all, you and I had many conversations over the years about the joys of mother-daughter communication via letters. Likewise, we shared our fascination with journals—letters to oneself. You encouraged this by giving me journals of Narcissa Whitman and Vera Brittain, and also books written as journals, by Agnes Newton Keith and Gerda Weissmann Klein.

A few years after your death, I enrolled in a Ph.D. program in counseling at the University of South Dakota. The dissertation requirement allowed me to explore a topic of deep interest to me: the experience of daughters losing a parent in midlife. Although I found many studies on the impact the death of parents had on their young children, I found few that focused on the experience of the midlife daughter upon the death of her mother, and quickly chose that topic. A plausible approach might have been to administer a grief inventory to a group of motherless daughters. Instead, I chose a qualitative research method where I could interview several women to explore both their relationships and their experiences of loss. I knew better than to think of this as a therapeutic way for me to continue processing your death. To understand the experiences of the bereaved daughters who volunteered for my study would require me to set aside my personal feelings of loss. Because these women were strangers, I could become a detached but empathetic observer. My tactic seemed to work.

After I completed my dissertation, my grief, which I had kept at bay while I completed my degree, returned with a vengeance. I needed a way to deal with it. For the next few years, I taught courses in counseling at Wayne State College. Then Chris and I retired and moved to Nevada. With Brenda and her two sons, Devin and Noah, there was no shortage of things to do. Still, my sense of loss never left me.

In the summer of 2018, I picked up your five diaries, hardbound, some with gilded edges and one with a leather locking strap. I had little idea of what I might find in them. I could almost feel your eyes on me as I began reading. You were giving me "The Look." I knew I had better listen carefully to what you had to tell me. I knew your writing style from my earlier browsing, but now I would come to know you as I had not during our forty-five years together.

To digress for a moment: Your "look"—which surely goes back centuries on your mother's side—usually conveyed a certain disapproval of something you suspected I was doing or planning, which your following words would confirm. Your opening, "I certainly hope. . . ," which I imagined you saying as I annotated your journals, came directly from 1982, when you first suspected that Chris and I were getting serious. I had said something to the effect that Chris had asked me out to dinner. Sitting on the sofa in my cozy "red barn" rented house on Valencia Street, you spun your head toward me, gave me The Look, and announced, "Debi, I certainly hope you're not getting involved!"

Well, yes. I was indeed getting involved. I not only responded in kind, but I never let you forget that outburst. But you came around: within weeks you had become one of Chris's biggest fans and celebrated our decision to marry that summer. Many times in your remaining years, we relived and giggled about your remark and change of heart.

Back to your journals: I pored over them for weeks. I thumbed through the pages and placed sticky tabs where you had noted key days and events. But I knew I needed to delve deeper, to do more than simply read them. I would have to transcribe all your journals, beginning with your freshman year in high school through the subsequent six years, including two years at Whitman College. So I began typing them, along with letters to your parents that you either copied or later snagged to glue onto blank pages. I kept my transcriptions in a ring binder, on the front of which I had attached a portrait of you from the time you would have written them. To inspire me while I worked, I also kept in front of me a photograph of you in your late sixties, from when you were doing a program on your grandmother Nanmy. You are wearing one of Nanmy's hats, smiling knowingly into the camera.

I then boiled down those seven years of writing from 189 pages to 49, to 8, and ultimately to 3 typed pages. It felt like I was trying

Wearing Nanmy's hat.

to force the script of your school years through a sieve—sifting out the extraneous details of your daily activities—to come up with a "Young-EJay Concentrate." I thought that if I could just set aside the playful, the philosophical, and the poetic in order to pare your

Transcribed Journals and Earlier Writing, 2018.

narrative down to a few key paragraphs, I would capture the essence of your youth, the "real you."

While doing this, I would sometimes forget to look up at your photo. But staring at it this morning, I caught your eyes on me as if you were waiting for a chance to speak. You were giving me The Look once again, your silent reprimand sending a clear message, "I certainly hope you aren't thinking you can capture my life by making a *Reader's Digest* condensed version of my journal writing!"

Well, yes, that is exactly what I was trying to do.

It was only while choosing how to condense my transcript that I saw a similarity to what I had done during my graduate program. But I knew that, your being my mother, I could not be an impartial observer. If this were to work, it would have to be a team effort, a collaborative research project across time. You were in charge, providing the source material for my project. Your journal entries were pieces of an incomplete puzzle, a portrait of you as you were then. My job was to supply as many of the missing pieces as possible, hints of the person you would become. What conversations might we have had if we were going through your journals together? What would you have wanted me to understand about you as a young girl?

Your journals cover the years from 1930, your freshman year in high school when you received a journal as a gift, until 1936, when you met Dad. Some of the recurring themes are music, travel, socializing, and food. But you also wrote about grades, poetry, letter-writing, death, female friendship, and—guys! Below, I have selected some that I thought were especially interesting or revealing.

Five-Year Diary, "From the Joe Bauer Family for graduation, June 11, 1930" (first diary)

Page 1: When read, start with the 1st day of September 1930, then continue in natural order.

Preface:

I plan for this to keep my record of my high school days. No doubt I shall have discouragement in both my studies and my music. But may it be that these experiences will give me will power to go ahead again and thus making them a point toward my goal instead of subtracting one.

May I write of many happy days filled with both work and fun. And in the next 4 years may it be my reaching the goal (music) shall have a good beginning and I shall continue from here when I go to Germany!

Emma Jane Kirsch. Aug. 30, 1930 [age 15]

As I mentioned earlier, you studied and taught piano during high school. Figuring out early that solo recitals were not for you, you found your niche as an accompanist and playing in small ensembles. You described how much you enjoyed working with some of your committed students.

While still in high school, you attended memorable concerts and recitals given by some of the greatest artists of the twentieth century:

February 25, 1931

Saw Sergei Rachmaninoff perform! His shadings, technique, and everything was marvelous.

Oct. 13, 1931 (I am writing this Thursday night, the 14th)

I heard [Lawrence] Tibbett last night and even got his autograph! I stayed all night at Mrs. Chamberlin's. I enjoyed it very much. Oh! So much.

Jan. 18, 1933

Althea and I [had] dinner at her house. We went to hear Fritz Kreisler and his accompanist. Was a wonderful program. Althea stayed overnight.

Although most of your entries are legible, some words required real effort to decipher. Once in a while I could read a word without having a clue about its meaning. In some cases I would ask Chris for help. For example, we could read the word "chinwag," but neither of us had any idea what it meant. Chris thought it might be a food item, which made sense to me. Thanks to the Internet, we learned it's a synonym for "gabfest" or "friendly conversation."

May 24, 1934

Miss Nelson and Miss Barquist were down to dinner. We had a good "chinwag"—something which we really haven't had for four years.

You learned to bake and to love entertaining:

March 29, 1933

Dad's birthday. Baked a sponge cake—and it was a "fizzle."

March 31

Got a new cake recipe for sponge cake from Mrs. Willets and tried it—and it really turned out after the two other "flops."

July 18th, 1934

A big day and evening. Bob, Anita, and Bert were here for dinner—company dinner, including sherbet and cakes iced by Chef Kirsch. After this dinner and the ugly and hot process of dishwashing, we all went to the Green Lake Fieldhouse to a dance. The Little Dutch Mill was the theme (especially appropriate for all of us four). I wore for the first time my lavender organdy. After the dance we all had a hamburger at Horluck's and we got home early. 11:45 or a quarter to 12. (What's this younger generation coming to, the parents wonder. . .)

Your Grandfather Kirsch and your favorite cousin, Billy, died within a few months of one another. Billy's death was especially painful for you.

Aug. 8, 1932

New—News—Terrible Happenings! Billy was killed in an airplane accident! Mother and Daddy left for Sat Lake by train at 4:30.

Aug. 13

Got a letter from Daddy Not much, but enclosed a newspaper article which gives quite full details.

Aug. 16

Got a letter from Mother—a wonderful letter. Daddy got home. Aunt Leah sent me Billy's class ring which he had on when he died.

June 28, 1933 [During their family trip to visit relatives in Utah, Colorado, Kansas, Illinois, including the Chicago World's Fair and a preview of Midwestern colleges]

Dad drove us to the mausoleum where Bill is. This is a most beautiful place—the location, the stained picture windows, and the solemnity and beauty of it all. In the evening Rollie and his girl came over. Rollie was one of Bill's very, very good friends.

You wrote your own poetic descriptions of hiking with friends. For example, this report from near Snoqualmie, Washington, during a camping trip to Lake Hancock with seven friends and a chaperone:

June 24–July 4, 1934.

I still think that this hike is one of the grandest trips there could be since the trail is through virgin timber, the mosses, fungi, and numerous wild flowers all add shards of green and beauty to the natural rusticness of the entire trail. The creek—splashing and playing—can be heard, too. Tall cedars draped with mosses stand guard here and there like ancient sentinels.

A 4-hour hike to the lake. Hiked to Lake Callaghan with Winfred. Had lunch of 24 raisins.

Had quite a feast in the evening. "Best ever!"

It was a "grand bunch, one swell time—one good pal and one wish—to repeat the event in a year."

Your return to Seattle after your freshman year at DePauw University was especially poignant for me. Arriving at your childhood home in Seattle, walking into your bedroom, seemed at once familiar and strange. It was as if you felt at sea, having left your innocence behind and were experiencing a transition you didn't yet know how to put into words.

Sept. 1, 1935

Dearest Diary—My heart is so full tonight that I can hardly suppress the desire—for some silly reason—because I get so darned homesick that it's terrible. I think of Indiana and Louisiana, Bob, Virg, Joe, George and memories crowed unhaltingly before my mental eyes. Oh, I'm going to miss them all so!

Today Anita, Bert, Bob (a different one) and I went to Shadow lake. I swam out to the raft and back twice. Am I improving! It did turn out nicely although it was so terribly foggy. We were boat riding. The Tri Delt moon—the songs—Mount Rainier is a haze. All was very beautiful. But coming home since I had nothing more to occupy my attention I began to think and I did get so homesick it's awful. Bob is so darned unemotional—at times he doesn't seem humanly possible. Gosh, how I remember how darned sweet Bob was. I'm perhaps just a silly Ole gal—but all of us like to have a little attention. My, I'm to blame—some might say I'm that way too, but I myself think otherwise. But that's life too.

Recalling my own experiences of moving to and from New Jersey, I can empathize with your experience of leaving home for Indiana and returning a year later. Of course, I was younger and the circumstances were very different. You left when you were ready and returned having changed dramatically after your year of college. I left before I was ready and returned to discover that my high school had changed, but I had not. I wanted to continue where I had left off from my freshman year in Walla Walla. But kids change a lot between their freshman and junior years. I felt adrift in my classes, but far more so socially. Fortunately, my dearest friends had saved my place in their friendship circle, where I felt welcome and totally loved—one of the best gifts of my life.

Thank you for not trying to explain to me that you understood the feeling of devastation I had when we moved to Chatham in 1959. You could have said you felt similarly bereft as a young girl, but you didn't. You knew that I wouldn't have believed you. Instead you gave me the gift of time—allowing me to read your journals eighty years after you wrote them to make these connections on my own.

You were drawn to Sara Teasdale's poetry:

February 1935

I read Sara Teasdale and learned these four grand lines:

Moon's Ending

"Moon, worn thin to the width of a quill,

In the dawn clouds flying,

How good to go, light into light and still

Giving light, dying."

It has a very perfect application to life and death. How I love Teasdale. . .

[Sara Teasdale committed suicide in 1933 at the age of 48.]

You included self-reflections:

March 1935

Gee I do hope I get some mail tomorrow—guess no one loves me anymore. I would like to know what it is like to be in love—that burning passion that consumes all else in its way—and so oft it seems that it leaves only a handful of echoes and a few broken memories to hold—We can't help to wonder where it will end. It seems as if so much of the time we're only groping toward the unknown.

November 1935

I wonder why I'm here—where I'm going—sometimes it all seems so unreal that it's almost an insanity in my mind. I fear I could be terribly unhappy if I were to let myself—but I mustn't—I can't.

Dec. 1, 1935

Oh, there are so many things to think! I used to think that at 20 one was very much grown up and ready to be married, but I feel very much as a little girl—who doesn't yet know what she wants.

By Feb. 1936,

I wonder—I wonder—I wonder—I wonder—I wonder—and I wonder.

In 1935 you transferred to Whitman College; you found a couple of violin students with whom to perform. You found joy and laughter in your music:

Tuesday October 8

Today was a student recital. I accompanied for Peggy Oliver and Betty Lou Kennedy. I made up my mind that I was going to hit those end chords with Betty Lou in Drigo's "Valse Bluette" if it were the last thing I'd do— and I did!

I listened to that piece on YouTube and could imagine your nailing the final chords to complement the violin's notes. Betty Lou Kennedy also performed with Dad on cello a few years later. When she quit playing the violin, she gave her instrument to me, as she learned I had picked up the violin after years of not playing after Dad's death.

Later that semester you wrote about your own efforts on violin:

Maxine [roommate] has lent me her violin. I promised to practice from only 9:30 to 10:30 at night in my room, so that the entire dorm can get the whole benefit of my progress. To further the agony, we are to play in recital sometime during the year. I'll likely be giving a recital the first shot out of the basket. . . Genius, you know.

That same month you record an incident with your piano instructor, Mrs. Bowers, who saw you talking with two guys near the music building when you were almost late for your lesson:

'Sfunny today when Mrs. Bowers yelled out the window, "Do you want me to bring the piano out there? Next time I'll invite you in, boys." This

remark was directed to Keith and Scotty who were conversing in front of
the library with me.

Some other things I learned about you: You were passionate about
learning German, evident in your eagerness to receive letters from
German relatives and acquaintances, to practice talking with your
Grandfather Kirsch when he visited you in Seattle, and to write an
occasional German phrase in your diary.

You related especially well to adults as a young person and found
conversations with them easy and stimulating. For example, you wrote
about Mr. LaVatta, a family friend, who came to dinner when you
were in high school. After he left you wrote, "He is one of the most
intelligent people I have ever met."

You always loved letters. Even as a young girl you couldn't wait
for the postman to deliver the mail, hoping there would be a letter
for you and feeling disappointed when there was none. You yourself
were a committed letter writer. In a January 1936 letter pasted into
your journal, you wrote: "I figured up last night how many letters I
wanted to write during this week—only 20! I'm beginning to believe
that I need a personal secretary—no fooling, but it's a cinch that you
would not do!!"

You wrote enthusiastically, as if talking with a close friend who
both understood you and could read between the lines.

Males figured prominently in your entries. You likely set your lifetime record for most males "met" on a single occasion your freshman
year at DePauw.

Sunday September 30, 1934–Open House

This was one of the most wonderful evenings ever. All residents of the
fraternities and men's halls were introduced to us. It really seems unbelievable to say that we met about 800 men. After we had been introduced to all
the men, we grabbed whomever we could. I don't remember just who was
who, but I talked to several of interest—a Beta who had been to Monroe,
Washington; Villapiano, a Lambda Chi; Elmer Carribur from Seattle; some
boy from La Grande, Oregon; and an Alpha Tau Omega with whom I have
a date Sunday; Bob Koss, a Phi Gamma Delta; and last but not least by a
long way, Willard Youngblood, a Phi Kappa Psi, Norma's [Mom's relative]
pick as my boyfriend.

Before the Phi Kappa Psi men arrived, we were given orders to "do our best." Of course Willard is plenty popular, and as he came down the line and I was introduced, he said to me, "I want to see you afterwards." After talking for quite a while, he asked me for a date Friday. I imagine that this made an impression on the Tri Delt girls. Anyway it should have.

Among your many suitors, crackerjack writers got your attention, while you quickly pushed away the mundane and plodding. Although strong language skills might be necessary, they were not sufficient to win you over. A couple of them wrote clever letters, often quoting poetry or writing their own. But while you acknowledged their command of words, you wrote that they didn't "awaken a spark in this lonely soul of mine." Ernie, a high school boyfriend, and Virgil, a college beau, tried to win you over through their writing, but instead seemed to be stuck, writing the same sentiments over and over. Neither advanced to the top tier.

One of your professors at Whitman had assigned a project to explore the question "Do men marry women who are less intelligent than they are?" I think as you pondered your own prospects, you wondered what it might be like to settle for a partner who was less articulate than you.

> *There is something about words. In expert hands, manipulated deftly, they take you prisoner. Wind themselves around your limbs like spider silk, and when you are so enthralled you cannot move, they pierce your skin, enter your blood, numb your thoughts. Inside you they work their magic.*
>
> —Diane Setterfield, *The Thirteenth Tale*

Walla Walla nurtures wordsmiths. There is something about the place—perhaps its warm-summer Mediterranean climate, its tree-lined streets and graceful mansions, its views of the Blue Mountains, or the waters of Mill Creek and the Walla Walla River—that inspires the writing instinct. Even its Native American name—meaning "place of many waters"—calls to mind a flowing river of words. Years ago, two local newspapers, the *Walla Walla Union-Bulletin* and the *Whitman*

College Pioneer, were the channels between whose banks flowed the thoughts and stories of two restless and masterful inkslingers who would become part of your life—one a decades-long friend and the other your beloved husband.

In early 1936, near the beginning of your second term at Whitman College, Pat O'Reilly entered your life. Writing to your parents, you described him as someone who seemed to like you. Although he had not asked you out, an intriguing idea occurred to you: Why not invite Pat to the upcoming Mortar Board Spring Formal? It might just "start something." In your entry dated February 29, you wrote, "Am I only moonstruck or is it really love?"

You and Pat dated much of that semester. In November, well into the following term, you met Roly Miller. Pat and Roly knew each other before you arrived at Whitman for your sophomore year. Pat, editor of the *Pioneer*, would eventually move on to the American Broadcasting Company in Hollywood. Roly was a reporter for the *Union-Bulletin*.

After a rather unspectacular beginning—Roly drove you home from a football game—you quickly discovered there was much more to this newspaper reporter. He had "been [to] places like Europe" and played "terrific jazz piano." By early December, you saw "Rolly" as the "only path now. . . . Everything seems so worthless besides this one thing now." You were not moonstruck; you were thunderstruck and in love. As you wrote to your parents on November 4:

> Life is so complex. Last Tuesday a Rolly Miller, he works on the paper here in town and is a good friend of Frank's [Frank LeRoux, whom she was dating at the time], brought me home from the intramural football game. I mentioned something about it to Frank and Frank said that Rolly had asked him about me, but Frank had said nothing very much. Only that I was O.K. (Or whatever is boy's vernacular). So, tomorrow evening Rolly and I are going out. However, as I said before it's getting to be rather one-sided on this campus for me. (Watch out, Ejay. . . You're slipping. . . And how! That's me talking to myself on paper.)

Nov. 5–Thursday

> My first date with Rolly Miller—nothing too awfully exciting. We went to the Capital and saw two good shows interspersed with a few kid squawks, etc. "Mary Burns, Fugitive" & "Postal Inspector" Of course he

would need to stop into the cabin—where Frank was hopping busily around in an apron—looking somewhat similar to a bartender—

But he asked me to the Beta Formal—Dec. 12th and we made halfway plans concerning Saturday—about going to Pullman.

Things escalated quickly, as you reveal in your journal between December 5 and 12:

December 12—

Well, behind as usual—but everything has been so heavenly there has been nothing else to think about. I come in from a date and I wander around in a dream. We wonder where the time has gone but we certainly can't figure it out. Tonight we were figuring up that Thanksgiving Day ('member?) was less than two weeks away and yet each time we go out time flies by in no time. Paradox, truly—but I'll let "Binx" figure out that one! I see only one way now but it's a hard time to say anything to Virg. Oh, it must be Rolly—we get along so perfectly swell. I've never said it [I love you] but I likely will. There are so many things that can't be placed here—Everything seems so worthless besides this one thing now.

Frank called—and we had about a 30-second conversation. But what was there to say?

Tuesday—it was Rolly

Wednesday—it was Rolly

Thursday—it was Rolly

Friday—it was Rolly

It has been only he for it would seem ever and ever so long.

Saturday—the Beta formal—12th

I guess the date of December 12, 1936, will long be remembered by me and Rolly. I'm now wearing a Kappa Alpha pin—and it would seem quite as if it has been for some time. Each date seems to have the time go faster and faster. Now I suppose I must write Virg—but there is nothing too imperative concerning that.

I wore my white dress and my corsage was lovely—red roses with silver leaves.

We had journalistic trades—Pat (how very, very far ago that seems)

I'm so extremely happy.

In your letters home you often included newspaper clippings about

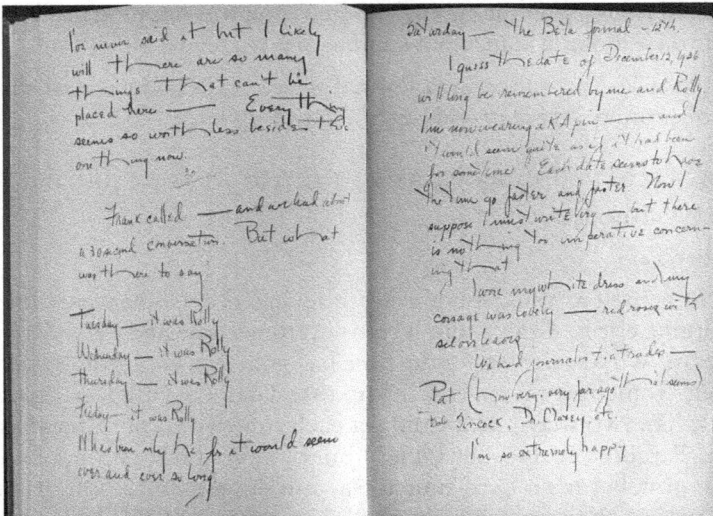

campus goings-on and other noteworthy events. (Sending clippings you thought might interest your recipients became a lifelong activity for you.) A pair of articles about a heavy snowfall in Walla Walla in early January 1937 stand out for me.

You clipped the side-by-side pieces and folded them into the January 14, 1937, envelope addressed to Mr. and Mrs. Frank Kirsch, 8th Avenue N.W., Seattle, Washington.

At the top of each story you had penciled the names of its author: "Pat O'Reilly" and "Rolly," as if you were presenting your parents with a sample of their writing to compare, each author displaying his verbal chops. I can hear you saying, "It's one thing for me to tell you how well each of them writes. Now you can see for yourself. Impressive, don't you think?"

Pat's piece, "Snow Brings Both Cheers and Votes of Disapprobation," focused on people's reactions to the new snowfall and their ways of keeping warm: "Winter Scene. . . Ruddy-faced youngsters, swathed to the chin, gleefully ride a la 'Alaskan' on sleds drawn by their mother, while dignified businessmen plowing through drifts mutter about "that blasted snow is going to freeze my spine."

After describing the complaints of shoe repairmen and cheers from "java-dispensers," he continued:

But of all the businesses, that of vending earmuffs seems to be the best. Hundreds of Walla Wallans have taken a fancy to the coverings, which are available in plaids, checks, stripes, solid colors or almost any design desirable. Professor Hart, college French instructor from North Carolina, wends his way through the snow with blue and white checked muffs; one of the local sports writers has a brilliant-hued orange pair (and wonders who got the other pair in stock); and Mayor Dorsey Hill is sporting black ones lined with grey.

When Pat referred to the "local sports writer" with the bright-as-neon earmuffs, could he have been referring to Dad? After all, Dad regularly wrote "The Sports Mill" column, one of which you clipped to put into the envelope along with the articles about the snowfall.

I'm imagining Dad—wearing a smirk in anticipation of your reaction—showing up at Prentiss Hall to pick you up for a date, bright orange thermal patches cupping each ear. I can almost hear you shriek with delight at his outrageous headdress.

In contrast to Pat's colorful column, Dad's piece about the snowfall was more straightforward, reporting the weather and its effect on traffic and farming.

When Roly Miller answered the casting call for your leading man, it was soon clear that he got the part. You and he experienced an almost magical synergy that was evident to you and others around you. Life became sweeter, the future seemed unlimited. Your journal writing and Roly's summer 1937 letters to you are dizzying in their excitement. All the speculation and wondering in your journals resolved into a partnership that would last until his death in January 1957.

You and Roly saw the first 1936 Walla Walla showing of George Cukor's film *Romeo & Juliet* soon after you started dating. In a note to your parents, you described the movie as too wonderful for words. In his newspaper review, Roly found the words to encourage readers to see Shakespeare brought to life on the silver screen. It's hard to imagine a better example of two lovebirds watching the story of two lovebirds.

Shakespeare Nobly Done

"Romeo and Juliet," Shown at Capital, Is Brilliant Film Well Handled.

In filming "Romeo and Juliet," which had its first Walla Walla showing last night at the Capitol Theatre, the motion picture industry did more than produce a brilliant picture—it took a long step, many people believe, toward giving the cinema a high place in the legitimate drama.

For in "Romeo and Juliet" the script of the play for the first time is given its proper prominence. In the past Shakespeare and other great dramatists have been given some attention by the movies, but it has always been felt necessary to chop the dialogue and action to pieces and bring forth something which resembles the original about as much as hash looks like beef on the hoof.

By some miracle, however, the producers found courage to recall that Bill Shakespeare was a pretty fair scenarist in his own right, and only such cutting was indulged in as was absolutely necessary to adapt the play to movie mechanics. The lines are Shakespeare's, not those of some anonymous adapter, and it seems certain that the Bard himself would be proud of the version of "Romeo" that has now appeared in such striking fashion.

All the artistic, histrionic and scenic resources of Hollywood have gone to make this cinematic version of one of the world's great tragedies. Norma Shearer plays a lovely and entirely capable Juliet; Leslie Howard a sympathetic, arresting Romeo, and the remainder of the cast measures up in every way to the exacting standards of the play. Edna May Oliver, in the important part of the nurse, makes screen history, and a list of other players—John Barrymore, C. Aubrey Smith, Basil Rathbone, Reginald Denny, Conway Tearle, Ian Wolfe and many others—reveals the care taken in casting.

Costuming, settings and scenic effects in "Romeo" are superb, but it is the play itself which deserves the greatest credit. The greatest romance of history has come alive again under the deft touch of Director George Cukor and the actors, and it is difficult to see how it can escape becoming a real box-office attraction.

Roly—the winner of your heart—was magical in ways beyond your previous suitors. Besides being musical and articulate, he had a spectacular sense of humor. He crafted sentences that turned your mind loose, creating new images and possibilities. His words were like silken melodies that drew you in. And they held you captive. You swam in his glorious sea of words and music for two decades.

The day after Dad died, Pat O'Reilly wrote to you from Hollywood:

January 22, 1957

Dear Emma Jane:

I am extremely saddened by the news. Roly was a good friend and a fine working companion. He was a real fresh wind for the newspaper, and I have often thought with pleasure of our association in those first days of re-vamping the *Union-Bulletin.*

Even more. . . you, Roly, Helen and I all have common threads which make the break more poignant. Our love to you and the children.

Pat

In my self-appointed role as family historian, I have attempted in this letter to bring to life a small slice of your and Dad's lives. The story of "Roly and EJay" is one of the main attractions in our family history.

Besides your many letters and journals, I have a paper that you wrote for a college biology class in 1938 on your genetic history and characteristics. The following excerpts especially interested me:

Not prone to believe superstitions.

We seem to have no tendency toward T.B. or cancer, about which there is still some discussion as to whether this is hereditary or not.

Longevity: From all the ages of grandparents who have lived quite a normal life and have died without outside causes it would seem that this is a definite [possibility].

What is to come: Predicting what is to be in the future is the same as attempting to peek into the crystal and see what is in one's future. However, it is possible for me to picture the future "Utopian me."

I expect to be very happily married and have started a family by age 35. I'll be very interested in my home and liking and getting the very best of what there is. Club work, too, will likely claim my attention—but, my home shall be first. I shall hope to be doing something worthwhile in the community, possibly a couple alumnae groups will claim my attention. I'd not likely lack for things to do [understatement!].

By age 60, it's possible that I'll be lessening my pace a little and become a little more reflective—begin to sit back and enjoy what has gone before and what is going on at the time. [Sorry, Mutti, you never slowed down, and it was a joy to watch you in high gear.]

Newlyweds in Canada, 1938.

Emma Jane at 1019 Alvarado.

Maybe I'm putting too much faith in the future, but I do believe that there are going to be some very swell things in store—and to make the sweet appreciated, there will need be some disappointments, too. But I'm really looking forward to the years to come!

Your journals and letters are a priceless gift. Through them, I have come to know you not only as my mother but as a young girl and young woman. Every page reveals your undiminished passion for life, music, travel, and connection with others.

Roly and Emma Jane chaperoning a Tri Delt formal, 1949.

In a world unspecified in time and place. A world not of gods or spirits. Not a world dreamed up by me. It was a world made up by words and only words. No images, no sounds.

Words fall short, but sometimes their shadows can reach the unspeakable.

One can and must live with loss and grief and sorrow and bereavement. Together they frame this life, as solid as the ceiling and the floor and the walls and the doors.

—Yiyun Li, *Where Reasons End.*

In my imagination I return to your hospital room in December 1989, carrying my transcription of your journals. Rather than being stone silent, I read to you from your youthful musings and reflections, a shared activity that can transport the two of us to a place where we can wander in the field next to your girlhood home. Two young girls on the cusp of adventure.

S'mores on the beach.

One of Mother's last trips to Wayne, Nebraska.

Mother, you told me many times over the years that, as an only child, you longed for a brother or sister. In your genetics paper you wrote, "I learned to be good company for myself and I was content to fashion doll clothes, play house, read, and other solitary occupations. I had my friends, but I didn't have to be with someone for a good time."

In your high school years, you made genuine friendships, some through music. In particular, you found great camaraderie with two females, both of whom were singers you accompanied on piano.

The first, a classmate of yours named Althea, took voice lessons in downtown Seattle. You often attended her lessons, sometimes to accompany her at the piano. Her teacher coached you both in preparing for high school and other local concerts. You and Althea continued to write to each other during your first two years of college. Second was Mrs. Pryor, a singer and family friend, mentioned dozens of times in your journals. She remained your close friend and mentor through your high school years. You visited her frequently and accompanied her at the piano. She would take you to concerts, movies, and other activities. Days after your high school graduation, you wrote the poignant entry: "June 23, 1934, Mrs. Pryor's funeral—a very sad affair for me."

It was, however, during your college years that your relationships grew in number and intensity. Each relationship brought new discoveries and interests.

I'll mention just two examples of your deep college friendships.

Upon your arrival at DePauw University in 1934, you met your roommate Jane Preston Howard, who became one of your dearest friends. Jane brought energy and vitality to your life as you settled into your first prolonged time away from home. Your diary, "Book of K—1934–35," includes an exchange you two had on her birthday just months after you both arrived at DePauw:

January 16, 1935

Jane's birthday. In the morning she came down and asked for her birthday present—"to take you (me) home as sweet as I first knew you." And tears came to her eyes—usually though I don't know why—when one is deeply moved, tears come to your eyes. I promised her I would try.

Reading it a half century later, I am moved as well. Jane likely influenced your ability to express affection toward others, a behavior you noted as being absent at home with your parents.

At the end of your freshman year, you took the train to see Jane before returning to Seattle.

June 21, 1935 Friday

Saw Virg for the last time ere I start home. Left from Evansville. Grace and I had lunch ere I left at 12:31. Jane met me at the train. In the evening,

Jane, and I drove to Centralia—and I—the proper guest—went to sleep coming home.

Sept. 1, 1935 [Newly arrived at Whitman College to begin sophomore year]

Dearest Diary

This year there won't be any Jane—dear pal that she is—for me to discuss all my what it's over with. But I can't live forever in that one year, for surely there must be several more exciting things to come. But this year did mean so much!

December 30, 1935

Monday—30th

Permanent in morning. Letters from Jane—glory, a 28 pager

February 25, 1936

A letter from Mother and a card from Jane. Jane writes, "I can't understand you sometimes—people like you aren't supposed to run around down here on earth without your halos and wings."

Jane included in one of her letters a fine pencil sketch of you that captures your bright eyes perfectly along with your permed curls surrounding the face she loved. Unfortunately, I have not found a photo of you and Jane, although I know you would have had some. You and

Photo sent to Jane Preston Howard and her drawing.

she, who lived in New Jersey much of her life, saw each other when you could and wrote or talked on the phone when you couldn't.

Unable to be in Seattle for the 1938 wedding, Jane sent a Western Union telegram: "Pleasant dreams Matey on wedding Eve and a good wish for every mile between us. Jane Preston Howard."

Jane and her husband, Leon Schmehl, attended Walter's and your wedding in 1958 in New Jersey. Jane's endearing letter, which included a diagram of the reception seating, made it possible for the rest of us to imagine being there with you. Jane kept tabs on us kids beyond that day as well. For example, she saw Sally Smethurst and me off to France the summer of 1965, helping us to settle into our quarters on the SS *France.*

The second friend, Anita Blucher of Seattle, began her freshman year at Whitman College in 1935, at the same time you transferred from DePauw. Anita pledged Delta Delta Delta sorority, a decision that was to forge a deep connection during your college years and beyond.

In your diary, you described an overnight train ride with Anita as you traveled from Seattle to Walla Walla:

January 2, 1936,

Anita and I had a berth together—talk about wiggle worms! We've tried to sleep together three times now—maybe that should be the last.

September 22, 1936—Just to think back a year ago—

A gorgeous moon on our tiled roof, the girls in a delta and then our silver, gold, and blue ribbons—and today Anita had the colors pinned on her. Was I ever happy although we both cried and I had only one hanky and, too, I spilled the nuts. Nuts! Oh, but her pledging is one thing I wanted. I think we have the grandest bunch of girls—Beth Armand, Madeline Albert, Helen Ruth Maddox, Maxine Conover, Anita Blucher—well, anyway 21 pledges all together.

And so ends one of my life's dreams—to have Anita a Tri Delt. No, I should say, "Not end but the beginning," for I'm sure it will grow lovelier as the years go on."

Anita wrote the day before your wedding that Tri Delts attending and participating in the wedding had arrived, and concluded with, "Rehearsal, then supper at the Kirsch's." The next (wedding) day, she wrote, "E.Jay got married and safely on her way. Everything went off nicely, but my feet ache & my hand hurts from shaking hands. They are going to Alaska."

I love the picture of Anita and you curled up in a window frame from those Tri Delt days. Anita was a bridesmaid in Dad's and your 1938 wedding. You and she remained close for fifty years, and it was great fun for me to be in her daughter Margaret's class in high school. Margaret discovered that her mother, a lifelong diary keeper, included entries about your wedding from June 1938, which she shared with me.

Emma Jane Kirsch and Anita Blucher Cornelison, Tri Delt sisters at Whitman, ca. 1936.

While transcribing your journals in 2018, I began thinking about the myriad ways you contributed to Walla Walla society and institutions. I felt overwhelmed as I tried to list the hundreds of news articles reporting on your activities. How would I ever be able to summarize all that? Then, a stroke of good luck: I found Iris Myers's writeup about you in 1988 as you replaced her as editor of the *Whitman College Fifty*

Plus newsletter. A veteran staffer on the *Union-Bulletin,* Iris crafted a summary of your contributions to the college, the symphony, and the Walla Walla community.

Introducing . . . Editor-Elect Emma Jane Kirsch Brattain

"I've never been employed."

That modest statement of Emma Jane Kirsch Miller Brattain, '38, who takes over editorship of *The News* with the Spring '88 issue, scarcely tells the whole story.

While Emma Jane may never have been on a conventional employee payroll, she certainly epitomizes the full meaning of the words "effective volunteerism."

Just reflect on her service to her Alma mater alone. For five years she was chair of the Alumni Fund and also served in similar capacity for Friends of the Penrose Memorial Library. One of her ardent interests is books. In 1972 she was given the Alumna of Merit Award by the Alumni Association. Now, at the 50-year milestone of her graduation from college she is assuming the editorship of *The News.*

But Whitman College has not absorbed all of her energy. The community of Walla Walla has benefited immeasurably from her volunteerism—the Walla Walla Symphony and Symphony Guild, League of Women Voters, the Archaeological Society, the Congregational Church, the Y.W.C.A. Board, the Walla Walla Art Club, P.E.O. Sisterhood—all reflecting her wide interest in cultural activities. Such contributions of time, energy, and expertise resulted in her selection by the Walla Walla Chamber of Commerce as its Woman of the Year in 1976.

. . . Transferring to Whitman as a sophomore, she received her degree with a major in public school music. The scope of her activities on campus is attested to by the listing of her affiliations: president of her sorority, Delta Delta Delta; member of Mu Phi Epsilon, music honorary; college Y.W.C.A.; and president of Mortar Board, senior women's honorary.

"My one journalistic attempt," she recalls with a smile, "was as society editor of *The Pioneer.*"

(Editorially we happen to know something of her writing skills, which are more than sufficient.)

As for the statement that she had "never been employed," there is a simple explanation. Two weeks after receiving her diploma from Whitman she was married to Roland Miller, Walla Walla newspaperman who eventually became publisher of the *Walla Walla Union-Bulletin*, a position he held until his untimely death of cancer in 1957.

Your role as newsletter editor ended in December 1989. Just as you left your peers at Whitman bereft, you left several dear friends feeling a huge loss.

Your two closest female friends in Walla Walla, Dorothy Robinson and Mabel Groseclose [see Chapter 7], were integral to your life and to our family as we kids were growing up. Each played a crucial role in providing grounding and stability to our lives after Dad's death. And again after yours. By phone and in person, they encouraged us to carry on during those achingly painful days. I remember in particular Dorothy's reaching out to me as I wondered how I would get through the weeks and months following your death.

Many other friends told us how important you were to their lives and how crucial your presence was in theirs. I'm including a few of their notes, which go beyond the standard bereavement messages.

From Frances Casper:

> I will miss her so much—she enriched my life in so many ways; as a dear friend for so many years, she shared her experiences in books to read, music to hear and places to go, and I loved her dearly. You have beautiful memories of a very special lady, special mother, friend and one who loved all of you with great pride and joy in everything you did.
>
> My love, Frances

From Ruth Kimball:

> Dear G, D, & W,
>
> What is there to say except that we are all together in feeling the loss of one of the world's loveliest persons?
>
> I've never known anyone whose goodness and intellect was shared so lovingly and humbly with so many.
>
> The blessings of her presence surrounded us whether she was here or far away—and that's the way it will always be.
>
> What a legacy you have! And how fortunate I am to have known and loved your mother as long as I have!
>
> That same love belongs to you and your children.

I am constantly in awe of the vitality of your mother's continuing presence in our lives.

Other beloved persons have left us and soon are wonderful memories, but Emma Jane is still here. We all feel it, and everywhere I go someone says, "She's still here. She's with me all the time."

If we feel that way, how much more strongly you must feel her strength and love everywhere. That should make it all easier—and will eventually—but right now I'm sure it make it increasingly difficult because of the repetition of adjustments to reality. I guess when you have possessed something so special, you have to pay a special price for that privilege.

Devotedly, Ruth

From Maxine Sires, Alvarado Terrace neighbor:

January 2, 1990

Dear D, G, B, and W,

Mari just phoned me that Emma Jane's ordeal is over and I feel, as I hope you do, that death is a friend. The briefing began with the first shock of the diagnosis. My fear was that this vital, wonderful human being might have to suffer the indignities of helplessness and slow degeneration which she had had to live through with Walter. Now she has been spared and was able to die peacefully surrounded by the people she loved best.

I cherish the memories I have of her and all of you over the years. I wish there could have been many more years. But I can tell you that after too many of those "golden" years, the gold becomes a bit tarnished.

She knew how to live fully and to die valiantly. I have been with you in spirit these past weeks and will be thinking of you through the next stage of celebrating her life and facing the many tasks of bringing it to an official close.

I will miss hearing about each of you as I have done through Emma Jane, and I hope not to lose you completely. You have shared the pain together and I hope that 1990 will bring peace and fulfillment in your separate lives.

Love, Maxine

These were the kinds of friends you cultivated: those who generously looked after you and your offspring, as you did theirs.

It took me years to grasp the impact you had on Southeastern Washingtonians. Your legacy extends far beyond the gifts you gave to your immediate family. Just days after your death, Douglas Clark sent the following poignant remembrance to the *Union-Bulletin*:

A Tribute to Emma Jane Brattain

With the sudden and untimely death of Emma Jane Brattain, a giant in our community has fallen. Her life and contributions represented what was best in Walla Walla and among the people who live in this valley.

With interests and involvement in the affairs of Whitman College, the local chapters of the American Institute of Archaeology and the symphony, among too many other endeavors to mention, she was the quintessential Renaissance woman.

Our lives are the poorer in her absence. The place in which we live is missing an important element of its richness, cultures and diversity and we witness sadly the passing of a saint.

Now we depend on someone—some ones—to step into her place, to pick up where she left off and to carry on the traditions of involvement and service which have so characterized her life and so enriched our community.

Douglas R. Clark, Walla Walla College

I will always be grateful for the kind and generous thoughts others wrote about you. They complement your loving role as mother and grandmother to your four kids and grandchildren. What a gift to have these reflections and memories of others who also loved you!

Mourning in many ways is like falling in love. . . It shares with falling in love total surrender and withdrawal. It is the only thing that counts.

—Toby Talbot, *A Book About My Mother*

After your death, I felt at sea, disoriented. My inner child was now an orphan. I desperately needed something that could help stabilize me. I found a book by Toby Talbot titled *A Book about My Mother*, which tells of her own bereavement. As I began reading, her writing took my breath away. Her words rang true—they could have been mine. She too felt the carpet of her life being yanked from under her when her mother died. I wanted Talbot to guide me along this unstable ground, to help me through those months of despair. If she could hold it together, I could as well.

That book helped me get past my sense of loss, but there was still a piece missing. What that piece was became clearer the more I worked on the family history. From the start, I had been looking to get closer to you by reading your diaries, journals, and letters. I imagined myself looking over your shoulder as you wrote your revealing letters and journal entries. In them I would find the "essential" you, with whom I could bond. That would satisfy me.

Besides having to survive your death, I wanted to understand how you yourself lived through loss and change. You never lost your equilibrium after Dad and Grammie died within the space of three years.

Your greatest challenge came in 1957 with Dad's death. You, a young widow [age forty-one] with three kids, needed to remain grounded in your relationships and routines. As your youngest child, I watched how you got through those days. Although I was too young to know what you were going through, you were showing me how it is possible to carry on after such a loss. Strange as it seems to me now—with my later research on daughters and mothers—I don't think I ever asked how you dealt with your mother's death following that car accident. Although Gramps lived an additional decade, he never recovered from Grammie's death. He did not share your survival stamina.

Archaeology holds all the keys to understanding who we are and where we came from.

—Sarah Parcak

After their deaths and your marriage to Walter, your passion for archaeology became a flood tide that never receded. Either you were on a trip with Walter or were planning the next one, it seemed. No matter where you were on the planet, you had an extraordinary sense of being present. Despite your eagerness to travel, you never seemed to be in a hurry. Traveling was as natural to you as your morning cup of coffee. You moved smoothly through life as I have seen few others do.

When I finally moved from focusing on my life to looking at yours, I needed to know how you did it. At first I thought I might find out by transcribing hundreds of pages of your diaries from high school through college. Although they were full of colorful adventures and observations, they shed little light on your passion for exploring.

My breakthrough came when I was reading obsessively about Egypt. As I sat steeped in books about Egyptian history, art, and archaeology, I felt like I was finally seeing the world as you had. Suddenly it appeared, spread before me as if I had seen it in a flash of lightning. I saw your craving to experience ancient civilizations as giving focus to your life. A sense of purpose that would see you through the rough patches.

Reading your travel journals and reflecting on your wanderlust, I have finally found the connection to you I have craved. You were always my mother, and I always loved you. But your outlook on life, your need to see as much of the world as you could, was a closed book to me. Now, for the first time, we stand side by side looking out at the world through similar lenses. Through your words and pictures you have given me the special glasses to see the world as you saw it.

A memorable exchange you and I had in 1986 during your move from our family home to Rustic Place triggered this sense of connection.

Individuals have spent their entire lives researching and writing these books. Someone has to read them!

—Emma Jane Brattain, July 1986.

It was the summer of your move from 1019 Alvarado Terrace. Your new home was a tidy single-story condominium with a view of the Blue Mountains from your back yard. It was just the right size for a single senior with relatively few possessions. But mountains of memorabilia blanketed four floors of Ten-nineteen, plus the garage and its overhead guest house. Fitting it all into your new abode would be like stuffing a camel into a Mayonnaise jar. Sorting and packing the accumulation of forty years would require a Herculean effort. Some extreme paring-down would have to happen.

The books were only part of it.

The scene in question took place in a basement room that was your auxiliary library—two walls lined with books—museum catalogs,

Chris's post card design Mother used to announce her move.

travelogues, stories of the world's lost cultures. Exhausted from our seemingly endless packing, I felt overwhelmed and a little disgusted at what seemed like pointless excess. I turned to you and said with only a hint of rebuke, "Just look at all these books…"

Your response, that someone had to read them, stung. Although I felt immediately humbled, it took years for me to see the judgment behind my comment. My snide observation had ignored a defining feature of your life. Even as a child in Colorado, you had an insatiable drive to learn about past civilizations and those who discovered them. That yearning never left you. During your final Thanksgiving visit to Nebraska—just weeks before death took you—you excitedly talked of future plans. You would need only a decade more to reach one goal: to travel with all of your grandchildren, a tradition you started by taking Megan and Mari to Europe. Brief trips could spark lifelong interests.

For over two decades you and Walter explored the world together. As his cognitive powers faded—thus ending your travel partnership— you needed to fill the void. Your readiness to roam was evident in that always-open suitcase on your bedroom floor. Never completely emptied, its gaping leather shell held the promise of another sojourn. A few unworn shirts and slacks in the bag meant you were already preparing for the next departure. Soon you would add to its contents in anticipation of the next trip. I imagine you looking at it fondly, its scuffs and scratches a record of faraway places, thinking: More travel ahead.

Like Tennyson's Ulysses, "unable to rest from travel," you were "always roaming with a hungry heart." You lived a similar wanderlust:

> I am a part of all that I have met;
> Yet all experience is an arch wherethrough
> Gleams that untravelled world, whose margin fades
> For ever and for ever when I move.
> How dull it is to pause, to make an end,
> To rust unburnished, not to shine in use!

I had not understood that those books I called "pointless excess" were a monument to your passion for exploring other cultures ancient and modern. I missed the significance of those volumes for decades. But I heard an echo on a recent trip to Oregon.

Chris and I visited the Pacific Northwest in October 2021, which included the obligatory pilgrimage to Powell's Books in Portland. Upon entering the full-city-block building, I dashed to the Egyptian history section and feasted my eyes on the myriad volumes. Within minutes I was lugging a hefty stack of books. Decades ago I dismissed your library as extravagant. I now viewed the books in Powell's like an opened archaeological tomb in which everything was riveting and valuable.

Since then, I have located many more texts at our local library and online. And I don't yet see an end to it. I have already read a dozen of them, with more in the queue. Egyptologists' notebooks from explorations along the Nile River; different perspectives of the international obsession and rivalry over finding and claiming antiquities; assessments of the consequences of foreign colonialism on Egyptians; it's all there.

Back home, surrounded by my books, I imagined myself once again in your basement, with its shelves of Egypt books, but this time noting ones I wanted someday to read—books once dismissed as dead weight, now coveted. For the first time, we were looking out at the world through mother-and-daughter field glasses, side by side, separated only by the passing of time. Then an epiphany: I have become my mother!

> *All I remember [is] the excitement in 1922 of the*
> *find. . . . Maybe there will still be another find someday.*
>
> —EJB, Trip diary entry, 1977, recalling the discovery of King
> Tutankhamun's tomb when she was seven years old.

Two thousand twenty-two. You would love to be part of the centenary of the opening of Tutankhamun's tomb. One hundred years ago Howard Carter and his team discovered the long-searched-for tomb of the Pharaoh Tutankhamun. Your learning of that astounding discovery sparked your love of archaeology.

Egypt is celebrating the centenary with the opening of the GEM (Grand Egyptian Museum) in Cairo. It stands just miles from the Egyptian Museum that you explored during your two trips to Egypt. This new structure—the largest archaeological museum in the world—has been a work in progress since its groundbreaking in 2002. One wing will include virtually all of the 5,000 items from Tutankhamun's tomb. (It took ten years for Howard Carter and his team to identify and document each object.)

Egyptian archaeologist and former antiquities minister Zahi Hawass has even produced an opera based on the life and death of the boy king. Described as a successor to Verdi's *Aïda*, it will be performed with much fanfare at the time of the official museum opening.

Remember what I wrote about stuffing a camel into a mayonnaise jar? That's how I feel now about the prospect of cramming all my thoughts and written reflections about Egypt into this letter. Once again, extreme paring down has to happen. I have a plan, however. I have included a few items that seem relevant to this segment: post cards, a travel diary, a newspaper clipping, a sketch Chris did of you, and a few photographs, including one of you perched on a camel.

These items have become my portal into your fascination with Egypt. Surrounded by them and my books about Egyptian history, art, and archaeology, I am transported into your world. Suddenly I can see all at once your approach to life, your lust for travel—through time and across distance—to absorb diverse cultures and lost civilizations. You were constantly weaving new golden threads into your life's tapestry, a magic carpet of knowledge and experience carrying you through the changes and losses in your life.

First, I want to share a few items that reflect your fascination with Ancient Egypt.

> *[I have a] great interest in archaeology (no one ever mentioned that as a career) and with all the travels that Walter and I did in various parts of the world, I have been able to indulge my interests in that with specialized trips to Etruscan Italy, Egypt, Greece, China, Korea, and Sicily. . .*
>
> —EJB, 1988 Whitman College 50th Reunion booklet

When I read your comment about no one mentioning archaeology as a career, I became curious and checked it out. In 1934, when you left Seattle to enroll as a freshman at DePauw University [Greencastle, Indiana], teaching was the most popular career at forty percent. Today (2022) at DePauw you could major in Classical Studies and take classes in eastern Mediterranean art and archaeology, enabling you to explore some of your passions from when you were little. You could even minor in classical archaeology. Over sixty colleges and universities listed archaeology as a major in 2019 [https://www.collegevine.com]. The University of Washington, less than ten miles from your girlhood home on 8th Avenue NW in Seattle, now offers a bachelor's degree in archaeological sciences, as well as a handful of programs in Egyptology.

The decade of the 1970s was a golden opportunity for you and Tutankhamun to get acquainted. By my count, you had at least four encounters with treasures taken from the Valley of the Kings' site, known as KV 62. In 1972, you and Walter saw the Tutankhamun exhibit at the British Museum in London; the following year, you and Walter traveled to Egypt (although I do not have your itinerary);

in 1977 you went with Lenny Bell's group to Egypt (for which I have your travel diary and a few photos tucked inside); and in 1978 you saw the Seattle Tutankhamun exhibit, about which you gave a program in Walla Walla.

You made travel accessible in my imagination through your postcards and travel diary. During your 1972 visit to the Tutankhamun exhibit at the British Museum, you sent us a postcard showing the pharaoh's sarcophagus. On the back was the following message:

Dear Kids—

Your good letter was here to greet me. We saw 4 hours plus of War & Peace opera by Prokofiev last night and then to this fantastic exhibit this morning.

We only had to wait 50 minutes to get into see it—better than 3 hours I read about at first. It was opened in April and is now extended to end of December.

Needless to say, we'll have plenty to do, and only a couple days left for Mary [friend traveling with them] to see the end of her first trip.

I may not get a full letter off again but I have liked hearing something. You'll have a special cancellation on this, too. Love, Mother

I loved reading about the 1972 London exhibit, described in Christina Rigg's *Treasured: How Tutankhamun Shaped a Century* (2022), where you first saw some of the tomb items during that exhibition. I got excited about what was going on in the long queues that formed at dawn, according to London journalist Anne Sharpley! She described those waiting in line as exhibiting "the air of a cheerful shipwreck" as they appeared toting "picnic baskets, folding chairs, and sporting transistor radios to pass the time." (I wonder if you and Walter saw any people in line listening to their pocket radios, unaware that his invention had made their listening possible.)

During your 1973 trip with Walter to Egypt, you visited Tutankhamun's tomb. On a postcard you wrote:

This, with many other things, was one of my real thrills to visit. I remember as a little girl when King Tut's tomb was discovered.

We lost one day here by not making our Paris connection. So today we have much to see, to go to Abu Simbel where the whole temple was removed by UNESCO when dam waters would cover. No school we've been told, and yesterday was at heat 105 degrees! We return to Cairo later today by plane. We came by train and almost too much to see of life along the great Nile. All fascinating. Love, Mother (June 1973)

I was impressed by how you were both tourist and scholar, writing in 1977 about your own experience and commenting on the state of present and future archaeological research:

Tuesday January 11 [1977]—Luxor—pleasant weather

#113 New Winter Palace

We left Cairo about 9:30 and Egypt airliner—very full and about 45-minute flight. Checked possibility of staying in Old New Winter Palace, but I ended up in New Part. (Later stories told it was cold, and not all that convenient.) As soon as we were settled in, we walked to Luxor Temple and came back to Hotel for lunch.

About 623' long and 164' wide.

Visit to Luxor Museum—new and very fine!

(Egyptian pound was equal to about 68 cents, so roughly 1 1/2 times the amount)

Valley of Kings: tombs of Tut, Seti I, Ramses VI & Ramses II, a special treat. Just being reworked by Brooklyn Museum and everyone was terribly excited! James Manning in charge.

Tut's tomb small by other's—when one thinks of the treasures to be seen, and all I remember the excitement in 1922 of the find—maybe there will still be another find someday. Ramses' VI rubble protected the entrance.

Tomb Seti I—one of best preserved—colors are beautiful. King's sarcophagus now in London Museum was found empty. Constellation on ceiling especially impressive.

Ramses II—James Manning from Brooklyn Museum—we were first American group to go in—this was work in the "raw"—shortly, maybe discoveries will be made.

Wednesday January 12

In what would be afternoon, we visited Funerary Temple of Ramses II—quite impressive—Ramesseum. Quite good repair.

An enormous statue of pink granite of Ramses II lies broken in court yard. If it were standing, it would be over 60'. We continued straight through until it was nearly 3 when we returned to Hotel for sandwiches in bar. Found out that imported beer is $2 a bottle.

Last item to see was Medinet Habu (Funerary Temple of Ramses III) Large and impressive. Especially interesting were the storage areas in back.

In evening attended "Sound and Light" at Karnak—very worthwhile— magical at night.

Bought doll for Brenda at Funerary Temple of Ramses II—the little girls "hawking" their dolls will long be in my memory.

Your Egypt Travel Diary from 1977 had pictures tucked inside the front cover that both delighted me and caused me to giggle. Of course, seeing you perched on top of a camel was such fun, where you appeared determined to hold still for a photo, but grateful your fee did not include a ride of any length. My favorite photo reminded me of a sketch Chris did of you on a skateboard before our 1988 trip, which he called "EJB Does China." Although Chris had not seen the

Riding a camel at Giza.

EJB DOES CHINA.

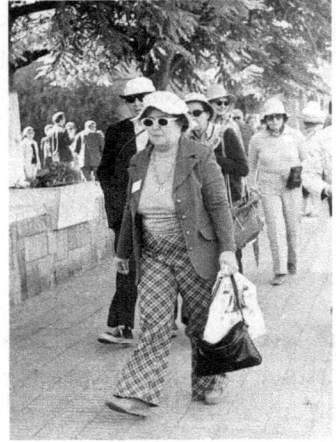

photo of you when he drew the sketch, he was familiar with your determined style of walking. Your hustle is a clone for the drawing. The two images belong side by side. Even the necklaces are similar.

The following year, 1978, you gave a program in Walla Walla to share slides of your trip to Egypt, in connection with an upcoming group tour to the Seattle showing of Tutankhamun artifacts.

Tours from city to see Tut exhibit

"Tut-mania" has struck Walla Walla well in advance of the July opening of the exhibit of King Tutankhamun's treasures in Seattle.

The exhibition of ancient Egyptian artifacts will be housed in a building in the Flag Pavilion at the Seattle Center July 15 through Nov. 15.

Tickets are sold out for two Walla Walla group tours of 100 persons each offered through Carnegie Art Center. Tour patrons have paid $10 per person for the evening showings in September and October.

To provide groups or individuals who plan to see the exhibit with some background on the Egyptian art treasures, Emma Jane Brattain will give a free public slide lecture April 10 at 8 P.M. in Maxey Hall on the Whitman College campus.

Mrs. Brattain saw the exhibit in London in 1972 and has participated in a three-week educational tour out of Luxor, Egypt. She is a member of the Walla Walla Society of the Archaeological Institute of America.

The Seattle Art Museum estimates an attendance of 1,000 viewers per hour will see the exhibit during public hours—Sunday, Tuesday and Wednesdays from 10 A.M. to 5 P.M. and Thursdays, Fridays and Saturdays from 10 A.M. to 9 P.M. Admission during public hours will be $1 for adults and 50 cents for children and senior citizens, but no tickets will be sold in advance.

—*Walla Walla Union-Bulletin*, April 2, 1978

I happily joined you to see the Tutankhamun exhibit in Seattle in 1978. As tickets could not be purchased ahead of time, waiting was part of the plan for most visitors. Some showed up with sleeping bags the night before to secure a place in the queue the following morning. The Tutankhamun exhibit contained only fifty-five artifacts. Of the more than 5,000 items found in the four rooms of the chamber, these represented a handful of the total trove. My memories are few of the exhibit proper beyond the gold death mask, but I remember going to the Seattle Center that day and the gift shop, which held promise for me. There I could grab mementos, reminders of the gold masks and other treasures I had seen. You got a small Tutankhamun mask and a gold-colored pendant (both of which I have). I chose a small, turquoise-colored owl amulet. And, of course, post cards.

My sister is the only woman I know who talks favorably about yeast.

—Webb Miller, June 6, 2023, 4:00 A.M.

One of the items not on display in Seattle was bread. In her book, Christina Riggs mentioned baskets of bread. That got my attention! I was as excited to read about bread as I was about any of the Tutankhamun tomb finds. I located tomb photos of loaves of bread online, including pieces loosely placed in plaited strands of grass. This is another connection to you. Bread means bakeries. You loved bakeries. I adore them. You and I frequented bakeries, starting with the Delicious Bakery on Second Avenue and Chestnut Street in Walla Walla.

Your nose for bakeries matched Gramps's radar for locating carnivals or even carnival ads. On one of our trips in the 1970s to Seattle to stay with Mari, you decided to stop at a bakery in Issaquah. When you asked me what I wanted, I casually quipped I would pass.

I was "on the wagon" that day. Still eyeing the array of goodies, you replied, "Well, you're no fun!" It was a wasted opportunity for me, one that we joked about for years. I doubt that I ever tried that line again with you.

You wrote in your travel journal about visiting the tomb of Ti at Saqqara with "many scenes of everyday life." Did you notice the elegant drawing on the walls that detailed the bread-baking process?

If only we could visit the new Egyptian museum, I know just what we would do: race to find the 3,500-year-old bread from Tutankhamun's tomb. Planting ourselves in front of the display case, we would stare, point, and giggle. Can't you imagine other tourists walking by, wondering what the heck was up with us?

Mother and daughter sharing a moment of levity with, of all things, unleavened bread.

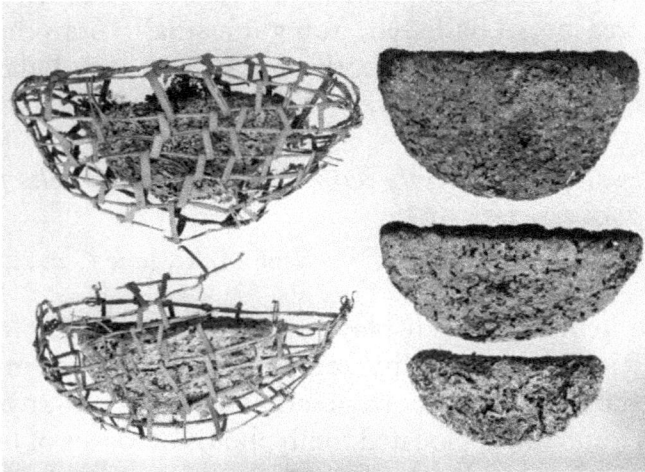

Bread from Tutankhamun's tomb. Scan made from Harry Burton's original glass plate negative.

I must share a delightful postscript to the Tutankhamun bread story: In June 2022, I discovered the Griffith Institute's online library of materials related to Tutankhamen, including Howard Carter's journals and diaries along with Harry Burton's stunning photographs. As I scrolled through the images online, I was most excited to see photos of bread found in the tomb and immediately wrote to the Institute, asking to use the photo in our family history project. Permission granted.

> *My mother let go. I let her go. Yet always I am car-*
> *rying her in me. Even find myself picking up some of*
> *her habits. This eternal attachment. Women–mothers.*
> *Daughters–mothers. The daughter leaves the mother at*
> *times by anger, rebellions, rejections. Then rapproche-*
> *ment. Finally the ultimate separation, the inevitable task*
> *of adulthood. Accompanied by numbness, hurt, anger.*
> *And then . . . What?*
> *Slowly I find myself being weaned from her material*
> *presence. Yet, filled with her as never before. It is I now*
> *who represent us both. I am our mutual past. I am my*
> *mother and my self. She gave me love, to love myself,*
> *and to love the world. I must remember how to love.*
>
> —Toby Talbot

I recently revisited Talbot's book. Although her quest to find an endur-ing connection to her mother took her a year, my journey took decades.

As I dug deeper into your life, it became clear that, to create a more lasting bond to you, one that would carry me through the rest of my life, I would have to write myself into your story, by reflecting on both our lives simultaneously, the warp and weft of a mother–daughter tapestry. In doing so, I have found, like Talbot, that I contain some essence of you and see myself as living for both of us. Now and in the future.

In a poem for a hospice program on the death of a parent, I wrote that I sometimes could hear your voice in my own. Today I am learning to see the world through your eyes.

I no longer imagine an afterlife when you and I will again be together. However, you are not gone from my memory. I want to grab the phone, dial your number (which I still know by heart), and wait for your perky "Oh! It's you!" In my mind's eye I see you hustling down the street in your trench coat. I feel the touch of your hand as I grasp your timeworn fingers. These things comfort me. It is through them that you will be such a vital part of my remaining years, and that is enough.

After you died, I told everyone how glad I was that you and I had said everything that we needed to say to each other while we still could. That prattle was short-lived. This family project is testament to the volumes we left unsaid.

We have a lot to talk about. More importantly, I have a lifetime of questions for you.

But first... How about a trip to the bakery? You can drive.

Love forever, Debi

Emma Jane and her four children before she moved from 1019 Alvarado.

II

Gretchen

A sister is like yourself in a different movie, a movie that stars you in a different life.

—Deborah Tannen

The highest forms of understanding we can achieve are laughter and human compassion.

—Richard Feynman

My dearest Sister,

You died on Friday, March 13, 2015. Just hours after Deborah called with the heartbreaking news, I told her and Katharine I wanted to speak at your memorial. But as the day neared, I truly did not know how I was going to deliver my message to hundreds of people. Although I didn't mind addressing such a large group, I doubted I could hold it together while remembering you. How could I stand amidst this giant loss, lift my protective veil, and face the flood of my grief and longing?

One way I could stay grounded would be to organize my thoughts as "House Rules," a takeoff on your time in the Oregon Legislature. Call them your values, your personal philosophy of life, lessons I learned—reluctantly—from you. Then I could add stories from our lives as the Miller sisters.

The chorus of friends and family who understood my anxiety united in a chorus of encouragement, assuring me I would do just fine. Even though I had written out what I would say, the prospect seemed iffy. But all I had to do was to read the text. Word by word.

Your memorial service was on Saturday, April 4 at the First Congregational United Church of Christ in Portland. That morning, Jim Matthews, a friend, said to me, "Look. Every person in that audience is there for the same reason you are. They care about Gretchen and are hungry for details about her. They want to hear what you have to say. Look around and let them support you."

Compassion. It would be right there in the room.

Humor. I had something I could use.

The day before, a few of us were in your condo, crowded around your writing desk, smiling at the collection of pigs we had given you over the years. They came in a variety of sizes, materials, and facial expressions. Deborah gestured toward the porcine array, saying, "Take a pig with you. Take several." She opened a square box containing a pair of incredibly ugly rubber pig earrings. The others stared in disbelief as she held up the grinning little porkers.

"One of us needs to wear these," I insisted.

"Go for it," Deborah said. "You'll never see those on me." "Nor on me," echoed Katharine.

As Brenda shifted her gaze from the pigs to my smirk, I felt her eyes boring a hole through my sense of playfulness. "Mom!" she said. "Promise me you will take those earrings off right after the service, that you won't wear them the entire day." I glanced around to see if anyone else thought my idea was outrageous. Smiles. Nods. Settled. The pigs were on for the next day.

As we walked into the sanctuary on Saturday, I touched the rubbery nubs hanging from my ears. In my other hand was a small blue ceramic pig I had picked out from the collection the day before. I imagined you nodding approval as I carried this talisman from your collection to help me get through my reading. Scanning the stage, I saw a small table that was the perfect place to set my pig.

I was first to speak. Before getting up, I exchanged glances with fourteen-year-old Alex, who would speak last. It seemed right that we two should be bookends for your service. I would reflect on your past, while your oldest grandson would carry your legacy into the future. His eyes told me we were thinking the same thing.

Steadying myself on Chris's arm, I rose to walk the short distance to the podium, carefully setting the pig on the table facing your grandchildren. I stepped behind the dais and adjusted the mike.

Just breathe. Don't think about why you are here. Think about the message. And remember the compassion and the humor.

"Before I begin, I have a favor to ask." I described the pig-earring exchange with Brenda as my eyes flitted around the crowd for support. "If any of you catch me at the reception still wearing these, please signal me to take them off and put them in my pocket. Immediately!"

Laughter. Salve for my soul.

Now I am ready . . .

First Congregational United Church of Christ
April 4, 2015, Portland, Oregon

Thank you for coming today to celebrate Gretchen's life. It is an honor to be here with you. Like all of you, I am humbled by her record of public service to the State of Oregon and to the residents of Portland in particular. I know Gretchen touched many of your lives in deep and diverse ways. As Commissioner Nick Fish noted, "Everyone has a Gretchen story!"

It is my privilege to share a few stories about my big sister and friend—about what she meant to me and the lessons I have learned from her. I call these "Gretchen's House Rules." The little stories may ring true to you, because in all the important ways there was no difference between the public and the private Gretchen. She seemed to have few secrets; everyone was entitled to her opinion!

Rule #1: When you enter the room, let people know you have arrived.

Gretchen lived at Broadway volume from the day she was born on June 23, 1942. Our father, who became editor and publisher of the *Walla Walla Union-Bulletin*, announced her birth in the form of a concert review:

Production of Millers' Heard

Walla Walla witnessed today the world premiere of a new production which is expected to prove of considerable future significance—Opus 1, No. 1 by a new team of collaborators, Emma Jane and Roland Miller.

The new work, which is entitled "Gretchen Elsa Miller," was ushered in before a small but select audience in St. Mary's hospital.

Mrs. Miller was the soloist for the occasion with Dr. Nathaniel Beaver directing the somewhat protracted performance.

Listeners recognized at once that this new production heralded an important new phase of activity for the versatile Millers. The work showed vitality and originality, with excellent tone production though perhaps slightly too much cacophony to suit this reviewer.

For all its weighty subject matter—the first edition alone weighs 7 pounds, 9⅛ ounces—the opus has a number of interesting variations. At times it soars to unsuspected crescendos; at others the theme is almost dripping. From the opening notes, one is impressed with the power of the material, and it is obvious that no one would be able to sleep through its performance.

All in all, the work is a promising beginning for the team of composers. The waiting public can expect a consistent improvement as the Millers gain experience to go along with their natural talents.

Thanks, Dad! Indeed, who among us ever slept through any of Gretchen's performances?

Rule #2: If people look to you for leadership, don't disappoint them.

Even as a young girl, Gretchen was organizing groups and creating a sense of community. At age ten, she gathered neighborhood girls to come to our basement at 1019 Alvarado Terrace to rehearse and perform in-home dance recitals, which she choreographed. I remember sitting upon the curved red bench with the other recruits as Gretchen showed off her new favorite steps to such songs as the Mills Brothers' "Glow Worm" and Johnny Ray's "Walking My Baby Back Home." Only when she decided we were ready did we deliver the hand-printed programs around the neighborhood.

Rule #3: Whatever you do, do it well.

When our father died in January 1957 (Gretchen was fourteen, Webb thirteen, and I twelve) Gretchen seemed to take on a new drive—a deeper motivation—to excel. And excel she did: at home, at school, with friends, and in music.

Gretchen seemed well organized and prepared for every job with which she was entrusted. For example, her strong work ethic saw her through the many hours of practice required to master the challenging works chosen for her senior piano recital at Whitman College.

Rule #3 and a half: It's good to be a fan of something or someone.

Having come from a musical family (when first married, our parents lived in an apartment with two grand pianos—and could play them), Gretchen and I shared a passion for all music. We loved to sing Broadway musical tunes at Broadway volume. Some years ago we were thrilled to meet one of our pop heroes, Johnny Mathis, and have our picture taken with him! How thrilled he was, I'm not sure.

Rule #4: Stand up for equality.

Her Peace Corps years in Iran opened her eyes to many examples of inequality for women in a male-dominated, religious society. Visiting her classroom, I saw her treat her female students respectfully and as equals. She was not one to dominate or dictate.

Rule #5: Know yourself and be that person always; don't say one thing in public and another in private.

One day in September 1980, Gretchen and I met as true sisters. During a time of upheaval for me, she came to Idaho Falls, and we vividly experienced each other as sisters for the first time, discovering the coveted bond that was given to us at birth.

I flew to Portland soon after to observe her in session at the Oregon Legislature. As I had done in Iran, I watched her with her peers and saw no "performance mode" masking her private personality. In public as in private, she was congruent, consistent, and convincing.

Rule #6: Use profanity as a teaching tool, not to hide your inability to speak intelligently.

Oh, there was perhaps one difference between her private and public personas. She used four-letter words freely, mostly in private company. I've not heard anyone else use the f-word with such authority and—would you believe—grace.

Rule #7: Whining will get you nowhere. Bring something tangible to the table.

I want to go back to when Gretchen and I were kids. Being older, she got to stay up later. I hated crawling into bed at night, staring out across the hall at her closed door, a faint, uneven slit of light creeping across the shag carpet. One night, eager to ease my anguish, I grabbed a few coins from the little dish on my shelf and headed across the hall.

When I tapped on her door, she cracked it open and demanded, "What?"

"It's too dark in my room," I whined in my most pitiful voice.

No reaction.

I opened my fist, "Would you leave your door open until I fall asleep . . . for ten cents?"

Still no reaction.

"How about fifteen?"

"Deal!" she snapped, snatching the coins from my hand.

That became a nightly ritual.

I soon learned that the more I paid her, the wider she opened her door.

It was not until years later that I came to appreciate her reaction to my behavior. She always had time for people in need, but had little patience with people who whined. There was no time for complainers. She didn't like it in herself, and she hated it in others. She believed in having a strong backbone and saw the irony in her own back being the source of her physical weakness and pain.

Rule #8: Find your place of peace.

Gretchen's great love was Arch Cape on the Oregon Coast. She spent days walking on the sand and reading in her loft— often a book a day after her retirement. She had a picture on her wall in Portland with the caption "I come to the sea to breathe."

Rule #9: Share the love—and the cinnamon rolls.

At the beach, I learned some things from Gretchen about sharing. Unlike me, she did not inherit the bakery-enthusiast gene, a passion our mother nurtured and nourished in me. It seemed no one else cared about yeast as much as I did. I felt deprived. Whenever I arrived at the beach, I would race to the Cannon Beach Bakery. When back at Gretchen's, I would deposit a community sack in the kitchen before heading for the bedroom where I could park my private stash. That incensed her! She was all about justice and shared commodities. All goodies brought to the beach house automatically became house property in her eyes.

Rule #10: Be an example and encourager for others.

In 1990, I finally got serious about graduate school. About the same time, Gretchen's passion for gay rights was raising my awareness of LGBTQ issues and carried over into my expanding roles of teaching classes and mentoring students at our local college in Nebraska. One of my most rewarding experiences was serving as co-advisor of the PRIDE student organization there.

So in a genuine sense, Gretchen's influence extended halfway across the country.

And so here we are. Today is day 23 without her. Gretchen and I were sisters for 25,658 days. One of my close friends described the impact of Gretchen's death on my life as a "cavernous" loss. She was right. I cannot yet fathom my life without her physical presence. For 25 years she and I had almost daily phone conversations.

Rule #11: Cherish your "raisins."

I'm thinking as well about the loss—the deep loss—for so many people. However, I am most aware of her three "raisins:" Alex, Jacob, and Anna. Her raisons d'être. Her lifelines. Her young trio, who brought her unparalleled joy. The lift in her voice when she talked about time with her grandchildren was heartwarming. The sparkle that I saw in her eyes when they walked into her living room could have lit up Broadway.

Gretchen and her "raisins" Alex, Anna, and Jacob.

Rule #12: Seize today.

After our mother's death, I finally learned what Gretchen seemed always to have known: On the stage of our life, we get to perform only once.

Our lives are our moments on stage—both our debut and our swan song. We hope to make a difference, to be remembered, preferably in a good way.

I can think of no better example of someone who has lived with the *carpe diem* mantra than my favorite sister, Gretchen.

Thank you.

Debi wearing Gretchen's pig earrings.

Grandson Alex talking about his extraordinary Grammie.

Alex spoke without notes about your love for his siblings and him, giving several examples of ways you showed it. "She watched every single X-Men movie with me. In one sitting." He thought of you as his best friend. Your death left him adrift, unsure how he would navigate his life without your guidance and influence. He especially loved those days when he would take the bus to your condo to watch movies or grab lunch.

In one of his most humorous and moving moments, he contrasted your literary tastes with his, describing how he somehow talked you into reading Aaron Dembski–Bowden's apocalyptic teen novel *Helsreach*. Even though it wasn't a literary tour de force, you waded through the complex tale, humoring him by discussing such details as the Orks' attack on Armageddon. "If that isn't a clear example of unconditional love, I don't know what is," Alex said.

Andrew Theen, journalist for the *Oregonian*, wrote a generous piece about your years of service to the State of Oregon, Multnomah County, and the city of Portland. He described you as "a trailblazing and tireless advocate for political outsiders: poor people, gays and lesbians, women."

As soon as we reported your death to your nieces and nephews across the country, each was eager to fly to Portland to celebrate your life. All but two East Coast nieces were there. Your death triggered a circling of the family wagons, reminding all of us of the importance of savoring our relationships and family connections, while respecting diversity in our family and beyond.

Bill's dinner celebration at Alexis, Gretchen's favorite Greek restaurant. L to R: Deborah, Megan, Katharine, Sarah, Andrew, Brenda, Karen, Scott, and Ross. Missing are Mari and Kathleen. April 4, 2015.

You would be stunned by the grace and stamina which Deborah and Katharine showed. A grieving public immediately inundated them with demands for information and comfort. With little opportunity to focus on themselves, they dove into your political archives and personal memorabilia left in your condo, the beach house, and storage. You were, indeed, your mother's daughter, skilled at stashing treasures—in your case—political.

March 13, 2016. One year after your death, the Nevada Chamber

L to R: Deborah, Gretchen, Katherine.

Orchestra performed Chris's "Simple Gifts," ten variations on the Aaron Copland theme from "Appalachian Spring," a piece you loved. Chris dedicated his composition to you. Deborah flew to Las Vegas for the event.

You shared a love of classical music with Chris. At the beach you two played your favorite Mozart two-piano sonatas.

Chris and Gretchen playing Mozart at the beach.

You and I grew up with similar experiences of female friendship—
intense loyalty and deep, lifelong support—yet as young girls we
didn't reach out to one another. I contributed to that estrangement,
watching you from a distance, fearful of both comparison and rejection. Despite not wanting others to compare us to each other, I often
did just that. I pictured you as a member of a great Broadway theater
company, doing Tony-award-winning work, while I was only a bit
player in off-Broadway (way off) companies, never able to land a part
in a production with you. I wanted to be close to you, but didn't see
myself as measuring up. It was as if I were auditioning for a part for
which the character had not even been written into your life script.

The picture below captures perfectly the psychological distance I
felt between you and me growing up. You were fourteen, Webb was
thirteen, and I was twelve when we lined up for this Easter 1957 photo.
Dad's death catapulted you (and Webb) toward adulthood—as, along
with Mother, you assumed your roles as family stoics, setting aside
your own grief.

Webb, Gretchen, and Debi.

Everything about that picture shows the childhood contrast between you and me. You look like a blond Carol Lawrence, one of our favorite Broadway stars, standing with poise, assurance, and elegance. You wore a fashionable black dress with colorful sash, red pumps, and a white hat over your blond curls. Although just two years behind you, I appear a decade younger, decked out in a pastel pink dress with a matching ribbon at my waist and pink leather shoes.

For the first few decades of our lives, we seemed to live in different worlds. It was easier for us to judge each other than to take an interest in the other's feelings and desires. I thought you were too focused on politics and didn't bake enough chocolate chip cookies for your daughters, whereas you thought I baked too many cinnamon rolls and did not care enough about your social justice campaigns.

Although I did visit you and Stephen in Iran in the 1960s, it was in the 1970s that we began to warm up to each other. It could well have started when we showed up at Mother's in similar purple pants suits.

Gretchen, Emma Jane, Debi (wearing a loaf-size wiglet).

Sisters misbehaving.

In the late seventies, at Mother's suggestion, you traveled to Idaho Falls, during what was a difficult time for my marriage. This was for both of us an opportunity to empathize. As we talked for hours, we became close in ways that would carry us through the next four decades.

We also learned how to become comrades in mischief. My 1980 Portland visit marked the start of a "chemical" bond between us—the chemical being nicotine. Even though the educated middle class was coming to view tobacco use as somewhat tawdry and definitely unhealthful, its value to us in forging sisterly bonds would soon override any concerns we might have had about shortening our life spans. Our shared vice leveled the playing field and freed us from our longtime big-sister–little-sister stereotypes.

We kept up our bad behavior through our 1988 trip with Mother to China, where we were continually searching for places to smoke. Upon settling into each new hotel, you and I would meet to scout out places where we could do our business: sheltered walkways, private areas, even a hotel bowling alley. No one caught us in the Shanghai bowling alley, but Marilyn, then your mother-in-law, strolled by as we puffed away in the bushes outside our Xian hotel. She seemed to enjoy confronting us: "Come on, you two! Aren't you a little old for this?"

As the health alarms mounted up, we decided that smoking in secret was losing whatever appeal it once had for us, and we discovered other playful ways of connecting. We bonded when I flew out to be with you in 2000 when you had back surgery. After you returned home from your ten-hour operation, feeling thoroughly miserable, we camped out together in your living room: you in that trendy portable hospital bed and me on the faded purple futon. You were itching to take a shower, forbidden because of your incision. But we devised a method for washing, donning a pair of your most fashionable black garbage bags with carefully clipped head and arm holes. We could barely squeeze into your guest bathroom stall, howling during the team effort. We both loved telling that story and likely came up with the term of feeling "velcroed" together during that visit.

Of course, we had planned a similar shower sequel to your hip-replacement surgery scheduled for March 16, 2015. But I never got to tell you the best part: I was planning to take a selfie of us in our twin shower bags! Timing was crucial as I knew you would never have agreed to a picture had I told you ahead of time. But once on your feet, eager to get in and out of the shower, you could not have escaped.

I traveled to Oregon several times over the years to see you in action: as an Oregon state representative in Salem, as a Multnomah County commissioner, as a Portland City Council member, and as a lecturer at Portland State. As I watched you in your elected official positions, you maintained the same tone that you did in your classroom of young female students in Zanjan, where I had visited you in 1965. You spoke passionately and respectfully to individuals about issues, urging them to hold themselves to the same standards which they expected of others.

Open house Invitation to Wayne, Nebraska friends.

You also traveled to Wayne, Nebraska, to visit us a few times and to attend Brenda's and Scott's high school graduations. In 1987, for one of your first visits to us, Chris and I planned an open house for which he sketched an invitation with four of your life experiences: piano major at Whitman College, Peace Corps volunteer in Iran with Stephen, Oregon state representative, and Multnomah County Commissioner.

Wayne, Nebraska: Debi and Gretchen with four desserts baked by Debi.

For your fiftieth birthday in 1992, you offered to take anyone to dinner who could meet in Lucca, Italy. The dinner was worth the trip.

*Scott and Gretchen at the 1999 Washington, D.C.
Alliance to End Homelessness ceremony.*

Bringing up the Italy trip a few years later, Scott said, "Mom, it was my decision not to go to Italy, right?" "Well, no . . . ," I began. As I explained that you and I decided to include Deborah, Katharine, and Brenda and make it a girls' trip, I could see my logic did little to assuage his aggrievement. I reminded him that he did get to meet you in Washington D.C. for your award from the National Alliance to End Homelessness. He retorted, "A single event does not equal a trip to Europe." Scott is still waiting for his family trip abroad.

Johnny Mathis was one of our favorite singers, and as kids upstairs

Gretchen, Johnny Mathis, Debi (eager for an autograph).

at 1019 Alvarado Terrace, we would blare his songs at Broadway volume. What fun it was to hear him live at the Blosser Winery in Portland. You framed the photo and displayed it in your office at Portland City Hall. Glancing at it, a co-worker asked if he was our brother.

L to R: Gretchen, Debi, Lynn Riegel, Julie Larson. Lynn is holding a soft sculpture gift to Gretchen from Julie.

Strong female friendships have been a sustaining theme in our lives, a tradition started by Mother and extending to our children and grandchildren. We especially loved those times when we could gather with friends. You hosted one such weekend at the beach house for Lynn Riegel and Julie Larson.

In advance of your retirement in 1998 from the Portland City Council, Terry Anderson, a close friend and colleague, interviewed you at length about your life and work. Using material from that interview and other sources, Marian Yeates wrote a booklet commemorating your personal and political history. Titled "Gretchen: The Story of Gretchen Miller Kafoury," it is a whirlwind chronicle of your life from childhood in Walla Walla through your tenure on the City Council to 1998.

At your City Council retirement gala in 1999, colleague Eric Sten

unveiled a photograph of "The Gretchen Kafoury Commons," an
affordable apartment complex in downtown Portland.

*Eric Sten unveils a photo of the Gretchen Kafoury
Commons as he invites Gretchen to join him.*

Deborah and Gretchen listen.

In your reflections at the end of Yeates's booklet, you wrote:

"If there were to be a next time around: I would surround myself with even more people who would challenge me intellectually. I like to think, reflect, argue, and debate, and I think I make better decisions because of this. Other than marrying three times, I don't know of anything else I would change."

Gretchen's three husbands at daughter Deborah's college graduation in 1989. Front row: Eric Hosticka, middle row: Stephen and Marge Kafoury with Emma Jane Brattain. Back row: Larry Picus, Katharine, and Susan Picus.

Your three husbands included two great guys and one maverick.

You and Stephen Kafoury met at Whitman College and married in 1963. The assassination of John F. Kennedy came just two months later. His death was a call to political activism for both of you. From 1964 to 1966, you and Stephen served in Iran in the Peace Corps, which President Kennedy had created in 1961. It was there that you learned about the subordination of women in the Middle East. That knowledge would inform your political life after your return to Portland.

Bobby Kennedy's 1968 presidential campaign coincided with your settling into life in Portland, giving voice to many of the passions already ignited in you for social and political justice. You became a district leader for southeast Portland, making phone calls, passing out leaflets and planning rallies for your candidate.

Gretchen's handwritten schedule for Bobby
Kennedy's Portland visit, May 1968.

Kennedy's assassination on June 5 in Los Angeles came only days after you met him. His death was a devastating blow both to the country and to you and Stephen. Reporter Kenneth Walsh reflected in a 2015 article that Kennedy's murder was a key event in the year in which the country "experienced a national nervous breakdown." Losing RFK was for you a seismic event that opened up a chasm exposing your unhealed wounds from Dad's death as well. Your repressed feelings from when Dad died now flooded to the surface and intertwined with your grief for Bobby.

RFK's death became an inspiration for you to carry on the cause of social justice. Afterward, in your office, you hung a photo of Bobby walking with his dog, perhaps contemplating Goethe's well-known quote: "Some see things as they are and ask why? Others dream things as they could be and ask why not?" It became a symbol for your deepening commitment to the rights of women and opportunities for the disadvantaged.

Although you and Stephen divorced in 1973, you remained close friends and political colleagues.

In 1976 you married Larry Picus as you were beginning your own political career as a member of the Oregon House of Representatives. Larry was an important figure in Deborah and Katherine's formative years. He has remained close to both of them, as he did to you. All of us love Larry, as we do Stephen.

After seven years with Larry, you fell for the swashbuckling Eric Hosticka. Your mysterious attraction to Eric caused a good deal of head-shaking among your network of supporters. It may have been politics that first drew you together, but it was soon clear that your relationship was not based on a shared commitment to social justice, as your previous marriages had been. To the rest of us he was an enigma. He bought a struggling local media business and made it profitable. He enjoyed the *Batman* movies and hot dogs at the ballpark, things which held no interest for you. He sometimes spoke of his friends and relatives, but they were his, and he didn't introduce them to us.

You seemed addicted to him as you were to nicotine. Having let your guard down, you became needy in a way that you found repulsive in others. In opening up to him, you gave up the self-control that you had guarded most of your life. You became vulnerable. There was no reciprocal opening-up, however. Outwardly affable, he remained a closed book emotionally. I didn't think he was interested enough in you—and by extension, in the rest of us. Despite Eric's apparent fascination with Mozart—whose music he used to show off his fancy speaker system—I felt as if I had little in common with him and was always relieved when I would call and you would answer instead of him.

Eric once told Chris that his favorite movie was *The Good, the Bad, and the Ugly,* starring Clint Eastwood. In hindsight, that could have been a tipoff about his priorities, where his treasure lay. It wasn't with you, although you didn't know that. With the wind in your hair and your mustachioed sea captain at your side that day on the coast, you thought that this was a match that would last forever.

Gretchen and Eric Hosticka's beach wedding, Arch Cape, Oregon, 1984.

Eric was a wanderer on the earth, and you were powerless to keep him in your life, or more aptly, to keep yourself in his. He packed up his belongings and his memories, and sailed off to a new life seeing the world from his boat, like Clint Eastwood riding off into the desert at the end of his favorite movie, never to return.

In making yourself an open book, by trusting him completely, you felt bitterly his rejection of this deeply private and newly discovered part of you. He violated your trust by disappearing from your life.

As your grief over Eric changed to resignation, you came to accept the likelihood that you would not find another person with whom to share your remaining years. Despite this reality, you held onto your desire for companionship, satisfied in part by your deep friendship with Mohammed Rakha, your neighbor in your condo. His daughter Naseem, also aware of your bond with her father, shared with me that she once asked him why he chose not to propose to you. His response was that, since he would probably die first, he didn't want to break your heart.

In 2012, I approached you about collaborating on a family history project. You suggested the time was not right for you, but that if you did at some point, you would want to write about our family history in the form of vignettes and anecdotes. Although you never got around to it, you did have a folder in which you collected clippings about Dad as well as this brief handwritten note:

> As the eldest child of R and EJM, perhaps I have the "clearest" memory of our Dad, as he was known. In the first fourteen years of my life, due to personality, birth order, or other factors, I was very, very close to him. Our entire family was musical—the parents' first furniture was two grand pianos. Special memories for me were in his last year when we both [played] in the Walla Walla Symphony together. That he was snatched or taken from us so early was painful—a loss I have never recovered from, admittedly.

Fast-forward to 2023: You would be thrilled to know how involved Webb has become in this project. His writing would take your breath away, as it does mine. As an added incentive, his letters and reflections could have convinced you to add your own pieces to the project. It would be so easy. You and Dad were both naturally gifted storytellers.

I have traveled my own highway to you, a journey that began with my going across the hall and paying you to send some of your light into my bedroom so I could go to sleep. Over the years, as I have said, we grew close. I had earned a part in the screenplay of your life. I admit to guarding that special relationship a bit jealously. Intellectually, I knew that you had many close relationships during your career, but emotionally I held on to the thought that ours was the most special. When you died, I was bereft. I guarded my own heartache as jealously as I had our relationship. It was at your memorial service that

I saw things differently. Seeing the people there—friends, neighbors, colleagues, cousins, children, grandchildren, exes, even sometime enemies—feeling the love in the room, I understood that each of them felt the loss as much as I did, or nearly so.

So my screenplay needs a proper ending. Final scene: I'm at the Portland Plaza, exiting the elevator at the nineteenth floor, walking toward that familiar door. With a firm downward press on the handle, I push the weighty door open, hearing it caress the mat just inside. I slip off my shoes without fully stopping, moving down the hall toward the Steinway grand piano, the same one from when we were kids, on which Dad would make us laugh when he played a jazz song that sounded like a braying donkey. I hear your singsong "Hello" from around the corner as I walk the short distance to your living room, with its window-wall view of downtown Portland and the Highway 26 tunnel, your gateway to your beloved Arch Cape, to your beach house.

And suddenly you and I are face to face. You rise slowly from the small blue recliner, in which you spend your days reading. "Oh, you're finally here," you say as we hold each other. Once again I am in the comfort of your arms, the familiarity of your grasp that greets me each time I make my pilgrimage.

I am safe.

Like we used to do, we hop into your "blue bomb," the Honda del Sol—your freedom machine—roof removed and you at the wheel. We stop for groceries, then head for the coast, a place of peace and replenishment, traveling past urban traffic, suburbs, lowland farms, forests of pine and spruce, talking of this and that. Finally, catching glimpses of the Pacific along Highway 101, we have arrived at your beach house, your sanctuary. You park in the drive and jump out of the car, disappearing inside. As I carry in the groceries, I call your name. But there is no answer. I set the bags on the kitchen counter and hurry to the front window.

You have flung open the deck door and have already hit the sand. It's low tide; treasures of the sea await. As I step onto the deck looking for some sign of you, I find myself surrounded by a host of fans and supporters: relatives, friends, and colleagues, who have materialized, hoping to be cast in one more Gretchen story. It's no longer about my solo ache for you. It's not about asking you to rescue me from the dark. Standing among the growing crowd, I no longer need to keep you for myself. You belong to us all.

We scan the beach in silence. Someone points. Look! There you are, heading straight toward Humbug Point, where starfish are. You are home. And free.

Ta-ta, my favorite sister, I shall remain forever yours,
D

Clockwise from top left: The Miller siblings as children and adults; Bill and Gretchen at Arch Cape; Gretchen and Debi at Rustic Place.

Stories from Family and Friends

Remembering Walter Brattain—Chris

In 1975 I was teaching music theory and violin at Whitman College. Located near the Blue Mountains of southeastern Washington, the city of Walla Walla is in an idyllic setting. Coming from the greater Milwaukee area, I found Walla Walla to be the ultima Thule of places to live and work. In those years you could drive out of town in any direction and pass only a few farms and wheat fields. As the dean who interviewed me for the job said, "It's a good place to go to seed [if you're not careful to stay current academically.]" Nevertheless, Whitman had a good reputation, generous donors, and a fine concert hall that drew well-known artists. And some of its faculty were world-renowned.

One of the first concerts I attended at Whitman was a recital given by the Hungarian pianist Andor Foldes. At the reception, Emma Jane Brattain introduced me to several people well-known in Whitman and Walla Walla society. I quickly learned that Emma Jane had deep connections to both Whitman College and the Walla Walla Symphony, which I had also just joined.

Emma Jane first introduced me to her husband, Walter, an older gentleman wearing a Clan Stewart Tartan blazer. Walter was then teaching physics at Whitman, having previously worked for Bell Labs. I was told that he had, along with John Bardeen and William Shockley, received the Nobel prize in physics for the discovery of the transistor effect. I was in awe of that (even more than I was of his jacket). I had never talked with a Nobel laureate before and wasn't sure how to act. I nodded to suggest that I was listening attentively and did not offer any opinions that might make me look foolish. I asked him what he thought of the changes in society that his and his colleagues' discovery had brought about. He was clearly not pleased that transistor radios had inundated the world with silly rock and roll music from which there seemed no escape. Years later, I learned that this was a story he enjoyed telling often.

Between 1979–1981, my work took me out of Washington for a couple of years. Shortly after my return to Walla Walla, I met Debi, who was looking for someone to give her violin lessons. As we got to know each other, she invited Walter and me to dinner at her place. It was there that I noticed how Walter's dementia was taking hold of him. He was interested in telling his story but had lost much of his vocabulary. It was painful to listen to him as he groped for words. Still, he enjoyed driving around in his yellow Toyota.

The bluegrass band I was playing in had organized a concert of bands in Cordiner Hall on the Whitman campus. Our band, the Ryegrass String Band, was the show's opener. Debi and Walter were in the audience. To close our set, we performed one of our signature numbers, a rousing twin-fiddle tune called "High Country." When we came on stage, Walter recognized me and said, "There's Chris!" As we finished, Walter led the audience in giving us a standing ovation (the only one that evening, I have to add!) He seemed able to respond well to music even as he was steadily losing his speech and memory.

As the months passed, Walter's condition worsened. The changes were painfully obvious. I could still see in him the Walter of old in brief moments. It was like being in a thick fog, which at times would lift a little and I could make him out, then the fog would settle in again and he—the person inside—would be gone. By the time Walter and Emma Jane visited us for Thanksgiving in Nebraska in 1982, he had lost much of his ability to converse. I took him on a short tour of the campus and introduced him to our music department chairperson. Then I took him to the library, thinking it might perk him up a bit to see an article on the transistor in a reference book. When I showed him the article, he smiled and said "yes, that's . . . that's . . . it." He clearly was struggling for words but couldn't remember how to say what it was he and his colleagues had worked on. He recognized the diagrams on the page but couldn't say the word "transistor." I was seeing for myself the destruction of a great mind by a devastating disease.

Our next visit to Walla Walla the following summer found Walter much worse. Only when something triggered a powerful memory would he react. One such occasion was a picnic lunch on the Brattain patio at 1019 Alvarado. Conversation was lively, but Walter was off in his own world. Then the conversation turned to Bell Labs and the work of Bardeen, Brattain, and Shockley. The name "Shockley" aroused Walter from his reverie and he loudly interrupted the conversation with "Shockley's *nuts!*"

Ultimately, Emma Jane found it necessary to move Walter to a nursing home. Seattle was a logical choice—Walter's sister Mari lived in Seattle, very near to a good care facility. The last time we visited him, he was able to walk around but unable to speak. I doubt that he recognized us. We went outside to enjoy the air. As we talked, Walter sat staring vacantly at nothing. A fallen leaf scudding along the sidewalk caught his eye. He reached down and grabbed it with great purpose. I had the thought that his brain was grasping for anything tangible that it could before it flickered out completely. Although I never heard him say anything when he was in Seattle, Emma Jane told us a fascinating and heartening story about one of her last visits. The nurse took her in and said to Walter, who was lying in bed, "Emma Jane is here." His eyes opened, and he said, "That's my girl!" It may have been the last thing he ever said. Walter died not long after that visit.

Remembering Emma Jane Brattain—Chris

I met Emma Jane Brattain through the Walla Walla Symphony and my work at Whitman College, where I was hired in 1975 to teach music. She was part of Walla Walla's high society. Other than that, I knew little about her until the party after Mr. Foldes's recital. In addition to Walter she introduced me to several of her colorful friends, including Maria Stein, a retired German physician. Dr. Stein seemed to know a lot about music. She also was not shy about sharing her opinions. When I asked her what she thought of the pianist, she grimaced and said in her thick German accent, "I don't know what he thought he was playing, but it wasn't Brahms!"

In 1976, Jose Rambaldi, conductor of the Walla Walla Symphony, resigned. The search was on for a new music director. In the past, the Symphony had relied on a member of the Whitman College music faculty to serve as its conductor. But this time the board decided to do an outside search. Three finalists were selected and invited to conduct one concert apiece during the 1976–1977 season. As concertmaster, I had some say in the process. The third candidate was R. Lee Friese, a music teacher from Texas. After his concert, I wrote an enthusiastic letter to the board, concluding with "Make no mistake: Lee Friese is our man!" I'm not sure how much that influenced the board, but they offered the job to Lee and he accepted. I may have discussed his candidacy with Emma Jane as well.

I left Walla Walla in 1979 and didn't return until the summer of 1981. (My wife and I had separated a year or two before that.) I rented a room in the home of a guy I knew and was pondering what to do about my future. One day I got a phone call. The voice on the other end identified herself as Debi Agenbroad, quickly adding, "I'm Emma Jane Brattain's daughter." She wasn't just anybody.

"I just moved back to town and am looking for a violin teacher with whom to study. You were highly recommended." I replied that I did know her mother and would be glad to give her lessons. (Debi had recently gotten a divorce and had moved from Idaho Falls with her two young children, Brenda and Scott, and was taking classes at Walla Walla College.)

We got off to a rocky start. I missed the first couple of appointments, but Debi agreed to give me one more chance to show up, which I did. One thing led to another, and we started dating. Emma Jane of course found out about this, and remarked to Debi, "I certainly hope you're not getting involved!" She thought that a romantic relationship would compromise Debi's career plans.

Perhaps knowing Debi's independent spirit and determination to make a life for herself and her children, Emma Jane accepted me. She invited me to join the family for dinner several times that year. It was a bittersweet time for me. I still didn't know where my own life was headed. I was getting a divorce and had no job offers. Debi was eager to adjust to being a single mother and to study speech pathology.

Walter's Alzheimer's was beginning to assert itself. It appears all of us were at a crossroads with no clear signs of direction.

As winter turned to spring, I got a call from Wayne State College, where I had had a one-year appointment in 1980–1981, inviting me to apply for the job, this time as a tenure-track position. By this time, Debi and I had discussed marriage. I did not want to get married unless I had a job, and I knew I would have to go wherever I got an offer. When Wayne State offered me the job, I told her I had to accept, but that I would understand if she said she couldn't come with me. It would mean leaving Walla Walla and the Northwest as well as a second move for Brenda and Scott. I was overjoyed that she decided to take that jump into the unknown. We got married on August 1, 1982. Emma Jane and Walter threw a post-wedding party for us at their home. The Ryegrass String Band provided music—I might have sat in on a tune or two. Soon after that, we packed up our belongings and moved to Wayne, Nebraska.

The last thing I remember as we pulled away from 1019 Alvarado was waving goodbye to Emma Jane. She stood stoically in the drive-way, seemingly fighting back tears, as her youngest once again left her.

I was now officially a member of the Miller–Brattain family. For many summers after that we would pack up the big Ford LTD and drive halfway across the country to Walla Walla, listening to 8-track tapes of Abba and the soundtrack from *Grease*. These trips most often included a vacation on the Oregon coast, a place Debi's sister Gretchen loved dearly, as do we. There our extended family would gather at a rented beach house for several days. Walter and Emma Jane were the senior members of the party the first year, at a run-down house on the beach at Manzanita, which Gretchen co-owned. (After her mother's death, she purchased her own beach house in Arch Cape, a few miles south of Cannon Beach.)

We would stay at 1019 Alvarado on our visits to Walla Walla. Sometimes we had a bedroom near the sleeping porch upstairs; other times we camped out in a room above the garage, which had a sink and toilet, but no tub or shower. I found the big house fascinating. There was living space from the basement up through first and second floors to the attic, which had been converted to a bedroom decorated to look like a first-class cabin on a steamship. That had been Webb's room as a child. The main floor, besides having a living room, dining room, and kitchen, featured a small library. At the foot of the staircase was a large wall of glass brick, which flooded the area with natural light during the day.

There was interesting stuff everywhere. One day I was investigating the contents of a small bookcase at the top of the stairs. I pulled out a slim book that was hidden behind others on the shelf. It was Timothy Ferris's *Galaxies*. I thumbed through it, interested. I showed it to Emma Jane. "Say, I found this upstairs. Would it be OK if I borrowed it for a few days?" She looked at me with one eyebrow raised and said, "Well, I suppose, if you don't mind getting your birthday present early!"

In 1986, Emma Jane decided that 1019 Alvarado was too much house for her to maintain. She put it up for sale and bought a condo on Rustic Place near the Country Club. Debi, along with our violinist friend Sharon Thompson, helped Emma Jane in the Herculean job of clearing out 1019 and getting stuff ready for an estate sale. I came out to help after they were well into packing. There were four floors of stuff that had to be sorted through: books, bolts of cloth, letters, scrapbooks, cooking gear, toys, phonograph records, knick-knacks, Navajo rugs, souvenirs from around the world, exploded cans of what had once been peaches. This was archaeology, although on a smaller scale than exploring Egyptian tombs.

A basement room where Emma Jane's father, Frank "Honeychile" Kirsch, had stayed was lined with bookshelves containing travel books and museum catalogs. I was pulling out books and thumbing through them when Emma Jane came down to check on the progress. I said, "This is amazing! You must have a catalog from every museum in the world here!" She replied, "No, these are just the ones I've been to."

Another time, Debi and I were in the kitchen pulling out kitchen stuff to pack. I was on a stepladder clearing out a high cupboard. I took out an amber-colored glass object in the shape of a lily, with what appeared to be a glass stopper at the base. I couldn't figure out what purpose it might have served. I asked Emma Jane, who was busy setting out things to pack, what it was. She glanced up, mumbling something that sounded like "appear." Uncomprehending, I asked again. She said, the slightest bit of annoyance in her voice, something that sounded more like "e-pair."

"What was that again?" I asked. That was one ask too many.

"IT'S AN EPERGNE! E! P! E! R! G! N! E!"

I wanted to drop it on the floor and say "Oh. I guess it *was* an epergne." We were able to laugh about it later. And I had learned a new vocabulary word.

What I didn't know at the time is that the glass lily was part of the art-nouveau epergne that Roly had broken before he rejoined the family in Europe in 1955. He had written to Emma Jane about it, and she had answered, saying it wasn't "fatal." It clearly had been an heirloom from Nanmy, but she had many things that were of more value to her.

We visited Emma Jane a few times at her new home on Rustic Place. It was clear that she had not fully downsized from the move out of 1019. She seemed not to mind that she was crammed into a much smaller space than she had been used to. On one occasion Emma Jane and I were in her kitchen. She was making me a sandwich. I was at the table. As we talked, I mentioned casually that I had plans the next day to have lunch with a female friend of mine from the Symphony, whom Emma Jane also knew. The clinking of knife on china stopped. She turned slowly, gave me "the look," and said slowly, with just a touch of menace in her voice, "Didn't you use to *date* ___??" I mumbled something about that being a long time ago. The look softened but didn't disappear entirely. I had to admire her protectiveness toward her youngest daughter.

In mid-February of 1988, Emma Jane called. That was nothing unusual—Debi and her mom visited every Sunday on the phone. I had just come home. Debi was sitting at the table talking to her in our "music room" in Wayne. As I approached, she scribbled a note and shoved it across the table to me. It read "Are you interested in going to China?" I wrote "Nah . . ." and passed it back to her. She said to her mom, "That's one 'yea' and one 'nay.'" I immediately said, "Wait, wait! I changed my mind!" Emma Jane was inviting us to travel with her on a Whitman College tour to China that would take us to seven major cities and several famous cultural places. First-class hotels all the way.

The trip, which included Gretchen and her then-husband, Eric, was a great success. We walked on the Great Wall, took a Li River cruise leaving from Guilin, saw the terra-cotta soldiers in Xian, and much else. We spent our first night in Hong Kong, where Emma Jane had a friend who took us, jet-lagged, to dinner at the exclusive Hong Kong Club. Emma Jane's social contacts extended from Walla Walla to the world.

The "gig" with the Guilin String Quartet, 1988.

On our first evening at the Holiday Inn in Guilin, a string quartet was playing Mozart in the lobby. The next night it was a trio. I asked the concierge about it. He explained that the first violinist wasn't feeling well. I volunteered to sit in the next night if he were still feeling ill. He approached the musicians and asked them if they approved. They did. I supposed I would fill in on second violin, but they insisted I play first and handed me his fiddle. We played the first movement of Mozart's G Major Quartet, K. 387. Our tour members loved it—especially Emma Jane—and the musicians seemed appreciative.

Before we left for China, I made arrangements to visit the Conservatory of Music in Chengdu. My host was a composer, Huang Huwei. He organized a class of violin students to perform for Debi and me, after which I was invited to make comments. Although Emma Jane did not attend, she was very supportive of the idea and applauded my initiative in arranging the meeting. Professor Huang also gave me one of his violin pieces, which I played on a faculty recital the following year.

Chris (center), Professor Huang Huwei to his right.

Emma Jane's last visit to Wayne was in November of 1989. Debi and I traditionally hosted a family Thanksgiving dinner each year. Emma Jane would fly to Omaha, and we would drive down and bring her up to Wayne. We would invite our friends Ray and Barbara Kelton, and later Vic and Ann Reynolds. One reason we invited Vic and Ann is that Ann is from Walla Walla, and her mother, Bundt Tuttle, was a friend of Emma Jane's. Debi thought that it would be nice to bring EJay and Ann together. After the guests had gone, Emma Jane remarked that Ann was a "clone" of her mother, in a tone of voice that suggested "and everything that implies."

On this last visit, Emma Jane and I were sitting at the little table in the kitchen. I had a photo biography of the Swiss psychologist C. G. Jung open on the table and was showing her the picture of his home in the Swiss village of Bollingen, with the tower he built as his study. She was very interested to learn even a little bit about a new person and subject.

My memories of that visit are tinged with sadness. It was our first clue to what we would soon learn, that Emma Jane had a malignant brain tumor. I was never to see her again after she boarded the plane back to Washington.

Emma Jane was naturally social. Her journals were all about friends and their activities together. Her letters to family and friends were full of stories about what various women she knew were doing and talking about. She wrote the same way she talked. The sentences spilled out and landed on the paper as things occurred to her, one incident reminding her of the next, and that of the next, a daisy chain of events and people connected to each other by virtue of residing in her head. She stuffed her envelopes with newspaper clippings—pictures and stories about people she knew the recipients would be interested in. For Debi and me, she included articles about food, stories about concerts she had attended, interviews with concert artists, and book reviews. Gretchen continued the tradition of sending packets padded with pertinent newspaper clippings.

Emma Jane Brattain was a person with remarkable and wide-ranging interests, who also had an phenomenal memory for names, faces, and what other people were doing. She was unflaggingly curious about other people. Her commitment to culture and community was unsurpassed. My life is richer for having known her.

Ejay and Chris, Hong Kong, 1988.

Remembering Emma Jane Brattain—Sharon Thompson

One of the most memorable times I spent with Emma Jane was the night we attended a string quartet concert at the Hanford Theater in Richland. I don't recall who was playing or what they performed, but I will never forget the drive back home that night. But first I must take a little detour.

I had always been in awe of Emma Jane Miller Brattain after learning about her involvement in arts and culture in the Walla Walla valley. I would read her name and see her photo from time to time in the Sunday Society section of the *Union-Bulletin*. She, along with other prominent citizens, regularly held fundraisers and other activities in support of the arts. Her name would also come up in Whitman College news.

It was through the Walla Walla Symphony that we became better acquainted. In addition to playing violin in the Symphony, I was its music librarian and personnel manager during the time Emma Jane was president of the Symphony's board of directors. We saw each other often and developed a lovely friendship. I always looked forward to our meetings and chats about symphony stuff, especially decisions about buying scores and parts for the orchestra library. Some purchases were paid for from the Roland E. Miller Trust Fund that she had established within the Symphony's endowment as a memorial gift honoring Debi's father. I reminded myself that her dad continued to play an active part in Symphony performances whenever I was playing from a violin part stamped "Roland E. Miller Music Fund" on its pages.

Over time, I grew to respect and admire Emma Jane as a remarkable person of great insight and intellect who could get things done and, I might add, was swift of foot at doing it. I remember how quickly she would always walk, focused on her next order of business, notebook in hand heading out to her next meeting. One had to hustle to keep up with her!

So, about our drive home from Richland after that concert. As it turned out, this was one of the most memorable, wonderful, but nerve-wracking and heart-pounding nights of my life! As I pulled up

Emma Jane and Sharon.

to the stop sign at Wallula Junction, about thirty miles from home, I glanced down at the gas gauge and, to my horror, saw the needle about three whiskers above the empty line! How could I have been so stupid as to leave Walla Walla without checking my gas? My head was spinning, thinking about all the scenarios that might play out if we were to run out of fuel on that dark, lonely road so late at night, with *no* services between there and Walla Walla. No cell phones in those days either! How could I have put this VIP Grande Dame of the Arts in such a predicament??? This lady was *royalty*! I soon had to share with her the awful news of my discovery back at the stop sign. Her reaction was one of the most astonishing things ever. She wasn't upset with me at all and showed only compassion and understanding for my visible distress. Thoughts raced through my head. Did I have enough blankets in the trunk to keep us warm? How long might it be before someone would come by and help us? Could we trust them? Oh dear Lord, what would we do if we got stuck out there in such darkness so late at night?? I thought, maybe if I slowed down a bit I could save on gas, so I did my best to hold a steady fifty mph from then on. Occasionally, she would look at me and ask how I was doing—that dear lady asking *me* how *I* was doing. Wow! I kept moving along at what seemed like a snail's pace, continuously watching that damn gas gauge. At long last, by some miracle, we crept into Walla Walla close to midnight. The gas gauge had been sitting on empty for God knows how long! I was a basket case, and Emma Jane was as cool as a cucumber! I headed straight for the WW Farmers Co-op where I had a gas account. Standing at the pump, I was so rattled that for the life of me, I could not remember my passcode to unlock it! That just about did me in. I knew I wouldn't be able to get the car started again at this point to drive Emma Jane home. I said a quick prayer and turned the key. Incredibly, the engine started, and I managed to get Emma Jane home safe and sound—though I'm not sure how sound she would have been after those thirty nail-biting miles with me in that car. I could not have felt worse, but she kept reassuring me that everything was going to be just fine. Bless her heart. I loved that woman and will treasure her and our many times together forever.

I've heard it said, you won't always remember what people say or what they do, but you will always remember how they made you feel. That couldn't be more true.

Remembering the Brattains—Chuck Templeton

As to memories of Walter, here are two special memories and something extra-special. First one: One day in the Hall of Science secretary's office (back long before we remodeled the building and added the new wing), Walter was trying to make some ditto copies for the physics class he was teaching, using the old mimeograph machine. I happened to walk into the office to find him fuming. He was frustrated because he could not figure out how to install the stencil on the drum and was getting pretty irritated at the whole thing. I offered to help, and he gladly turned it over to me.

I remember thinking, "How come Walter is brilliant enough to invent the transistor, but can't figure out how to run a simple mimeograph machine?" Of course, there was no necessary connection between his scientific brilliance and his mechanical ability in running an office duplicator. But the memory of that event has stuck with me all these years, and I felt pretty smug at the time in being able to help him out. I was a young assistant professor and he was a world-famous scientist.

Another fond memory was the time Walter and Emma Jane invited Lillian and me to their beautiful home on Alvarado Terrace for dinner, or maybe it was just for wine and cheese, I don't recall. But I do remember Emma Jane being the perfect hostess, showing us around the house, explaining about the antiques, etc., while Walter just sort of followed us around, letting her "do her thing." He was very gentle and supportive, but I could tell his mind was someplace else, dealing with something more technical and scientific than beautiful furniture and family history. I think he and I eventually got to chatting about something scientific, but I forget what it was. I remember it just as a fun evening with two lovely people.

Now, the real "keeper" or special memory relates to the photos below. I had learned from Walter that these stamps were coming out, so I purchased the entire set of first day cover envelopes, one of which was cancelled. I asked Walter to autograph the envelope and he offered

First Day Covers, "Progress in Electronics" Series, July 1973.

to send it to Bardeen and Shockley for their autographs. As a result, I may be the only person in the world who has such a collector's item. I have kept these in my safe deposit box all these years, but recently brought them home. I have since framed all five envelopes, as shown in the photo, since they are such a unique item and would generate a lot of fun conversations, because I was a personal friend of Walter's, as well as his neighbor just down the street. (I photographed the envelopes on our granite kitchen counter top, hence the interesting background.)

There you have it—some fond memories of an amazing man and friend for quite a few years. Both he and Emma Jane were charming, unassuming, lovely people. Lillian and I treasured our association with them over the years.

Remembering Gretchen—Lynn Riegel

Henry David Thoreau said, "Friends cherish one another's hopes. They are kind to one another's dreams." He also said, "Friendship is never established as an understood relation. It is a miracle which requires constant proofs. It is an exercise of the purest imagination of the rarest faith."

Gretchen and I met when we were starting college at Whitman; she was seventeen and I eighteen. We became sorority sisters, later roommates, and finally lifelong friends. I was a poli sci major and Gretchen chose music and education. She married Stephen Kafoury right away and took a year off before heading overseas in the Peace Corps. The world was calling to me right away, and Army Special Services would even provide me an income!

After a year in Korea, I traveled to Zanjan, Iran to visit newly-arrived Gretchen and Steve. Gretchen, who was outgoing and social, was now finding herself in the background because of the place of women in the culture. Stephen was always asked out to join the men at the end of the day—no women allowed.

During the brief time I was visiting, we three were asked to family homes, mainly out of curiosity. Young men, still living at home, found a single woman traveling alone quite alluring. Even so, with

Lynn Riegel and Gretchen.

the Shah in power, women's rights were, at the time, becoming less restricted. Gretchen, as an American teacher, would have had some great discussions with the women of the village about their own hopes and dreams for the future.

Fast-forward almost thirty years and our friendship was demanding to be rekindled. Individually our dreams were becoming tarnished and faith in ourselves challenged. Although she was now successfully involved in politics, she was on her third marriage, her mom had died, and arthritis was taking its toll. I was a grieving mom, now single, with a teenage daughter and a new job. So the miracle of friendship sparked a need in both of us. We were opposites in some ways, but complementary in others. We could laugh, cry, reminisce, argue, and find ourselves rejuvenated over a weekend together at the beach.

We found a very special bond through our spiritual journeys. By spiritual, I mean the work that defined who we were and how we related to the world. I had found mine through the organized church and more recently in the field of grief and loss. Gretchen had found hers in the political arena, with issues of homelessness, women's rights, et al. In the end, we were both deeply spiritual beings who needed healing. We found that in the ensuing twenty years of visits, travels, and endless conversations, basking in our love and friendship.

Memories of Bob Brattain—Joanne Brattain

Bob Brattain, my father, was the youngest of the clan. On the surface, irascible (had the Brattain need to be right) and underneath a puppy dog. Fiercely loyal. He was proud of his pioneer heritage and loved telling stories he had learned from his father (with some embellishment I'm sure). He was a scientific pioneer in his own right and world renowned as a spectroscopist: designed the first mass spectrometer, led projects to identify low-volatile fuel for our ships during WWII and to synthesize penicillin. He was a lover of the arts—I learned my love of theater and opera from him—he would quote Shakespeare at the dinner table. And he was a "present" father, playing, tutoring, and counseling. He encouraged us to make our own decisions (I set my own curfew) and live with the consequences. In the twilight of his life, he spent eleven months bedridden due to cancer. To everyone's amazement, he was a good patient. Terrified of the Alzheimer's that claimed Walter, he was determined to have all his marbles to the end, and he did.

Childhood memories. . . . My mother was not a morning person, so there was a coffee pot by her side of the bed and beginning at the age of seven, I cooked breakfast every morning for Dad, Fred and myself until I left home. My father adored my mother and put her on a pedestal—probably not a comfortable place to be in retrospect.

Dad came home from work every day at 6:20. Cocktails in their bedroom by the fireplace and then dinner. We had no TV until after I went to college. I believe the objective was to teach us to entertain ourselves—reading, games, etc.

Lots of bedtime stories. When I was quite sick at about age five, he recorded bedtime stories for me so I would have them while he was gone. Another time, I was sick during the World Series. He taught me to keep score (radio only) and then checked me against the box score in the paper. In later years, we loved going to baseball games together—both the Giants and the A's.

We entertained my father's colleagues from all over the world. One evening, a guest accidentally broke something valuable. Dad was very gracious and said "we own our possessions; they don't own us." A good lesson I've carried with me.

Christmas—we had stockings in my parents' bedroom by their fireplace. There would be a sign on their door saying what time we could come in. Fred and I would play games from when we woke up until the appointed hour. After stockings, breakfast where my father would dawdle and read every section of the newspaper. Then *finally* we could go into the living room, where gifts were doled out one at a time. And we had to write thank-you notes before we could play with any gifts. In later years, I was aghast when kids ripped into their gifts and chaos reigned.

For high school, I went to a girl's school in Berkeley. Dad drove me to school most mornings, top down in the Austin-Healey. He loved his cars! I learned to drive a stick shift on a hill in that car—I suspect the clutch was never the same, but I can drive a stick shift on the San Francisco hills to this day.

My junior year was the dreaded Chemistry class—rumored to be the hardest A ever. (This daughter of a scientist has not a scientific bone in her body). The only school bribe I got was the promise of a lunch at Trader Vic's with an A. There was a test every Friday. Every Thursday night, he would tutor me. I would in turn tutor my friends on the phone (great lesson—the best way to learn something is to teach it!). And voila—an A, followed by a lovely lunch, just the two of us, at the original Trader Vic's. We continued the tradition of lunches throughout his life.

When I left for college, Dad told me, "If we haven't succeeded in teaching you a strong sense of morals, there's nothing we can do from 1,200 miles." There was a checking account with money in it. In order to get additional money, I had to account for every expenditure, and "misc" could not be the largest category. So I got a job on campus.

He always encouraged my career. After graduating college and planning to go to DC, the Census Bureau asked me to take an aptitude test for computer programming. This was 1967: This history major said "What's a computer??" He told me, "You got an A in logic, you'll be fine." And he was right. Best decision ever.

Family thoughts. . . . When Mari, his older sister, had her terrible auto accident on Christmas Eve 1983, he and Bee (second wife) rose to the occasion. They cleaned out the Mercer Island house and helped her find an apartment in Seattle. And, if memory serves, they also helped when she had to move to an assisted living facility in later years. (Sidebar about Mari: I was visiting her in the facility. The staff assumed I was her daughter and asked me to please make her follow the rules. Good luck with that. Guess the Brattain genes were pretty strong).

My parent's divorce in 1971 almost broke him emotionally. He had adored my mother and was devastated to think she had been unhappy. I believe that the stroke, resulting from a fall and skull fracture, altered the balance of her personality. Nevertheless, he never forgave her.

The other major disappointment in his life was that he ran out of money and couldn't finish his thesis for his doctorate at Princeton. In later years, he petitioned Princeton to award it based on his scientific work but was denied. A former colleague, who documented Dad's early work for some conferences and the museum at Beckman Instruments, said that he thought if Dad had petitioned earlier in his career, it would/should have been granted. He was a pioneer in his field.

Bee, his second wife, was very different from my mother. They were happy, traveled extensively and played lots of golf. For a few years, we all went to the San Francisco Opera on Sundays. They were in a box, and I would join them at intermission for champagne.

His relationship with Fred (my younger brother by three and a half years) was complex. Fred, based on testing, was brilliant. And he had a strong dramatic flair—enjoyed acting in high school and music. Since we were four years apart in school, I was not around for his puberty. Somewhere, in my opinion, he went off the rails. He dropped out of college, joined the Navy, and then pursued a musical career with his first wife. He borrowed money several times from Dad and removed himself from the family. He had several careers, always chasing some mythical big kill. His second wife, Lynne, was his college sweetheart.

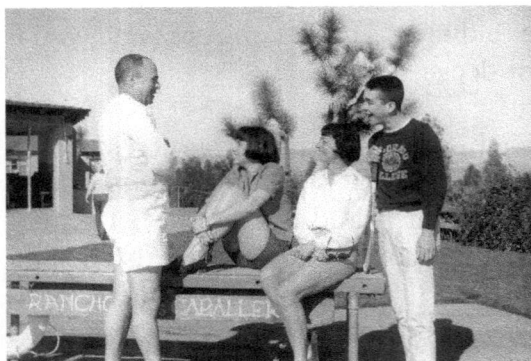

Bob, Joanne, Helen, Fred at Rancho de los Caballeros, Wickenburg, Arizona, 1964.

Joanne, Bob, Fred, 70th birthday.

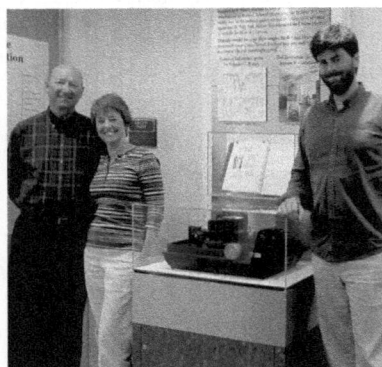

Beckman IR-1

The First Commercial Infrared Spectrophotometer

Designed by R. Robert Brattain at Shell Development Corporation and manufactured by National Technical Laboratories, the Beckman IR-1 was widely used for the multi-component analysis of C_4 mixtures in petroleum applications. In 1945, Shell scientists first determined the ß-lactam structure of penicillin based on IR-1 spectra.

Originally intended for C_4 gas phase samples, the IR-1 used 18 pre-selected wavelength turret stops. The unit displayed here was modified to use a micrometer adjusted wavelength control.

Composite Hydrocarbon Spectra Six Component C_4 Mixture	Shell Development Laboratory Beckman IR-1 Installation

Joanne and husband Chuck Hohos, and nephew Eric Brattain at Beckman Museum, Pasadena, California. Bob's Mass Spectrophotometer, the Beckman IR-1 and description.

Fred adopted Lynn's son Eric. Their relationship was tumultuous. Dad always tried to be supportive and was hurt by the lack of connection. During Dad's convalescence, Fred was supportive and I think some wounds were healed. (Fred's son, Eric, and I have a nice relationship now—the positive from Fred's early death). (Sidebar—interesting that both Bill and Fred appeared to have rejected the family educational and professional expectations—too much pressure?).

Three generations of Brattains. L to R: Standing: Mari, Keren, Walter, Helen, Bob. Seated: Joanne, Ross, Fred, Bill, Ottilie. Mercer Island, Washington, ca. 1952.

I rarely saw him with Walter and Mari together. My most distinct memory is how shocked I was that he was very quiet when around them. I now realize that when with family, we all tend to revert to our childhood roles. He was the youngest and I think somewhat cowed by Walter.

For his eightieth birthday, I snuck his address book and contacted friends and colleagues, asking them to send their thoughts and memories. He loved it and was quite moved. I still have the responses. His

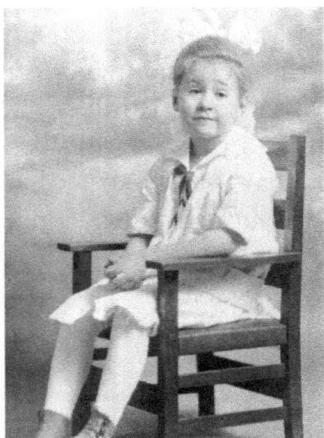

Young Mari Brattain.

Walter, Mari, and Bob at Joanne's wedding, 1977.

Remembering Mari Brattain, Seattle, 1992. L to R: Gretchen, Karen, Debi, Fred, Joanne, Evelyn, Bill, Ross.

loyalty to friends and the respect for his work and integrity shone through.

Memories of Bill Brattain—by his daughter, Karen Brattain

My father was a wanderer, and I was privileged to join him on many journeys. Given the scientific achievements of his father and mother, it's natural to imagine him carrying on their legacy, conducting and publishing his own research. But that was not my father's way. He had a life of ups and downs, success and sometimes underachievement or failure. Yet he found his path, found happiness, and made others happy in the process.

Bill (William) Brattain did admire his parents, and he did share their scientific inclinations. He earned two bachelor's degrees, in mathematics and in microbiology. Around the time of my birth, he worked in a steel foundry, where he took samples and analyzed their chemistry. As I grew up, he taught a science-focused extracurricular class for honor students, cooked at a school and at an assisted living facility (food preparation being its own kind of science), and worked as a nurses' aide in a memory care facility. In his meandering professional life he combined his technical skills with his interest in understanding other human beings.

My father loved puzzles, mental and physical. I have inherited sketchbooks where he hammered out math problems and drew diagrams. My brother remembers the band saw in our basement in Ellensburg, Washington, which my father used to craft wooden puzzles. Some of them he composed so cleverly that he himself had trouble fitting the disassembled pieces together. He liked to figure out how things functioned: his philosophy for broken electronics was to take them apart, bless them, and put them back together again. When that worked, success! When it didn't, he still learned something.

He was curious about nature as well, especially insects and reptiles. If I found a beetle or odd-looking bug, I would point it out to him. This was a lifelong interest with him; as a boy, he owned a pet praying mantis that he named Sylvia. He had a guidebook to reptiles

and amphibians of America, which we would page through in fascination as he told us about coral snakes and snapping turtles. He was
interested in fossils and gave me a book about them that he read in
his childhood. He even had a small collection of rocks with imprints
in them from ancient shells. Had it not been for my father, I would
not have encountered any of this knowledge.

There is wandering in thought, and there is wandering in the world.
My father loved both. I grew up listening to his stories of working a
food service job in Alaska, going to his great-grandfather's gold mine
in Idaho, and learning the "carney" ropes from his step-grandfather
Frank Kirsch, carnival sage. My father loved to take us on trips through
the Northwest, planned our unplanned, of long or short duration.
Of the former, I remember dearly our visits to Aunt Mari on Mercer
Island and cousin Gary Houser in Pomeroy. These were two different
realms, urban West and rural East, both endlessly fascinating to my
brother and me. As for unplanned trips, we would ride down back
roads through the wilderness of Central Washington, where one of
my father's favorite pastimes seemed to be looking for rattlesnakes.
He wasn't always the most responsible parent, but he had abundant
enthusiasm.

In 1980, he worked for the US Census and covered miles of ground
in a sparsely populated area. A few times, he took me or my brother
with him on the road. My memories of those days are distant, faded,
but always beautiful. On one trip, we passed a field of elk grazing.
He stopped the car. We got out and stood watching them. Tentatively
we walked closer, as close as we could. I was only five and had never
before seen creatures so wild and in such large number. As I said
before, I was privileged to journey with him.

We traveled to family gatherings in the Northwest and Midwest.
From my earliest years, I remember with great love our vacations on
the Oregon coast, where Bill's sister Gretchen rented a beach house.
In the evenings, my father would play card games in the house or help
us cook s'mores on the beach. When it was his turn to provide breakfast, he made oven-baked German pancakes. Years later, after we had
moved from Washington to Illinois, my father drove us to Nebraska to

spend Thanksgivings with his sister Debi and family. He loved classical music and would play cassette tapes in the car. I have clear memories of driving across the snowy plains under the winter sun, accompanied by Dvořák's *New World Symphony*—the landscape and music fit so perfectly that they blended into each other. Then we would reach our destination, with my father always so happy to see family.

Bill had a sensitive heart that reached out to humanity. His curiosity and compassion made him seek out connection. At a private school in Illinois, my father worked as a maintenance man and later a cook. He played chess with the school's head of maintenance—a tall, stern man that I feared but later came to appreciate due to my father's friendship with him. In the school cafeteria, he worked with a man and woman from the Philippines. My dad, always interested in exotic recipes, would talk with them about their favorite meals.

One of his greatest acts of generosity came later, when we had moved to Portland, Oregon. A homeless man named Pete began attending our church. After the service, my father would offer to drive Pete back to wherever he was staying. My father stood by Pete for nearly a decade, giving him rides, spending long hours listening to him, connecting him with possible resources. This was not easy. Pete had a mental illness that led to encounters with law enforcement and admission to various institutions. There were times of light, when Pete stabilized and was able to rent his own apartment. Always my father was there, a confidant and conscience. When Pete was institutionalized

Bill, Seattle, 1974.

Bill's Graduation, Carleton College, 1966.

for the final time before his passing, Bill cleaned out Pete's apartment and adopted his beloved cat. I did not always understand this commitment to someone who could be so problematic, but I admire my father's willingness to be present in a challenging relationship. Frankly, it was his calling.

In the last years of his life, my father's greatest pleasures were reading, sitting with his cats, going to restaurants, and playing bridge. His wandering took on a more sedate pace, but he still wandered. He loved Chinese, French, German, Italian, Korean, Lebanese, and Thai food—really, any food the world presented to him. I was glad he and I tried Ethiopian food, at a restaurant that became a birthday destination we both loved. He had an endearing habit of finding new restaurants, picking up their takeout menus, and scrutinizing each menu item carefully to decide what dishes he wanted to try.

His unfailing desire to meet and make friends flourished at the bridge games he played. Among others, he befriended a retired newspaperman and a spry 100-year-old lady. For the many years that he played in senior centers, he was happy to help set up for the games, even when it wasn't his turn to, and he gave much thought into what he would bring when it was his week to provide snacks. Until the very last weeks of his life, my father helped his bridge friends by giving them rides to and from the meeting place. When he died, I was overwhelmed by their feelings of grief and appreciation of him.

To my father, living a humble and meaningful life was comparable to achieving greatness or creating a work of art. He remarked to me, more than once, that his idea of fulfillment lay not in personal achievement but in service to others. He did not always succeed in this: he lacked social graces, made remarks without thinking, and in the process sometimes offended people. His blithe approach to life made him easy to please but frustrating to those who set goals and made plans. He was gentle, though, and good to the core. In my mind, I still see him wandering, bringing to every place and person an open heart.

Bill and Evelyn, Oregon Coast, ca. 1980.

Karen, Bill, and Ross, Elgin, Illinois, ca. 1984.

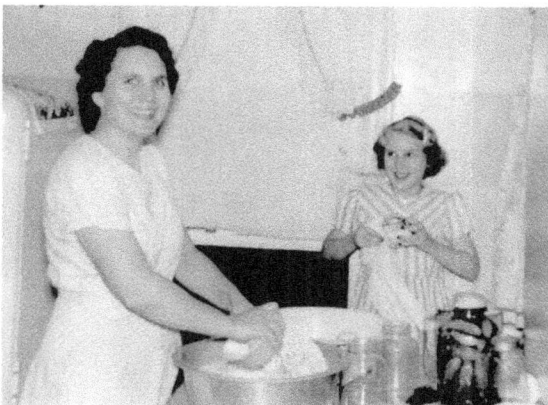

Evelyn in the kitchen helping her mother,
Ethel, Norfolk, Nebraska, late 1940s.

Evelyn, Seattle, 1974.

Bill and Evelyn's wedding at Aunt Mari's house,
Mercer Island, Washington, February 1974.

Walter holding his granddaughter Karen, November 1974.

Memories of Evelyn Brattain—by her daughter, Karen

Evelyn was a child of the Northwest and Midwest. Her mother and father met when they both worked at Diamond Lake, Washington. They married and moved to live with his family in Norfolk, Nebraska. Ethel and John Henry Herbert Ehrichs raised their four girls in what were often rough times. Evelyn, third of the four, remembered helping her mother can food and pluck chickens. There was an effort to use everything wisely and for as long as possible. This included getting the most out of education: Evelyn was valedictorian of her high school class. In the midst of frugality, though, was enjoyment of life. She made lifelong friends, played the French horn in high school band, and cruised around with the other young Nebraskans of the 1950s. Notoriously, she waited in the getaway car as her sister and sister's future husband stole a few watermelons from a farmer's patch. Yes, this is how I remember my mother: she embodied the practicality, civility, and friendly warmth of the Midwest.

She was the driving force in my family. She enriched all our lives. My parents met and married in Seattle, where Evelyn had moved to be closer to her Washington family. After my birth but before my brother's, my mother and father decided to move to Ellensburg, two hours east, because they thought we would be happier and safer in a small town. We were. I have many fond memories of growing up between the Cascade Mountains and Columbia River. My parents, however, struggled to find enough work. Evelyn, a college graduate who had taught sixth grade in Nebraska, worked as a teaching assistant and playground supervisor. Then she found a job listing in a national newspaper to which she subscribed. I didn't know where Chicago was: my six-year-old mind couldn't conceive of it. Nonetheless, Evelyn applied, flew out for an interview, and accepted the offer that followed. In the summer of 1981, we moved to Illinois.

Our eight years in the Chicago area changed the course for us all. My brother and I grew up knowing so much more of the world than we might have otherwise. Even the move across the country opened our minds: a moose by the side of a lake in Montana, the Corn Palace in South Dakota, the vastness of the Great Plains. Our destination, Chicago Junior School, was a phenomenal place of old buildings on sixty acres of land, much of it still forested. During our five years there, my brother and I explored every corner of the campus.

My mother worked as secretary to the school's development officer. She quickly made friends with her coworkers as they worked their way through mailings, phone drives, and fundraisers. Diligent, principled, and organized, my mother also oversaw our education. When we lived in Ellensburg, she used to bring home extra worksheets from her class so that my brother and I could get a jump on reading and math. In Elgin, she enrolled us in after-school classes of our choosing. She always showed interest in what we learned, whether it was Greek mythology, Medieval customs, or (for me) a summer session of "circus camp." (It was a blast. Thanks, Ma.)

This I am thankful for: her unflagging efforts to educate her children while allowing them to pursue their own interests. And Chicago was a great place to do this. I remember so many spots in the city, but dearest of all are the Art Institute and the Field Museum. Exploring these institutions gave my life breadth—the Art Institute, which exposed me to works from Europe, India, Belarus, and China and thus showed me the world's expanse—and depth—the Field Museum, where I saw dinosaurs, mummies, and Indigenous American artifacts and thus witnessed the vastness of history. All of this, always, with my mother eager to hear my thoughts, take them to heart, and present me with more opportunities to develop my interests.

Illinois enlightened us for eight years, but we grew to miss the Northwest. My mother felt that my graduation into high school provided an opportunity to move back. We chose Portland, Oregon. This time, neither job nor home awaited us, but my parents made it work. Soon my mother had a new administrative position, to which she brought her characteristic alacrity. She did well, and her work provided her means to take an Alaska cruise with my father and a tour of Switzerland and Germany with my cousin, my father, and me. She had always wanted to see these parts of the world. She even visited me during my internship in Russia, where she instantly charmed my coworkers.

In my adulthood, I see my mother's contributions to my career—not only in the education she made sure I received but also in the qualities she modeled for me. In high school, she offered to read my writing assignments. She would come back with my draft marked in light pencil; among other errors, I was prone to writing run-on sentences. After college, she helped me write résumés and cover letters. She taught me how to phrase sentences carefully, positively, to present my best self. In doing so, she showed me the value of every word. I now have a master's degree in book publishing and have worked as a copy editor for fourteen years. When I compiled my final portfolio to graduate, I dedicated it to two people. One was to Evelyn, "my first and finest editor."

Life with my mother was not always good. She was raised in Christian Science, a religion that relies on prayer for healing and refuses all medicine and medical care. Her deep, lifelong commitment to Christian Science provided her with professional opportunities and cherished friendships. The job posting that moved us from Ellensburg to Elgin was published in the Christian Science Monitor, and we enjoyed many social gatherings with church members. But Christian Science betrayed her. She died at age sixty-six of untreated cancer. While I began graduate school, she suffered at home, trying to heal the "illusion" of disease. While I broadened my horizons, she dwindled in isolation, rejecting her family's efforts to help, choosing instead to call church members to pray with her. She died before I earned my degree. The religion led her down a path of perfectionism and control, always control, of every word, thought, and deed. Of the many lessons she taught me, I did not learn how to swallow a pill, take my temperature, accept my flaws, or talk about negative feelings. I don't know what else to say: we all choose the path that seems best for us. She poured into her religion the same self-discipline, intelligence, and care that she brought to every aspect of her life. She was true to herself to the very end.

Despite the grief, her goodness remains. After Walter and Emma

Jane Brattain had both passed away, our family inherited many boxes of correspondence and personal papers. My mother went through them one at a time, applying the full force of her secretarial skills. She organized, labeled, and filed documents. She consulted my father and family members. She got facts straight and made notes. Then she sent these records to the Whitman College archives. If there is handwriting on a document—gentle pencil marks that explain the sender or recipient, the place or time—it may be my mother's handwriting. I am grateful that in this and so many other ways she reaches out and carries on.

Afterword

I had an inheritance from my father,
it was the moon and the sun.
And though I roam all over the world,
the spending of it's never done.

—Ernest Hemingway, *For Whom the Bell Tolls*

I began writing the letters for this book more than a decade ago. They are filled with searching for, and discovering, details of the lives of Dad, Honeychile, Grammie, Nanmy, Hattie, Walter, Gretchen, and Mother. Webb signed onto the project in 2015. His uniquely expressive voice and our collaborative way of working have added immeasurably to the project.

My goal has been to bring to light the events—even seemingly inconsequential details—that shaped the lives of these individuals. I fantasized about pulling up a chair and conversing with each of them one-on-one as they told their stories. I hope that I have portrayed them fairly, such that readers can relate to them as well. For Hattie, whom I never met and knew little about before 2013, I relied mainly on documents from the Pueblo Hospital and Carthage, Missouri. Luckily, I found just the right people to ask for help in accessing her records. Without these, I could not have understood what multiple tragedies and a thirty-year hospitalization meant to her life. For Grammie, Honeychile, and Nanmy, I made use of their letters, photos, and journals when available. For Gretchen, I spent much of the year following her death reflecting on our sisterhood. At her memorial, the memories and views by several of her colleagues of her passionate life and legacy blew me away. I wove some of these impressions into my letter. Dad's letters, editorials, and talks helped me better understand his perspective on life. My letter to him tells of my journey from a grief-stricken adolescent to a daughter who could celebrate him with breath-catching admiration. Through reading Walter's early, affectionate letters to Mother, along with his personal and professional writing, especially his account of traveling to Sweden to receive the Nobel Prize, I came to see him and his place in our family in a completely new way, not as a surrogate or usurper, but as *my* stepfather. And without Mother's passion for genealogy and commitment to preserving decades of documents from her family history, this book would not have been possible.

Legacy is not leaving something for people. It's leaving something in people.

—Peter Strople

I have always strived to connect meaningfully with others. But it's one thing to form relationships and another to maintain them. As I wrote, I wondered if the connections I was making to these loved ones might fade away after I finished the project. Would I soon forget the passion and excitement I felt in telling their stories? I know now that I will not. As an example, I did much of the research and writing about Hattie in 2013. Ten years later, she remains just as alive in my imagination as she was a decade ago. As long as I have memories, these individuals will remain key parts of who I have become.

July 2023: The cousins from the 1995 picture on page xxxiii. L to R: Deborah Kafoury, Megan Miller, Katharine Kafoury, Mari Fox, Sarah Simmons, Andrew Miller, Brenda Barranco, Karen Brattain, Scott Agenbroad, Ross Brattain, Kat Miller.

July 2023. First gathering of next-generation cousins. L to R: Alex Blosser, Lauren Woodard, Devin Barranco, Jacob Blosser, Anna Blosser, Noah Barranco, Emme Rhee, Sydney Agenbroad, Anni Rhee, Naia Mendenhall–Miller, Nile Mendenhall–Miller. Missing from picture: Tia Rexine, Frank Baltimore, Jr.

My foray into my family's history has enriched my life. We all have a chorus of ancestors whose voices are waiting to be heard. Their stories should be passed on to future generations. That is why I decided to write this book with Webb. It pleases me to see that several family members from the next generation are showing a similar interest in storytelling.

This became evident at the 2023 family reunion on the Oregon coast. For example, Webb's son, Andrew, is carrying on the narrator tradition. He can turn most any get-together into a group conversation. He did that at a gathering in Arch Cape when he encouraged all present to introduce themselves and reflect on family members who had died. Andrew led the way by describing his life in Washington, D.C., including his work focused on human rights and indigenous peoples in South America. He then recalled some of his summer 1994 Portland internship experiences in Gretchen's City Council office. Whenever Andrew needed a car, Gretchen insisted he take her blue Honda del Sol, with her favorite Dire Straits songs in the tape deck. As he and I walked on the beach earlier that day, Andrew told me about listening to "Tunnel of Love" at Broadway volume.

Another example: Scott got a big laugh as he riffed on having been left behind when several of us went to Italy for Gretchen's fiftieth birthday. He also told of attending in 1999 an important ceremony in Washington, D.C., where she received an award from The Alliance to End Homelessness. Scott watched in amazement as billionaire philanthropist H. Wayne Huizenga received the same award from home-repair expert Bob Vila. This was a really big deal. In contrast, Gretchen, modest as always, was at the same time downplaying her accomplishments. As family members listened to Scott, all who had known Gretchen were nodding, confirming this self-effacing element of her persona.

At another moment, Brenda told of Bill's generosity in taking the cousins on hikes decades ago. Strong in her memory was Bill marching his charges into Mariner Market in Cannon Beach to get as many snacks as they could carry. But he also insisted that they haul out all their trash at the end of the hike.

Small stories such as these serve both to humanize the figures from our past and strengthen our ties to them. As family members spoke about their lives and memories, I watched the faces of those listening for the first time to those stories. I imagined the seeds being planted

Andrew, raconteur.

Nile, emerging raconteur.

Scott, entertaining storyteller.

in the young people's minds that could one day germinate into their own investigation of their family histories.

The making of connections did not end with the reunion get-togethers. As Chris and I were flying home, Devin and Noah were watching the new IMAX film *Oppenheimer*. Immediately afterward, Devin texted me, excitedly telling of having seen this three-hour "incredible" film. When Brenda picked us up at the airport, I mentioned that we had Robert Oppenheimer's autograph (among others) on Mother's menu from the 1962 White House dinner. Word quickly spread. Within minutes, Devin texted again, "Mom just said you have Oppenheimer's autograph. Is this true!?" A series of rapid-fire messages ended with, "Can Noah and I see the autograph?"

This film, which feels both contemporary and historical, has the potential to form other links for Devin and Noah to our past: Oppenheimer's presence at the White House dinner; Mother sitting next to Glenn Seaborg, who first isolated plutonium; Niels Bohr, whom Walter met in Copenhagen in 1956. And of course the Atomic Energy Site at Hanford, Washington, seventy miles west of Walla Walla, where the plutonium used in the Los Alamos and Nagasaki bombs was produced. It is connections like these that I hope Devin and Noah and our younger family members will make to past, current, and future events and individuals. Learning of them requires only curiosity and eagerness for exploration. One point of entry might be to ask why Oppenheimer, who was at the 1962 White House dinner, was not attending as a Nobel Prize laureate.

As a complement to the seriousness of Oppenheimer's legacy, we showed the boys the lead medallion from Walter's induction into the playful "Society of the Ever Smiling and Leaping Frog." It feels like a friendly signal from Walter, carrying energy to Devin, Noah, and others in the family.

May they be forever chased by shadows.

—Debi, August 2023

Noah and Devin with White House menu signed at bottom by Robert Oppenheimer.

Noah wearing Walter's frog medallion.

Appendix I
Genealogy

*"We all grow up with the weight of history on us.
Our ancestors dwell in the attics of our brains as they do
in the spiraling chains of knowledge hidden in every cell
of our bodies."*

—Shirley Abbott

Our Ancestors in America

In thinking about family history, we learned how easily incorrect familial relationships get propagated. Internet sites like Ancestry.com make it simple to just copy parts of another person's reported family tree, regardless of its accuracy. Twice, we were fooled into thinking we had discovered an ancestor on the Mayflower in 1620, only to later become convinced that a claimed parental relationship was wrong. (In each case, Webb invested $25 with an application to the Mayflower Society to confirm that the proposed Mayflower link was invalid.) We haven't found convincing evidence of our ancestors among the couple hundred British that immigrated to New England before 1630 (or any coming to other parts of the Americas). However, as described here, several were among the more than 2000 that came to New England between 1630 and 1635. The tree that we are reporting omits portions that didn't seem convincing, or where we didn't locate interesting background information.

Before getting into the details, we give a simplified family tree that summarizes what we found. To keep the picture to a manageable size, we collect people with the same last name, and single out only a few of our closest ancestors. It is oriented so that an individual is pictured below the parents, with the paternal line on the left.

The chart is complex, so we will explain it in steps. First, starting at the bottom (that is, with us), follow the connections to our mother,

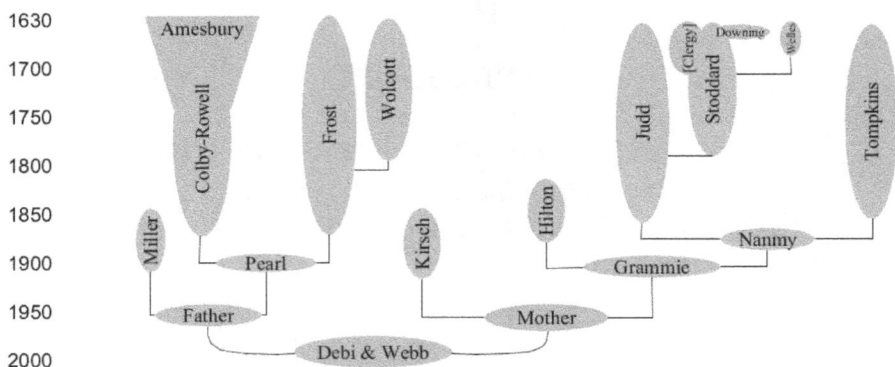

Overview of our family's genealogy.

then to her mother (Grammie), then to Grammie's mother, Nanmy. Nanmy's American ancestors on both sides (Judd and Tompkins) can be traced back to the 1630s. Nanmy's father's sixth great-grandfather, Thomas Judd, came to New England in 1634. Similarly, Ralph Tompkins, Nanmy's mother's sixth great-grandfather, arrived in 1635. While *maternal* lineages are often difficult to trace (*i.e.*, because census records before 1850 didn't record the wife's name), the picture indicates that around 1800 a Judd man married a Stoddard, and her paternal lineage goes back to a man who married Mary Downing (more about her later), who came to Massachusetts in 1633. Finally, around 1700, a Stoddard man married a Welles, and her paternal lineage goes back to Thomas Welles, who arrived in 1635. Since the picture indicates that our father's side has at least three equally old American lineages, the chart suggests that we have a total of at least eight lines of descent dating back to the 1630s. In fact, there are a few more (see below).

We now turn to the details of Nanmy's American ancestors, starting with the Tompkins lineage. It shows that Ralph and Katherine had a son John, who married Margaret, and so on.

	Ancestor	Married
	Ralph Tompkins 1585–1666	Katherine Foster 1577–1650
Son	John Tompkins 1610–1681	Margaret Goodman 1612–1672
Son	Nathaniel Tompkins 1633–1684	Elizabeth White 1642–1698
Son	Nathaniel Tompkins 1678–1732	Elizabeth Cornell 1680–1745
Son	Nathaniel Tompkins 1703–1790	Mary Forshay 1707–1758
Son	Amos Tompkins 1742–1802	Mary Chatterton 1740–1809
Son	Brundage Tompkins 1765–1832	Phebe Thorn 1786–1841
Son	Samuel Thorn Tompkins 1806–1840	Jane Ricketson 1807–1857
Daughter	Maria Tompkins 1833–1909	Randall Stoddard Judd 1829–1912
Daughter	Ida Judd (Nanmy) 1859–1953	John Edwin Hilton 1849–1909

Our Tompkins lineage.

A book on the Tompkins family (see below) proposes that this lineage extends back to "Thom the Saxon", who came to Britain with William the Conqueror, and fought in the Battle of Hastings (1066). While the lineage back to Ralph Tompkins is confirmed by numerous independent sources, we find the full proposed British lineage difficult to believe. (In general, we didn't try to trace European ancestors because we don't know how to judge their reliability.)

	Thomas Judd 1608–1688	Sarah Freemen 1612–1678
Son	Thomas Judd 1637–1702	Sarah Steele 1639–1696
Son	John Judd 1667–1717	Hannah Hickox 1671–1750
Son	Benjamin Judd 1710–1755	Abigail Adams 1716–1755
Son	Joel Judd 1748–1779	Mercy Hickox 1752–1842
Son	Randall Judd 1773–1803	Mary Stoddard 1771–1845
Son	Stoddard Judd 1797–1873	Elizabeth Emigh 1803–1885
Son	Randall Stoddard Judd 1829–1912	Maria Tompkins 1833–1903

Our Judd lineage.

In Nanmy's paternal lineage, the older Thomas Judd was in Boston by 1634, but soon became an early settler of Connecticut. He went to Hartford in 1636, perhaps with the first group of settlers coming from Massachusetts. By 1646 he had moved to Farmington, just west of Hartford, which remained the home of Thomas Jr. and John of our lineage. Another ancestor, Thomas Jr.'s father-in-law, John Steele, arrived in 1633. Notice that Randall Judd (1773–1803) married Mary Stoddard (specifically in 1794), connecting us to the Stoddards.

	Anthony Stoddard 1600–1686	Mary Downing 1615–1647
Son	Solomon Stoddard 1643–1729	Esther Warham 1644–1736
Son	Anthony Stoddard 1678–1760	Prudence Welles 1682–1714
Son	Eliakim Stoddard 1705–1749	Joanna Curtis 1708–1802
Son	John Stoddard 1730–1795	Mary Atwood 1733–1802
Daughter	Mary Stoddard 1771–1845	Randall Judd 1773–1803

Our Stoddard lineage.

Esther Warham married Solomon Stoddard. Another of our ancestors, Esther's father, John Warham, arrived in 1630. Also, Prudence Welles married into the Stoddard lineage (on October 20, 1700, to be precise). She was a great-granddaughter of Thomas Welles (1590–1660, arrived 1635), the first governor of Connecticut.

Mary Downing came to Massachusetts in 1633 as an unmarried teenager. Nowadays it is almost impossible to imagine the hardships she faced. No doubt things were better in 1633 than in 1620, when half of the Mayflower passengers died the first winter at Plymouth Colony, but Mary's sister Susan who made the trip with her, apparently died within a few years. Indeed, Mary lived only thirty-two years. Extending the study to include Mary's half-brother, Sir George Downing, after whom Downing Street is named, prompted Webb to even learn a bit about the English Civil War.

Solomon Stoddard was a well-known preacher in Northampton, Mass. He dealt with Puritan churches and Indian attacks, two additional topics about which we knew essentially nothing but were inspired to learn a bit. As described in Solomon's Wikipedia biography, his professional and personal lives were closely tied to those of other famous Puritan clergy, such as Cotton Mather. Broadening our search to other relatives, such as direct descendants of Solomon's daughter Esther, brought in some other interesting characters, such as Jonathan Edwards and Aaron Burr.

That completes our dive into the ancestry of our maternal great-grandmother, Nanmy.

On our father's side of the family, we are able to identify some ancestors of his mother, Pearl Colby Miller. The paternal lineage of Pearl's mother, Ellen Ada Frost, was easy to trace. Edmund Frost came to Boston in 1635 with his wife and infant child. He quickly settled in Cambridge, Mass., where he spent the remainder of his life.

	Edmund Frost 1593–1672	Thomasine Clench 1600–1633
Son	Samuel Frost 1638–1717	Mary Cole 1639–1673
Son	Samuel Frost 1664–1739	Experience Miller 1673–1731
Son	Joseph Frost 1694–1775	Zerniah Cooley 1709–1781
Son	Abner I. Frost Sr. 1748–1834	Dinah Cooley 1758–1796
Son	Abner I. Frost Jr. 1780–1852	Hannah Conklin 1788–1823
Son	Benjamin Frost 1806–1899	Margaret Mooney 1811–1889
Daughter	Ellen Ada Frost 1836–1924	Charles Clifton Colby 1831–1895
Daughter	Pearl Leone Colby 1873–1954	Armand Rudolph Miller 1874–1942

Our Frost lineage.

Another interesting part of the tree extends from Henry Wolcott down to the Frost lineage. Henry had a number of well-known and extensively documented successors. For instance, one of Joanna Wolcott's brothers, Roger Wolcott (1678-1767), was an early Connecticut governor. One of Roger's sons, Oliver Wolcott (1726–1797), was also a governor, and another, Erastus Wolcott (1721–1793), was a Major General in the Revolution.

	Henry Wolcott 1578–1665	Elizabeth Saunders 1584–1655
Son	Simon Wolcott 1625–1687	Martha Pitkin 1639–1719
Daughter	Joanna Wolcott 1668–1755	John Colton 1659–1727
Daughter	Joanna Colton 1695–1765	Jonathan Cooley 1686–1752
Son	Jabez Cooley 1729–1800	Abigail Hancock 1734–1815
Daughter	Dinah Cooley 1758–1796	Abner I. Frost Sr. 1748–1834

Lineage from Henry Wolcott to Abner Frost Sr.

The only part of the above graphical summary of our ancestors in America that may be controversial concerns Pearl's paternal ancestry. In particular, Pearl's belief in her descent from Anthony Colby (arrived 1630) is based on deductions she made around 1920. She worked with her nephew, Charles Clifton Colby III, over the course of several years, multiple trips to major libraries (*e.g.*, in Boston and New York City), and correspondence with historical societies and family members. Much of their effort went toward an unsuccessful attempt to confidently identify Pearl's paternal great-grandfather. According to Colby folklore, the family bible containing a record ending with Pearl's grandfather, John Colby, had been sent to Chicago to be re-bound shortly before the Chicago fire of 1871, and perished in the fire.

The key observation by Pearl and Charles was that the paternal grandfather of John Colby's wife, Hannah Rowell, was Thomas Rowell. Once the tree was pushed back to Thomas Rowell, it connected with multiple generations that lived in Amesbury and Salisbury, Massachusetts, as documented in *Old Families of Salisbury and Amesbury, Massachusetts*, by David Webster Hoyt (1897). The book has two

Plaque at Amesbury, Massachusetts.

additional volumes and a supplement published at later dates. In particular, p. 1081 of the Supplement (1919) tells that the Thomas Rowell born in Amesbury is the individual that moved to Bradford, Vermont (where John Colby met Hannah Rowell). Other critical observations are on p. 133 of *The History of Warner, New Hampshire* by Walter Harriman (1879), on p. 241 of *A History of Guildhall, Vt* by Everett Chamberlin Benton (1886), and in Thomas Rowell's probated will. Pearl and Charles found these documents with considerable effort, whereas we simply got them from the Internet. (Books mentioned here are free at Archive.org).

	Thomas Rowell 1594–1662	Margaret Milner 1594–1649
Son	Valentine Rowell 1622–1662	Joanna Pinder 1621–1690
Son	Philip Rowell 1651–1690	Sarah Morrill 1650–1731
Son	Jacob Rowell 1672–1746	Hannah Barnard 1671–1731
Son	Aaron Rowell 1701–1769	Mary Challis 1707–1777
Son	Thomas Rowell 1737–1816	Mary Barritt 1732–1817
Son	Aaron Rowell 1770–1846	Polly Putney 1770–1849
Daughter	Hannah Rowell 1806–1894	John Colby 1806–1876
Son	Charles Clifton Colby 1831–1895	Ellen Ada Frost 1836–1924
Daughter	Pearl Leone Colby 1873–1954	Armand Rudolph Miller 1874–1942

Lineage from Thomas Rowell to our paternal grandparents.

We have summarized the painstaking work by Pearl and Charles in a table that starts with Thomas Rowell. The result is that while Pearl's maiden name was Colby, her purported relationship to Anthony Colby (1605–1660) was not though an unbroken line of male Colbys, but rather through the Rowells. Namely, the first Aaron Rowell's mother-in-law was Mary Colby Challis (1673–1716), daughter of John Colby (1633–1674), son of Anthony. This argues that Webb indeed is a descendant of Anthony Colby, after whom he was named.

The founding families tended to stay in Amesbury or Salisbury for generations. As a result, the Hoyt book implies that we are direct descendants of the founders Thomas Barnard (1617–1677), Anthony Colby (1605–1660), John Hoyt (1615–1688), John Colby (1633–1674), Phillip Challis (1617–1691), Valentine Rowell (1622–1662), William Sargent (1606–1665), and perhaps Jarret Haddon (1608–1689), if the Susannah that married Anthony Colby was Susannah Haddon, as believed by many.

Almost all of the tree that we were able to reconstruct ends with either our maternal great-grandmother, Nanmy, or our paternal grandmother, Pearl. The three small paternal lineages in the overview tree, *i.e.*, for Miller, Kirsch and Hilton, have the following specifics. Our paternal grandfather's father, Jacob Miller (originally Müller) (1840–1908), came from Switzerland in 1857 and fought with the Union Army for most of the Civil War to gain citizenship. Jacob married Laura Huesselmann (1851–1919), whose parents, Frederich Huesselmann (1811–1892) and Anna Henrichs (1815–1898), came from Germany. The father of our maternal grandfather (*i.e.*, Gramps, AKA Honeychile), Martin Kirsch (1848–1932), came from Germany. He married Emma Koerner (1855–1913), whose parents, John Koerner (1812–1892) and Louisa Koerner (1825–1880), came from Germany. Nanmy married John Edwin Hilton (1849–1909), *i.e.*, Grammie's father, whose parents were Edwin Hilton (1820–1899) and Deborah Slack (1823–1890). Edwin came from England in 1844.

Nowadays, thanks to the Internet, it is relatively easy to investigate family histories. For the cost of a dinner at a good restaurant, one can get three-month access to either Ancestry.com or the online databases at AmericanAncestors.org, which provide good starting points for the kind of family-history exploration that has enriched our lives.

Our reason for highlighting the ancestors that arrived in New England by 1635 is that each one is extensively documented in the definitive *Great Migration Study Project*, available at AmericanAncestors.org. Thus, it easy to start learning about any of those ancestors.

Ancestor	Arrived
Mary Downing 1615–1647	1633
Thomas Judd 1608–1688	1634
John Steele 1591–1665	1633
Ralph Tompkins 1585–1666	1635
John Warham 1595–1670	1630
Thomas Welles 1590–1660	1635
John White 1600–1684	1632

Early ancestors on Mother's side.

Anthony Colby 1605–1660	1630
Edmund Frost 1593–1672	1635
Henry Wolcott 1578–1655	1630

Early ancestors on Dad's side.

The Welles family is highlighted in the pictorial representation of the ancestry because it arguably has the best documentation, namely the book *The Descendants of Governor Thomas Welles of Connecticut and his Wife Alice Tomes,* vol. 1, 3rd edition (2015) by Barbara Jean Mathews. It is available at a very reasonable price ($20 for 672 pages in paperback) from the Welles Family Association (Wellesfamily. org). The book contains many facts about our Welles lineage down to Prudence Welles Stoddard, *e.g.,* that (p. 417) Prudence died in her thirty-third year, after the birth of her ninth child in thirteen years. Another example is that when Prudence was sixteen, her mother died; eight months later, her father, Robert Welles, (re)married Mary Stoddard. Two years later, Prudence married Mary Stoddard's younger brother. Complicated.

Several books that mention our ancestors are freely available on the Internet at Archive.org, including:

1. *The Tomkins–Tompkins Genealogy* (1942) by Robert A. Tompkins and Clare F. Tompkins

2. *Thomas Judd and His Descendants* (1856) by Sylvester Judd

3. *Genealogy of the Family of Anthony Stoddard of Boston* (1949) by Charles Stoddard

4. *The Frost Family in England and America* (1909) by Thomas G. Frost and Edward L. Frost

5. *Wolcott Immigrants and Their Early Descendants (The First Six Generations)* (2002) by John Benjamin Wolcott and Charles V. Waid

Also, although he arrived too late (1639) to be in our table of pre-1635 arrivals, Solomon Stoddard can be easily studied, perhaps starting with his extensive Wikipedia entry. Another example is that John Warham and Anthony Colby arrived with the well–documented Winthrop Fleet in 1630.

It is probably impossible to anticipate who will become deeply interested in their family's history, or when in their life that might happen. Also, once someone looks beyond their immediate family, there is no telling which relatives will capture their imagination and prompt a deeper study. In Debi's case, a main fascination was with Hattie Judd Cooper, who was not even a direct ancestor, but rather one of Nanmy's sisters. This fascination, or rather obsession, resulted in a year of gathering information from multiple sources to help Debi understand a life much different from her own. Later, Webb got involved. The findings appear in pages 25-51.

One of Webb's motivations was to better understand the sources of his names, "Webb" and "Colby". As a boy, he was told that Anthony Colby and Richard Webb were his earliest ancestors in America, according to Pearl. As mentioned above, the ancestry back to Anthony Colby and the Amesbury crowd has some uncertainty. Worse yet, the multi-page entry on Richard Webb in the definitive work on this period, *Great Migration Study Project,* says simply "CHILDREN: none recorded." Apparently, all the public-school abuse that Webb endured because of his name was based on an error. However, Webb's appreciation of Pearl, initially based on his fond memories of learning to read with her, was strengthened when he discovered that she obtained a Master's Degree in Mathematics from Stanford in 1904 (preceding his degree from another university by sixty-three years). Webb completely forgives his grandmother.

We will be pleased if anyone is prompted to learn more about these (or other) ancestors. We have provided an overview of our ancestors in America, and suggested some Internet resources for possible follow-ups. We invite you to continue our journey, and hope you have as much fun as we have had.

—Webb Colby Miller, Debi Miller Bonds and Chris Bonds (editor and graphics designer)

Headstone (Fox Lake, WI) of Nanmy's grandfather, Stoddard Judd (1797–1873.)

Appendix II
Family Trees

In June of 2023, Webb's daughters Mari and Megan visited him, during which time Mari read drafts of most chapters of this book. Her primary concern was the difficulty she had keeping track of the many relatives mentioned. She recommended including ancestry trees showing their relationships, an idea that Megan heartily seconded.

With Mari's artistic assistance, Webb prepared trees for the chapters about Roland, Emma Jane, Walter and Hattie. Relatives mentioned in the chapters on Frank, Ruth and Ida are located within the trees for Emma Jane and Hattie. Webb also included a tree of those few blood relatives of Roland's sister Marian (Anderson) Miller whose names appear in the book. Following Debi's recommendation, he created trees of our immediate families and one of our sister Gretchen.

We hope that these trees will help interested readers find their way through our family "thicket."

—Debi and Webb

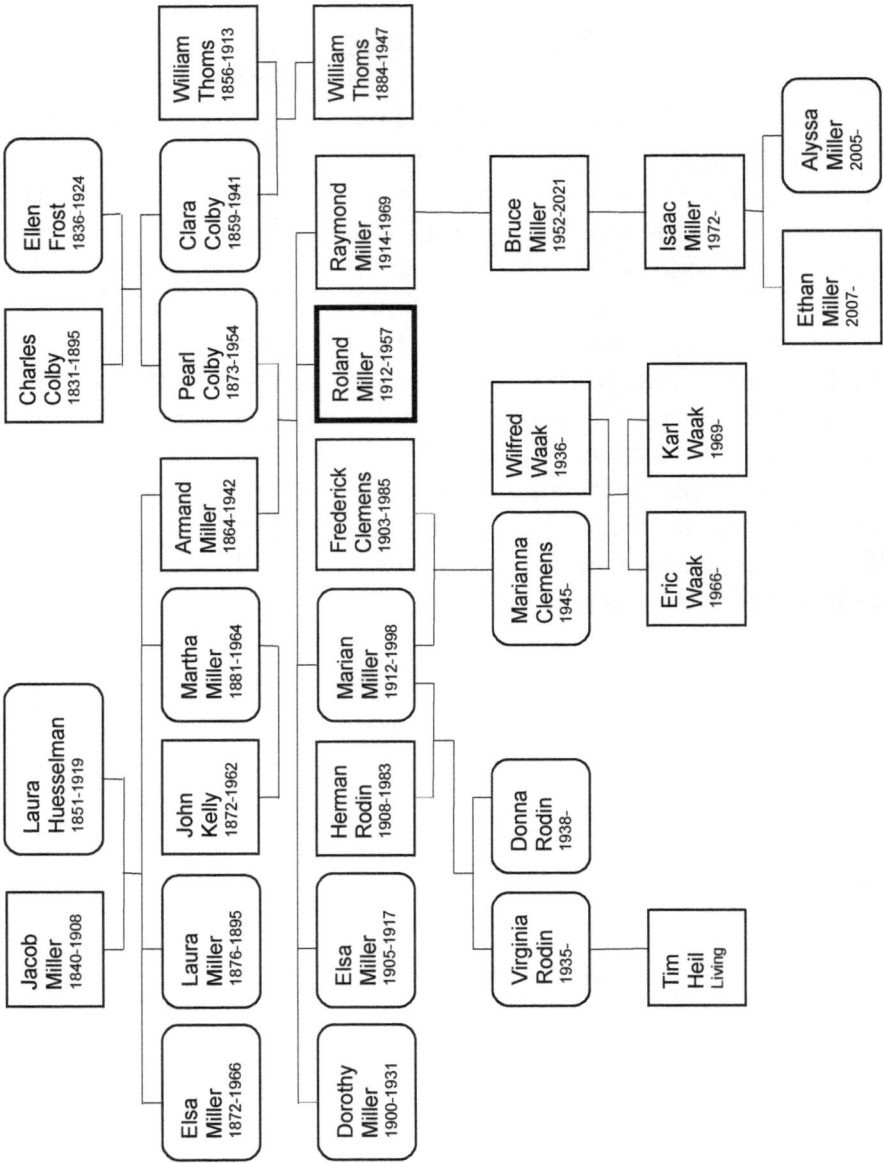

Roland Miller.

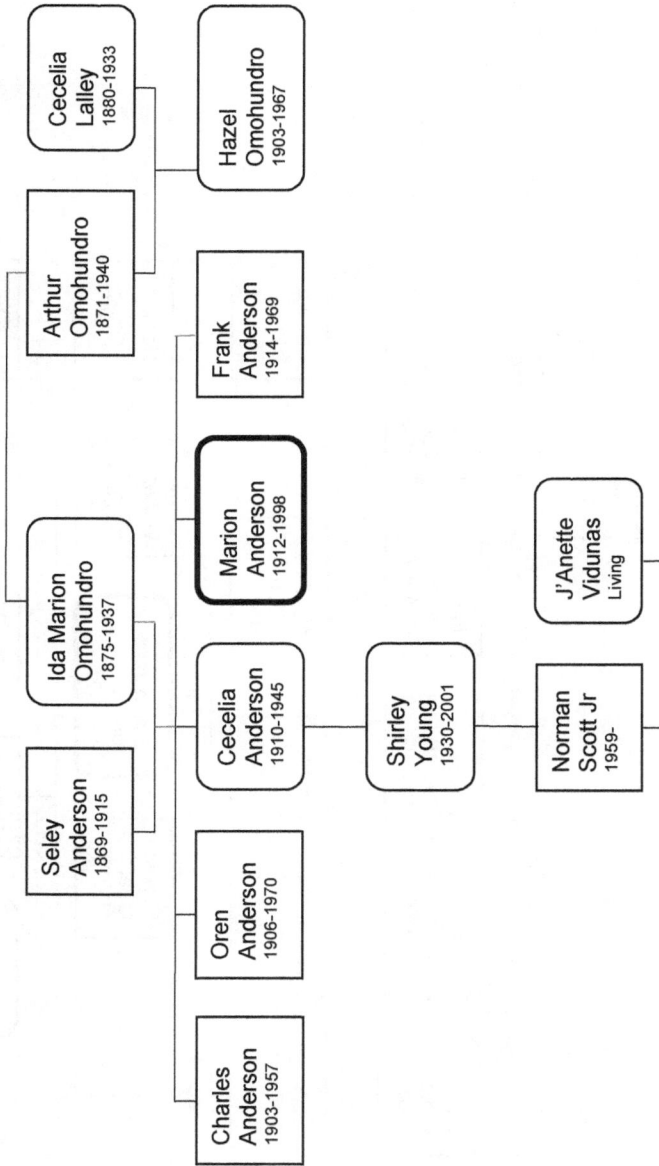

Marion Anderson.

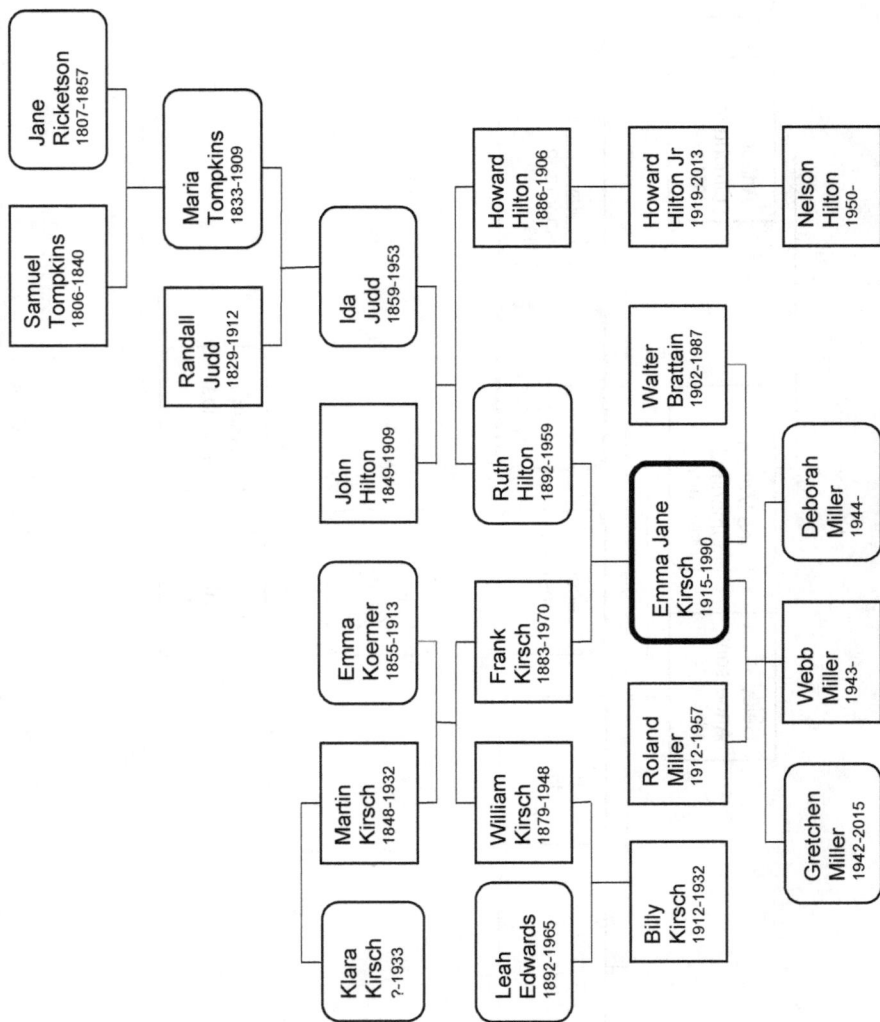

Emma Jane Kirsch.

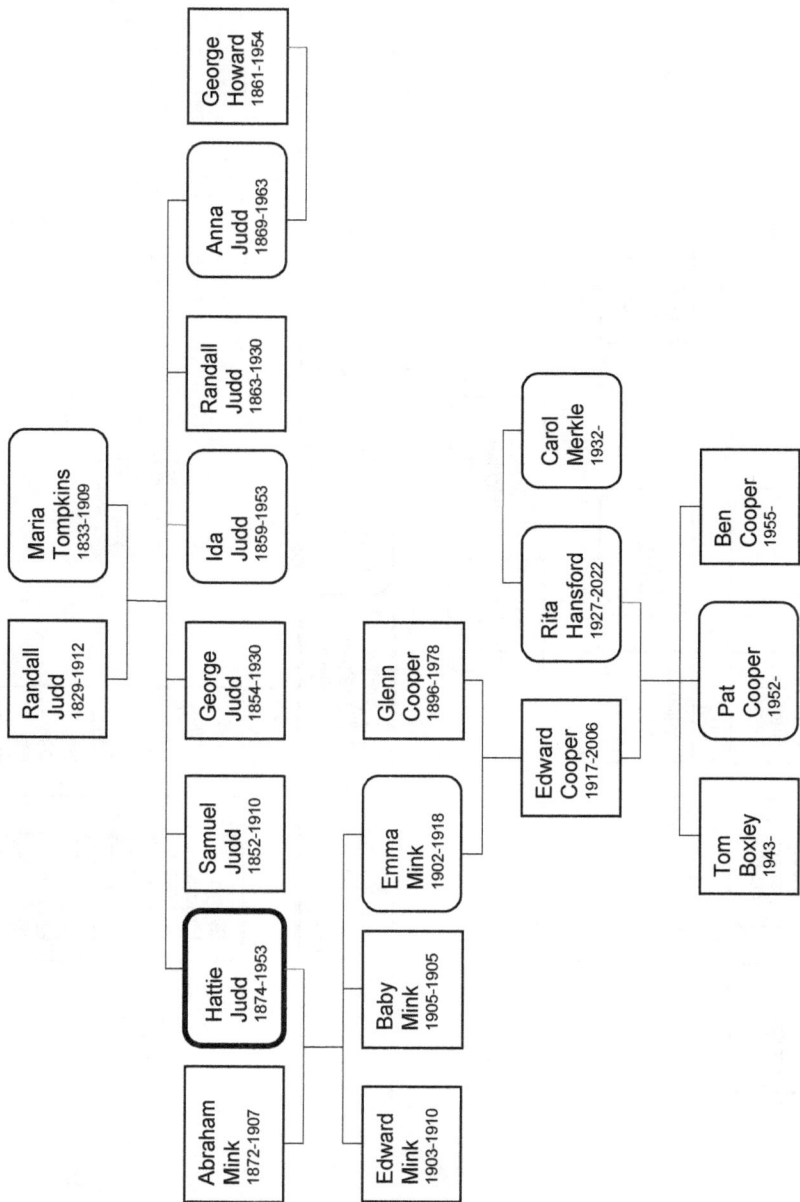

Hattie Judd.

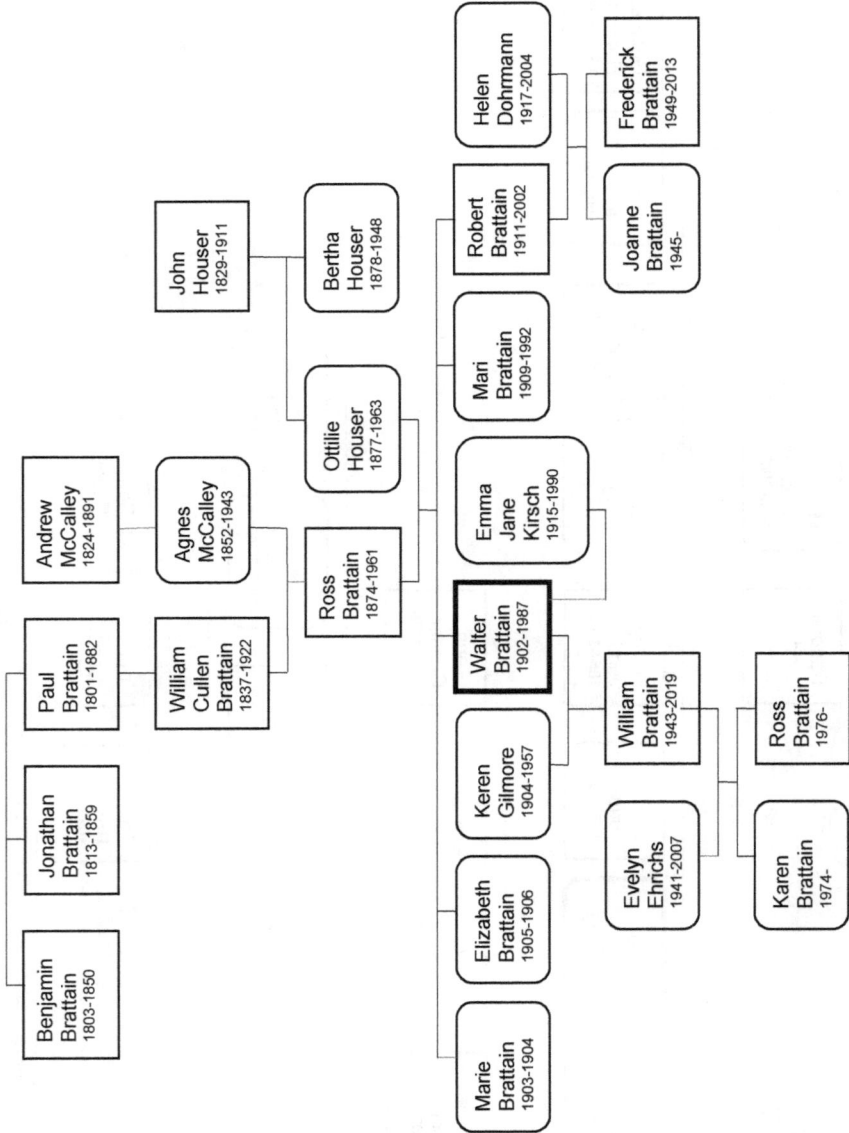

Walter Brattain.

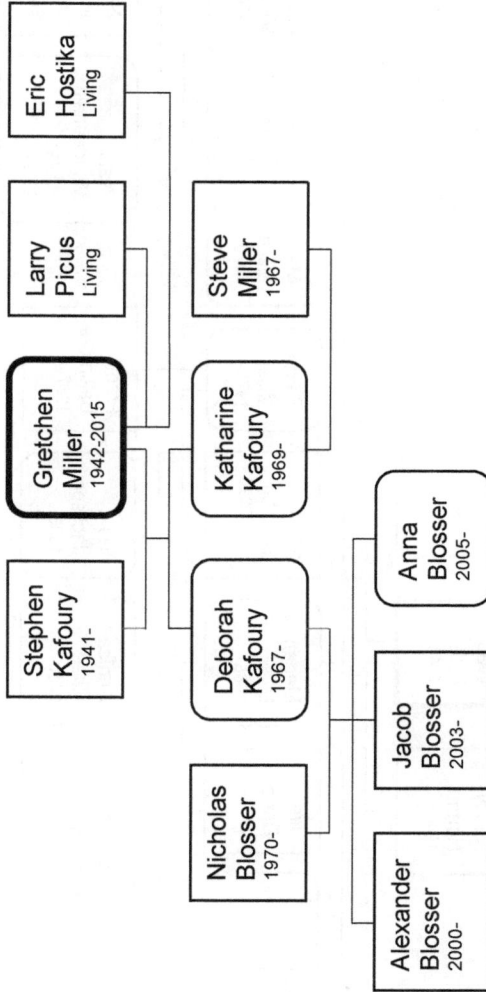

Gretchen Miller.

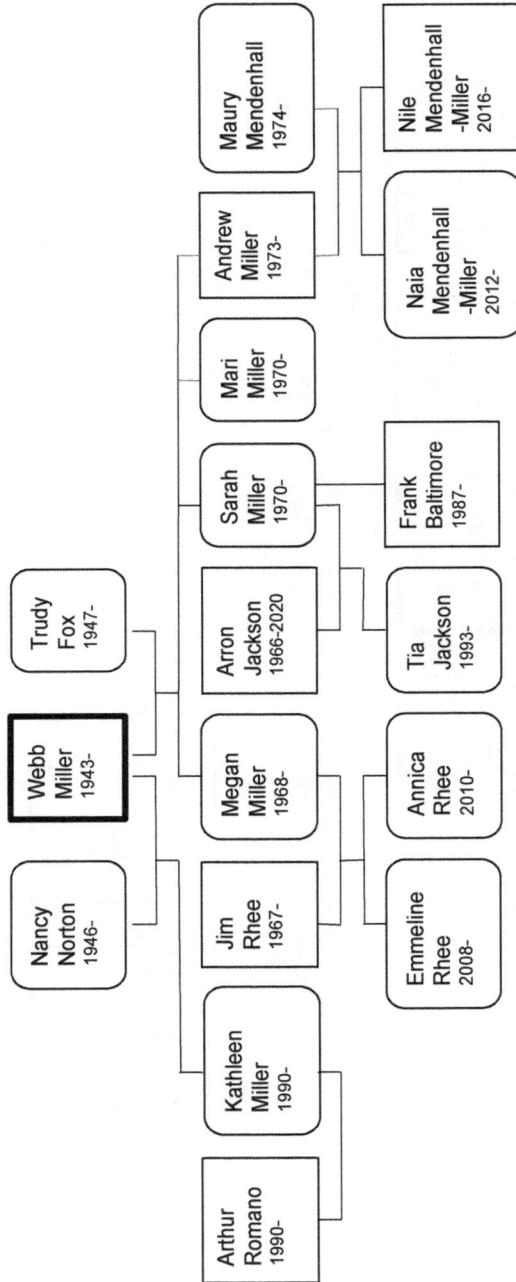

Webb Miller.

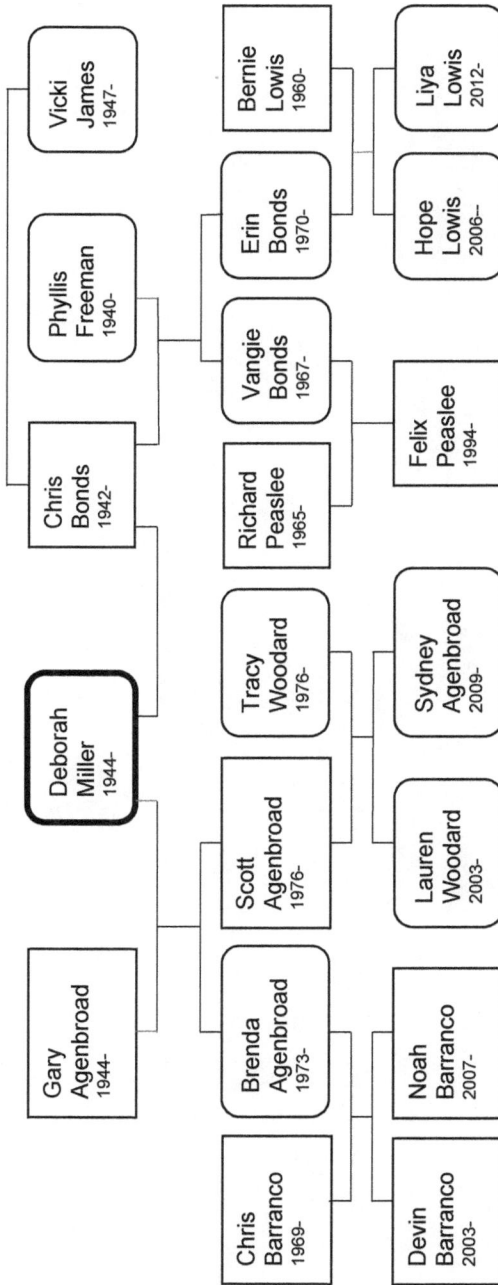

Deborah Miller.

Acknowledgments

The highest tribute to the dead is not grief but gratitude.

—Thornton Wilder

Deep gratitude to our mother, Emma Jane Miller Brattain, who must have hoped that her trio would stumble into the family thicket, where we couldn't help but become storytellers. She left enough letters, documents, and photographs to generate several books. All we needed was the courage to begin and the tenacity to complete the project.

A giant thank you to my children, Brenda Barranco and Scott Agenbroad, for their love and support. Brenda's encouragement and life energy have kept me focused on this project. Although she doesn't yet admit it, she inherited the writing gene; Scott is a master storyteller. His poignant reaction in 1990 when seeing his grammie's kitchen calendar filled with six months of planned activities, continues to remind me of the importance of preparing for the future while focusing on the present. Grandsons Devin and Noah Barranco have greatly enriched my experience of planning and writing this book, all the while putting up with my endless demands for pictures. In keeping with the family goofball tradition, their playfulness is on display on page 435. And special pats to Husker, our "day dog."

My gratitude to Deborah Kafoury for reading several letters and finding the White House folder containing the missing autographed menus! To Karen Brattain for editing many parts of the book and discovering the green lead frog! Thanks to Kat Miller for reading early drafts about her grandparents and to Megan Miller, Sarah Simmons, Mari Fox, Andrew Miller, Katharine Kafoury, and Ross Brattain for their feedback and insights. To Vicki James, Vangie Peaslee, Erin Lowis, and Phyllis Bonds for their support. May this book encourage them to write some of their untold stories. Thanks to Tia Rexine, Lauren Woodard, Sydney Agenbroad, Hope Lowis and Liya Lowis for their shared enthusiasm for the stories in the book—especially the elephants—and to whom I pass the torch as future writers and storytellers. To Alex Blosser, already an articulate raconteur, I am especially grateful for his stunning remembrances of his grammie at her 2015 memorial.

I could not have written this book without some treasured longtime friends who have put up with me over the years. Their encouragement when it was time to celebrate small victories or provide much-needed distractions kept me going. The Wa–Wa Sisters—Karen Reich, Sherry Matthews, Sally Raker, Gayle Bush, Lynn Knauss, and Brenda Voshell—were in my life long before I realized I could write anything beyond vacuous teenage letters.

Thanks to dear friends who have added invaluable support and read segments of the book: Markella Hatziano, Kathleen Conway, Karen Granberg, Piyali Dalal, Branis Knezevic, Annie Nguyen, Ying Wang, Richard Quine, Lauraine Dalton, Susan Batenhorst, Ginny Otte, Linda Anderson, Betty Stimmel Blegen, Ron Holt, Glenace Melton, and Don and Mary Halverstadt; also very special thanks to Julie Larson for her reading, her many stimulating conversations about the project, and for printing a version of my Hattie Judd story in a booklet, the first part of the book to appear in print. Members of my 100-Day Book online class, especially Karen Bergmann and Sue Muller Hacking, deserve mention for their recent involvement and in-depth feedback of chapters. Thanks also to Bill Raker and Stephen Kafoury for suggestions and insights; to Margaret Hoglund for sharing her mother's journal from 1938; and to Caroline Houser, with whom Mother felt an intense personal and intellectual connection. The two could have traveled and written together. Caroline and her brother, Gary, cleared up some of the mysteries surrounding Walter's aunt, Bertha Houser.

Without Chris Cutler and her memoir group's guidance and support, I would not have had the self-confidence or the tools to write. Ever-present in my peripheral vision as I write, Chris remains an inspiration. Joy Bellis, Temple Kinyon, Nabila Khanam (who gets the prize for most frequently asking, "How long do I have to wait for the book?"), Beth Parker, Linda Sandborn, Penny Yazzie, Nancy Craddock, and Ronnie Tee Smith have all supported my work and kept me on task for the past decade. The poetic words of Imelda Agustin-Ruiz both challenged me and encouraged me to take risks.

Dana Bronson, my "personal" archivist at the Whitman College and Northwest Archives, patiently responded to my endless requests while sharing my excitement during the four-year hunt for Brattain memorabilia.

I am grateful to Joseph Esposito, author of *Dinner in Camelot*, for further stimulating my interest in Walter and reading portions of my "Dear Walter" letter. Our cross-country email friendship has been a great joy and an unexpected bonus to my work on this project.

Thanks to Lillian Hoddeson and Michael Riordan for their book *Crystal Fire*, which tells of the astonishing discovery of the transistor effect and of the scientists' histories and personalities, including Walter's deep friendship with John Bardeen. Special thanks to John's son William Bardeen for sending the one photo Walter tolerated of the three transistor discoverers.

To Nell and Bob Mitchell and Margie O'Leary, who spent a morning with Chris and me in 2013 at the Colorado State Hospital Museum in Pueblo and encouraged me to ask for Hattie's medical records again. To Steve Welden, archivist at the Records Department of Jasper County, Carthage, Missouri, who spent time with us researching Hattie's life prior to Pueblo.

To Rita Cooper, who married Hattie's grandson, Edward Cooper, I offer my love and deep appreciation for welcoming me into her life and family. Her willingness to connect through email and a couple of phone calls meant so very much to me. She sent photos with Edward, including the only picture I have of his mother, Emma. Thanks also to Rita's sister Carol, and to her daughter Pat, for the ongoing connection to their family.

Special thanks go to those who contributed their own stories of our family members: Chuck Templeton, who also gave feedback on many segments of the book; Sharon Thompson, whose contribution to the book began with helping Mother move from 1019 Alvarado Terrace. Her love and laughter carried us through many long days in the mid-1980s; Karen Brattain, whose narrative about her parents adds both to the richness of the book and to my appreciation of her father, Bill; Joanne Brattain, whose material and insight into her father's life and relationship with his brother are a gift; Lynn Riegel, who remained one of Gretchen's closest friends from their days at Whitman College.

A huge thank you to Ginger Rodin Heil and Ethan Miller for responding to Webb's eager search for photographs and information about Dad's siblings, Marian and Ray Anderson, and to J'Anette Vidunas Scott for information about Marian and Ray's blood relatives. Marianna Waak signed on as Webb's and my first-ever cousin and also provided—along with her sister Ginger—much historical material for the Roland chapter. Marianna's generously detailed comments on the early chapters were an unexpected and welcome gift!

Our appreciation goes out to Bonnie Peterson and her daughters Kristen Amidon and Kami Ginder, the current residents of the house in northwest Seattle built by our grandparents. The magic of elephant stories lives on in that house.

Thanks to Amy Field for inviting me to share the elephant stories with her second-grade class and to Addison St. Pierre for capturing the energy of the morning in her art. To Bob "in Elephants" Lee for his generous private tour of the Portland Zoo's Elephant Lands for our family in 2016.

Special appreciation goes to my dear brother, Webb Miller, for stepping somewhat willingly into this project in 2015, not realizing how this might consume years of his life. What a gift it is for me and readers that he did. And thanks also to Nan Miller for tolerating the interruptions to their lives.

Without my husband, Chris, I could not have found the writer within me. Even when I was in graduate school, he had a sense of what worked and what didn't in my sentences. He has given me the extraordinary gift of not only reading my efforts but also editing my work to make it sound even more like me. Beyond editing, he has scanned hundreds of photos and formatted the entire manuscript. I wanted to heap more praise on him, but he did his job and edited it out. Now, he's stuck with my daily shout-outs of appreciation.

Photo Credits

All photos not mentioned here are the property of Debi Bonds or Webb Miller.

Page xxxiii, top: Larry Picus.

Page 20: Amy Field.

Page 21: Top right, Addison St. Pierre; bottom left: Courtesy Oregon Zoo.

Page 48 and page 49, top left: Rita Cooper.

Page 49, top right: Pat Cooper.

Page 105, bottom: Marianna Waak.

Page 107: Top, Ethan Miller; bottom, Marianna Waak.

Page 108: Marianna Waak.

Page 209: Karen Brattain.

Pages 214–215: Whitman College and Northwest Archives, Penrose Library.

Page 216: https://www.washingtonruralheritage.org/digital/collection/pomeroy/id/1020/rec/1. Courtesy of Gary Houser.

Page 217: Joanne Brattain.

Page 250, top: William Bardeen.

Page 253, top: Niels Bohr Library and Archives, American Institute of Physics.

Page 253, bottom: Whitman College and Northwest Archives, Penrose Library.

Page 280, bottom, page 281 and page 282, top: Courtesy of the John F. Kennedy Library.

Page 364: © The Griffith Institute, University of Oxford.

Page 377: Michael Lloyd/The *Oregonian*.

Page 382: Larry Picus.

Page 410: Chuck Templeton.

Page 412: Lynn Riegel.

Page 416: Joanne Brattain, except for bottom left: Courtesy of Science History Institute.

Pages 423–424: Karen Brattain.